KU-216-524

PENGUIN BOOKS

Hellish Nell

Malcolm Gaskill is Emeritus Professor of Early Modern History at the University of East Anglia. An authority on the history of witch trials, his books include *Witchfinders: A Seventeenth-Century English Tragedy* (John Murray, 2005) and *Witchcraft: A Very Short Introduction* (Oxford University Press, 2010). His most recent work, *The Ruin of All Witches: Life and Death in the New World* (Allen Lane, 2021), was a *Sunday Times* bestseller, shortlisted for the 2022 Wolfson History Prize. He is a regular contributor to the *London Review of Books*, and lives with his family in Cambridge.

Hellish Nell

The Curious Case of Britain's Last Witch Trial

MALCOLM GASKILL

PENGUIN BOOKS

PENGUIN BOOKS

UK | USA | Canada | Ireland | Australia
India | New Zealand | South Africa

Penguin Books is part of the Penguin Random House group of companies
whose addresses can be found at global.penguinrandomhouse.com

First published in Great Britain by Fourth Estate 2001
Revised edition published in Penguin Books 2023

001

Copyright © Malcolm Gaskill, 2001, 2023

The moral right of the author has been asserted

Set in 12.5/14.75pt Garamond MT Std
Typeset by Jouve (UK), Milton Keynes
Printed and bound in Great Britain by Clays Ltd, Elcograf S.p.A.

The authorized representative in the EEA is Penguin Random House Ireland,
Morrison Chambers, 32 Nassau Street, Dublin D02 YH68

A CIP catalogue record for this book is available from the British Library

ISBN: 978–1–802–06199–4

www.greenpenguin.co.uk

Penguin Random House is committed to a
sustainable future for our business, our readers
and our planet. This book is made from Forest
Stewardship Council® certified paper.

My father, Ed Gaskill, was not only the first to tell me about this story but much earlier made me fascinated by the past. This book is for him, with love and gratitude.

And in memory of
Donald West (1924–2020)
and
Hilary Mantel (1952–2022)

Now, don't, sir! Don't expose me! Just this once!
This was the first and only time, I'll swear —
Look at me — see, I kneel — the only time,
I swear, I ever cheated — yes, by the soul
Of her who hears — (your sainted mother, sir!)
All, except this last accident, was truth.

Robert Browning, 'Mr Sludge, "The Medium"' (1864)

The belief that disembodied spirits may be permitted to revisit this world has its foundation upon that sublime hope of immortality which is at once the chief solace and greatest triumph of our reason.

Charles Mackay, *Extraordinary Popular Delusions and the Madness of Crowds* (1841)

Contents

CONTENTS

PART III

Helen Vindicated

Prologue: Under Fire

Towards the end of March 1944, Donald West, a nineteen-year-old medical student, boarded a train from Liverpool to London. News from the capital was bleak. At night the air-raid shelters, deserted for over a year, were once again full of people escaping what the newspapers were calling the 'Little Blitz'. Days earlier, Islington had been in flames, and the previous month the theatres of the West End had emptied. In wartime Britain a poster asked rail travellers if their journeys were really necessary. But Donald paid little heed to this, nor did he think much about the danger. For he had heard there was going to be a witch trial and was determined to see it.

Donald, a member of the Society for Psychical Research (SPR), had been invited by its leading light, Mollie Goldney, to join her for this remarkable event. A redoubtable flame-haired midwife from genteel Putney, Mrs Goldney was as indifferent to the Luftwaffe as to the protests of the fraudulent mediums she exposed, and ignored the drone of the sirens as she crossed the capital to keep her appointment with young Donald. They met outside the Old Bailey, London's Central Criminal Court, which was situated in an area of the City from Cripplegate to the Thames that had been burned and blasted by bombing. So far, St Paul's Cathedral had been spared, but the 'Bailey', as barristers called it, was severely damaged. As in most shops and offices, however, 'business as usual' had been declared and the Clerk of the Court got on with his work.

A long queue of people extended down the street. Some were Spiritualists, but most just curious citizens, successors to the Londoners of Hogarth's day who had gathered there to follow the condemned to Tyburn, cheering, jeering and sharing the latest from the Grub Street presses. In a boarded-up, blacked-out city, people were drawn to any diversion, the terrifying exhilaration of the first Blitz having long faded into flat, predictable tedium. Apart from the cinema, where *Gone with the Wind* had entered its fourth year, sensational crimes were the best entertainment. Fleet Street reporters had only to stroll up Ludgate Hill to check the screens for forthcoming cases. This, however, was something altogether new.

The formidable Mollie Goldney, who held senior rank in the Women's Voluntary Service, jumped the queue and jostled her way into Court No. 4, a wide-eyed Donald in her wake. Never having been in such a place before, the magisterial setting stirred in him an anticipation felt by many spectators now filing to their seats, some of whom had waited hours to be admitted. Space was limited, the wrecked public gallery closed, and the front benches reserved for the gentlemen of the press. Mrs Goldney and Donald sat down. Ahead was the Director of Public Prosecutions' representative, E. G. Robey, and next to him the Clerk. To the right were the barristers, to the left the jury, alongside whom loomed the raised dock awaiting its accused.

Three sharp taps silenced the hubbub, and everyone rose. A door behind the Bench opened, through which the aldermen and sheriffs emerged, followed by the Recorder of London, Sir Gerald Dodson, in full-bottomed wig and scarlet robes. The usher intoned an ancient proclamation, Dodson bowed to the aldermen, Clerk, counsel and jury in turn, and all were seated. Little had changed in two hundred years. Only since the start of the war had pens replaced quills and customary charms against jail fever been discontinued – no more protective rue along the dock ledge, or dried flowers scattered on the judicial dais.

The Clerk alone remained standing. At his order that the prisoners be presented, the soft thud of footsteps up the basement stairs resounded through the chamber. And then Donald West caught his first glimpse of Helen Duncan, a bulky woman in her mid-forties, with a bluish-red complexion, flashing dark eyes, and the hair beneath her hat as black as her fur coat. Beside her stood a diffident-looking man in horn-rimmed spectacles, then two other women, one built like Mrs Duncan and also enswathed in furs, the other smaller in stature, almost bird-like. The Clerk raised a sheaf of papers tied with a pink ribbon and the accused confirmed their names. Then he read the charges:

Helen Duncan, Ernest Edward Hartland Homer, Elizabeth Anne Jones, and Frances Brown, you four are charged upon an indictment which contains seven counts. In the first count that between 1 December 1943, and 19 January 1944, you conspired together and with other persons unknown to pretend to exercise or use a kind of conjuration, to wit, that through the agency of the said Helen Duncan spirits of deceased persons should appear to be present in fact in such place as the said Helen Duncan was then in, and that the said spirits were communicating with living persons then and there present contrary to section four of the Witchcraft Act 1735.

Other charges followed: actual pretence to exercise conjuration, monetary fraud and 'effecting a public mischief' – a catch-all charge used against the builders of shoddy bomb shelters, but here intended to mean exploiting anxiety at a time of national crisis.

The accused all pleaded not guilty, Mrs Duncan alone, her Scots brogue reduced to a croak, adding 'sir' as a deferential flourish. The Clerk then swore in the jurors, and prosecuting counsel, John Maude KC, the Eton-and-Oxford educated son of a theatrical actor-manager, took the floor. The stage was set. For forty minutes the defendants came under fire in a speech of such self-assured wit and poise from Maude that his junior colleague, Henry Elam, could only look on in awe.

Maude's point was that the trial concerned common fraud alone. Donald West remembered the bogus medium whom he himself had exposed in Liverpool in 1942, for which he was booed and hissed from the seance room – 'a most revolting episode'. The Duncan case had nothing to do with religion, Maude continued, still less witchcraft, overlooking the inevitability that using the Witchcraft Act would determine how it would be perceived. Mediums were usually just fined under the Vagrancy Act of 1824 and in most minds the Witchcraft Act meant witchcraft.

Maude's sole concern was the opinion of the seven jurors (in wartime cut down from twelve): six men and one woman, all from the suburb of Barnes. 'In olden days,' he told them, 'it was almost a popular matter to chase poor deluded creatures who were thought to be witches, or indeed sometimes may themselves have believed themselves to be witches, and the mass of the public believed in that sort of thing being possible.' Yet by the reign of George II, Maude continued, witchcraft trials were thought ridiculous, and an Act was passed to end them – a watershed in British beliefs and values.

So we reach a position in 1735 which would no doubt be welcomed by any person who may call himself to-day a Spiritualist; for those persons . . . would no doubt be the warmest supporters of any measure directed by the State against the fraudulent and deplorable activities of any persons who would be pretending anything such as the calling back of the dead into a room.

Mrs Duncan sipped her water, exchanging glances with her daughter Nan sitting below, as Maude condemned the return of the war dead as a 'false and hollow lie' and a cruel entertainment. He knew well how the public's weary indifference to the war masked anxiety for servicemen overseas and never more so than in the run-up to the invasion of Europe.

Maude sketched events leading to the arrests. Stanley Worth, a naval lieutenant, had attended several feeble seances at a place known as the 'Master's Temple Church of Spiritual Healing', a room above Ernest Homer's chemist's shop at 301 Copnor Road, Portsmouth. Once, a medium sensed from Worth's pocketknife that it belonged to an aspiring sea captain, a reading made less impressive by the fact he was in uniform. In December 1943, however, Elizabeth Jones (who called herself Mrs Homer) promised something more special: in the New Year a Mrs Duncan was coming, a wonderful medium able to materialize spirits from ectoplasm. This flowed from her body, then surged back with such vitality, Mrs Homer enthused, it sucked up dust and litter such as cigarette ends and matches, just like a vacuum cleaner. The price of admission – 12s 6d (today, equivalent to about £25) – might have been reasonable, Maude suggested, 'if one were going to see the ghost of Napoleon or the Duke of Wellington, but not of much value if you were going to see a bogus conjuring trick'. Worth was intrigued, though, and bought tickets for himself and a fellow naval officer.

In the seance room the chairs were arranged in three rows facing the 'cabinet', a corner sectioned off by a curtain. Mrs Duncan sat there in a black gown, drawers and shoes which three women appointed to search her had watched her put on. Blackout material covered the bay window, the only illumination a red bulb dimmed with a handkerchief. Mrs Homer, who had entertained troops in France in the last war, led the circle first in prayer and then song – as Spiritualists said, to raise the vibrations; it was the medium's favourite, 'South of the Border'. Entranced, head on one side and snoring softly, Mrs Duncan began generating ectoplasm, which crept sinuously from beneath the cabinet and built up into 'Albert', her spirit guide and impresario. Frances Brown, Mrs Duncan's travelling companion, watched intently from the back row. Just as Donald West had snared his medium by inventing an Aunt Lilly, when Worth was called to summon a spirit, he asked if it was his aunt, even though all his aunts were alive. 'Yes', came Albert's husky reply. Worth's sister also appeared, even though she too was alive and well and driving an ambulance in London.

Afterwards, Worth pretended to be amazed, but he was indignant and went to the police. A Detective Inspector Ford asked him if he would attend another seance as a stooge. On the evening of 19 January 1944, Worth and War Reserve Constable Rupert Cross visited the Master's Temple and the seance began as before. Suddenly Worth blew a whistle to summon policemen waiting outside and shone a torch at the cabinet. Cross, meanwhile, lunged at one of the spirit forms, which he swore was butter muslin, but it vanished, and the police found nothing.

'It is not too much to say', intoned Maude, 'that the mockery of the dead will cease in the little room over Mr. Homer's shop.' By now the court was spellbound, appalled and amused. Calling spirits 'ghosts', he invited the jury to consider the afterlife of a cat: 'What the cat was doing before it was summoned to make its appearance in Portsmouth one can only imagine: whether it was hunting pink mice in the Elysian fields one does not know. All one knows is that a miaow came from behind the curtains; so, I suppose, if one is a cat, one does not make much progress.'

A ripple of laughter left only the Spiritualists unmoved, as Maude, also poker-faced, extended the ectoplasmic menagerie: 'A parrot is alleged to have appeared, his name is Bronco. It came fluttering round from somewhere; it was called up by Albert from some heavenly forest, and it appeared in Portsmouth. It was followed by a rabbit. We do not know its name; we know the parrot was called Bronco.' More laughing and the Recorder shifted in his seat. Maude pressed on, relating how a materialized policeman had nipped back to collect his helmet. 'No doubt all policemen,' he suggested to the court,

> hope that, when they pass into the next world, they will not go on being policemen for ever . . . Can you imagine anything more disappointing than a policeman having passed through life and apparently not having risen as high as an Inspector, because he still had a helmet? Finding himself in the next world, not in plain clothes, not at ease in a shirt and a pair of plain trousers, but having to look for his helmet?

Now that he had the jurors in his thrall, Maude asked them to put all the insanity to one side and try to think of anything more thrilling than asking 'Is that you, Dad?' and receiving the answer that it was Dad. And with that deft switch between the masks of comedy and tragedy, Maude stole the show.

For the Defence, the Spiritualists' National Union had appointed Charles Loseby, a veteran of the trenches and an ardent Spiritualist. His strategy was to prove Helen Duncan a genuine medium, thus precluding fraud. Of three hundred witnesses he claimed to have waiting in the wings, he called forty-five, some of whom had attended dozens of seances. And their stories were extraordinary. Conjured up in ectoplasm, the spirits of loved ones had returned, as many as twenty at a sitting, spectral hands reaching out, lips planting warm kisses on tear-streaked cheeks.

The reporters scribbled down the witnesses' words. Here is Alfred Dodd, an authority on Shakespeare's sonnets, remembering a seance in Liverpool in 1936 where he was reunited with his sweetheart, who had died in 1897 aged twenty-one:

> She stood there dressed in a white flowing robe, and over that white flowing robe was a fine curtain of net. I was so astonished that I stood up in my seat, which I ought not to have done . . . The girl did not come to me direct, she came right round the room from left to right, and she stood before me, a living, palpitating woman. The same hair that I knew so well, dark and ruddy; the same eyes, hazel; they shone with animation; her face, the same ivory pallor on her cheeks . . . Then I heard her speak, and she spoke in the same soft Scotch accent that I knew so well.

As the testimony floated out into the courtroom, so the Spiritualists felt Maude's sting abate, not least Mrs Duncan, who wept when Dodd described her as an 'absolutely straight materialization medium'. The witness who most impressed Mrs Goldney was Jane Rust, a well-spoken midwife like herself, who had examined Mrs Duncan, and was convinced she had been reunited with her deceased husband, mother and aunt. Each witness, invariably of good standing, clear-headed and articulate, added to a chorus which, by the fourth day, began to seem endless. But this was Loseby's fatal mistake: far from being over-whelmed, the jurors became increasingly bored, the press began to crave novelty and the Recorder was irritated. What for the Prosecution had been a stage had become a pulpit for the Defence. Only psychical researchers like Donald and Mollie sustained their fascination and even they suppressed the odd yawn.

More tantalizing was Loseby's offer for Mrs Duncan to hold a special seance for the jury. Mrs Duncan held a hand to her forehead as if she might faint and, staring straight ahead, motioned away a cup of water. The Prosecution knew this was coming, and junior defence counsel Henry Elam had begged Maude to consent if the Recorder approved. But the Recorder refused to let his court become a cheap sideshow. Dodson was no killjoy; indeed, as the co-author of a successful West End musical, he had a passion for popular theatre. Instead, he did merely what the Crown paid him to do: he applied the law. If no phe-nomena were to appear, he averred, Mrs Duncan would be condemned before trial, constituting 'a reversion to the Dark Ages, and to something very akin to trial by ordeal'.

On the Friday – judgment day – demand for a place in the chamber was greater than ever. This time Mollie Goldney went with her friend Harry Price, Britain's foremost psychi-cal researcher, but in the crush she alone was admitted and only then because she was waving a letter from the High Sheriff. It was so cramped, the atmosphere so charged, that when one of Mrs Goldney's SPR colleagues offered her his seat, the police took exception and ejected him. As proceedings began, it was clear that Loseby's optimism had waned. Until now, apart from the odd plaintive sob, Mrs Duncan had maintained a composure bordering on the cocksure. 'On one occasion,' noted a reporter, 'she came up from the cells as if to a reception. After smiling at people in court, she sat down with as much elegance as a woman of her size could muster. Shortly afterwards, she took a wrap from her shoulders, and, with the manner of a queen, handed it to the wardress behind her.'

As the proceedings reached their climax, however, her emotions fell into disarray. Discharged from reaching verdicts on all counts except what related to the Witchcraft Act, the jury retired at teatime to consider the Recorder's lengthy summing-up. For twenty-three minutes spectators waited patiently, speculating in low voices, before the jury returned and the foreman rose and cleared his throat. When Mrs Duncan heard that she and her co-defendants had been found guilty, she was at first too shocked to display anything other than an eerie calmness.

Prior to sentencing, the Recorder called upon the Chief Constable of Portsmouth, Arthur West (no relation to Donald) to provide some background regarding the lives of the accused. The court heard how Mrs Duncan had in fact been fined at Edinburgh in 1933 for a similar offence and had threatened and cursed the woman who exposed her. At this, as if emerging from a trance, Mrs Duncan snapped, 'I never did!' West pressed on. Intriguingly he referred fleetingly to the principal defendant having breached security regulations in 1941 when she had predicted the sinking of a warship before its loss was announced – a solitary hint at what, behind the smoke and shadow of the seance room, the trial might really be about. She was, in any case, 'an unmitigated humbug and pest' with no redeeming features the Chief Constable could think of. Emboldened by Mrs Duncan's outburst, Frances Brown shouted her denial as West exposed her as a convicted shoplifter, to which the Recorder retorted that if she had something to say she should have said it under oath in the witness box.

At Loseby's request, the Recorder postponed sentencing until Monday and the court was adjourned. As Mrs Duncan was led down to the cells, she cried out something which Mollie Goldney failed to catch, but others reported as: 'I never heard sae mony lies in a' my life. I dinna ken why they should get away with thae lies!' And as her muffled noises off faded from the courtroom, her followers closed their brimming eyes in disbelief. Nan Duncan screamed that prison would kill her mother, brushing off the police officers who tried to pacify her.

On the following Monday, the Recorder sent Helen Duncan to prison for nine months, a pronouncement which she received with bewildered despair. She wept and groaned her innocence, then cried out, 'Oh God! Is there a God? I never done it, is there a God?' before swooning to the floor of the dock, knocking over her chair. The warders, police officers and three other defendants, who had scarcely broken her fall, helped her up and handed her back her hat. As she was taken downstairs, she continued to rail, the Recorder waiting for her cries to subside before continuing. Mr Homer and his pretended wife were bound over for two years. Frances Brown received four months. Thus martyred, Mrs Duncan was escorted to a van waiting to return her to North London. Her supporters, who had begun to disperse, flowers wilting, reassembled momentarily, and, as Charles Loseby observed, 'cheered her as though to encourage her but not excitedly'.

The trial had lasted eight days. So much had been said that the appeal hearing for which the Defence applied was delayed while the shorthand writers finished their transcript. A sallow-cheeked Loseby suddenly looked ten years older. He had been humiliatingly upstaged by John Maude, and now faced the combined wrath of the Spiritualists' National Union, the editor of *Psychic News*, the Duncan family and even Spiritualists in the SPR. Those who sympathized with him felt that the guardians of British justice had denied a demonstrable truth about life and death – and the life beyond death – and had pilloried an innocent woman into the bargain. Psychical researchers took a more detached, clinical view. On the Saturday between verdict and sentencing, Mollie Goldney wrote to Harry Price to reassure him that he had not really missed much:

> As you see, a verdict of guilty. The Judge's summing up was very feeble. He did not *comment*; he merely recapitulated, telling the Jury with every word that she was a

fraud . . . The fanatical conviction of 50 or 60 witnesses is a most amazing psychological study; they all averred that no argument, no alleged fact would shake them in their conviction that they had verily seen their relatives.

Yet the key issue had been whether the defendants were guilty according to law, never the possibility of post-mortem survival or the fallacies of human perception, however much anyone wanted these matters to be aired. As the Recorder stated: 'Whether genuine manifestations . . . are possible, the verdict does not decide.'

Donald West's opinion was that, although Helen Duncan was a fraud, the Crown had failed to prove its case. Instead, the court had resorted to a statute which made the four accused guilty from the moment of indictment – a strategy which gave poor Henry Elam stage fright, not least because his senior, Maude, had been only occasionally present in court to ensure they 'got home'. Mollie Goldney, who had declined the Prosecution's invitation to give evidence but lent them one of Harry Price's books, spotted Elam's six-and-a-half-foot frame outside the court and engaged him in conversation. 'Thank heavens that is over,' he confessed with a deep sigh.

And as Elam wound down, so reporters, editors, compositors and printers rushed to get the witch trial onto the front page and into waiting news vans. Of course Helen Duncan was not a witch, and the Crown had protested that the trial had nothing to do with witchcraft. But in the public eye the law had cast her in that role. To borrow a term from the Middle Ages, Helen had been branded *invocator spiritum* and, by that token alone, in wartime London the days of old and the burning times were recalled to mind even as bombs fell from the skies.

PART ONE
Helen Valorized

1. You'll be Burned as a Witch!: The Child-Prophet of Perthshire

In 1697, two centuries before Helen Duncan's birth, a Dumfriesshire woman named Elspeth McEwen sat in jail awaiting trial. In the previous year her neighbours had complained to the kirk of Dalry that she was a witch who spirited milk from their cows and stopped the eggs in their hens. Elspeth was carried to the kirk sessions and imprisoned while the wheels of superior justice were set in motion. Other angry, fearful parishes had identified witches. At Kerrick an evil spirit had pelted a house with stones and fireballs, a white hand was beating the walls, and when a cloth was pulled from a figure that materialized by the hearth there was nothing underneath. The local minister committed their tale to print at Edinburgh, and in due course the London presses brought out an edition of this saleable sensational news story.

It was not until April 1698 that poor Elspeth was examined by a commission of justiciary, before whom she confessed to making a pact with the devil, which ensured her conviction. The Chief Commissioner, Sir John Maxwell, recommended that she be burned to death, and she was returned to jail for five months pending sentence from the Privy Council, in which time she was so badly mistreated she begged her tormentors to kill her. On 24 August, Elspeth was taken to a public place in

Kirkcudbright and set in a barrel of tar stacked up with peat and coal. The Provost read out the sentence, accompanied by a drummer beating a solemn rhythm, whereafter the executioner throttled their witch and then kindled the fire. The burgh treasurer recorded the costs in his account book, from the tar barrel and coals down to the executioner's ale. A total of seven Scots pounds and nine shillings was spent on the death of Elspeth McEwen.

Quite what they got for their money now seems obscure, but imagine a world where witches were a real threat, their execution reassurance that a divinely ordained state was resisting Satan. The punishment of Elspeth McEwen and 50,000 Europeans like her (four-fifths of whom were women) constituted not just random slaughter; rather, it was a consequence of rapid religious, political and economic change in the sixteenth century. Competing faiths sharpened the definition of a moral universe poised between good and evil, and of a physical environment where wondrous manifestations of the supernatural were commonplace. The prosecution of witches may seem like folly, but how could early modern people ignore the devil in their midst? And so it was that virtually every Scottish generation from the 1590s to the end of the seventeenth century experienced its own regional witch panic, each lasting no more than a year or so.

The fate of witches was determined by the law, which in itself was essential to godly state building. Abiding by the injunction in the Book of Exodus, 'Thou shalt not suffer a witch to live', in 1563 the Catholic Mary, Queen of Scots, and her Protestant English counterpart, Elizabeth I, both passed legislation against witchcraft. Mary's son James was a lonely boy-king whose academic interest in politics properly embraced demonology – the study of forces liable to undermine order and authority. His interest peaked with the first of the Scottish witch crazes, which began in 1590 after the ship carrying James and his new bride, Anne of Denmark, was beset by storms blamed on witches hostile to a union between nascent Protestant states. A maidservant and healer, whose name, curiously enough, was Geillie Duncan, was said to attend secret gatherings in a North Berwick church with other witches, some people of substance whom she identified under torture. On her throat they found the devil's mark, which was pricked with pins to see if pain was felt or blood drawn.

James interrogated personally those named by Geillie Duncan, among them Agnes Sampson who told James snippets of pillow talk from his wedding night, upon which the King called the witches 'extreme lyars' – like their master the devil. Mostly, however, he took the witches seriously because to insecure European states the occult information gathering was potentially treasonable. James approved the witches' executions, and in 1597 published a short treatise entitled *Daemonologie*, republished in London after he ascended the English throne in 1603. The capital's most famous playwright wrote a short play (the king was known to fidget) about a usurper destroyed by ambition driven by the false promises of witches:

> And that distill'd by magic sleights
> Shall raise such artificial sprites

As by the strength of their illusion
Shall draw him on to his confusion

The manner in which Hecate's advice to the 'weird sisters' regarding Macbeth's fate emphasizes diabolic delusion rather than diabolic possession would prove significant for the legislative history of witchcraft in the next century and beyond.

The Witchcraft Act of 1604 was distinguished from its predecessor by a clause prescribing death for invocation and conjuration of diabolic spirits alone. In England, James soon lost interest in witches, and in his lifetime there was no craze south of the border to match that of his homeland. Even so, his law became the statutory basis for several hundred witch trials in England spanning more than a century. In Scotland, too, the social and legal idea of the witch persisted, resulting in over a thousand executions all told. By 1698, however, when Elspeth McEwen was executed, doubts among the educated elite were hardening into scepticism.

The prosecution of witches owed as much to folk tradition as to learned demonology. Ghosts, revenants, demons and fairies populated a dreamscape where nature met supernature and the mundane and the miraculous were conjoined. Cunning folk diagnosed, healed and prognosticated, interpreting omens and resisting curses, offering the poor and powerless a measure of control over their own lives. Trials depended on the testimony of ordinary people; had the farmers of Dalry not feared for their produce, Elspeth McEwen would not have died.

The courts established truths that served the needs of communities and there, too, declining witch beliefs among the elite were mirrored until witchcraft became legally defunct. In 1736 the Scottish and English statutes were replaced with a single Act (dated 1735) which made pretence to conjuration an offence, which, according to one Scottish antiquarian, turned the witch into a cheat and impostor and substituted the pillory for the stake.

In the nineteenth century, however, men from the same class that had ended the witch trials became fascinated by ancient superstitions. Like anthropologists in their own land, they discovered collective memories of remarkable longevity. Early in Queen Victoria's reign, one inquirer met an old man in Renfrewshire whose great-grandmother had seen witches burn at Paisley in 1697 and shuddered to recall the smell. Beliefs and customs enshrined in oral tradition, and in countless libraries and parish chests, suggested to these researchers a mentality distanced in space and time from their own. What they failed to appreciate was the extent to which such beliefs had outlived the repeal of the witchcraft statutes. In 1841, Charles Mackay, a lexicographer of Lowland Scots, filled a book with stories of archaic prophecies, delusions, apparitions and devils, including a whole chapter on 'the witch mania', seemingly unaware of the still living thread that joined the Dark Ages with the age of industry and empire.

Callander, situated on the River Teith and backed by the crags and glens of the Menteith Hills and Trossachs Forest, had long been a site of strategic significance – a place where

Lowlands met Highlands. Traditionally, the vulgar tongue was Gaelic. A reforming minister resigned his living in 1596 because his parishioners had but 'a poor pennyworth of the English', a state of affairs which a visitor in 1724 found unchanged, although the anglicization of speech spread in the eighteenth century. Half an hour north of Glasgow, it is the sort of town you might drive through without paying much attention. Houses built from the flecked granite natives call 'plum-pudding stone' flank Main Street, along which cattle were once driven to the great lowland fairs or trysts. Now the shops there sell Celtic knotwork, clan certificates and tartan from the woollen mills. An older British generation may remember Callander as the 'Tannochbrae' of the BBC drama *Dr Finlay's Casebook*, a nostalgic evocation of small-town Perthshire life.

The nostalgia was misplaced. Time out of mind, generations of Callander folk had toiled on crofts on the sour moors, or out in water-logged fields, hiking across hill slopes, shepherding, felling timber and longing to be home by the fire. Even men with trades grew vegetables or kept chickens and cows in the long, narrow gardens behind their cottages and eked out starchy diets with trout and salmon from the Teith. Life was short, opportunities for self-advancement few. By 1800, smelting and weaving had been added to the staple occupations, and men carried cartloads of bark, wool and wood to the lowlands, returning with coal, tar, grease and small luxuries to sell. But even a witch on the blasted heath could scarcely have foreseen that the town's future would lie not in manufacture or commerce but in poetry.

Callander's weather forecasts varied little: it was either 'exceptionally cold and wet' or 'phenomenally mild'. In the nineteenth century the roads were forbidding, facilities rudimentary, people inscrutable and intractable. The Trossachs resembled the safe world broken open and exposed to the elements, with little to attract lovers of comfort. Sensitive souls, however, began to find inspiration in its savage beauty, an antidote to the prissy correctness of classicism. In 1803 the Wordsworths arrived in Callander and spent a rainy evening by the fire in their hotel room learning about the town from a pamphlet by the minister, Dr James Robertson. Soon Sir Walter Scott's verse romance *The Lady of the Lake*, published in 1810, was inspiring visitors with melancholic scenes of primitive life: dark hills and darker passes, myth, magic and the primordial contest between good and evil. For in the raw vastness of nature the poets had been touched by the immanent power of the supernatural.

The impact on the world of letters was matched by the effects on the local economy. Public and private coaches brought in waves of tourists to the point that a Romantic poet could barely hear himself sigh. In 1818, Keats sniffed that the area was 'vexatiously full of visitors', of whom three steamer-loads per day were being ferried up and down the loch by the 1840s. The Dreadnought Hotel and Callander's handful of boarding houses were packed. The turning point came a decade later with the Oban railway, which lured the urban working classes too, prompting this cynical appreciation of Scott's legacy: 'All the world, rich and poor, including crown-princes and *noblesse*, crowded to visit the scenery which he had depicted. Instead of being, as usual, a dull, stupid village, whose inhabitants were all in a state of *cabbageism*, Callander of Menteith became a rallying point for all classes, a place wherein to study varieties of character. Truly *that* study was not very consolatory or edifying.'

Cabbages, perhaps, but busy cabbages. By 1870 there had been a dramatic expansion in the variety of shops and services at the disposal of visitors; there were also now six hotels and sixty-six lodging houses. By the time Helen Duncan was born there in 1897, the Callander Recreation Company had invested in a bowling green and a nine-hole golf course, and tennis courts had been built and a keeper employed to look after them. At a time when decent working-class housing was scarce, houses were built specially for well-to-do families – the so-called 'carriage folk' – who rented them for the summer. It was at refined consumers like these that fashions such as tweed suits and ladies' capes were being aimed by 1900, likewise the 'Women's Chat' column in the *Callander Advertiser*, which offered royal gossip and style tips: 'The handkerchief of the moment is white,' advised 'Madge', together with a distinctly proletarian-sounding recipe for Balmoral pudding.

By 1897, Helen Duncan's parents would have known an improved physical environment and broader mental horizons in Callander. Burgh status was conferred in 1866 and the provision of public amenities overseen by a council of commissioners. Gaslighting was extended, kerbs and gutters laid, sewers rebuilt and shrubs planted to hide the ash pits. Ratepayers took these matters seriously and civic-minded businessmen sat on innumerable committees. But life remained a mixture of old and new. Street dung was used to grow hay sold for public funds. Rabbits and sheep dip were advertised in newspapers alongside French millinery and women's pills to 'quickly correct all irregularities, remove all obstructions, and relieve the distressing symptoms so prevalent with the sex'. Deaths in boiler explosions were reported, as was tubercular infection in milk. English did not banish Gaelic so much as establish bilingualism. The middle classes prospered disproportionately compared to labouring families dependent on seasonal wages, Christian charity and the Penny Bank, a change reflected in Queen Victoria's impression that Callander had 'a few good houses and many poor ones'. Petty thieves frequently appeared before the commission chairman (also the chief magistrate) as did fraudsters – weavers who adulterated linen with cotton, for example. Occasionally there were suicides. It was only natural, then, that many young people were seduced by visions of the New World conjured up by the emigration agents who visited Callander to recruit farmworkers and domestic servants for Canada and Australia.

Hopes were also pinned on religion, which offered eternal life in the hereafter and, until then, dignity in adversity. Worship was as pluralistic as in any Victorian town, embracing Free and United Presbyterians, Catholics, Episcopalians and the Church of Scotland. Protestantism of the most straight-backed kind dominated, an ethos that pervaded Callander's clubs and societies, such as the Ben Ledi Masonic Lodge and the Fiery Cross Lodge. The magistrate, Colonel Robertson, presided over the Abstainers' Union, his wife the YWCA Bible class, which met in the Mission Hall, where Mrs Chenevix-Trench also held her Band of Hope meetings. In 1892 the Free Kirk School became a high school committed to promoting 'the sound religious and moral training of the young in the parish and neighbourhood of Callander' and offered adult evening classes in shorthand, bookkeeping, drawing and mensuration. Public lectures advanced ideals of prohibition and self-improvement – for instance, condemning swearing, cheating, lying and smoking among youths, before whose eyes exemplars of morality were held up. This was, therefore, a formative environment characterized by censure and restriction. In 1908 the Callander Literary Society, a focal point of cultural life, debated the enfranchisement of women, but the motion was defeated thirty-four to eighteen.

There was another side to this rational existence of civic discipline and muscular religion. When the Dreadnought Hotel was built in 1802, the McNabs, who owned it, had the severed head of a rival clan chief carved in relief and set into the gable wall. Doubtless his ghost returned. The hotel is reputedly haunted by a mother who died giving birth to an illegitimate child, and the window of her room is kept blacked out. To stray beyond Callander's main streets, up the winding paths into the crags, is to enter an altogether darker world of bloody deeds and their spectral legacy, where the looming presence of Ben Ledi – the Hill of God – and the enveloping chill and mist propel the mind back through the ages. This was, after all, where Romantic poets found truth in folklore and imagination, and reason was redundant. Here roamed Robert MacGregor, the outlaw lionized by Sir Walter Scott, and the novelist's senses were beguiled by the supernatural. The witch-hunt had been most intense in the Lowlands, where the kirk was most anxious about the presence of Highland beliefs in curses, charms, sacred ponds, fairy hills, ghostly warriors, angels, hags, necromancers, werewolves and banshees – the Celtic spirits whose wailing foretold death.

Then there was second sight: the gift of prophecy. Dr Samuel Johnson, of whom his companion Boswell maintained 'he did not affirm anything positively upon a subject which it is the fashion of the times to laugh at as a matter of absurd credulity', returned from his tour of the Hebrides in the 1790s utterly convinced of its power. In the seventeenth century opinion had been divided. Did it come from the devil or the 'good folk', tribal mountain fairies who could blind humans but were repelled by iron? The authority was Robert Kirk, minister of Aberfoyle, a parish not far from Callander, who was interested in his parishioners' folk beliefs and defended them to repel advancing atheism. Spirits might live in the air, he said, as easily as in a body, and might be called upon to do good, just as witches summoned demons to do evil. This fascination persisted into the nineteenth century when the journalist Charles Mackay, like Kirk a Perthshire man, collected true supernatural stories, and in the twentieth century with a twelve-volume conspectus of ancient customs, *The Golden Bough*, published in 1915, by the Glasgow-born anthropologist Sir James Frazer. Frazer's work stressed the enduring vibrancy of such beliefs and propagated them in a new generation of writers.

One Thursday evening in January 1908 the Callander Literary Society welcomed a visiting speaker, Dr McDiarmid, an authority on Gaelic and the folklore of Breadalbane. McDiarmid regaled the Society with an evocation of the days of romance and cruelty, long-dead rituals and supernatural beliefs from a past as mysterious as the mountains on a moonless winter night. After he had finished, the society's chairman, primary school teacher Alexander Cumming, offered his appreciation of McDiarmid's vivid portrait of this lost world and elicited applause. Appearances were deceptive, however. If some in the audience supposed that McDiarmid's arcana belonged entirely to legend, there were others who knew differently – not least Mr Cumming, who at that time had rather an unusual, not to say disturbing, little girl in his class.

This was the cultural ground in which Helen Duncan's life took root, terrain mapped by past and present – Presbyterianism and progress jostling with the spirits and sprites of the hills. Helen was born a MacFarlane, a clan deeply rooted in and around Callander, their graves scattered across the kirkyard at Kilmahog. The wife of an ancestor killed at Waterloo, it was said, wore her widow's weeds for the rest of her lonely life. In an age when ties of kinship were the sinews of local power, the MacFarlanes had produced numerous influential men, among them John MacFarlane of Kilmahog, a teacher respected at the parish school for thirty years. Later, Norman MacFarlane had given his name to a salmon pool on the Teith. By the time of Helen's birth this prominence had declined, although the MacFarlanes still cropped up: the town librarian, a secretary of the cycling club, a finalist in a YMCA draughts tournament.

Archibald MacFarlane, Helen's father, was a slater and builder, the sort of upper-working-class skilled artisan who, though not recorded as a town councillor or magistrate (as descendants claimed), was industrious, God-fearing and loyal to the Crown. By tradition, when his wife Isabella was a girl, an open coach en route to Balmoral was caught in bad weather and her family were asked to shelter the Queen. The tale, however improbable, was repeated many times in the Rattery household, the embossed letter of thanks, like the crest on a marmalade jar, somehow confirming that the family were 'by appointment'. It was a pride that Isabella Rattery brought with her when she married Archibald, and set up home at 96 Main Street, a respectable house rented from Daniel Melrose, an ironmonger, for the princely sum of £14 a year.

In June 1897, during Queen Victoria's Diamond Jubilee celebrations, Isabella MacFarlane was three months' pregnant with her fourth child. Across the nation, glittering pageantry and ebullient festivities marked the height of British imperial pride and Callander did its bit, despite controversy over plans to spend good money planting commemorative trees in Main Street when the town's water pipes needed overhauling. Isabella's baby was born at three o'clock in the morning on 25 November, a healthy girl whom she and Archie named Victoria Helen in honour of the Queen. They celebrated modestly but did not make an announcement in the *Advertiser*. Christened into the Presbyterian Church, Victoria slept through most of the ceremony, waking only for the naming and blessing when the minister looked into the deep, dark brown eyes that Helen's followers would remember long after her death. The birth details were lodged with the registrar, who used the schoolhouse as his office, and the MacFarlane siblings began adjusting to the new arrival in the family home.

Early in the new century, Archie and Isabella moved to Bridgend, a road crossing the river and the oldest part of the town. Their small, whitewashed house, Cherry Cottage, had a slate roof and three front gables and sash windows; some say Archie built it himself. Perhaps because her first name was too grand for daily use, the MacFarlanes' baby was known as Helen, and even that soon became 'Nellie' or 'Nell'. She grew into a plump, sturdy child, more handsome than pretty, with her flashing eyes and hair so black it had a shimmer of blue. As in many households in Callander, her father's regime was loving but austere. Though not exactly poor, by the time Isabella's eighth child was born, the MacFarlanes couldn't afford to be profligate even if profligacy hadn't been a sin. Christmas emphasized the festival's religious aspects over its excesses. Luxuries were few. Helen, however, had a sweet tooth; the local delicacy was tablet, a brittle fudge made from sugar, cream and butter. She played hard with her brothers, forming a solid bond with Peter. It may be significant that in a photograph she looks very much like a boy in her jacket, collar and tie. There was an enduring memory in Callander of her scaling a building to retrieve a ball and standing on the roof in triumph soaking up the applause and cheering from children below. It was for such tomboyish antics that she acquired the nickname well known in her home town: 'Hellish Nell'.

Like her brothers, Helen spent her summers outside and could be found playing down by the Teith where kingfishers swooped low over the water. The weather was unsettled: when it was hot the river sank (spoiling the salmon fishing); then it rained and there were floods. She may have known the old Scots saying that when the sun shines through rain it means the fairies are baking; perhaps she believed it. Activities thought fit for girls were not to Helen's taste. Up in the hills the MacFarlane children hid among the oak and birch or surveyed their land from the earthworks of Dunmore Fort where the kicked-up ground occasionally yielded Roman coins. Closer to home, on the site of the old parish church, sprawled the disused graveyard with its watch-house built in the previous century to deter bodysnatchers. Rarely far from mischief, the children once released the coal from a freight wagon on to the railway track and were made to pick it up lump by lump. It seems, though, that the more Helen was corrected and restrained, the more she resisted and persisted in her hellish behaviour. The MacFarlanes had long cherished their reputation as champion swimmers, but even this outlet was forbidden to her, Norman's Pool being considered unsafe for a child and disporting oneself in one's undergarments unseemly for a girl. She did it anyway.

Growing up in Callander, Helen would have known about 'pancakes', a hiding-and-stalking game where an appointed 'witch' would steal children (the 'pancakes') from a 'mother', and a 'maid' had to stop her. Its symbolic origins – a harvest festival where 'witch', 'maid' and 'mother' were names for the last corn sheaves depending on when they were cut – show how deeply living customs were rooted in the past. And when Helen reached the age of about seven, her nascent sense of herself met with the belief in Highland second sight. The trigger may have been just a fireside tale or an encounter with a fortune teller, but it gave meaning to her life. Helen suspected that her mother had psychic powers, because she always knew when her wayward daughter had been swimming. Even when she discovered the truth – Isabella MacFarlane noticed whenever the child's petticoat had been laced up at the front – she clung to the idea that her mother was clairvoyant, by which time her own suspicions about herself had intensified, especially once she started to see strange things.

The memoirs of many psychics tell of powers emerging in childhood, for which they were chastised and punished. No surprise, then, that when Helen had visions of a soldier (long dead) and a man lost in a snowdrift (alive), her mother warned her she would get a reputation as a 'glaikit' or even 'fey' child possessed by unnatural power. For good measure, Isabella added she would be burned as a witch or thrown into Loch Sloy. 'Noo, dinna ye be sayin' these things ootside,' Helen recalled her mother saying. 'When ye have anything like that to say come to me with it and to no one else.' But Helen stubbornly thought her behaviour to be natural, and so refused to suppress or disguise it. Nor did she avoid the church, as a witch might have done. In fact, she was rewarded for good attendance, an achievement slightly marred by her guessing in advance what her prize would be – a copy of *Oliver Twist* – and her pious disdain for 'a book that tells you how to steal'. Family lore had it that the minister was sufficiently alarmed and offended by her 'dreams and visions' to condemn them during Sunday service. By contrast, Dr Todd, the family physician, considered her a remarkable child.

In 1908, Rev. William Morrison wrote an introduction for a collection of instances of second sight, a phenomenon he attributed to the 'racial genius' of Highland people. Like Robert Kirk two hundred years earlier, he believed that children were powerless to resist a gift which came to them through the bloodline, a gift which 'is in every case regarded as troublesome to the possessor of it'. Morrison cited medical as well as cultural factors. Clairvoyant episodes, he said, were preceded by 'nerve storms' when spirits became visible, ending with utter prostration. In its mildest form, second sight was a raised sensitivity, enabling seers, as Kirk had put it, to 'perceive things, that for their smallness, or subtlety, and secrecy, are invisible to others'. And with this uncanny perceptiveness, Helen wrapped herself in a cocoon. Every day she passed a doorway above which the text of John 3:16 was set in stone, a reminder that God so loved the world he promised everlasting life to the faithful. Of this she had no doubt, and yet the wall between heaven and earth – the barrier which required a leap of faith – was crumbling as the spiritual traffic between life and afterlife shimmered into view.

Helen could not stay in her cocoon all the time. She attended the school in Craigard Road, whose traditions prior to the appointment of Mr Cumming in 1879 had been poor teaching and attendance, as well as mismanagement by the School Board. Scholarly and sober, Cumming (nicknamed 'Tiger') was remembered with fondness and respect by everyone he taught. Attendance remained a problem, however, especially in May when girls prepared the houses of the carriage folk and boys ran errands and delivered messages. Even a committed teacher could only achieve so much, especially with a pupil like Helen, whose own estimation of her psychic gifts compensated for, or at least excused, a lack of academic aptitude. Her sense of difference was compounded by the discovery that she was less popular with her peers when not retrieving balls from roofs. In the playground she saw into their pasts and futures, issuing portentous advice and fearful warnings – and they didn't like it at all. One girl was told she would marry a chauffeur who, exotically, *would not be from Callander*; worse, a boy in a sailor suit was told he would end up at the bottom of the sea in a coming war. Helen was treated with both fear and contempt and, like Elspeth McEwen, became the subject of persistent rumours, which pushed her to the margins of normal social life. Perhaps the children played 'pancakes' without her – or perhaps she was always the witch.

The child-prophet's ostracism was self-perpetuating.

A curious memoir from 1933, of which Helen was supposedly the author (one detects the hand of her husband), rationalized the blessing of foresight using the benefit of hindsight:

> Strange sayings fell from my lips. I could not control my tongue. I simply had to express the thoughts that came to me. The result was that I was left pretty much to my own resources, but this was no hardship. On the contrary, it allowed me to develop my personality free from the influence of others, and I believe this was a factor in fostering my psychic gifts.

And yet she was far from at ease with herself and the world. Her character traits – crippling diffidence, timidity and passivity, punctuated by outbursts of hysterical rage – suggest that her personality was not developing as it might. A few stories stand out. She was fond of recalling how she never needed to study, because knowledge would pop into her head from an unseen source (she thought heaven), and that whenever she was asked a question, 'I would lift my downcast head and sing forth the answer'. Once, an inspector of schools, suspecting she was hiding a book, ordered her underwear to be searched. On another occasion, when the dates of famous battles miraculously appeared on her slate during a history test – she had clasped it to her chest and prayed for God's help – Tiger Cumming accused her of cheating. She denied this to the point where she snapped, hurled her inkwell at him and ran home to Cherry Cottage. Another version of the tale has it that with the date '1066' in her head, she predicted Cumming's death, and that he succumbed to a heart attack during a lesson about the Battle of Hastings.* She feared similarly for Dr Todd shortly before he died in a car crash.

Like all children in Edwardian Callander, Helen struggled to reconcile her parents' social world with the scenes of gracious living that swam before her eyes each summer: the sleek, chauffeur-driven cars, the young women draped in silks or furs depending on the barometer reading. In fashions and manners, the rich visitors advertised an era of change. The Cockhill Fair in May, a traditional highlight of the year, declined and the influx of private motor cars prompted town commissioners to impose a speed limit of ten miles per hour. Popular recreation was no longer determined by the agricultural calendar, and even the YMCA's limelight lectures lost their allure after the first visit from Frame's Vaudeville Company, which included demonstrations of the Anglo-American Bio-Tableau Cinematograph. Watching luminous images in the darkness was like peering into a secret garden and glimpsing an alternative reality. Reading Helen Duncan's life backwards, we might feel that something stirred in her in these years, a longing that would carry her away from Callander and virtually everything that went with it. Quite how this would happen she couldn't foresee, although she probably pinned her hopes on love and marriage.

* In yet another version the teacher's name was Fulton and the battle Bannockburn, 1314.

Indirectly, though, for her, as for thousands of others, the crucible of change would be war.

In February 1914, sitting before an audience of nearly a thousand people, Sir Arthur Conan Doyle, the creator of Sherlock Holmes and a committed Spiritualist, received this chilling prediction from an Australian medium, Mrs Foster Turner:

> Now, although there is not at present a whisper of a great European war at hand, yet I want to warn you that before this year, 1914, has run its course, Europe will be deluged in blood. Great Britain, our beloved nation, will be drawn into the most awful war the world has ever known. Germany will be the great antagonist, and will draw other nations in her train. Austria will totter to its ruin. Kings and kingdoms will fall. Millions of precious lives will be slaughtered, but Britain will finally triumph and emerge victorious.

Predictions of war were commonplace, some made before the outbreak of hostilities, others, less impressively, afterwards. Since the 1850s rumours had circulated in Germany about Prince Wilhelm meeting a gypsy who, Macbeth-style, hinted at his becoming the first Kaiser – but forecasts of imperial greatness soon gave way to more apocalyptic visions. At a private psychic sitting in 1909, a medium in Teddington, Middlesex, saw poppies, waxed mystical about the reign of Mars and, like Mrs Foster Turner, warned of a blood-soaked world to come. For the more popular market, *Old Moore's Almanac* did not get into the swing of things until 1916, prompting an Oxford don who studied such auguries to comment drily: 'What can one expect for a penny?'

War broke out in the summer before Helen Duncan's seventeenth birthday. All over Britain, popular patriotism and jingoism surpassed the Jubilee celebrations of 1897, and men who were either proud, bored or unemployed merrily queued down the street outside the recruiting stations as if, as Philip Larkin would reflect, it was all an August Bank Holiday lark. For one thing, it was work — and exciting work, too. The average weekly wage of these men, assuming they had jobs, was £2. In Callander, as elsewhere, boys keen to escape the fields, factories and pits (where many earned less than 10s a week), arched their backs and looked the recruiting sergeant in the eye as they gave their age as nineteen. Not that most needed to fear rejection: the sergeant's per capita bonus saw to that. As men of the town marched off to France with the Black Watch, and the flags were put away until victory, so refugees arrived from Belgium, and by Christmas 1914 – when they had said it would all be over – the casualties began to fill the beds at the requisitioned mansion house of Inverleny, soon to acquire permanence as Callander Military Extension Hospital. Life was transformed in countless small ways. The woods beneath the crags where Helen had played as a child were cut down for timber, and as an economy the *Callander Advertiser* shrank in size.

Archie MacFarlane, who also thought the war would end within months, scoffed when his doomy daughter predicted it would last for three or four years, killing thousands of men, and especially at her vision of horseless war machines which moved on their bellies and smashed through houses. She alone saw the horror and her prophecies were both abundant and accurate. News of the first casualties from Callander trickled in during 1915, one of the first being Private William Ferguson, a plumber, severely wounded in the neck by shrapnel. That was in April. By June the trickle of stories about soldiers injured, gassed, captured and missing had become a steady stream. The first death was that of John Cameron of the 1/6th Black Watch, aged twenty-nine, on 11 August 1915; before the war he had been the keeper of the Callander tennis courts. Memorial cards went on sale in the Main Street shops, 'specially suited for our Fallen Heroes', and, like the rest of the town, the MacFarlanes did what they could to accept grief and keep the men fighting. A photograph dated April 1915, depicting a group of schoolgirls raising money to buy an ambulance, contains three MacFarlanes. Their clan did not emerge unscathed. Like her Napoleonic forebear a century earlier, in April 1918 Mary MacFarlane of Kilmahog donned her own widow's weeds when her husband was killed during the last great German push on the Western Front.

Not that any of this meant much to Hellish Nell, however, for by the outbreak of war she was gone, banished from her family under the blackest of clouds, and so too from the community whose traditions had instilled in her a sense of the mystifying and the miraculous. As the war dragged on, and Mrs Foster Turner's vision turned into

ghastly reality, at night in her dreams Helen was trans-
ported to the trenches. There, she sowed the seeds of a
future where her life's purpose lay in not just Highland
second sight but an ability to communicate directly with
the spirits of the dead.

2. Developing God's Gift: Labour, Love and the Arrival of Henry

In 1966 a nightwatchman at Edinburgh University was discharged from the City Hospital after suffering a stroke. Haunted by the memory of his wife, who died ten years earlier, he had sold their big house in Rankeillor Street, lock, stock and barrel, married his cleaner, Anna, and moved into a two-bedroom flat. When his granddaughter Sheila visited him there as he convalesced, she found him sitting in a dream, naked and unabashed while Anna got ready for work. Notes, cuttings and photographs covered the floor, and he was reminiscing in a stream of semi-consciousness. Sheila had always known him as a strict, disciplined man, an old soldier who wore a stiff collar and tie, even at home with a cardigan with leather elbow-patches. He drank moderately, read voraciously and, though his health had been poor since youth, was a rock to all around him. Now there he was, diminished, stranded somewhere between death and the life spread out in paper before him. 'He's not talking to me, Sheila,' Anna said peevishly. 'He's talking to *her*!' She meant, of course, his first wife: his precious Nell.

When Henry Duncan died the following year, his eldest son Harry, who had emigrated to Australia, took care of his father's papers but lost most of them in a house fire. Fortunately, Henry's meticulous record of his wife's development as a medium survived, which Harry later sent back to Scotland to help his sister Gena write their mother's biography. Gena's daughter Sheila (Henry's visitor after his stroke) remembers her mother tapping away at the typewriter, shaping the story from childhood memories, family lore, remnants from the fire and, crucially, spirit guidance. A seventh child, Gena had professed psychic and spiritualistic powers from childhood – powers which gave her a unique insight into Helen's gift and which she, in turn, passed on to Sheila. Gena also bequeathed her book, which fixed the details of Helen Duncan's life, but demonstrates, too, how every family's knowledge of itself is shot through with errors and elaborations, secrets and lies. Like Spiritualist tales, however, ancestral tales don't need solid fact to tell people where they came from and who they are. If stories reassure and entertain, they seem as true as anything else.*

We can be sure, though, that when Nellie MacFarlane left school in her early teens, around 1911, marrying her off was not an option and even at sixteen the prospect was remote. The scarcity of regular employment in Callander meant that many men couldn't afford to marry and so migrated or emigrated, and in greater numbers than women, whose average age of marriage in 1911 was twenty-six. Helen would have to go out to work, and yet there's something fishy about Gena's account of the

---

* Even Helen's birth year is disputed. Formally registered as 1897, Helen herself sometimes said it was 1898; Gena thought it was 1895 and elsewhere 1896 is given.

cheerful family discussions about finding her a job in
Dundee – hard, badly paid toil associated with unskilled
married women too poor to subsist on a husband's wage.

What Gena could not say, even in 1985, was that in the
early summer of 1914 Helen became pregnant and was
sent away. Who the father was, she never said. When the
baby was born in February 1915 in Dundee Maternity
Hospital, Helen gave her address as Bridgend, Callander,
and her occupation as hotel waitress. Beyond a single
meeting before Helen's marriage, Gena doesn't mention
the family again. In fact, young Nell was banished for good
and may have returned to Callander only once to visit her
brother Peter. He had protected her since the days when,
fresh from the forbidden pool, they had learned to lace up
her petticoat at the back to avoid detection by their mother.
Poignantly, it was Isabella MacFarlane after whom Helen
was to name the baby that she didn't want but couldn't
bring herself to give up for adoption.

Helen's new life living in a women's hostel was not the
dormitory caper Gena made it out to be. Of the town's
two principal places of employment – the jam factories
and the jute mills – Helen chose the latter, where she
befriended Jean Duncan, who was a year her senior. They
spent their free time together, in winter ice-skating on the
quarry pond. After war was declared in 1914, they sought
work making munitions, attracted by the camaraderie and
higher wages, but Helen was rejected due to her obesity and
tubercular lung, and perhaps also because she was three
months pregnant. It was a blessing in disguise. Not
only was she spared the yellow skin and sickness of the

TNT-poisoned 'canaries' but, as Gena related, the sanatorium she entered instead restored her health and inspired her to care for others. Soon after Isabella was born, she was taken on as a Nursing Auxiliary at Dundee Royal Infirmary and in due course may have arranged for Isabella to be minded there when she was on duty. Helen's experience of the psychiatric wing left a lasting impression: the epileptics whose fits convinced her that demonic possession was real, the frantic woman who ate sanitary towels. Helen and Jean still saw each other when they could, and on one visit to Helen's hospital digs Jean, who doubtless already knew her friend's biggest secret, was entrusted with another.

In her dreams Helen had been visiting the trenches of Flanders, extending her dull, dread-filled life into what Byron once called 'a wide realm of wild reality'. On the Western Front the temporal and infernal were juxtaposed, the reality of dreams and the surrealism of life thrown into hellish confusion. There, Jean heard, Nellie had met a young private whose war-sick eyes told her at once that his soul would be joined with hers for ever. To bring Helen down to earth, Jean encouraged her to write to her brother, a *real* soldier at the front and Helen's age, which she did – but the reply she received further fused the material and the spiritual, fulfilling her sleep-borne prophecy and satisfying a yearning to love and be loved. So far, her experience was still shaped by Highland ghosts and omens rather than a conviction that spirits communicated with the living. This was the central tenet of Spiritualism, a religion of which she had heard but whose claim to have

opened up the kingdom of heaven she regarded scepti-
cally. As in the hearts of many thousands, however, the war
would change that.

Spiritualism originated at Hydesville in Upstate New York.
In 1848 the teenage daughters of a Methodist farmer, J. D.
Fox, heard strange rapping noises, which they deciphered
as messages from the spirit of a murdered man whose
bones were subsequently discovered in their cellar. As word
spread, the Fox sisters attracted attention from investigative committees and a huge number of people wishing
to sit with them. The movement swept across America,
spawning 'spirit depots' and periodicals, and winning
converts among academics, writers, politicians and indus-
trialists, unchecked even by the girls' confession that it had
all been a hoax. Before long, the enterprising showman Phin-
eas T. Barnum had hired them and money began to change
hands. Mediums proliferated and spirit communication
diversified. Automatic slate writing, levitating furniture,
spirit hands cast in plaster, direct speech and the appearance of shadowy faces became standard. In their remote
Ohio township, the Koons family put on spirit shows in
darkness, playing musical instruments, waving phosphores-
cent hands and calling through trumpets – the standard
repertoire of physical mediums for a century to come.

Spiritualism married religion and entertainment, displaying something of the Catholic Apostolic Church's
desire to speak in tongues, and in America the ecstasies of
the Shakers and the radical nonconformity of Mormon-
ism and Adventism. But it was also a union with science,

especially hypnosis and the 'animal magnetism' developed as a healing science in pre-Revolutionary France by Friedrich Mesmer. At his sittings – or *séances* – patients and visitors linked hands to allow free passage of an invisible fluid, which Mesmer said exerted an electrical force upon human bodies. By the mid-nineteenth century, mesmerism had inspired 'spiritism', which, under the direction of the philosopher Allan Kardec, treated the quest for physical phenomena as a red herring and preached reincarnation as the royal road between this world and the next. Even earlier than Mesmer, the Swedish mystic Emanuel Swedenborg had as a child entranced himself by holding his breath and by the 1740s was venturing into the spirit world to converse with its inhabitants, for which he is hailed as the father of Spiritualism.

The idea that people could talk with spirits stretched back into ancient civilizations and, cave paintings suggest, prehistory. Spiritual encounters occur throughout the Bible (the lives of the prophets were *controlled* by spirits), which influenced the early Christian Church. St Augustine believed 'the spirits of the dead can be sent to the living and can unveil to them the future which they themselves have learned from other spirits or from angels'. Protestants and Catholics alike preached the reality of the spirit world. Queen Elizabeth I, who legislated against witches, employed an astrologer, Dr John Dee, who conversed with angels through a medium, Edward Kelley. Spirits prophesied various things, including the foiled invasion of the Spanish Armada. In the next century, educated men continued to see the spirit world as proof of the doctrine of immortality and a bulwark against 'atheism' and Deism, which pushed all spiritual creatures, including God, off the cosmic stage. Belief, however, was dominated by ambiguity and ambivalence, and it's easy to forget that Newton was as fascinated by angelic wisdom as by gravitating apples. The interest in nature of virtuosi like Newton was consonant with their reverence for God's design, even though, unknown to them, it was gnawing away at the traditional world view from within.

Many ordinary people encountered spirits who revealed secrets, issued warnings, accused the guilty and exonerated the innocent. For these were not historical ghosts but the familiar dead – friends, relatives, neighbours – and they had something to say. In the 1760s a murder trial was initiated by a female spirit who, as in the Fox household, communicated by raps received by an eleven-year-old girl. When Dr Johnson questioned her, he was doubtful but in private he grappled with more uncertain feelings. Not only was he convinced about Highland second sight but prayed that his dead wife would revisit him 'by appearance, impulses, dreams, or in any other manner'. Uncertainty lingered in middle-class mores well into the next century, by which time technology and industry were breeding trust in material progress, and scripturally based faith was receding like an ebbing tide with Matthew Arnold's 'melancholy, long, withdrawing roar'. Spiritualism, however, offered a tonic. Research into invisible impulses – light waves, magnetism and electricity – and the invention of the telegraph coincided with interest in thought transference and spiritual communication, heralding a glorious dawn rising over a world darkened by secularism and disenchantment. 'It seems to me that a new era in the history of humanity has actually commenced', Rev. S. B. Britain declared in the first ever public lecture on Spiritualism, delivered in New York City in 1850,

> and that those tremendous and unexplained mysteries that we have called in the earliest ages 'Magic', in the Biblical dispensation 'Miracle', and in the Middle Ages 'Witchcraft' are now coming to the front as the work of human spirits, ever aiming to communicate with the earth-friends they have left behind, and ever striving to impart that knowledge of spiritual life and possibilities, of which mankind has been so lamentably ignorant.

Critics noted the irony that Spiritualism, far from routing materialism, had capitulated to it. Replacing faith with tangible truths was indeed Spiritualism's unique selling point and explains its appeal to the respectable working class, to whom it offered an alternative to ecclesiastical dogma and authority. Spiritualism, Conan Doyle promised, was 'a religion for those who find themselves outside all religions'. No surprise, then, that the Catholic Church feared it as a lethal contagion and condemned mediums as halfwits or whores prostituted to a wicked trade – even as witches.

No surprise either that, as a progressive and idealistic movement, Spiritualism embraced socialism, and thrived in the nonconformist halls and mechanics' institutes of northern industrial towns. The social reformer Robert Owen lived to see Spiritualism nourish the ideals of working-class unity and freedom he held dear. As with friendly societies and trades unions, and as had happened in America, the engine that spread Spiritualism was the popular press. The first of many Spiritualist periodicals was published in 1853 by the husband of an American medium, Mrs Hayden, who held seances and counted Owen among her converts. In the same year, the first English Spiritualist church opened its doors, at Keighley in Yorkshire. Around this time Emma Hardinge, an actress from London's East End, who as a child had seen visions of dead relatives, met the Fox sisters in America and returned home a decade later as a performing trance speaker. A skilled publicist – she had campaigned for Abraham Lincoln – she developed skills from levitation to healing, which she took on a world tour before settling in Manchester. There in 1887 she used the text of Rev. Britain's New York lecture to launch a weekly newspaper, the *Two Worlds*, whose masthead showed Truth perched atop the earth, exhorting the crouching figures of Science and Love to rise up. At the back was a directory of mediums from Bradford to Bloomsbury, among whom Mrs Hardinge Britten (as she had become) discreetly included herself.

Half of this list were women, who were regarded as natural mediums worthy of respect and attention. Class and education were no obstacles: the simpler the soul, the purer the results. In a deeply patriarchal society, liberation by seance could be sexual as well as social. At seances young women held hands with strange men in dark rooms; light, mediums maintained, inhibited psychical phenomena.

Satirists were amused by this: one newspaper cartoon from the 1890s depicted male and female sitters abandoning decorum as soon as the lights went down. But to moralists seances were no laughing matter. What they saw were women – mediums and clients alike – craving power, crossing boundaries, and breaking rules of class and gender.

None of this altered the fact that respectable people, women and men, took Spiritualism seriously. Seance-going was part of the afternoon tea ritual indulged in by society hostesses who invited guests on printed cards. And female curiosity was notable among the intelligentsia. George Eliot showed an interest, as did Elizabeth Barrett Browning, although her husband Robert was cautious. Dickens, Trollope, Thackeray and Tennyson went to seances, among whom Tennyson was *the* Spiritualist poet:

> The Ghost in Man, the Ghost that once was Man,
> But cannot wholly free itself from Man,
> Are calling to each other thro' a dawn
> Stranger than earth has ever seen; the veil
> Is rending, and the Voices of the day
> Are heard across the Voices of the dark.

And yet this spiritual renaissance only reflects the depth of religious despair in an era of profound scientific and cultural change. The anti-creationism of Darwin (who disdained both mesmerism and Spiritualism) didn't help either.

Drifting from their faith, three Fellows of Trinity College, Cambridge – Henry Sidgwick, Frederic Myers and

Edmund Gurney – progressed from the University Ghost Club to active investigation of paranormal phenomena. Alternating between open-mindedness, credulity and scepticism, they established a defining spectrum of opinion for the Society of Psychical Research, which, with Professor William Barrett, they founded in 1882. It drew members, Spiritualist and non-Spiritualist, from all walks of intellectual life in Cambridge and beyond. Sidgwick, who was Professor of Moral Philosophy, and Myers, a classicist and philologist, were frowning bearded men of scruple with impeccable intellectual credentials. The same was true of another budding avatar of psychic science, the physicist pioneer of wireless telegraphy – and Myers's friend – Sir Oliver Lodge. The SPR thrived into the Edwardian period, challenging old orthodoxies and constructing a new framework for investigation and debate. The evidences for Spiritualism seemed very real, a breakthrough imminent.

Then came the First World War. Across Britain, mechanized slaughter and the vast, unmastered grief it inflicted raised the profile of Spiritualism and increased demand for the services of mediums. Private readings and seances brought comforting messages, and spirit photographers captured tired-looking women in black, the faces of servicemen hovering above in a fuzzy aura. Like bereavement, interest in Spiritualism knew no boundaries of class or education. When Rudyard Kipling, devastated by the loss of his son in 1915, asked 'Who shall return us our children?' a growing army of mourners felt the answer was obvious. Like many, Kipling was ambivalent, which he expressed in a poem about Saul breaking God's law by visiting the Witch of Endor to speak to Samuel's spirit. Spiritualism could seem irrational or sinful – but parents, widows and siblings were desperate to ease their pain.

In May 1915, Sir Oliver Lodge received a letter from Alta Piper, the daughter of a Bostonian medium, Leonora Piper, who had persuaded him of the reality of life after death. Miss Piper said the war horrified her soul and enclosed a script from an automatic-writing session at which Lodge's friend Frederic Myers, who had died in 1901, foresaw a better world but warned that 'some of our earthly helpers must be sacrificed ere this struggle ends'. The message impressed Lodge, whose twenty-six-year-old son Raymond was an infantry officer on the Western Front. Lodge had a sheaf of his letters, four from that month alone, describing trench systems, bombardments and messy meals of bacon and cheese. A note dated 12 September 1915, however, was Raymond's last. Two days later he was struck by a shell fragment and died within a few hours. As the family sat stupefied by the news, Lady Lodge received a letter of consolation from a fellow officer, Lieutenant G. R. A. Case. But the Lodges' suffering, and the sacrifices predicted by the spirit of Myers, were almost too great to bear. And even before Lady Lodge had assimilated his words, Case himself was dead and buried.

Like many others, including their friend Conan Doyle (who lost a son, a brother and a brother-in-law), Sir Oliver and Lady Lodge endured their grief through Spiritualism. Communications from their son, received through the medium Gladys Osborne Leonard, were compiled by

Lodge into a book, *Raymond*, published in November 1916. The message was clear: death was a rebirth into another state, and at worst exile to a world that was still connected to this one by a bridge of love.

Famous now as a Spiritualist as well as a scientist, Lodge received many messages from beyond the veil. His reaction to a letter from none other than William Shakespeare, in June 1918, is unrecorded. The contents had been whispered to an American medium, Sarah Taylor Shatford, and typed up in a New York hotel room. The bard, demented by time, spoke of his love for England and his striving to 'open the soft and thin partition which hides her sons out-gone from those on her fertile and worshipped land'. The spirit also reeled off four hundred pages of patriotic doggerel, including verses entitled 'Peace After War', which begin:

When wars have done and peace is come, and to a wounded
    world no longer torn,
By cannonshell, or doubts or fears, there comes sweet rest,
    new born,
To solace hearts and make men see how traitorous their
    itching greed,
O What a World wherein to live, where each man shares his
    brother's need!

However absurd this all seems, the idea that war might be banished by love and enlightened brotherhood was a sincere one, disclosing deep anguish and anxiety, and was shared by millions of ordinary men and women who had lived through the war. And it certainly represents the feelings of Private Henry Duncan, who, by the time Sarah Shatford was transcribing the voices in her head, was already a veteran of a world torn by cannonshell, doubts and fears, and was looking forward to a better life.

Henry Duncan had grown up in Dundee, where, in 1914, aged sixteen and a half, he ducked out of an apprenticeship and headed for the recruiting depot of the 4th Battalion, the Black Watch. After lying about his age, he was kitted out in tam-o'-shanter and kilt and sent off for ten weeks' basic training with many other Dundonian men – so many, in fact, they called the 4th Battalion a 'city at war'. With them they took body lice and sunken chests but left behind tenements, factories and mills. Most felt they had nothing to lose. Henry's father, an iron driller in the shipyards, joined up too. A Presbyterian with Spiritualist leanings, in 1895 he had married Annie Mearns, a Catholic from Arbroath, who as a girl had toiled as a herring gutter. They raised five children in a poky tenement flat where the spirits of the dead were never far away. Even by contemporary standards, the building was suffused with a gloom which was not only depressing but seemed to stir violent urges in Henry senior. One day his son, plagued by a recurring nightmare about a strange man in his bedroom, smelled gas and went out onto the landing. There Henry junior saw a pale, wraith-like woman he didn't recognize, but who, according to their landlord, was the wife of a bully who had gassed herself; the husband had been found hanged. The Duncans were moved to another property. There they found tragedy of their own when Henry's eight-year-old brother disappeared. After the police drew a blank, contrary to the doctrines of her church Annie Duncan went to a medium, who saw water and ships and predicted they would receive news within three weeks. Right on time, crewmen of a ship in for repair at Victoria Rock found a boy drowned between the hull and the quay. Imagining Annie's grief, a Fife man sent her one of his poems, which began:

> There is just a thin veil we almost see through,
> And one whom we love is dimly in view.

Originally written for Queen Alexandra on the occasion of Edward VII's death in 1910, it brought Annie some comfort. But in 1914 the memory of loss was revived by the fear that she was about to lose another son – and her husband.

At the front, the Black Watch lived up to its reputation for ferocity and fortitude, once serving seven weeks in the line unrelieved. Like all men in the trenches, Henry struggled to cope with the scenes of horror to which he was exposed. Once, the blast from a shell tore the uniform from a friend standing nearby, leaving him naked at the moment of death. Exhaustion brought sleep and escape into the wild reality of dreams. Many soldiers had their faith tested, inspiring the National Bible Society of Scotland's mission to provide every Scottish soldier with a threepenny 'active service' New Testament. In others, however, religious belief flourished as a primal reaction to danger. Even atheists followed superstitious rituals and clung to lucky mascots and talismans. Tales of bullet-stopping watches, cigarette cases and pocket bibles were legion, as were rumours of supernatural interventions on the battlefield, stories that in turn shaped experience. Everyone had heard of the 'Angels of Mons', the spectral archers from Agincourt who relieved the British Expeditionary Force in 1914; but the popular writer who invented them was a lone voice indeed among those soldiers who claimed to have *witnessed* the miracle. The moral truth of the fiction was unassailable.

Soldiers met the ghosts of the more recent dead, too, those whose mangled bodies lay all around, re-exposed by shelling or when rain dissolved the trench walls into which they had been built. It was inevitable that Spiritualism would flourish here, for, as one artillery officer explained in the *Occult Review*, 'in a world of Death one would expect to penetrate the veil when it hangs so constantly before one!' Most soldiers had heard of *Raymond*. A bestseller at home, it was read avidly at the front, and many a parcel of socks, jam and cigarettes contained a copy, much to the consternation of military chaplains. By the end of its first year Methuen & Co. had brought out six editions, twice that number by 1919. Other Spiritualist works addressed the hopes and fears of the infantryman. The medium Elsa Barker's *Letters from a Living Dead Man*, first published in 1914, appeared in successive editions and was still in print in 1932. Barker also published a volume of war letters in 1916, soon after J. Paterson Smyth's *The Men Who Died in Battle* had explored the same spiritual territory as *Raymond*.

In the years 1918–19, Frederick Bligh Bond, an ecclesiastical architect, published various spiritual communications
(including the vision of poppy fields from 1909), lifting a
nation weighed down by its emotional burden.

Almost as if fire had wished no trace to be left of Henry
Duncan, an air raid in 1940 destroyed 60 per cent of the
ordinary soldiers' service records from the First World
War and rendered unusable most of what survived.* Henry's war probably ended in 1915, when so many of the 4th
(City of Dundee) Battalion became casualties that it amal-
gamated with the 5th. Sickness was rife among poorly fed
soldiers continually exposed to the elements. The novelist
Eric Linklater – who like Henry lied about his sixteen and
a half years to join the 4/5th Black Watch – remembers a
downpour so heavy they wore their kilts as capes and
marched bare-buttocked. Henry's joints swelled and ached
until, after a spell of sustained fighting, he collapsed. The
last thing he remembered was the sensation of lightness
and of being raised by unseen hands. He woke up in a field
hospital a week later, lying next to a man with no legs, and
was told by a doctor that rheumatic fever had damaged a
valve in his heart, and he would be going home. Whether
from fever or morphia, Henry slipped in and out of delir-
ium and saw with marvellous clarity the round smiling face
of a dark-haired girl, her deep brown eyes reassuring him,
beckoning him back to Scotland. In Dundee, meanwhile,

* Records do exist for Henry's father, Henry Duncan senior. He was
discharged from the Black Watch in February 1915, probably before
he could be sent overseas.

Nellie MacFarlane's latest dream featured her soldier ailing but safe in hospital. Helen and Henry, the eternal soulmates, had met at last.

Henry was admitted to Craigleith Military Hospital, Edinburgh, where, as a convalescent, he was permitted to travel to Dundee at weekends. One afternoon he arrived at his mother's house to find the table laid for tea and was told that his sister Jean was coming with a friend. Annie Duncan was looking forward to meeting this Nellie of whom her daughter was so fond – but not as much as Henry, who at once knew that this was the girl who had written to him. Helen and Henry just stared when they were introduced, recognizing one another from their dreams; he also intuitively knew that she was a natural psychic. At what point he learned that she was also a mother is unknown, except that taking on another man's child seems not to have concerned him; perhaps a man in his position, jobless and infirm, couldn't afford to be choosy.

Baby Isabella probably explains why Annie Duncan had never met Helen before. Walking her home after tea, Henry did ask why she hadn't been to the house before, to which she replied that she had spent nine months in a sanatorium with a spot on her lung, adding that she and Jean rarely saw each other these days, especially now that her hospital was busy with the influenza epidemic. Later, their daughter Gena made more of this exchange than it would warrant if it were absolutely true: the influenza epidemic did not begin until 1918. What is significant, however, is that this was when Henry asked Helen if she knew what a clairvoyant was, and she wondered, with genuine concern, whether that was what doctors had said was wrong with him.

When Henry finally asked for Helen's hand in marriage, she replied: 'I'm sure it has already been arranged in heaven that we two will always be together.' Henry agreed and so they were engaged. When Henry was demobilized, Helen burned his kilt because it was infested – a symbolic goodbye to all that. Helen moved to Edinburgh, where Henry was still being treated, and found work in a baker's shop. Henry was hired as a labourer among other jobs. Together they would make ends meet. With two soldiers from the Royal Scots as witnesses, they married on 27 May 1916 at the Bank Street Registry Office (certified under the Sheriff's warrant as an 'irregular' marriage) and left temporary accommodation in Easter Road for a tiny rented flat in Forrest Road.

Married life was characterized by hardship and tragedy. In their first winter together Helen contracted pneumonia, Henry clasping her hand at the bedside until she surfaced from a coma. Without her income they lived on Henry's pittance of an army pension and, once Helen was back on her feet, were forced to return to Dundee where Henry was apprenticed to a cabinetmaker. He started a business in a tiny shop with a workshop to the rear, but progress was slow due to his infirmity, and the anxiety of failure hung over him like a cloud. While bedridden he devoured the books Helen brought to him from the public library, mainly treatises on psychical research and Spiritualism, ranging from the sensational and sentimental to the serious and scholarly. He also read cheap works of self-improvement – E. W. and M. H. Wallis's *How to Develop Mediumship* being a representative example.

Henry Duncan expressed his love for his wife very physically for one so weak. Helen gave birth to eight children in all – above the Scottish average but not uncommon in her social class – of whom only six survived childhood. The toll upon her body was worsened by her own poor health. Obesity and oedema were linked to hypertension and diabetes; later she suffered from pleurisy, abdominal problems and a chronic kidney condition leading to albuminuria – the abnormal passing of proteins in her urine. During labour, pre-eclampsia caused fits which damaged the limbs of her daughters Henrietta (Etta) and Gena, Etta living little more than a year after contracting pneumonia. Lilian was born in 1922, then the following January the birth of a ten-pound son brought especial joy; Helen called him 'my Henry', but everyone knew him as Harry. He was soon joined by Peter, named after Helen's beloved brother; born prematurely he was reared in a cardboard box and fed with an eyedropper. The death of the last child, Alex (from pneumonia blamed on a damp baby suit), devastated his parents, leaving Nan, the first child of their marriage, to take charge of her siblings. Nan was herself a sickly girl – like her father, she contracted rheumatic fever which damaged her heart – but took responsibility ahead of her elder sister, the aloof and awkward Isabella (or Bella as she was known). Bella's resentment at not knowing her true father's identity was compounded by anger at a disaster that befell her while Helen was in hospital giving birth to Lilian, four weeks after Etta's death.

Seven-year-old Bella had been taken to stay with friends who lived in a caravan and, left unattended, was mauled by a ferret, losing an eye and part of her nose. Helen was nonetheless strict with Bella, as short on praise as for all her 'bairns', who were made to be grateful for what little they had. The family saying remained 'God is good to us'.

But times grew harder. Henry's business was failing due to his over-generous credit, customers failing to collect ordered furniture (which had to be sold at a loss) and general low productivity due to illness. Henry had a nervous breakdown. Then one day Helen was seized by a premonition and found him slumped at his bench having a heart attack. Pregnant with Lilian, she had been trying to hurry along the orders by stuffing upholstery in the workshop, babies at her feet, but with Henry in hospital bankruptcy was inevitable. She also took in washing and mending, sold the contents of the shop to pay debts, and moved the family to a smaller flat. She found work in the bleach fields, where linen was spread on the ground to be whitened by sunlight – a cruel environment where she developed severe back pain and her overalls froze to her body. The housework was also demanding, and Helen was always the last to bed and the first to rise. Hauling washing from the boiler, she collapsed and was taken to hospital with kidney paralysis. When Henry regained strength he found a job as a postman, but in the hard winter succumbed again to rheumatic fever. And so he became what Dundonians knew as a 'kettle-boiler': a man who stayed at home while his wife worked, although Henry was often too sick even to boil a kettle. On one occasion, out of bed yet out of work, he took little Harry to hear an immaculate middle-class lady give an improving talk on how the unemployed could make soup from a cod's head. At the end, a plump man asked the threadbare audience if they had any questions. 'Aye,' shouted an old woman near to the Duncans, 'never mind the heid, wha eats the body?'

Things became desperate, and the family subsisted on porridge, bone broth with peas, 'stovies' (corned beef or sausages cooked with potatoes and onions) and 'mealy pudding': oatmeal, bacon scraps and onions served with turnip or swede. The children stayed in on Saturdays while their clothes dried ready for church and Sunday school the next day. Most women in Helen's area raised families in poverty and deployed robust strategies of mutual cooperation. They minded each other's children, shared hand-me-downs and donated food, especially for christenings, weddings and funerals. They even helped with the rent. After Henry's heart attack, the Duncans moved and found a friend in their new neighbour Mrs MacLain, who brought flowers and started watching out for them. Christmas was predictably lean: Henry, still sick in bed, made Harry a windmill with coloured paper sails, while Helen unravelled the wool from an old jumper to knit socks. Auntie Mac, as Mrs MacLain became known, made up stockings with rag dolls and sweets (and a bear for Harry). Already overwhelmed by this generosity, on Christmas morning Henry and Helen opened a small box from the MacLains to find a ten-shilling note for them to buy something for themselves.

Not everyone was so kind. Later in the century, Harry remembered that the Duncans were thought of as 'loonies' because of his mother's second sight and the fact that his father, the kettle-boiler, spent his days in bed reading paranormal literature. Helen liked Henry to read to her, her favourites being the poems of William McGonagall and various accounts of spiritualistic phenomena. At Henry's instigation, Helen had started developing her mediumship by giving clairvoyant readings. One night the Duncans heard a 'peculiar whistle' like a banshee. Helen dismissed it as a hawk, but they both knew the truth. At three o'clock in the morning with a jolt Henry realized his father was dying and jumped out of bed; but later that morning, before he reached the hospital in Leith, Helen saw an apparition of Henry Duncan senior, telling her it was too late. The time of death was confirmed as just after 3 a.m. She shared these supernatural experiences with neighbours. On Auntie Mac's first visit, Helen had seen the spirit of her son, David, who had died of diphtheria a year earlier; he asked 'Mama Duncan' to allay his mother's fears for her daughter who lay sick at the time. Auntie Mac was overjoyed.

Given that Helen was by now a de facto Spiritualist, she pooh-poohed Spiritualism per se for a bafflingly long time. It was Henry's father who first pointed out that her second sight and contact with the dead were 'one and the same thing'. And that was it. 'I caught a glimmering of the truth,' said Helen, 'and from that day I ceased to be sceptical of Spiritualism.' But the real turning point had been her pneumonic coma. Regaining consciousness, she had described to

Henry a vision resembling the hypnotic states of non-Christian religions: colours, lights, tunnels, barren landscapes. A man in flowing white robes led her by the hand across a river to a paradise and left her there alone. A bright light preceded a voice calling her name, upon which she was shown a book in which a record of her life to date had been wiped clean. The Christ-like guide led her back across the water and commanded her to serve others. Just before she rejoined the world, Helen saw her mother-in-law's coffin, complete with a date on the lid; they had never seen eye-to-eye, perhaps because of Helen's illegitimate child. Henry, normally ready to find spiritual significance in the most mundane occurrence, dismissed the prediction as a dream. But the night before the death of Annie Mearns Duncan – a poor forty-year-old diabetic exhausted by toil and motherhood – Helen and Henry were woken by an apparition of her hand tapping at their bedroom window, the lines of the scars from her herring gutter's knife visible across her palm.

These stories formed an important part of family and Spiritualist lore about Helen Duncan's life and explain why she hardly ever wavered, even to the hour of her death. Helen's time was coming, and she knew it. She was convinced of the reality of spirits, had discovered she could communicate with them, and was fired up by her heavenly mission and a desire to put the past behind her. It would not be long before she was ushering back the dead in physical form and her awed and astonished husband was recording in his journal visible effects of spectacular radiance.

3. Radiant Effects: 'Albert' and the Spectacle of the Seances

Imagine the scene. It is 1958, a dark living room in Edinburgh, where sisters aged six and twelve are messing about with their school friends, the coal fire casting tall shadows on the walls. They promised their mother Gena, who is at the theatre, that they'd be good. Suddenly a serving hatch slides open and out floats a disembodied arm in a glowing aura, a wagging finger reproaching the miscreants. The younger sister swings at the apparition with a poker; the others run to the kitchen to find no one there. The arm vanishes. Arriving home, Gena chides the children, having been informed of their mischief by the spirit of her mother, who had died two years earlier. But the elder girl, Sheila, already knows it was her grandmother's arm, owing to its gold wristwatch, which Sheila's mother Gena had inherited. It is inscribed: 'Helen Duncan – Double Chance'. In 1925, Helen shared a vision of a double-yolked egg with one of Henry's acquaintances, who was facing bankruptcy. Pinning his hopes on Helen's omen, he put all his money on a horse called Double Chance running in the Grand National. It won. The watch was the first of many such gifts of gratitude. On this occasion Henry received a 'Swallow' raincoat, the best of its kind.

Whereas Helen was driven by duty to love and watch over others (even after death), Henry was motivated by abstract intellectual curiosity, and perhaps the ambition to escape from poverty. A gold watch and a fine coat must have got him thinking; he may even have regretted not backing Double Chance himself. Whatever the spur, the objective was honing his wife's skill as a medium, for which he devoured every relevant printed work he could find. In 1917 for the price of a hot public bath (for the lower classes), one could send off for a pamphlet entitled *Psychic Science and Barbaric Legislation* by Dr Ellis T. Powell, a barrister who later (after his own death) became president of a Spiritualist group, the Society of Communion. It was published by the Spiritualists' National Union, the leading English association, established in 1891, and had originally appeared as an article in *Light*, the weekly periodical of the London Spiritualist Alliance. The LSA was founded in 1884 by William Stainton Moses, an Oxford-educated country curate whose mediumship began in his schooldays when he came top of the class for an essay written in his sleep. Dr Powell expressed the concern of both SNU and LSA, namely that the Witchcraft and Vagrancy Acts outlawed Spiritualism and psychical research – 'youngest of the sciences'. At the end of Powell's pamphlet, the SNU appealed for contributions to raise £3,000 to pursue legal change in Parliament – a vast sum. But, as with all such publicity, the tone was optimistic; it was a rallying cry not a lament.

Henry Duncan needed rallying. One of 26,000 rheumatics invalided from the war, he lived on eight shillings a week plus a small supplement for each of his children. As the postwar world piled on disappointment – too few homes for heroes, too few jobs – so he found hope in the things he read. Although there was little money for books, short works such as J. Arthur Findlay's study of John C. Sloan, a Glasgow warehouse packer who became a medium, were within his means. Periodicals too. In 1926 the first edition of *The Medium*, a sixpenny miscellany of short articles, was published in Scotland. These covered jealousies among developing mediums, censure of the BBC for broadcasting 'creed-bound theology in an age that has outgrown creeds', and news of how unemployed miners in the coalfields of South Wales were discovering 'latent psychic gifts'. These publications, mostly lasting just a few issues, bound the home circles, small churches and incorporated societies into a common Spiritualist culture: a defiant minority in a widening world of knowledge and opportunity. Even before they had left Edinburgh, Henry Duncan was familiarizing himself with different varieties of mediumship. Reading in bed one night, he described to Helen how the soul could detach itself from the body to travel great distances. When she next glanced over, he had become very still with his book over his face and his skin was clammy. Fearing it was another heart attack, she shook him and was about to call the doctor when he regained possession of himself and told her what had happened: he had just been to visit his sister Jean sixty-four miles away in Arbroath, a feat that Jean later verified.

Between leaving Edinburgh and settling in Dundee, the Duncans themselves stayed in Arbroath and there through devoted, patient endeavour, in an atmosphere of love and amity, developed Helen's mediumship. This began with experiments in psychometry – divining information from vibrations in inanimate objects – first using trinkets which Henry bought and of which she guessed the price; then graduating to personal possessions such as rings, watches, brooches, cigarette cases and pocket knives. She found she could see the contents of sealed letters by running the envelope across her head and down her spine. She learned to read the luminous auras surrounding bodies and perceived the invisible golden cords connecting people, which indicated they were related by blood. She showed real promise.

Henry watched her closely, puffing on his pipe, scribbling notes and occasionally discussing matters with his friend Jim Murray – conversations that usually excluded Helen. But she soon discovered that she needed more guidance. During a discussion between Henry and Jim, a bored Helen fell into a trance, which felt like rising into the air rather than falling as if she were fainting – and began speaking in the deep voice of 'Dr Williams', a spirit guide whose name was spelled out in smoke from an extinguished candle. The guide announced that work lay ahead that would require changes in the medium's body – and then, as his voice faded from Helen's lips, to show he meant business he materialized a bent tie pin belonging to Jim Murray (who had recently trodden on it). From such acorns of mundane experience oaks of revelation would grow. At any rate, Helen now had the attention of the men, who agreed it was time to start a home circle.

Henry had had this in mind since his father's death. Father and son had agreed that whoever died first would reach out to the other, and the night he died, after the ominous banshee wail, Henry had heard his father's double knock at the door and decided this was a good way to communicate. Much as Methodists knew of the travels of John Wesley, and Mormons of Joseph Smith receiving the lost gospel, Henry knew the story of the Hydesville rappings. Like the Fox sisters, the Dundee circle – Henry, Helen, Jim Murray and his brother Frank – heard knocks on the table, which they interpreted using a special code. Friends soon joined the circle, including Auntie Mac, who had recently discovered her own psychic powers. Seances were held every Thursday, interrupted only by Henry's spells in hospital and whenever Helen's kidneys were bad. During these intervals, Auntie Mac would care for the children and nurse Helen, bringing flowers and tempting her to eat. These crises reminded the Duncans of their fragile existence and, like the pre-mature deaths of Etta and Alex, spurred them to seek consolation and guidance from God – and Dr Williams.

Spirit guides – or 'controls' as they were known – were both servant and master, which suited young people who resented the superiors on whom they relied. Forced to use Helen's voice box to speak, Dr Williams had nonetheless taken her on as a novice – a signal honour for a marginal woman ostracized by her family. In home circles, all ambitious sitters would practise their psychic skills but inevitably a frontrunner would emerge, to whom the rest were meant to lend support – hence the advice in *The Medium* about dealing with jealousy. But even prodigious mediums progressed only so far. Helen's achievements knew no bounds, confirming what her excursion to the spiritual plane had taught her: that, like Joan of Arc instructed by the saints to liberate Paris, she had been chosen. And as with St Joan, this was greatness thrust upon the low-born, a sacred purpose for a woman otherwise denied one. It was power.

One of the most useful skills was Helen's ability to transfer a sick person's symptoms to herself. After her mauling by the ferret, Bella developed a swelling in her face from which her mother drew poison into her own body through prayer and touch, forming a dental abscess which meant she had to have a tooth extracted. Having accepted the reality of Spiritualism, Helen saw her powers as natural rather than supernatural; she was a channel for psychic energies, not the agent of the dead. Gradually, however, this changed as the spirits clamoured more directly and, it transpired, threateningly.

One evening Henry took Helen to a Spiritualist church to see a demonstration of clairvoyance. There she saw something unseen by anyone else: a lumbering ape dangling a noose above the medium's head. Helen became hysterical and tried to warn the medium's wife, but she was dismissive – until her husband was committed to an asylum in the paranoid belief that something was trying to kill him. Helen visited the man, laid her hands on his head and prayed. Back at home, Helen developed a blinding headache, which Henry surmised was due to an evil spirit. He attempted an exorcism from the family bible at the place where it fell open, Paul's Epistles to the Corinthians, and the room grew cold. An invisible entity then seized Helen, causing her nose to spurt blood. 'The Lord is my shepherd, I shall not want,' stammered Henry, continuing the psalm until the malevolent presence exited with a loud bang. They discovered later that Helen's nosebleed coincided with the moment that the medium, driven insane by the ape spirit, died.

The thought that this work should not be undertaken lightly preyed on their minds as the spirits intruded upon their Thursday evening meetings. As the atmosphere became more charged, the vibrations more intense, so wispy hands and faces appeared in the darkness. Helen extended a bridge of love into the void, dissolving her essential self even beyond the boundaries of the universe. But this bridge was open to sinister visitors. At one seance the circle gathered as usual, holding hands around a small candlelit table, when Helen felt something grab her leg. At first, she thought it was a prank, but peering down saw a spectral hand that ended at the wrist. When the others looked, they were petrified not just by the hand but by a severed head laughing at them. Helen closed her eyes but found the spittle-lipped face still there when she opened them. The worst was yet to come, however, for at the next seance Helen was to be visited by the ape spirit.

That evening, Helen complained of feeling tense and, unusually, put baby Gena in her cot upstairs before the seance began. She might have cancelled, but Henry played down her fears and, besides, she never liked to disappoint sitters. Panting softly, Helen rested in a chair to gather psychic energy, then they all sat at the table. This time not only did the room become eerily cold, but furniture and ornaments began to move in a violent crescendo. The candles were snuffed out. The Singer sewing machine sailed through the air, Henry's books were catapulted from the bookcase, a bed levitated, curtains were ripped down and the iron grate was wrenched from the fireplace. As the dust settled around them, the sitters sat petrified, listening to the sound of a creature stalking them, which then became visible: a hairy apeman who laid a cold, clammy hand on each of them in turn. 'Good Heavens! What's that on my head? Who's touching me?' cried two men present, probably Jim and Frank Murray, who then fled. The apeman followed them, allowing Henry to light the gaslight. He saw his darling Nell's pale face, her raven-black hair dulled with soot, the only brightness her terrified eyes and a streak of blood from her nose. Henry comforted her, tidied the room a little, then feverishly began writing an account in his journal, quizzing the Murray brothers once they had dared to return. When one of them said he thought there must be evil spirits abroad, a briar pipe flew from the rack on the mantelpiece and cracked him on the bridge of the nose.

Helen had mixed feelings. Her Presbyterian sensibilities told her they had seen the devil, not merely the manifestation of a bad soul, yet she remained certain that mediumship would do more good than harm. To proceed, however, they would need protection and guidance. Henry made a small wooden cross on a plinth and gave it a lick of luminous paint, and the circle resolved to start seances with a prayer or scripture reading and a hymn, which would also help raise the vibrations. At the first meeting after the apeman incursion, they said the Lord's Prayer and sang the Twenty-Third Psalm, after which Dr Williams told them to make a 'cabinet' — not a task requiring Henry's joinery skills, as at first he imagined, merely a curtain suspended across a corner of the room to create a private space for the concentration of psychic strength. Dr Williams said they should replace their candles with a dim red lamp that would allow sitters to witness phenomena without harming the medium. Henry found an old railwayman's paraffin lamp, which reeked but satisfied Dr Williams.

A new guide, 'Matthew Douglas', formerly of Kirkcaldy, advised the circle to invest in a trumpet, a narrow megaphone with luminous markings, which would float around the room bringing messages. The Duncans' one was made from tin and was such a hit that a second one was acquired. After Matthew Douglas came the spirit of 'Donald', an intelligence they found blustering and lewd. Henry complained that the spirit, who spoke through his wife, was too dominant to be her guide, and the last straw was Donald's flirtation with one of Auntie Mac's guests. Finally, Dr Williams stood Donald down for meddling with Helen's kidney medicine and replaced him with the man who would serve her for the next three decades, standing by her side in the darkness, of which, it is worth mentioning, Helen had a visceral fear.

As Dr Williams predicted, in 1926 the Duncans moved the sixteen miles back to Dundee, closer to most of their fellow sitters. Henry found a small gable-fronted house in the suburb of Monifieth, near where his parents used to live, and although at 12s 6d per week the rent for 59 Ferry Road was beyond their means, its electricity supply plus the extra space for their expanding family made it irresistible. In an atmosphere of amity and love, the seances resumed. Henry built a wooden box fitted with an electric bulb and a sliding red glass lid, the effect being to throw a dull glow up rather than out, allowing sitters to pick out shapes if they focused hard. The new control was 'Albert Stewart' – a spirit of dignity and good sense who directed proceedings and protected the interests of the woman he called 'Mrs Duncan'. Albert was a Scots émigré to Australia, apprenticed as a pattern maker but drowned in 1913 aged thirty-three. Given to cryptic comments such as 'If your love is as big as yourselves then I should like to have it', his accent was a hybrid: sometimes Scots inflected with Australian, or that of an Oxford don or BBC announcer, a voice British people associated with authority and wisdom. A sitter from York thought he was 'the nicest spoken man I have ever met'. Albert's reserve was tempered by the mischievous charm of another control, a three-year-old Scots girl, Margaret 'Peggy' Hazzeldine, Albert's trainee, who stood in when he was away on urgent spirit business. Peggy's mother Lena, grief-stricken when her daughter died of tuberculosis in 1929, attended a seance in Dundee and was convinced.

From this point there was really only one stage of progress left for Helen. Clairvoyance and clairaudience were second nature, witnesses reported remarkable feats of levitation and apportation (transporting small objects) and her psychometrical insights were infallible. So far, her visible manifestations had been either faint, silent and anonymous, or vivid, violent and uncontrollable. Now, however, Albert was ready to help Helen fulfil her destiny by refining a skill to eclipse anything achieved so far. And like a witch from the burning days, an ordinary woman with extraordinary powers, she would endeavour to join the proud traditions of the materialization mediums, who were able to summon the spirits of the dead and parade them before those who had loved them in life and mourned their absence.

In the later 1870s a series of seances was held at the Bloomsbury headquarters of the British National Association of Spiritualists, forerunner of the London Spiritualist Alliance. One of the first mediums engaged was William Eglinton. 'There were about sixty people present', recorded the explorer Sir Henry Seton-Karr, 'and the large room was lit by three or four gas jets, making a brilliant light. A small curtain was suspended on a rod across one corner of the room farthest from the door, and Mr Eglinton's feet were visible under the lower edge as he sat behind, breathing heavily in trance.' Seton-Karr, sitting a yard from the curtain, was astonished by a sequence of spiritual forms which built up in the cabinet. When the last of these, a tall black man in white robes, waved a substantial fire screen above his head to show his strength, he accidentally demolished the cabinet, exposing the unconscious medium. 'As I gazed,' recalled Seton-Karr, 'the figure melted into a white cloud which slowly entered Mr Eglinton's body.' After that the medium regained consciousness and staggered to his feet.

The *Western Morning News* reported in 1876 that if Eglinton was a conjuror he was the best there ever was, certainly better than Maskelyne and Cooke, who, styling themselves 'illusionists and anti-spiritualists', packed out the Egyptian Hall on Piccadilly twice a day and challenged any medium to perform a feat they could not reproduce. The way these public seances bridged devotion and

diversion is summed up by an escapology routine performed in Boston by a Mr Fay, and remembered in 1911
by Sir Hiram Maxim, pioneer of the modern machine
gun. Spiritualists, who took Fay's act to be the most marvellous evidence of spiritual power, were not disappointed
when finally he explained how he did the trick. Knowing
his audience, the old trouper explained that he simply
drew upon the 'spirits of the departed'.

By merging religion and entertainment, Spiritualism
also reconnected the Church of England with the people
for whom it was losing relevance. Formally, the clerics
were hostile, but more discreetly there was considerable
interest in how Spiritualist beliefs might reinvigorate
Christian faith. The problem was distinguishing genuine
mediumship from fraud. Thomas Colley, a seasoned Anglican clergyman, made no secret of his Spiritualist leanings
and believed that a former Baptist minister named Francis
Ward Monck could manifest spirits from a fibrous vapour
that billowed from his side like steam from a kettle. When
in 1876 Monck was imprisoned under the Vagrancy Act,
Colley ran to his defence, even though 'conjuring apparatus' had been found in Monck's room. William Eglinton,
however, did not impress Colley, who once edged towards
one of his spirit forms with a pair of scissors and snipped
off cloth and hair later found to match muslin and a false
beard in Eglinton's trunk. In the shape of battles to come,
charges levelled against Eglinton in the *Journal of the Society
for Psychical Research* were hotly repudiated by the British
National Association of Spiritualists.

Materialization mediums received academic approval.

'A living being, or living matter, formed under our own eyes . . . is surely the climax of marvels!' declared Charles Richet, a Professor of Physiology in Paris who, like Einstein, hypothesized that mechanical energy might be projected like light. Richet was first convinced by a materialization in 1905 at the house of a French general in Algiers. After the death of their son, the general's wife had discovered that his fiancée, Marthe Béraud, possessed remarkable psychic gifts and could manifest spirits such as 'Bien Boa', a sixteenth-century brahmin. Professor Richet applied vigorous tests and took photographs. The claim by an ex-servant that he had impersonated Bien Boa, Richet put down to alleged Arab mendacity; reports that Marthe herself had confessed to fraud, he attributed to press sensationalism and mental fragility. The photos survive – but it's hard to see Bien Boa as anything other than a man wearing a sheet, silver helmet and false beard, resembling not so much an Indian sage as Kaiser Wilhelm in a lacy frock.

In 1923, Richet published a book translated as *Thirty Years of Psychical Research*, dedicated to the Cambridge classicist and SPR founder Frederic Myers and the recently deceased physicist Sir William Crookes OM, discoverer of thallium, inventor of the radiometer and pioneer of electric lighting. Crookes was a committed psychical researcher drawn into a curious relationship with a teenage medium from Hackney called Florence Cook, whose full-form materializations were a sensation in Spiritualist circles. Her spirit guide (and doppelgänger) 'Katie King' also fascinated Crookes. He pointed to differences between the two girls – only one was a nail-biter, he said – even though photographic evidence indicates that they were one and the same. Sir George Sitwell – who at seances rarely lived up to his name – was positive of this in 1880 when he leapt up and seized 'Katie', only to find himself holding Florence, whose clothes lay in a pile in the cabinet. Confronted by these frolics, it's easy to overlook the academic stature of men like Crookes and Richet, who in 1913 were respectively elected as President of the Royal Society and awarded the Nobel Prize for Medicine. Like many great scientists, they were dreamers as well as empiricists, ready to reconcile contradictory intellectual positions. Frederic Myers defended a pair of young Newcastle materializers despite admitting there was an element of 'drapery and delusion' in their performances.

Opinion could be polarized but also came in subtle shades. The SPR pioneer Henry Sidgwick was free-thinking yet cautious, his Trinity College colleague Myers recklessly credulous. Richet believed in materialization but not that it proved human survival after death, and although certain cases intrigued him (including that of Sir Oliver Lodge's son Raymond) he believed beings of higher intelligence to be the cause. Sir William Crookes, who so admired Florence Cook, struggled to accept the most famous Victorian physical medium – but only because his phenomena threatened to overturn Newtonian physics. That medium's name was Daniel Dunglas Home.

Born in the Scottish Highlands in 1833, Home was a nervous child who inherited the gift of second sight, had visions and predicted his mother's death. Taken to

America, in 1850 he attracted rappings to the house of his aunt, who threw him out when exorcism failed. Arriving in England in 1855, Home awed polite society, floating out of a window in the presence of titled guests. He was banished from Rome for sorcery, for which attempts were made on his life. The newspapers were obsessed with him, and Crookes thought him the world's most remarkable medium. Himself an outspoken critic of charlatans in sheets, Home was investigated but never exposed, despite rumours he used police intelligence, carried a secret monkey and drew magnetic power from cats. Some had their doubts. After Empress Eugénie of France claimed to have been touched by a spirit, a spectator swore he had seen Home extending a naked foot. Robert Browning was so disgusted with Home's silliness – a wreath of flowers 'levitated' on to the poet's head – he composed the vitriolic satire, 'Mr Sludge, "The Medium"', which condemned Spiritualism *tout court*. Browning's wife Elizabeth, however, clung to her beliefs, even though she thought Home's seances were 'twaddle'.

Here's a dream, of sorts. Sir Oliver Lodge and Frederic Myers are roaming a deserted island in their pyjamas, Charles Richet is fishing for their supper. At night, they sit in a dark room watching strange lights and hands dance in the air. Sidgwick and his wife Eleanor arrive and are convinced by the phenomena, which include an enormous floating melon. Except this wasn't a dream: it's what happened in 1894 on the Île Roubaud, Richet's private resort in the South of France. Lodge and Myers wore pyjamas due to the heat, which they endured so they could spend time with a special guest, a medium named Eusapia Palladino, a middle-aged, illiterate Italian peasant. In the following year she was entertained at Myers's leafy Cambridge residence, where, even though she was taken shopping and allowed to win at croquet, she was unhappy with the food, weather and starchy social conventions. The earthiness for which the ladies detested her proved magnetic to their husbands; Sidgwick even had her photographed wearing his academic gown. Although suspicions about Palladino grew with every seance, the phenomena were remarkable, the oddest being lumpy protuberances on her back that sprouted into arms. Lodge and Myers were persuaded; the Sidgwicks less so now. Richet had found her phenomena 'absurd and unsatisfactory', yet still thought this insufficient reason to cry foul.

The story shows how far Spiritualism relied on materialism for its anti-materialism – or, put another way, the perception of materialized spirits depended on their physical rather than spiritual nature. The quasi-scientific substance of what Richet called 'mechanical projections' was ectoplasm (elsewhere teleplasm, psychoplasm or plasma), organic matter familiar to cell biologists as the complement of endoplasm but adopted by Richet and his adherents for Spiritualism and psychical research. Like Francis Ward with his steam-like discharge, William Eglinton was said to clothe his spirits in dingy white ectoplasm that poured from his body and pulsated on the floor as the shape of a spirit coalesced. Investigating Marthe Béraud, Richet noticed how:

A kind of liquid or pasty jelly emerges from the mouth or the breast of Marthe which organizes itself by degrees, acquiring the shape of a face or a limb. Under very good conditions of visibility, I have seen this paste spread on my knee, and slowly take form so as to show the rudiment of the radius, the cubitus, or metacarpal bone whose increasing pressure I could feel on my knee.

The properties of ectoplasm were those of gases, liquids or solids depending on how spiritual intelligence directed it; but Spiritualists and scientists never agreed what it was or was not – although it's easy to see why Sir Oliver Lodge's killjoy idea that real ectoplasm was invisible never caught on. Undoubtedly there was something seminal and ovarian about it, and sitters were sometimes advised to uncross their legs so as not to impede the confluence of imperceptible reproductive matter and the stream emanating from the medium's body. The exit point was the mouth, nose, ear, navel or genitals, and mediums displayed the simulacra of orgasm or labour. Some believed that ectoplasm picked up dust in the seance room to increase its substance.

The quality of ectoplasm varied between mediums. The child-visionary Elizabeth Hope, known in adult life as 'Madame d'Espérance', described it as a 'faintly luminous hazy material' which thickened until visible. 'To the touch it at first appears of a light fleecy character, resembling combed, finely drawn cotton wool,' she claimed, 'but quickly, even under the fingers, it seems to assume the character of a textile fabric.' All too often, though, seized ectoplasm *was* textile fabric, gauzy diaphanous stuff, several feet of which could be packed into the bent medium's capacious bloomers. But there were places that modesty closed off to investigation, even in the name of science. After 1900, however, the relocation of proceedings from the salon to the laboratory meant that etiquette could be set aside and a colder critical eye cast over the transmutations happening inside and around these women's bodies.

Instead of posed photos of artfully draped teenagers, the published research of the new era was illustrated with candid snaps of women in states of entranced abandon, straining, ecstatic. Ectoplasmic effluvia snake from beneath skirts, suggesting sexual liberation, perhaps, or objectification as male investigators flashed their cameras. A work epitomizing this style became the bible of physical mediumship. Freiherr Albert von Schrenck-Notzing was a Bavarian psychiatrist whose interest in hypnotherapy led him to renounce materialism (though not to embrace Spiritualism), give up medicine (he married into money) and devote his time to psychical research. One of his earliest ventures was to join the pyjamaed men of science on Richet's island to see Eusapia Palladino, after which he followed her across Europe. In 1909, Schrenck-Notzing shifted his gaze to Eva Carrière, a Parisian medium in her early twenties who operated under a patron, a sculptor named Juliette Bisson, much as Marthe Béraud had done under the general's wife in Algiers. Although few knew it at the time, Eva Carrière *was* Marthe Béraud, who had escaped adverse publicity in Algiers and formed an intimate relationship with Bisson, who took photographs for Schrenck-Notzing's *Materialisationsphänomene*, published in

1913. Bisson was Eva's Svengali, her influence literally hypnotic, and Schrenck-Notzing was struck by the medium's passivity as she submitted to Bisson's examinations *per rectum et vaginam* (to use Richet's discreet term) to check for concealed materials. Schrenck-Notzing himself consented to feel Eva's body only through her leotard. Eva moaned, her muscles racked with spasms of sexual or obstetric climax.

A famous picture shows a tangle of gauzy ectoplasm across Eva Carrière's bare breasts; another from 1913 shows her wearing nothing but a pained expression as she manifests a shrouded gentleman resembling the King of Bulgaria. Whoever it was, his face looked very flat, which was explained when the camera caught Eva's head at an odd angle, revealing part of the masthead of *Le Miroir*. To psychical researchers, this did not prove that Eva was a fraud, only that some phenomena were not genuine. Schrenck-Notzing even speculated that these images were 'ideoplasts' – sharply recalled images (a habit of hysterical women, he argued) projected externally. More plausibly, German researchers suggested, she regurgitated props. The escapologist Harry Houdini agreed, after noticing that Eva's papery images looked semi-digested. The fact that Eva sometimes bled from the mouth supported the idea. All this was refuted by Richet: 'How can masses of mobile substance, organized as hands, faces and drawings be made to emerge from the oesophagus or the stomach? No physiologist would admit such power to contract those organs at will in this manner.' Schrenck-Notzing made Eva drink bilberry syrup before seances and administered an emetic after she had sucked back her ectoplasm, but without result. So, the regurgitation theory lingered, and was discussed again by the Society for Psychical Research when Eva Carrière held seances in London in 1920.

That summer David Gow, a Highland poet and editor of *Light*, received a letter from Dr William J. Crawford, a thirty-nine-year-old mechanical engineer at Belfast Municipal Technical Institute, with whom he had corresponded during the war. Six years earlier, in 1914, Crawford, an intense man with a waxed moustache and rimless spectacles, had been mesmerized by a seance held by Eva Carrière, and won the trust of a working-class family in Belfast, the Golighers, who had developed psychic powers in their home circle, prominently the teenaged Kathleen. Crawford spent many hours above their shop, the gaslight flickering behind a pane of red glass, listening to spiritual raps and straining to see small feats of levitation. His theory was that ectoplasmic 'psychical structures' levered up the table, a process which decreased the medium's weight by as much as fifty pounds. Crawford studied every aspect of Kathleen's mediumship until depressive illness got the better of him. 'I have been struck down mentally,' he confessed to Gow. 'It is not the psychic work. I enjoyed it too well.' The letter was a suicide note, and soon afterwards Crawford drowned himself.

Although Crawford had been discreet, clearly Kathleen's ectoplasm, which he described as as solid as iron or as 'soft as the flesh of a baby's arm', came from her vagina. In a typical experiment, recorded with clinical precision, Kathleen wore clean knickers, stockings and shoes treated with coloured dyes to track the movement of the 'plasma'. Crawford was an avid photographer of the phenomena, and took advice from the spirit guides seriously, namely that the medium must be allowed to get used to the flash so as to withstand the shock it caused. 'Nor is this to be much wondered at', he noted, 'when it is considered the plasma is part of her body exteriorized in space.' The photos illustrated three books of Crawford's findings (one published posthumously), a body of research endorsed by Schrenck-Notzing. But those that were not used are even more revealing. In the SPR archives, in Cambridge University Library, there is an album full of them, one of which – '3f' – shows a seated Kathleen Goligher wearing a white blouse, plaid skirt raised above her knees. What we don't see, but Crawford did, was how she shuddered and writhed with each blinding flash of ignited magnesium.

But doubts set in even before Crawford's death. When Houdini met him at a dinner, where they discussed the Golighers at length, he thought him insane, especially when he saw Crawford's photographs. A cold-hearted obituary in the *Proceedings of the Society for Psychical Research* mentioned rumours of fraudulence. In 1921 the SPR sent Dr E. E. Fournier d'Albe to Belfast, where in twenty sittings with the Golighers he detected nothing paranormal and saw Kathleen lift a stool with her foot. Fournier d'Albe concluded that the family were 'an alert, troublesome group of well-organized performers'. But scepticism only galvanized the believers, some of whom said that the Golighers' powers had waned after Crawford's death, others that Fournier d'Albe was prejudiced. One believer was Ernest

Oaten, president of the Manchester-based Spiritualists' National Union, to which over three hundred local societies were affiliated, twice the prewar figure. In October 1917 Oaten had visited the Golighers and was impressed by the phenomena, which included a floating trumpet, all provided by 'splendidly co-operative and courteous' spirits. When Fournier d'Albe's findings were published, however, Kathleen Goligher withdrew from the limelight, claiming trouble with her nerves, although later she performed privately for her husband, a prosperous shopkeeper seduced by the enigmatic power of the mediumship.

After the First World War, physical mediumship and psychical research advanced together, each encouraging the extravagant ambitions of the other. In 1922, Schrenck-Notzing rented a room in Braunau-am-Inn, a town not yet famous as the birthplace of Adolf Hitler but notable for Spiritualism. There he began tests on a nineteen-year-old apprentice, Willi Schneider, who after hearing about soldiers dabbling in the occult had discovered in himself the trance personality of an adolescent mistress of King Ludwig of Bavaria. Through her, it appeared, Schneider produced astounding telekinetic and ectoplasmic phenomena, often becoming so sexually aroused that he ejaculated. His younger brother Rudi demonstrated similar skills, panting like a dog to sustain a trance. Willi held regular seances in Munich, which was nearer to Schrenck-Notzing's laboratory, attended by men of science and letters, including the novelist Thomas Mann, who, utterly convinced, was struck by the 'impure, obscene, spiteful, demonic' character of nature. Six months earlier the guests had been the English psychical researchers Harry Price and Dr Eric Dingwall, a shrewd but fickle observer who despite earlier criticisms of Schrenck-Notzing's methods was impressed.* Even though the red light was poor, Price and Dingwall thought many of the phenomena impossible to fake. Back in Britain, printed accounts of their experiences popularized the Schneiders, although Dingwall continued to waver in his views.

Through the Spiritualist grapevine these were the stories that shaped Helen Duncan's mediumship. The figure who made the greatest impression was 'Margery' – the *nom de séance* of Mina Crandon, the Canadian wife of Dr L. R. G. Crandon, a surgeon at Harvard Medical School whose passion for psychical research was sparked by a lecture by Sir Oliver Lodge and was nurtured by Crawford's work on the Golighers. He tirelessly promoted his wife's mediumship, which had begun with spirit messages from her dead brother Walter. In 1924 the Crandons made a bid for the $5,000 prize the journal *Scientific American* had offered to anyone producing a 'visible psychic manifestation'; the investigative committee included William McDougall, Professor of Psychology at Harvard, and Harry Houdini, whose scathing *A Magician among the Spirits* was published that year. The affair split opinion in the American SPR and at Harvard. Margery had many champions and social class enhanced her credibility. Her good

* Dingwall's friends called him 'Ding', but he was also known as 'Dirty Ding', owing to his job as an assistant keeper of erotic publications at the British Library.

looks, manners and humour elicited chivalric outrage when she was impugned, not least in Sir Arthur Conan Doyle, who found Margery 'charming, cultivated and heroic', and felt so strongly about suggestions of fraud from the Harvard sceptics that he rose on Christmas morning 1925 to write a counterblast for the *Boston Herald*, saying that 'there is no day so holy that one may not use it for the fight for truth'.

As with Eva Carrière, interest in Mina Crandon's mediumship was poised between scientific observation and voyeurism. A photograph from 1925 shows her seated, robe open, one stocking pulled down, ectoplasm at her mouth. In another she is naked beneath an overcoat, a cloth barely covering her pubic region and a hand like a bunch of overripe bananas coming from her navel. That year Eric Dingwall, in his role as the SPR's Research Officer, visited the Crandons in Boston. At 8.57 p.m. on 8 January, he heard a rustling as the medium fell into a trance, followed by snoring, upon which Walter, the spirit guide, invited Dr Dingwall to feel the clammy substance on her thigh, 'a round mass with knobbly prominences' which flinched at his touch. Professor McDougall, also present, likened it to placental cord. An hour later 'Margery' began coughing, which continued until 10.20 p.m., when, as a finale, she vomited. At other seances Walter dragged her into unconsciousness, causing her to moan, either in agony or in ecstasy. 'Pay no attention to her, let her groan,' ordered Walter. 'She must sit every night. Don't ask her how she feels.'

But Dingwall did ask. He suspected that the flabby ectoplasm, the whistles, bells and levitating luminous doughnuts amounted to 'a huge hoax got up for the purpose of discrediting psychical research'. He also believed that the Crandons used animal organs and regurgitation, a practice Walter sneered was common across the Atlantic because 'the British have ectoplasm served with their tea'. The spirit also ridiculed Dingwall for referring to 'little old Margery lying there like a beautiful corpse with lung tissue coming out of her ears'. An American conjuror, Grant Code, suggested that Crandon might have surgically enlarged the mouth of his wife's uterus, enabling her to produce fraudulent pseudopodia from what he called, horribly, her 'most convenient storage warehouse'. Houdini, fresh from an anti-Spiritualist lecture tour, was accused of trying to frame Margery; Walter also mocked his baldness.

But, for all this, psychical researchers remained fiercely divided. On 6 June 1928, having seen a materialized hand which dissolved as he went to photograph it, Professor R. J. Tillyard, a distinguished Australian entomologist, wrote to Sir Oliver Lodge to rehearse thoughts he went on to publish in *Nature* that August: 'Margery, in my opinion, is now the finest medium that ever lived. She would assuredly have been burnt as a witch if she had lived three centuries ago.' As it happened, like many a fading starlet and the Fox sisters before her, Mina Crandon was to sink into alcoholism, and died in 1941 at the age of fifty-three. Not even a psychic could have foreseen this tragic end in 1929, when 'Margery' was at the height of her powers and fame.

When in December that year, the Crandons disembarked at Plymouth from the SS *Mauretania* the British press were waiting at the harbour. A reporter from the

Daily Sketch was surprised to find Mina 'a charming, vivacious little woman, who almost danced into the room, a dainty smiling brunette in black velvet'. Bombarded by questions, she fingered her necklace, glanced at her husband and said: 'He does all the talking for both of us.' Margery was a sensation. People flocked to see her, as did the press. At the Crandons' London hotel, the telephone did not stop ringing until 2 a.m. on day one and their diary filled quickly around sittings already arranged with the SPR. The journalist Hannen Swaffer, inventor of the gossip column and a keen Spiritualist, opined that half the inhabitants of London would attend a 'Margery' seance if they could. Indeed, it seemed that news-addicted Britain, facing economic depression and political turmoil, was in need of a 'Margery' of its own.

Like the spirits at their table, opportunity was knocking for the Duncans. What Helen lacked in Mina Crandon's social refinement, she made up for in phenomena. She fell quickly into a trance – nerves steadied by a drop of Dutch courage and the morphine in her kidney medicine – and by the late 1920s, to outward appearances, had mastered the production of ectoplasm. Gena Brealey takes up the story from the moment the spirit guide Dr Williams asked people in the circle, bathed in muted rosy light, whether they were ready to experience this domestic miracle: 'As he spoke, out through the curtain . . . came a substance not unlike cheesecloth or butter muslin. The material continued to flow until there seemed to the sitters to be at least ten yards in a soft pile . . . Through the opening of the curtains they could see Helen sitting in the hard-backed chair, and the ectoplasm flowing from her nose and ears . . . down the front of her dress on to her lap, then down on to the floor and out to the centre of the room.'

A great task lay ahead. Every Thursday, sometimes other days too, Helen practised moulding diaphanous ectoplasm around invisible spirits, perfecting an impressive performance into something absolutely startling. Guests were invited. In 1928 family friend Harvey Metcalfe visited and arranged with the spirit guide Albert to take flash photographs of the materializations. As Walter had done for Margery, Albert would not allow Metcalfe to proceed until the medium was ready. Of about fifty pictures only a few survive. Helen is sturdily seated, wearing a velour dress and a protective blindfold, as Kathleen Goligher did when she faced Crawford's camera. Her hands are held fast by sitters, ankles secured with rope. From behind an aspidistra stand a spirit baby rises, attached to Helen's nose by an ectoplasmic cord. In another image, a figure looms further back behind the cabinet curtains, an apple-cheeked twenties flapper draped in white. This, then, was the Duncans' proof.

Interest grew in Dundee and beyond. In June 1929, Helen was introduced to James Souter, a local man who came to the home circle with an open mind and left intoxicated by images of the dead and their implications for science and religion. A subscriber to *Light*, Souter wrote to the editor David Gow to announce the arrival of a new prodigy in mediumship: 'The forms build up clearly and distinctly (as many as fourteen have manifested at one sitting); they speak clearly, giving their names and other convincing particulars, answer satisfactorily all questions put to them, they handle objects both light and heavy, [and] play musical instruments.'

The most important manifestation was Albert, described by Souter as a typically canny, level-headed Scot, six feet tall and neatly bearded. We get a sense of his classically idealized features from a bust entitled *A Disciple* by Frederick George, an Aberdonian sculptor, who exhibited it at the Royal Scottish Academy and then donated it to the Edinburgh College of Psychic Science. Helen was presented with a framed photograph of the piece. There are photographs of the spirit himself: at his best he resembles a cadaverous revenant, stooped and shrouded like a funerary monument; at his worst a rolled-up sheet of paper. From the early 1930s spectators were being shown his ectoplasmic voice box, 'a kind of vertebra with a larynx at the top', but also likened to a microphone stand wrapped in cloth.* By this time Albert had a companion: his infant apprentice Peggy, who, one sitter related, 'said in Scotch Dialect "Hoo air yeall" and sang a ditty relating to her discovery of the Mystery of Life'. Winsomely cheeky, she swung from the cabinet curtain until Albert told her to stop, answering back: 'Now, I ken my weight wudna pull the curtain doon.' She was partly Shirley Temple, the screen moppet who in 1936 reached her cinematic peak aged eight, and partly

---

* Walter, too, had exteriorized his vocal cords for Margery, gathered into an organic lump joined to her nose and perched on her shoulder like a lifeless pet.

seance-room stereotype. Twenty years earlier John Lobb, the editor of *Christian Age*, had reported the arrival of 'Mischief' – a young female apparition 'addicted to practical joking, often imparting a stimulus to those inclined to secrete articles just when they are wanted, and enjoying the fun when the search is going on'. This was Peggy to a tee. 'Mischief' agreed to be photographed, the grainy result of which Lobb printed. Today all we see is a sinister grinning face of a girl, her tongue protruding obscenely.

Under the stewardship of Albert and Peggy, materializations were witnessed by men influential in the world of mediumship. J. B. McIndoe, who succeeded Ernest Oaten as SNU President, was so amazed he invited her to Glasgow. Montague Rust, a doctor from Newport in Fife (later a witness at the Old Bailey), had also become a staunch supporter. To end a controversy about Albert's sex, Rust performed a strange examination from which he was pleased to confirm that Albert was all man. Most attendees at the Dundee circle, however, saw themselves as not students but helpers in family reunions. One of the earliest materializations was a boy who sang a hymn and threw his arms round his mother's neck. As she left 59 Ferry Road, she whispered to Helen: 'I am a new woman. I have now something to live for. I know now that my boy is not dead; he lives. How can I ever thank you?' But that was gratitude enough, for, as Helen said, only a mother could know what it meant for such a wound to be healed.

Such moments – and there would be many – mixed mourning and consolation with rapturous thrills. For all his gravitas, Albert was a Master of Ceremonies, an entertainer in his own right, and a family friend. Helen hung the photograph of his bust in her bedroom, reflecting an intimate relationship with the man her children adored as 'Uncle Albert'. They sat at his spectral feet, as before a party conjuror or Punch and Judy booth, and listened to his saws and parables. A favourite was that of the moth flying into the flame, from which they learned to seek only the true light of the Saviour. Albert also amazed them with tricks, such as when he held an armchair above his head, a feat worthy of Tarzan, with whom the Duncan boys were obsessed. One of them once grabbed an airborne trumpet, making his entranced mother groan; if he wasn't sorry then, he was when he saw the burn on her cheek. At night the children prayed to Albert and thanked him for his spiritual care. Particularly fond of him was Gena, whose life he supposedly saved by warning her parents that she had pneumonia. She attended her first seance at four days old, and by the age of three was a budding psychometrist. Once she started to 'talk funny' when Henry's brother Robert came to tea. Uncle Bob, who had served with the Royal Scots in India, hugged her saying she was just like her mother. Apparently she had accurately described a comrade killed in a rebel skirmish, her account all the more remarkable for being delivered in Hindustani.

To the Duncan children, then, psychic phenomena were normal, including the table that, by means obscure, participated in games of hide-and-seek. But it was the seances they loved most. Soon after they moved to Ferry Road, Harry, then almost five, got his first taste: 'We the children had been playing in the back yard and making a lot of noise. My parents were holding their weekly seance and we were brought into the house and taken into the seance room being told to sit still and be quiet. The room was dark but dimly lit by an Aladdin lamp. I remember people dressed in white shimmering "nightgowns" coming out of the curtains that were stretched across a bed recess and disappearing into the floor.' Harry attended many more seances, but never found the words to describe ectoplasm accurately. 'The closest I can describe it', he said, 'is to liken it to driven snow with bright sunshine shining on it. It appeared to sparkle with a million sequins.'

Other observers, though impressed, were franker about the grim physicality of it all. In March 1930, Montague Rust attended a Ferry Road seance where heavy curtains hung at the windows and the guests sat in an arc facing Helen in the corner. As the cabinet closed, white light was switched to red, and Helen entered a trance. But then she had a coughing fit, her chair creaking dreadfully, upon which Albert protested it was too bright. As the medium recovered, he said she was ready to manifest Adam, as in the husband of Eve – but first he had to lift the unconscious Mrs Duncan to her feet – 'my word this takes some doing', he croaked – then stood behind her on her chair. Stepping up to steady Albert there, Dr Rust took the opportunity to feel the umbilicus connecting him to Helen's body – like fine muslin, he said. Then Albert said: 'Thank goodness I love her – she is a poor beggar', explaining that the medium's coughing and retching were caused by a tightening of the cord. Next, he placed in a sitter's hands his bare foot, which felt like a human foot with a thin ankle, and showed everyone his umbilical cord. When Henry asked if the ecto-plasm had been drawn from the sitters, Albert replied: 'I get a certain amount, as I love you all.' When the house lights went up, Helen was slumped in the corner, dazed and con-fused, blood and slime dripping from her chin.

Between the end of the Roaring Twenties and the start of the Hungry Thirties, Helen Duncan realized, like Mina Crandon before her, that she was on the verge of becom-ing something greater than her workaday self. By now, the craft at which she excelled was performed all over the country: mediums advertised in newspapers and theatre programmes, and even exhibited at Wembley Stadium. Alive to the commercial possibilities, the Duncans began to charge visitors a small admittance fee and, for the first time in their married life, felt the chill of poverty thaw.

In the spring of 1930, Helen visited a studio photog-rapher in Dundee to have her portrait taken: she stares at us from a sepia-toned past – simple, unguarded, wearing plain clothes, but with unmistakably purposeful ebony eyes. Someone, perhaps Henry, wrote on the back of one print: 'Mrs Victoria Helen Duncan, Aged 32½ years', the 'Helen' subsequently scored through as if she was undecided how she wished to be known in the future. The one thing of which she was sure as she packed a suitcase for London, laying the photograph on top of her clothes, was that she was on her way up and out. The days of cod's head soup were over.

PART TWO
Helen Vilified

4. Darkness and Light: Research and the Search for Respectability

Helen Duncan's reputation grew in the early 1930s as more people fell under the spell of Spiritualism and desired the kind of mediumship at which she excelled. Ena Bügg, whose life Helen would later transform, was a shy teenager from a working-class family in Gosport, Hampshire, when in 1931 she attended her first materialization seance, with a Mrs Baylis. She was overwhelmed. Voices murmured through a floating trumpet, and spirit faces – men, women and children – crowded into the darkness, mirroring the joyful expressions of the sitters. Ena's experience was shared by tens of thousands of people at Spiritualist meetings in churches, public halls, scout huts, back rooms, cellars and attics. Some attended from deep conviction, others justified 'going to the spooks' as a bit of fun or a favour to a friend; few went alone. Many went to seances because the war dead haunted their hearts and minds, and there the act of memory offered hope of reunion. Writing on Armistice Day 1927, Rev. Charles Drayton Thomas of the Society of Communion urged mourners to focus on the afterlives of the fallen. It was apt, then, that Mrs Baylis's spiritual Master of Ceremonies should be 'George', a soldier from the trenches, and his assistant, 'Curly', a boy who perished in a Zeppelin raid.

By the mid-1930s, the number of Spiritualist churches

affiliated to the SNU had risen to over five hundred, to which should be added many unaffiliated congregations; Manchester alone had the Central Spiritualist Church, the Progressive Lyceum Church, the New Manchester Lyceum Church, the Spiritualist Mission and others besides. The total in Britain may have exceeded two thousand, serving as many as 250,000 members. The principal means of worship was not the seance but the service, where a clairvoyant might pass on messages, but only after hymns, prayers and readings. Spiritualists venerated Christ, but most rejected faith in him as the route to salvation, preferring to see him as a superlative medium, an idea popularized by Rev. G. Maurice Elliott's *Psychic Life of Jesus* (1938). The Bible was to the Spiritualist a compendium of paranormal phenomena: trance, clairvoyance, clairaudience, apportation, lights, spirit writing, veridical dreams and materialization. Spirit hands were first recorded in the Books of Daniel and Ezekiel; Jesus may have invoked the spirit of John the Baptist; and, most famously of all, there was Saul's 'seance' with the Witch of Endor.

Orthodox clerics reminded Spiritualists that Saul had been condemned for conjuration, heaven and postmortem survival were different, and seances were antithetical to faith – a heresy that lured man from God, back to human contrivances. Worse, spirits might be hellish deceptions to propagate error, a position advanced keenly by the Catholic Church. In 1917 the Holy See banned communicants from attending seances, even as onlookers or researchers. In 1926 the priest and historian Montague Summers, whose books were widely read, excoriated Spiritualism as a revival of witchcraft fuelled by wartime bereavement, a demonic illusion 'most foul, most loathly, most dangerous, and most damnable'. As in the previous century, the Church of England was less dogmatic. Committees of inquiry, set up in England and Scotland to investigate Spiritualism, were circumspect in their conclusions rather than hostile. The new religion may fill gaps in knowledge, they said, and could be part of God's plan to resist secularism. Nor were there many objections to Anglican ministers exalting spiritual experiences that suggested the truth of Christianity. Spiritualism might even revitalize religion, a moral anchor in an age of war, revolution and upheaval.

One area of upheaval was class. Victorian mediums had flouted conventions of deference and obedience suited to sex and station, and in the era of enfranchisement this could only increase. Mediums were new moderns, symbols of social restructure and, condescension aside, were in demand from a bourgeoisie with money to spend. Travelling to wherever they were needed, they bore out the Duke of Wellington's prediction that the railway would only make the working classes move about more. Unlike the phenomena of some other mediums, Helen Duncan's were spectacular even when she was away from home. As J. B. McIndoe's guest, she astonished sitters in Glasgow and subsequently at the Edinburgh College of Psychic Science. She invested in a small attaché case for her seance outfit of black dress, drawers and loose-fitting court shoes, and began keeping an autograph book, in which one client wrote: 'With grateful thanks to my friend

Mrs Duncan who has raised and taught me to keep within one's heart of hearts the beautiful ideal.' Under the patronage of Montague Rust, the next step was to achieve recognition by the SNU, whose diploma would open the doors to Spiritualist gatherings nationwide. Only then would she gain full credibility and earn a decent living.

Around this time, F. W. FitzSimons, a psychical researcher (and authority on snake venom), argued that women made fine mediums because they were naturally sensitive and unfettered by reason. There were, however, differentiating criteria. If a stereotype existed of the *clairvoyante*, it was of a diffident, middle-aged spinster in sensible shoes and owlish spectacles with a light wave in her hair. Not so the materializers, who were physical mediums in every sense. 'Vitality in a woman', George Bernard Shaw observed, 'is a blind fury of creation' – and so it was with those who rebirthed the dead, the super-mothers who, as one seance-goer put it, were 'sexually flush', an electric life-force surging through their procreative bodies. Best suited to the task, FitzSimons thought, were women of a 'gross material nature', most especially those of what he called 'a lymphatic temperament'. All of which defined Helen Duncan, the down-to-earth thickset mother of six. Even admirers rarely minced their words. She was described as coarse, gross, 'fishwifey' and, by a man she *amazed*, thus: 'She was in a brown tight-fitting dress . . . a large ungainly woman who moved slowly as though she suffered from heart trouble or glandular affection and had not to hurry. She had by no means a magnetic personality . . . rather a repellent one that aroused one's critical faculties.'

Between the time she failed her medical at the munitions factory and the early 1930s, her weight increased by almost thirty pounds to over seventeen stone, even though she was only 5 feet 6 inches tall. As for her other vital statistics, soon to be recorded by investigators, she measured 47 inches under the arms, 53 inches around the shoulders, and her bust and hips were 57 inches and 54 inches respectively. Her weight later rose by another five stone at least, and at seances the Laurel-and-Hardy contrast with the lofty Albert occasioned his quip: 'I have it one way and Mrs Duncan has it the other.' At a sitting in Dundee, Albert announced that she would levitate in her armchair, but the spirits only got her a few inches off the floor. She enjoyed porridge, stew, eggs, bacon and chips, and was often found in the kitchen wearing a wraparound pinafore, baking and chopping and pickling. When her children hugged her they had to stretch their arms; nestled on her lap, listening to stories or boggling at tricks, they toyed with the loose flesh of her arms. Once they begged their parents to take them on a flight to London, but Henry explained that with their mother on board the bottom might fall out of the aeroplane.

Helen's obesity exacerbated various ailments. While still reeling from baby Alex's death, she learned she was pregnant again, but was persuaded by doctors to have a termination and be sterilized, which left her gravely ill. Then there were pulmonary, renal, cardio-vascular, glandular, urinary and intestinal malfunctions for her ravaged body to contend with. Even when she was mobile, her erratic blood-sugar levels caused her to faint often and she was, in any case, prone to falls. In London she tumbled down a staircase, injuring her arm, and more than once appeared at seances with a swollen leg, shuffling towards the cabinet, a person on each side straining to support her. Travelling was invariably uncomfortable, and to perform she was usually seated on hard wooden chairs. Beforehand, she appreciated help in dressing, in particular putting on her shoes. Installed in the cabinet, her weight bore down on her bladder, muscles weakened by obstetric strain. Invariably, she visited the lavatory immediately before and after seances, but even then a mop and bucket were sometimes required. The endless flow of tea at these events didn't help.

But love and the memory of the Christ-like man from when she had been close to death spurred Helen on. And she was clear-sighted in her ambitions. To obtain her SNU diploma she decided to engage with the leading research institutions, perhaps in part to scotch a rumour that a member of the British College of Psychic Science had been sniffing around her seances in Scotland and thought she was a fraud. Time for a change of scene, perhaps. In August 1930, seeking to pre-empt the charge that her ectoplasm was regurgitated matter, Montague Rust arranged for Helen to be X-rayed at Dundee Royal Infirmary, where staff knew her well, and so obtained certification that her oesophagus and stomach were normal. That autumn Dr Rust arranged with the London Spiritualist Alliance for the Duncans to spend time in the capital to allow Helen to give a series of sittings, some for research, others for paying guests. In October the family boarded a ship at Leith and, as news spread of their impending arrival in London, respectable investigators sat back and waited, sharpening their senses and pencils.

William Crawford's album of Goligher photographs, and files relating to Helen Duncan, are among many weird relics in the archives of the Society for Psychical Research. One only has to browse the index for phrases such as 'tapes of telepathic baby', 'the flying armchair' and 'Barbados coffin mystery' to leap out. But like a Renaissance cabinet of curiosities, beneath the strangeness lies a coherent purpose: to solve mysteries about the natural world. Consensus, however, eluded the SPR from the start and by the 1890s tensions between Spiritualists and sceptics had led to a relative secularization of the Society and a boost to its intellectual prowess. In Lord Rayleigh and J. J. Thomson the SPR boasted two future Nobel laureates, and in William Gladstone and A. J. Balfour a past and a future prime minister. Gladstone, indeed, judged research by the SPR committees on mesmerism and hauntings to be 'the most important work which is being done in the world'. A census of hallucinations taken from 17,000 answers to a questionnaire showed that one-in-ten had experienced *something* inexplicable.

The fraudulence of Eusapia Palladino marked a loss of patience, however, as did that of the mystic Madame Helena Blavatsky and her Theosophical Society, founded to challenge the Christian monopoly of spiritual truth. The daughter of a Russian army officer, her childhood had been blighted by greed, tantrums and hallucinations, and as an adult she wallowed in burning sexual and super-natural fantasies, stoked with hashish at her headquarters in India. Her seances were satirized in *Punch* as the ancient wisdom of the Mahatmas manifested through party tricks, including the extrusion of ectoplasm and spontaneous rose showers – all dishonest stunts, according to her housekeeper. The SPR diverted its attention to trance mediumship and between 1894 and 1923 published no major paper on seance manifestations.

Interest in Spiritualism after the First World War did not re-enchant the SPR, but there were now more medi-ums to investigate and supporting funds. By the time Helen Duncan arrived in London, though, the SPR was no longer the only solvent research organization and some members had gone their own way, notably Harry Price, who had founded the National Laboratory of Psy-chical Research in 1923 and spent freely. Sir Oliver Lodge was dismayed to hear a rumour overseas that the British psychical research establishment had succumbed to 'a kind of insanity'. If so, it was an insanity that in the autumn of 1930 Helen and Henry Duncan were ready to exploit.

The London Spiritualist Alliance was located at 16 Queensberry Place, a grand South Kensington town house with four floors and a basement. Visiting mediums did not, as a rule, enter through its neoclassical porch but instead were directed towards the tradesmen's entrance. The Duncans arrived with Montague Rust for a prelimin-ary meeting so Helen could get the lie of the land. Rust introduced his protégée and her husband to the LSA's Sec-retary, Mercy Phillimore, who showed them the seance room with its double doors, the innermost padded with green baize, and in a far corner the cabinet, a plush curtain suspended from the ceiling, over which hung a wooden chandelier holding four red lamps. Helen noted the location of the ladies' lavatory and listened as Miss Phillimore went through the rules for the protection of mediums. Lights, smoking, striking watches and the touching of manifestations were forbidden, and on a point of honour proceedings were confidential. A copy of the code was pasted inside a book that sitters were obliged to sign (ladies on the left of the page, gentlemen to the right). Helen was satisfied – although concerned by malevolent vibrations she sensed from a tall, smartly dressed gentleman climbing the stairs to the fourth-floor flat he rented from the LSA as a laboratory. That man was Harry Price.

Montague Rust decided that the first spiritual communication for establishing Helen's credentials should be an act of clairvoyance. On Saturday 25 October he brought the Duncans to Queensberry Place, where they hung up their coats and hats and settled into their surroundings. Before an audience waiting in the spacious seance room, Helen sat at a small table on which paper and pencil had been laid. Dr Rust produced a wax-sealed envelope labelled 'The X Document, June 1910'. This, he explained, was a message given to him by a deceased friend William Martin and only to be opened after his death. As usual, Helen passed it across her forehead and up her back, staring silently into the sitters' faces – and seemingly beyond. In an atmosphere of great reverence, everyone watched as her pencil hovered before she began to write laboriously in her best curvilinear hand. When she had finished, the envelope was opened, and the messages compared. Apart from getting the date wrong and allowing for some predictability of content – Martin had promised to make contact post-mortem – Helen did well, especially in the way Rust was addressed as 'physician and friend'. The room was impressed with this appetizer for a seance and made encouraging noises.

Early the following evening, the President of the LSA, Dr Robert Fielding-Ould, welcomed Helen back into the seance room, where a crescent of sitters, who had inspected her black housecoat and underwear, were waiting patiently. Henry cranked up the gramophone, smiling encouragingly as his wife strode towards the cabinet, oblivious to the hushed whispers. As arranged, she was helped into a large satin bag tied loosely at the neck, and tapes wrapped around her body and secured to the chair. Dr Fielding-Ould tugged at the knots and then sealed them with wax.

As in a submarine preparing to dive, the white light was switched to red, casting a pinkish luminescence across the room. At five past six, trussed up like Houdini, Helen closed her eyes and the curtain was drawn. After a few minutes the sound of heavy breathing was heard over the scratchy, jolly music, and Henry asked everyone to be quiet and not touch anything. After twenty minutes a pale strand crept from the cabinet. Rust asked: 'Is that Albert? Can you show us more of that psychoplasm, Albert?' A pause of bristling anticipation followed. 'I will show you some, my lad,' came the sonorous reply, followed by the sight of an expanding human form. The guide then invited sitters to sample the matter now oozing from Helen's body. Phosphorus-white against the black of the room, a trail of ectoplasm hanging in the air coalesced into a rough cross, which Fielding-Ould felt and said it was soft like fine merino cloth. Albert also asked Fielding-Ould to smell the ectoplasm and was irritated when he detected nothing, owing to the fact, he said, that he was a smoker. Others approaching the cabinet reported a pungent odour that Miss Phillimore had noticed before at materialization seances – like old cloth, Henry suggested, but Albert protested it was nicer than that.

The rest of the seance set a pattern that would be repeated many times in the coming weeks with only minor variations. A child's face appeared, causing Albert to complain: 'If only I could get rid of the girl!', followed by several other shapes struggling into definition, including a figure 'like a little baby in long clothes'. Rustling and banging from within the cabinet suggested that the medium was also struggling, until, without warning and still entranced, she wandered out free from the sack and plumped down on a chair in the circle. As she was being helped back to the cabinet like a sleepwalking child, sitters had a chance to check that the sack was undamaged, which it was. Shortly afterwards Helen re-emerged from the cabinet and stood directly beneath the red light, twelve or thirteen feet of luminous matter streaming from her mouth to the floor, and then paraded left and right in a stately fashion, exercising obvious care not to step on the ectoplasm despite her apparently semi-conscious state.

At these London seances, much more so than in

Dundee, the dominant, spiritual Albert would use the sub-ordinate, corporeal Helen to put down the man who stood between them. At this first sitting, speculation about how she had managed to escape from the sack prompted Henry to propose 'an elongation of the medium', to which Albert replied: 'Nonsense, you fool. You are a perfect ass with your theories.' Henry, meek as ever before the control, tried to lighten the atmosphere by suggesting that Albert was as good as George Robey; but this only made things worse, for Albert made him explain who Robey was – Britain's top comedian – then took offence at the comparison.

Albert's shifts between formality, levity and sarcasm were sustained to the end of the seance, at which point he drew attention to the way the ectoplasm, like a skein of wool, was withdrawn, saying: 'I want to let you see it go right down into the mouth.' When Dr Rust said they were looking forward to the next *séance*, Albert cried with mock horror, 'Oh help! That is surely French!', before delivering a pious farewell: 'The Lord be with you.' The lights went up at 7.25 p.m. Helen, barely awake, bustled off to the lavatory with less ceremony than she arrived with, and returning found the LSA researchers re-examining the pristine seals. She lit a cigarette and watched them.

Helen sometimes needed smelling salts to leave her trance, but usually she was merely disoriented, a dull stupor eased by tea and nicotine. Waking up, she made unsettling cryptic pronouncements. 'I ken ye,' strangers were told, or, 'I dinna ken ye, but I ken of ye.' Once, affecting the air of a Highland seer, she revealed: 'I have been in a strange house, one that I have never visited before. It is a house with an unmade bed, and under the mattress there are some papers.' But informality was limited at the LSA. Albert was more assertive, which for Helen was just as well, for the inquisitiveness of her hosts increased after the first performance. At the second sitting, on 30 October, Dr Fielding-Ould examined her mouth, nostrils, ears and hair, and the restraints were tightened. 'I wish there were someone here to take this blinking bag off,' grumbled Albert as he tried to, he explained, deconstruct the medium atomically to squeeze her through the 27-inch aperture. In the end, the bag was removed and sitters had to be content with a few ectoplasmic hands, which grasped at them before dissolving. Helen bickered with Henry, then started spluttering and choking, a fearful sound that her smiling husband smothered with a happy tune from the gramophone.

The sittings continued on Tuesdays and Fridays throughout November and December. There were some changes: a woollen dress provided for Helen (at a cost of £1 4s) was exchanged for a larger size and an airy mesh sack introduced. There were surprises, too, as when for no obvious reason the medium's dentures were gently plopped into Mercy Phillimore's hand. Just as bafflingly, one minute Albert was talking about getting the medium's brain under his domination, the next he was offering to play the bagpipes at Miss Phillimore's wedding. Splashing was heard from the cabinet, where the floor was found to be sticky. And yet always the ectoplasm flowed – shimmering, numinous, pastel-tinged – and the manifestations were eye-popping, not least Peggy, who bounced a ball, sang 'Baa, baa, black sheep', then waved 'ta-ta'. Sitters treated the spirits obsequiously, yet shared Albert's contempt for Henry and his banal interjections. Albert once threatened to 'twist his blinking neck' after he proposed playing another record, and next time called him an 'old fathead' and accused him of wanting to bring down the moon when he suggested they adjust the lighting. Albert remarked scornfully that if Henry really wanted to control his wife, he should have her nailed into a coffin. As usual, the comedy, if it can be called that, was of the blackest hue.

The LSA arranged medical checks. After each seance, a loss of weight was recorded, as were increases in Helen's pulse and blood pressure; urine tests showed 'an amazing amount of albumen'. In December there were two other developments: procuring an ectoplasm sample and making a photographic record. On the 5th, Fielding-Ould placed a bowl of water in the cabinet, as Albert had instructed he should, and the seance began. The researchers, who were experimenting with a new type of illumination, accidentally let a painted glass shutter slip, catching Albert in the full glare of the white light. 'Though behind the curtain, and not directly exposed to it,' they recorded, 'the medium emitted a fearful groan, following as closely on the flash as if she had been shot, and Albert described the effect on him as resembling a horrible blow from a red hot poker.' A scrap of ectoplasm did reach the bowl; a larger fragment found on the chair was described as 'two inches square and rather more than an eighth of an inch thick, of a creamy white leathery-looking matter which floats readily on the water'. Meanwhile, it was noticed that Helen's jaw was inflamed and a patch of skin the size of a sixpence excoriated as if burned. J. A. Stevenson, a sculptor, sat in on two seances at which, under Albert's supervision, he made seventeen photographic plates for use in a magic lantern. All showed the opaque white forms, even if the fine folds and lustrous sheen were not well reproduced. After the second seance, however, Stevenson obtained an even better souvenir. While he was chatting with Mrs Duncan over a cup of tea, she complained of something icy cold in her seance suit. Miss Phillimore picked open the stitches to reveal a strip of ectoplasm stuck to Helen's chest. This strip Fielding-Ould removed with forceps, dropped into distilled water and later divided into several pieces. One of these was given to Stevenson, who made a detailed sketch for a lantern slide, recording it in his notes as a 'piece of substance resembling tissue – in parts apparently fibrous and in parts resembling fatty nodules'.

Almost from the start of the LSA sessions, doubts had been creeping in. Early in November a fleshy arm was seen beneath the spirit form of a child swaying in time to the music. Later that same month Helen stepped to one side of the cabinet, leaving a lifeless phantom there attached to her face by an ectoplasmic strand, which, as she turned towards the light, appeared to be tied in a knot under her nose. To Stevenson the sculptor, one manifestation looked quite solid, with cylindrical legs as if swaddled like a mummy. The swinging motion of another spirit form made it seem so unrealistic that

Albert apologized: the medium was nervous, he explained. Sitters likened the ectoplasm to muslin or dishcloths. Circular burns on Helen's body were attributed to the rapid reclamation of ectoplasm when it was disturbed, but only ever appeared after her post-seance cigarette. By the end, the LSA agreed that some fraud was involved but couldn't agree on how much, especially as some members had attended more often than others. So they invited Helen to return to London in the New Year. But over Christmas back in Dundee, Helen felt profoundly unhappy with the LSA and was open to fresh offers – even from Britain's most devious and sceptical psychical researcher, Harry Price.

Harry Price and Helen Duncan had more in common than they could have known, their lives a tangle of fantasies and conflicting facts, ambitions surging whenever people took them seriously. Price was primarily a ghost hunter and journalist and used his expertise in both fields well. He was reviled by Spiritualists and psychical researchers alike, even though (or perhaps because) his aim was only to publicize the truth by circumventing the polite conventions of the SNU and SPR. 'Good mediums do exist,' he said, 'but they are so few and far between that the casual inquirer is not likely to come across them.' The Schneider brothers impressed him in 1922, and a year later he met a shy nurse, Dorothy Stella Cranshaw, whom he nurtured as the physical medium 'Stella C.'. An obsessive bibliophile, Price spent years trying to foist his vast library upon any institution willing to give it a home.* The SPR stored the books before they were moved to the NLPR, then the LSA refused them (four times), until finally they were accepted by the University of London shortly after Price had offered them to Hitler, whom he admired and believed to be interested in psychical research.

Price was a peerless opportunist. Within weeks of Schrenck-Notzing's death in February 1929, he had snapped up Rudi Schneider for a run of sessions about which he published a book the following year. In October 1930, Price booked a clairvoyant of Irish birth, Eileen Garrett, who had married wisely, travelled widely and topped up her psychic energies by sunning herself on the French Riviera. Her Arab spirit guide 'Uvani' brought messages from Captain Walter Hinchliffe shortly after his aeroplane disappeared over the Atlantic in 1928. These communications were remarkable less for what his widow learned − 'Tell them there is no death but everlasting life' − than for their technical detail. Two years later Price invited a journalist to hear the spirit of Flight Lieutenant H. C. Irwin, pilot of the R-101 airship, which two days earlier had crashed, killing forty-eight passengers and crew, including the Secretary of State for Air, Lord Thomson. Again, the analysis was highly specialized and astonished Major Oliver Villiers, an intelligence officer at the Ministry of Aviation, who arranged seven sittings of

* This included a pristine edition of Reginald Scot's *Discoverie of Witchcraft* (1584), which in his way Price claimed was the actual copy Shakespeare used to research *Macbeth*.

his own. Seeking further proof, Villiers also attended Mrs Duncan's materialization seance on 9 December, as the LSA register indicates.

Price sold the story to the *Morning Post* (as an 'exclusive') and received another ninety guineas for the US rights. As SPR members began defecting to his National Laboratory, he moved to bigger premises, in Roland Gardens, not far from the LSA, and invested in new equipment. All he needed was a medium. Stella C. had married (and ended their friendship), Rudi had been poached by the Institut Métapsychique International in Paris and, however diligently he combed the Spiritualist press, Price could find no one suitable. The medium he most wanted was Helen Duncan, about whom he had first heard from James Souter's notice in *Light*. Although the LSA refused him entry to their sittings, Price did meet the Duncans privately and found them pleasant and intelligent; he was told they had accepted the LSA's offer but might be available at a later date. Price was dubious. Early in 1931, J. A. Stevenson gave him his LSA photos and ectoplasm sample, about which Price's suspicions were confirmed by chemical and microscopic analysis. In a sample taken from Eva Carrière, Schrenck-Notzing had found: 'numerous skin discs; some sputum-like bodies; numerous granulates of the mucous membrane; numerous minute particles of flesh; traces of sulphozyansaurem potash'. Mrs Duncan's was similar but also contained egg white. Price kept this to himself, but the knowledge was spreading from other sources. The following month a Mr Montagu Scott contacted the LSA to say that Charing

Cross Medical School had found his sample of ectoplasm to be just paper and cloth bound by albumen.

Helen spent February 1931 convalescing after a bout of bronchitis and mustering the courage to return to London. Henry was keener to get back than she was, fixated by the offer of £9 per week – three times the average domestic income. Helen relented and placed an advertisement with the Dundee Labour Exchange for a maid to join her on a long engagement, and so hired a young woman named Mary McGinlay. In the second week of March the Duncan household decamped to 8 Beulah Crescent, Thornton Heath, near Croydon, a comfortable villa arranged for them by the LSA at an annual rent of £85. On 9 March Helen and Henry signed a six-month contract with an option for the London Psychical Laboratory, the newly formed research branch of the LSA, to re-engage them for a further year; Helen signed 'Victoria Duncan', fluffing the first letters as if nervous or unused to styling herself this way. Excitement among the researchers was undiminished by the damning analysis of the ectoplasm, largely because the LSA chose not to publicize it. The ink was scarcely dry on the contract before the SPR was making overtures to Helen in a letter that she showed to her new employers; in turn, the LSA Secretary, Miss Phillimore, invited an SPR observer, disingenuously vouching for Mrs Duncan's honesty.

The twice-weekly seances resumed on 13 March, when sitters were treated to ectoplasm, at first the size of a cherry on Helen's tongue, then masses of drapery and a figure substantial enough to shake hands. On the following Tuesday at a sitting attended by, among others, a military staff officer, a theatrical producer and a continental baron, Peggy appeared, sang her usual 'Baa, baa, black sheep', said she preferred water to lemonade (because of the gas), then handed over to the medium, who stole the show by escaping from her seance suit naked except for a 'bridal veil' of ectoplasm. Dr Margaret Vivian, a general practitioner from Bournemouth, was astounded and told her friend Maurice Barbanell, the editor of *Psychic News*, and other Spiritualist pressmen, how impressed she had been.

Between March and May, new controls were adopted – stitching up the seance suit using a secret pattern, padlocking the suit shut, enclosing the medium's hands in buckram mittens – but still the phenomena enthralled guests, the names of which read like the society pages of the *Tatler*: Madame Destrees, Major and Mrs J. S. Swayne, Lady Harris and daughter, Lady Laura Culme-Seymour, the Hon. Mrs Wild, Susan Countess of Malmesbury, Countess Ahlefeldt-Laurvig, Mr and Mrs Staveley Bulford, Major Stewart, Countess de Lavradio, Lady Doreen Knatchbull, Dr E. S. Reid, the Hon. Mrs Cooper and the animal welfare campaigner Maria Dickin OBE, to name but a few. On 20 March, at a research session attended by the eminent German dowser Freiherr Gustav von Pohl, Albert was asked to leave his mark on an ebony hand mirror. Helen's fingerprints were taken and compared by an ex-police chief inspector to a blown-up photo of the mirror, though, to everyone's disappointment, inconclusively.

The LSA was not the Duncans' only source of income. Henry was still receiving his army pension and on days off

Helen held seances at home in Thornton Heath. They could now afford to live like a proper lower-middle-class family, eating well and travelling by taxi. They also had their maid, Mary McGinlay, who by now had begun to notice strange things. Mary's Irish grandmother materialized at a seance, although her grandfather – who, unknown to Helen, was a Scot – seemed to have acquired his wife's accent in the spirit world when he too materialized. Further suspicion was aroused by a spirit baby, allegedly one of Helen's own, which resembled a doll Mary sometimes helped the Duncan girls to dress. Mary also wondered why the children were tasked with cutting out faces from periodicals such as *True Story Magazine*, and why she was sent to buy butter muslin and told not to tell Henry. Rubber gloves, surplus to domestic need, she found stashed in a cupboard and again was instructed not to say anything; on another occasion she saw Bella burying a pair of these gloves in the garden. Mary also found, hidden in a drawer, the luminous star worn by a little spirit girl whenever she returned to see her mother.

Elsewhere, Helen's work was receiving even closer scrutiny. In the spring of 1931, the LSA published two broadly favourable reports on the Duncans, concluding that 'physical forces by some supernormal agency have been observed'. The weight of negative evidence, however, was considerable. In mid-April a safety pin found in the ladies' lavatory was identical to one found in the cabinet. A strip of ectoplasm removed a week earlier was discovered to be surgical gauze soaked in Canada balsam, a resin used in cough syrup, and later matched a sanitary towel Mrs Duncan had left in her dressing room. Ectoplasm was 'extruded by obvious movements of the mouth and throat muscles'. In Harry Price's opinion the stomach could not be searched without anaesthetic, so instead the LSA had Helen swallow a tablet of methylene blue stain. No ectoplasm appeared that day. The dilemma was that what was good for science wasn't good for business. The seances for members and guests, paying 21s and 25s respectively, over the full term of the contract could have been worth as much as £500, twice what the Duncans were being paid in that period. Business triumphed over science.

Although these concerns were not shared with the Duncans, they sensed all was not well and, like the alert Golighers and sensitive Crandons, 'watched the researchers with the eyes of super-researchers', as Mercy Phillimore recalled. When the code-stitching of the seance suit was tampered with no one said anything, yet the trick wasn't repeated. Henry tried to rekindle the LSA's interest with Helen's clairvoyant profiling of a murder suspect, but even if this hadn't been feeble – the man, she said, was sturdily built, married and wore boots – reconciliation was a forlorn hope. Only commercial gain and fear of ridicule kept the Executive Committee of the London Psychical Laboratory from tearing up their contract. In the meantime, antennae twitching, Harry Price wrote to Miss Phillimore asking to borrow Mrs Duncan, knowing this would be denied and, without waiting for a reply – indeed, the same day – offered Henry £100 as a retainer, £10 for a weekly seance and £100 at the end. This proved irresistible. After a meeting at 13d Roland Gardens, where the Duncans inspected the National Laboratory of Psychical

Research and found it congenial, Price sent out invitations to the first seance with what he called 'the most brilliant materialising medium ever seen in this country'. The NLPR's Treasurer, Mollie Goldney, a trainee at Queen Charlotte's Midwifery Hospital, he asked to perform a physical examination, recalling the days when midwives led juries of matrons to search suspected witches for the devil's mark.

The seance room, which critics likened to a hunting lodge decked out in trophies of exposed mediums, Price considered to be 'nothing so much as a gentleman's library, comfortably furnished with a home-like atmosphere'. The adjoining workshop, however, with its tool racks, bell jars, microscopes, and box cameras on tripods, was accurately likened to an operating theatre crossed with a torture chamber. Houdini's portrait on the mantelpiece was a warning to phonies. Arriving for the first seance at 7.30 p.m. on Monday 4 May, Helen Duncan seemed nervous as she was introduced to the sitters, among them Harvard's Professor McDougall, who had examined Margery. But after she had been searched and helped into her suit, the performance passed off normally with Albert hosting, the medium snoring and ectoplasm forming a veil and then an apron, its odour a curious mustiness tinged with latex.

Another four sessions were arranged, one a week for a month, at which Mrs Goldney was to examine Helen's rectum and vagina. This revealed nothing unusual, but suspicion lay elsewhere. A piece of ectoplasm fell, leaving a safety pin attached to the cabinet curtain. Another pin was visible in one of Price's flash photographs, as was a face cut from a magazine and a dangling hand that looked like a glove stuck to a length of muslin. 'I must say that I was deeply impressed,' declared Price. 'I was impressed with the brazen effrontery that prompted the Duncans to come to my Laboratory ... I was impressed with the amazing credulity of the Spiritualists who had sat with the Duncans for six solid months.' Things had gone quickly downhill.

The day after the first session, 5 May, Helen had returned to the LSA and was perturbed to see in the front row Mollie Goldney, who had been invited as an SPR observer. The seance commenced. Also there was Dr Nandor Fodor, a Hungarian journalist on Lord Rothermere's staff, who was hit by a stump-like thing and then approached by Albert, who ceremoniously handed him the medium's shoes. But the dramatic climax came when the train of ectoplasm became caught, or more likely was trodden on by Mrs Goldney, and had to be yanked free. Helen shrieked, always a chilling effect in the bristling darkness. Afterwards, Mollie hurried into the cabinet, and found Mrs Duncan with blood on her face, which the midwife dabbed at with a handkerchief.

Helen spent that night vomiting – a reaction which Mary McGinlay noticed had become frequent. The glory and the dream were fading. That same evening, Helen's naked escape from the LSA's seance sack was mocked at the Cambridge University Union Society, one debater spoofing Wordsworth to describe Mrs Duncan coming forth:

> Not in entire forgetfulness,
> And not in utter nakedness,
> But trailing clouds of teleplasm . . . .

The motion, 'That this House has no faith in the Black Magic of Spiritualism and the Occult Sciences', was carried by eight votes (26 to 18).

The next day Henry Duncan telephoned Harry Price to inform him about burns near his wife's navel and a letter she had written for the coroner were she to commit suicide. Price met the Duncans and managed to calm Helen, although that evening, at Queensberry Place, she was, Albert said, 'all shaking and trembling'.

At the second NLPR sitting at Roland Gardens, on 14 May, Price and a Harley Street doctor, William Brown, examined the livid burns and, as a precaution against shock from the flash of Price's camera, Mollie Goldney lent Helen a silk stocking to use as a blindfold. The performance was poor. Albert bowed out early, Peggy could not be coaxed out, even with chocolates, and Helen hurried to her tea and biscuits, smoking prodigiously. For the next fortnight she complained of chestiness, stage fright and money worries, and telephoned Price, who sent a cheque for £5. He was determined to press on and, having recorded Albert's voice, now prepared to use X-rays, hoping to detect a safety pin. His claim that Helen consented to this, and to having her stomach pumped, is improbable given her anxiety. Five-year-old Gena noticed her mother's anguish and overheard her say that a man called Harry Price would be the death of her.

At the fourth NLPR sitting, on the night of 28 May, David Fraser-Harris, a retired Scottish professor of physiology, was less than thrilled by the 'vague trivialities' uttered by Albert in his affected drawl and the muslin hanging from the medium's nostrils. At the first flash of the camera, Albert announced that all was not well, and the curtains opened to reveal Helen's nose trickling blood, a sample of which Dr Brown absorbed with his handkerchief. Amid the unfolding chaos, Price had to act swiftly to get his X-ray picture. It was getting very late. With theatrical sympathy, he led the wobbling Helen to the chesterfield, where she sat sweating, reluctant to lie down and even refusing a cup of tea. Professor Fraser-Harris described what happened next: 'Several times she tried to rise and leave the room, which was not easy as the bulky X-ray apparatus barred the exit. Her agitation increased with every request that she should lie down for the X-ray photograph, until at last she sprang to her feet, struck her husband a violent blow on the face, and fled from the room.' Price went after her into the entrance hall.

In a state of advanced agitation, Helen said she needed the lavatory, which request Price granted. But when he just stood there, she changed her mind and plonked herself down like a sulking child. As a glass of water was being fetched, she jumped up again, unfastened the front door and hurled herself into the street. According to Price, who had gone for some brandy, the clock was just striking midnight. Outside, Helen collapsed and clung to the iron railings, screaming hysterically and tearing at her seance suit. Henry, first on the scene, tried in vain to calm her. A policeman arrived and was disconcerted by the sight of several men in dinner jackets gathered around a seventeen-stone woman clad in black satin combinations wailing on the pavement; but once she had stopped swearing at everyone,

Price was able to get rid of him. He then turned back to the Duncans, suspecting that something had been passed to Henry – a suspicion strengthened by the medium's sudden insistence that she be X-rayed after all. When Price asked Henry if he could search *him*, he refused, giving the excuse that he was wearing dirty underwear; he also hinted that he was carrying sanitary towels, even though, as Mollie Goldney pointed out, his wife was not having a period. There was little point carrying on and everyone went home.

In the cold light of day, Professor Fraser-Harris reached three conclusions: first, Albert's voice was that of the medium 'altered by long practice so as to be unrecognisable'; secondly, fabric had been concealed in Mrs Duncan's body, hence her reluctance to be X-rayed; and, thirdly, her bleeding was meant to influence them, but may have been caused by pushing something up her nose.

The Duncans returned to the NLPR, despite the fact that Helen had a badly swollen arm due to an abscess and that she was obviously distressed. Most of her fear focused on Mollie Goldney, whom she accused of having set her up by planting a safety pin in the tuck of her seance suit. Henry speculated that his wife had been subconsciously aware of the pin, which had triggered a hysterical fit; he even proposed that Albert may have apported the pin from Mollie's handbag. Back at the LSA the sessions dragged on, signing in became lax and the reports briefer – for 2 June just: 'One piece suit sewn gloves etc. No other control. Substance seen coming from mouth. Medium tied.' Eve Brackenbury of the SPR also attended this seance and recorded how light was thrown into the sitters' faces and away from the cabinet, from which came a good deal of rustling. Helen arrived wearing a sling – now with a suspected *broken* arm – and the phenomena were disappointing, although a woman who recognized Madame Blavatsky in the medium's transfigured features saved the day.

For the next sitting, Harry Price requested that Henry leave them alone, suggesting he go to the cinema, which he did. This would allow time for a pair of doctors Price had drafted in from a London hospital (he said St Thomas's)* to explore the dark continent of Mrs Duncan's body before the performance: 'They brought a bag of tools with them, took off their coats to the job, and really got down to it. But they found nothing. Every orifice and crack where an instrument or a hand would go was thoroughly explored; every nook and cranny was examined; but at each fresh place they drew a blank.' Price admitted how terrible this sounded but blamed medium tricksters who necessitated such measures. The doctors could tell she was in poor shape: her eardrums had old perforations (probably from the mills), and there were signs of middle-ear disease, including a purulent discharge. The turbinate bones of her nose were infected and seeping pus. The doctors' report described her uterus as 'small and anteverted', her cervix 'small and scarred' and her rectum empty 'except for some soft faecal matter'.

Then the seance got underway. It had been agreed that

---

* Although these doctors were probably both men, to soften the impression left by the episode Price told the SNU president, J. B. McIndoe, that they had been women.

an ectoplasm sample would be taken, and to be sure of getting it Price issued each sitter with a pair of surgical scissors, which glinted in the half-light. But Albert was shy and sluggish. 'The helplessness of thwarted purpose seemed to have settled like an incubus on that gentle spirit,' sniped Price, 'for although not exactly inarticulate he uttered only indistinct and uninforming platitudes.' Helen extruded just a few inches of ectoplasm – but, within a second of Albert granting permission, one of the doctors pounced. Helen squealed, jerked back her head and the ectoplasm tore off like a slimy pancake; the remainder, of what was obviously a flattened tube of paper folded zigzag, she swallowed. As Helen left her trance, she rolled her eyes and flailed her arms until the doctors spoke loudly to her and panic subsided into a daze. Blood smeared around her face, they discovered, came from a prick on the nasal septum, and it was noted that an abscess on her arm was suppurating. 'I am in an awful mess', she whimpered.

Price concluded that Mrs Duncan produced artificial matter 'by regurgitation, or reversed oesophageal peristalsis, with the help of the diaphragm and the muscles of the anterior abdominal wall'. He had the chemical analysis; he was ready. On 11 June, seeking an explanation for similarities between Helen's ectoplasm and cheesecloth, the NLPR Council interrogated her husband, pointing at the warp-and-weft in enlarged photographs and suggesting that inflated surgical gloves were also used. Henry was philosophical. Citing the examples of Mina 'Margery' Crandon, Eva Carrière and Rudi Schneider, he was adamant that his wife's productions were supernormal – but conceded that he had suspected her of concealing things, albeit unconsciously. 'I have taken her into the bathroom and made her take all her clothes off,' he said, 'and I have on two occasions given her a vaginal examination.' He also had Mary McGinlay search her clothes before a seance. Amazingly, Henry left this meeting with another seance booked for 2 July. The next day, after a disastrous show at Queensberry Place, where Helen tried to pass off her protruding tongue as ectoplasm, he met the LSA Committee and admitted that his wife's materializations were the result of regurgitation. The contract was annulled – but even then the seances for paying guests continued and handbills advertising Mrs Duncan's 'Experiments in Physical Phenomena' distributed.

By now, the medium was in a bad way. She fell into a violent despair when she learned what had happened, besides which her arm had become septic, requiring admission to St Thomas's Hospital, where they drained the abscess and kept her in for observation. But, as her body healed, her mind curdled, and she drank half a bottle of Eusol, an antiseptic of chlorinated lime and boric acid, and had to have her stomach pumped. The doctor, who believed this to be a 'hysterical histrionic performance' rather than a genuine suicide attempt, nonetheless advised that she should cancel her seance bookings forthwith. The LSA, who were eager for the final curtain anyway, were informed by Henry in a letter received on 15 June, which said Helen had *twice* attempted suicide. The LSA's President, Robert Fielding-Ould, saw in Helen's hospitalization a chance to analyse her urine, but a pathologist found nothing abnormal. Feigning concern, Dr Fielding-Ould organized a contingent from the LSA to visit Helen as she recuperated, a gesture to which she responded by screaming obscenities until they left.

On Friday 19 June, up and about but feeling delicate, Helen met Mercy Phillimore at Queensberry Place to sign an agreement whereby the LSA would pay her the £7 1s 6d they owed (after deductions of rent, rates and tax) and, on condition the Duncans were gone within a week, foot the £40 bill for sending them and their possessions back to Scotland. Meanwhile, for purposes of comparison, Harry Price was busy taking photographs of his secretary Ethel posing with a length of Woolworth's cheesecloth, including stuffing all six feet of it into her mouth. Only by chance on the Monday did he learn that Helen and Henry were going home before the sitting he had booked for 2 July. That evening Mollie Goldney tracked the Duncans down to a seance in Eaton Terrace, SW1, where Henry explained they were leaving because Helen needed a holiday. Mrs Goldney, who was used to getting her own way, took him back to Roland Gardens, where Price attempted to cut a new deal, offering Henry £100 for the opportunity to film Helen regurgitating cloth. So desperate was Henry to quit London that he declined – but before he left Price showed him the two sets of photographs: Helen in full flow and the mock-ups with Ethel. Henry was confused and needed Price to point out that Ethel was half Helen's size before he could tell the pictures apart.

On 23 June the Duncan family boarded an overnight steamer and breathed the fresh air of liberty from the disgruntled London research societies. The next morning little Gena was nauseous from the pitching of the boat but mostly from over-excitement, her constitution not helped by the sight of her jubilant father downing a plate of kippers as they sighted Leith in the distance. Over her tea and first cigarette Helen, too, contemplated with satisfaction their homecoming and what had been achieved. After all, the trip had not been a complete failure: they had been well paid. In the space of a few months, including their expenses, the Duncans had cost the London societies over £500, which, according to Harry Price's NLPR, had been money well spent in the public interest. Helen left behind some semi-digested blotting paper and a few of her photographs, including the portrait of herself she had packed the previous autumn, on the back of which she had written 'Return to Mrs Duncan, Ferry Road, Dundee' before lending it to Price. But Price never did return it and used it without permission for the frontispiece of his next book.

Having seen off the Duncans, Harry Price prepared to trounce the LSA – 'the people down below', as he called them at Queensberry Place – as revenge for their slurs and slights. Early in July 1931 he finished a draft of *The Duncan Mediumship: A Study in Regurgitation*, although on legal advice he made cuts and retitled it: *Regurgitation and the Duncan Mediumship*. With insufficient time to publish before the LSA's own report appeared, Price gave an interview to the *Morning Post* reporter who had covered the R-101 airship disaster and lent him an advance copy.

Price didn't mention the LSA but innuendo about a well-known Spiritualist society sufficed. On 14 July the news broke with the headline: SPIRITUALISTS HOAXED. TELE-PLASMS FROM CHEESE CLOTH 'MEDIUM' EXPOSED, REMARKABLE FACULTY OF REGURGITATION. Readers were regaled with stories of wood-pulp ectoplasm and told that the Duncan episode was 'one of the cleverest frauds in the whole history of Spiritualism'. The story also appeared in the *Liverpool Post* and on Sunday in the Manchester *Empire News*. Just three days before the publication of *Light*, therefore, the LSA had been humiliated – 'spitting blood', according to Mollie Goldney. A furious volley of letters was fired from Queensberry Place towards Roland Gardens. Dr Fielding-Ould refused to believe that Price had not written the article himself.

The report printed in *Light* on 17 July 1931 stated that 'on nearly all points the conclusions are disappointing to those interested in psychical research'. Months of suppressed doubt now came flooding out. As soon as she'd finished reading Mrs Goldney wrote to Eve Brackenbury: 'They were a long time coming to this!!' The SPR Executive Committee met to discuss the LSA and NLPR reports and decided the most astonishing thing was the LSA changing its mind about Helen Duncan's credibility. Mercy Phillimore had tried to ease things by informing the SPR Research Officer that 'Mrs Duncan was greatly under the adverse influence of her husband and that he, in one way, deserves more blame than she.' Furthermore, the LSA alleged, Henry had confessed to being more interested in 'the lure of gold' than in psychical research, hence his defection to the NLPR. Over the summer the Duncans put their side of the story to Ernest Oaten, the editor of the Spiritualist newspaper the *Two Worlds*, who wrote a leader that started a debate with Dr Fielding-Ould about the relevance of Jungian analysis to the case.

Reactions to Price's book were mixed. The SPR declared the psychical research content nil and doubted even that regurgitation had been proved. Price defended his work as a contribution to medical science – but to him profit and publicity were paramount, so the book had a soft cover (meaning it cost only five shillings) and plenty of pictures, including a set of stereograms – pairs of identical photographic images for which readers were advised to buy a 3-D viewer. Despite William McDougall's opinion that Helen Duncan was a fraud, the American SPR was even more equivocal than its English cousin and refused to publish Price's findings because, 'the principal facts are in controversy'. In Italy the editor of *Luce e Ombre* reminded readers that ectoplasm *always* looked like cloth! Spiritualists were even more indignant. J. Arthur Findlay, the Vice-President of the Glasgow SPR, sent testimonies to Price, who returned them with the stinging reply: 'When these people produce as good evidence for the abnormality of Mrs Duncan's alleged phenomena, as we have produced for the fraudulent side of her mediumship, I will listen to them. I have not seen or heard a shred of real evidence which would persuade me that Mrs Duncan had any psychic power whatsoever.'

Meanwhile, Helen had resumed her seances in Scotland.

The Glasgow SNU was wary, J. B. McIndoe told Price, but so far had detected no sound, smell or sight of regurgitation, and doctors who X-rayed her in Dundee had scoffed at the idea. Ernest Oaten disputed that Price had seen what others had seen, to which an exasperated Price replied: 'If you had felt, smelt, and photographed the stuff as I did, you would have not the slightest doubt that it was cheesecloth, swallowed and regurgitated.'

But Price was wasting his time, for Helen had risen to new heights in the estimation of her supporters. Montague Rust, who had attended over fifty Duncan seances, continued to exalt the phenomena. He recalled one particularly good session where the cabinet opened to reveal 'Mrs D. standing, one foot on the chair, and masses of white material streaming from nose, mouth, ears, breasts and from the region of the vagina'. In November 1931, Rust told Mollie Goldney that they had always known London would be a fiasco and that sceptics would never get good results from such 'a *very* sensitive human creature'. Sarcastically, he referred to all her miracles as regurgitations: 'In fact she *regurgitated* my brother-in-law, Charles Ross, and my driver, Andrew Barclay, and my dog Hector. We had long conversations with them in their own characteristic voices and varying memories, Hector being life-like in all his actions and ran about the floor as he did in life. Forms came out and sat on some of the sitters' knees and spoke and ate apples and drank water, and also others who removed my boots forcibly and put them on and walked about with them.' Rust had also seen Helen dematerialize, levitate, suck back a spirit in a split second, and produce a football-sized lump of ectoplasm, which crashed to the floor.

With this support behind them, the Duncans complained about an article in the *Empire News* bearing the headline HYSTERICS OF CLEVER WOMAN MEDIUM, which showed a touched-up picture of Helen, a clump of ectoplasm obscuring her face. The editor rang Harry Price about a solicitor's letter he'd received asserting that their client had 'never been photographed in the position indicated and she is satisfied that the photo is really one of a person whom she knows as Ethel who is a typist with Mr. Harry Price'. To cap it all, an expert certified that the picture was a fake. 'The Duncans fly from one folly to another', grumbled Price. 'What *are* you to make of such people?' But the SNU showed what it made of them by granting Helen its prized diploma, for which she thanked the LSA, who 'definitely put me on the map as a medium'.

Work flooded in. Price realized his report had, in effect, been an advertisement. 'Spiritualists on both sides of the Tweed', he later recalled, 'began falling over themselves in order to obtain sittings with her.' In December she accepted Margaret Vivian's invitation to Bournemouth Spiritualist Church, where sitters were delighted by an apported cucumber, the feculent smell of the ectoplasm and the headaches they suffered as creative juices were sucked from their bodies. The resident minister, Rev. Frank Blake, declared Helen 'the most valuable medium for physical phenomena in the British Isles'. In the same month, a *Two Worlds* reader wrote in to say how Albert had been asking sitters to consider Price's interpretation, jesting that if it were true Mrs Duncan must have the swallowing powers of a crocodile! When not in a trance, Helen conducted herself at seances with an air of abused innocence – a rehearsal, it turned out later, for full-blown martyrdom.

The Duncans moved back to Edinburgh and for a while lived in a one-roomed tenement flat where Henry and Helen slept in a bed recess in the kitchen – but they still had money earned in London and soon were able to swap this for a three-bedroomed house with a bathroom. However, with the exception of sixteen-year-old Bella (and the maid Mary McGinlay) the family were rarely at home. To allow her to travel, Helen sent her children to a corporation-run home forty miles away at Kelso, where, traumatized by the regime there, Gena wet the bed and prayed hard to God and Albert, especially for her sickly sister Nan. But Helen had taught her girls the principles of the Fatherhood of God and Brotherhood of Man, and they accepted that she had a duty to spread the message.

Helen kept herself busy. In the spring of 1932, the President of the Southend Society of Spiritualists died, only to reappear at a house in Leigh-on-Sea thanks to Helen, who at the same seance manifested a woman proud of her ectoplasmic dress, reunited a man with his singing grandmother and had Peggy draw pencil kisses on a pad. Next, the Duncans were in London, where Will Goldston, founder of the Magicians' Club and the author of forty books on legerdemain, attended a seance where Helen consumed a double helping of coffee and teacakes before materializing eight spirits. At Easter they were in Bristol – Gena remembers them returning with chocolate eggs – then back to London.

At the invitation of Maurice Barbanell, Goldston attended another seance, where he tried in vain to incapacitate Mrs Duncan with sash cord and handcuffs, and he then wrote up the experience for Barbanell's newly founded *Psychic News*. As with Rudi Schneider in 1929, Goldston swore he had seen things no trickery could achieve.

Seances were even impressive when things didn't go as planned. At a service at a Spiritualist church in Manchester, a woman kissed by a male spirit screamed, causing the entity to lurch back into the cabinet. Helen said she felt as if she had been bashed over the head, a physical reaction apparently confirmed by her nosebleed. For the rest of the seance, ectoplasm emanated not from her head but 'from the lower part of her body', shooting up to full height before collapsing to the floor. One awed witness, aware of the recent bad press, swore that the ectoplasm was like thin steam, not drapery. At another Manchester seance, Albert informed sitters that spirits often seemed confused, because 'they think they are alive and that it is you who are dead'. After the ectoplasm had been and gone, Mrs Duncan staggered from the cabinet, breathing heavily and drenched in sweat, the pupils of her eyes turned completely upwards. As she came to her senses, the room agreed it had been 'a most magnificent experience'. In Brighton soon afterwards Helen seemed on edge, then became hysterical as the spirits started appearing, and finally vomited, although, witnesses reported, 'what came out of her mouth was ectoplasm in significant quantities'.

But, for all the adulation, from this time Helen Duncan's enemies refused to leave her alone. Early in 1932 a man, probably a journalist, stopped Mary McGinlay and Bella Duncan in the street and in exchange for £10 – probably as much as the maid was paid in a month – was told that the family kept masks and a dummy in the bathroom. Back at home Bella told her father what had happened, causing him to exclaim that the price of Judas had risen. Mary was dismissed and returned to Dundee.

Helen may have been right to think that Harry Price was behind the betrayal. In February 1932 he received a letter from the scorned maid, who had read a newspaper article of his and thought he might like to hear her stories of 'the Great Materialized [sic] Medium, Mrs Duncan'. She claimed to have been made ill through overwork and asked him to send a cheque so that she could buy clothes and a railway ticket. On the evening of the 15th, she arrived at Euston Station and was taken by taxi to the Harrington Hall Hotel in South Kensington. The next day Mary told the NLPR Council what she had seen and heard: the rubber gloves, the doll, the luminous star, the vomiting and, of course, the ectoplasm: 'Mrs Duncan used to get me to wash out a length of this muslin. The muslin had a rotten smell. It put me in mind of the smell of urine . . . occasionally it would be stained a little as if it had been washed beforehand. At other times she would give it to me just as she had used it, and then it would be much stained and slimy.' Not only were the rips shown in Price's photographs the same as she remembered in the muslin, but she had been made to separate egg whites, which her mistress claimed were for her abscess. Before every seance, Mary said, Mrs Duncan had tea and biscuits, then took a bath, before disappearing into the potting shed. Why, she didn't know. There was more. On the night of the hysterics at Roland Gardens, the Duncans had arrived home and proceeded to row until Henry stormed out and Mary was sent after him. Telling the maid that the game was up, Henry handed her the cloth that Helen had given to him in the street.

Mary McGinlay's statement was incorporated as a statutory declaration, sworn before a Commissioner for Oaths, published by the NLPR and reproduced in the *Daily Mail*, which had covered the story the previous October. Two days after Mary left London, Price refused to give her more money to get married, which seems to have turned her against the psychical investigator. Back in Scotland, when J. B. McIndoe interviewed her, she said she had no reason to think Mrs Duncan fraudulent. He wrote to the *Daily Mail* to report this change of heart, but they declined to print his letter.

Like cat and mouse, in December Harry Price travelled to Edinburgh, Helen to London. At a Spiritualist society in well-to-do Wigmore Street, sitters felt Helen's hands and then Albert's – the former calloused, the latter soft – and an old man was invited to compare his materialized mother's gums with the medium's dentures. In Edinburgh, meanwhile, Price visited the Theatre Royal, where the variety bill included Marie Lauton and her Harp; the Harum-Scarum girls and their Merry Madcaps; and Michel & Nan: the Dancing Xylophonist and his Stepping Sister. Price, however, was interested in only one act, Kanichka the Human Ostrich, to whom a female contact in Edinburgh,

'E. M.', had alerted him. In her opinion Kanichka's proficiency as a regurgitator indicated that Helen Duncan was nothing of the kind. True, she vomited paper, which would explain why many of her materializations were coughing old women, but the swathes of cheesecloth seen by Price surely originated elsewhere. After seeing Kanichka perform for himself, Price agreed and may even have reconsidered Helen's denial: 'I did not swallow the cheesecloth; they give me credit for far more than I can do.' He certainly started taking an active interest in a forthcoming 'government inquiry' into fraudulent mediumship, alluded to by E. M., for now he knew that impostors could not be defeated by rhetoric or experiments. The law alone had teeth, so that was where Price would now watch for opportunities, assuming the law did not seek his help first. Helen's days in the limelight were numbered and dangerous times lay ahead.

5. Changing Fortunes: A Brush with the Law and the Coming of War

During an American tour in 1922, Sir Arthur Conan Doyle attended one of Mr and Mrs Tomson's seances in New York. As a parade of spirits drifted to the earth plane, he grew suspicious, especially when his own mother appeared. Having tirelessly preached the comforts of spiritual communication, Conan Doyle accepted that fraud was rife. And the Tomsons did have a questionable reputation and had been brought to the attention of the New York Police Department. Three nights later the Tomsons manifested 'Aunt Emma' for a Mrs Martin, whereupon she and her 'husband' – both undercover police officers – leapt to their feet, a whistle was blown and an NYPD squad came crashing in. Willie and Eva Tomson were fined $100 under the Fortune Telling Act, similar to legislation in Britain. 'All of us are eager to know, of course, what becomes of our loved ones after death,' observed Harry Price, reporting the story in a newspaper. 'So deep-rooted and sacred are these longings to open communication with our departed that it is difficult to conceive anything more cruel and heartless than deception in such a matter.'

A witness at the Tomsons' trial described the circumspection of the true believer: 'If a spirit fades out of your grasp it is indeed a spirit. But if it screams and rolls over on the floor – it is just another fraud.' If only things had been that simple. The truth was that even manifest imposture could be hidden by a dazed and emotional medium falling this way and that, creating a smokescreen of chaos, protesting ignorance or diminished responsibility. Spooks stitched from bedsheets, furthermore, could be spirited away almost as fast as the real thing. Most fraudulent mediumship, moreover, was not physical but mental and therefore almost impossible to prove – unless, of course, one presupposed that seances, irrespective of intent or outcome, were de facto illegal.

The problem was an old one. In eighteenth-century England property was deified and fleecing the credulous was one area where the state sought to protect the haves against the have-nots. By 1800, the authorities were committed to suppressing gypsies, but the 1735 Witchcraft Act, which proscribed fortune telling, was not commonly used against them, because it required a jury trial. More often, offenders were summarily tried as vagrants – a policy given definition by the Vagrancy Act of 1824, Section 4 of which specifically outlawed soothsaying and palmistry as crimes of deception. Arrests under the 1824 Act increased in the 1850s when county police forces were established, and plain-clothes officers used marked coins to prove that money had changed hands. By this time, because fortune tellers could be prosecuted not just for who they were – vagrants – but solely for what they did, it meant that the Act could be applied more generally to Spiritualist mediums at work in their parlours.

The first high-profile trial was that of the floating society medium D. D. Home. He had been cut into the will of a deluded widow, but when her 'golden-haired boy' refused to have sex with her she saw through communications from her husband and likewise Home's promise that her artificial hand could be brought to life. Home was made to return the deed of gift by a judge, who condemned his 'mischievous nonsense'. In 1876, Henry Slade, an American medium whose speciality was automatic writing on sealed slates, was exposed in London by the zoologist Edwin Ray Lankester. Despite a ringing endorsement for Slade from Alfred Russel Wallace, a naturalist whose theory of natural selection anticipated Darwin's, the magistrate at Bow Street Police Court reached a decision based on 'inferences to be drawn from the known course of nature' and sentenced Slade to three months' hard labour under the Vagrancy Act (although the sentence was later quashed). This case, and the prosecution of Francis Monck, a physical medium who did serve his sentence, raised public awareness not just about the possibility of fraud but its associated tricks: masks, veils, gloves, wires and double slates hinged to conceal a pre-prepared message until the climactic moment.

Such cases also provoked debate about the persecution of Spiritualists, the pro-lobby decrying medieval superstition, opponents the folly of witch-hunting. Police action continued into the twentieth century, although the gentility of many mediums and their clients was a restraining factor. Questions were asked in Parliament, to which successive Home Secretaries replied by citing the 1824 Act and reaffirming that whenever prophecy led to imposition the law would intervene. In 1912 a surge in fortune telling in London's West End led to a police clampdown: raiding premises, issuing cautions and banning advertisements. An Egyptian medium who predicted tragedy at sea for an undercover policewoman, in the year that 1,500 lives were lost on the *Titanic*, pleaded at Bow Street that he only tried to make people happy. The fillip that war gave to occult services animated the police, sparking complaints that mediums were at the mercy of obsolete legislation and agents provocateurs. In 1915 the Home Office opened a file containing a letter from Sir Oliver Lodge claiming that 'there is an Anti-Occult League afoot, anxious to put in force an antique Act against necromancy of all kinds'. Lodge had tried to draw in A. J. Balfour, First Lord of the Admiralty and a former SPR President, but received only a tight-lipped legal disquisition and a comment about impostors 'cruelly trading on the feelings of bereaved relatives'. But Lodge had a point: the rules *were* unclear. Another metropolitan purge in 1917 caused the magistrates' periodical *Justice of the Peace* to observe that, although this evil had to be curtailed, 'the law concerning alleged dealings with the supernatural has fallen into such a tangled condition that the public, even the educated public, has but a very confused idea of what it actually is'.

And so, from police heavy-handedness and a confused legal position a culture of persecution grew up around Spiritualism. In 1920 the foundation of the British College of Psychic Science was inspired directly by wartime prosecutions, especially that of an American medium, Almira Brockway, who was deported. The following year, a petition to the King requesting that mediums be protected from the law was signed by Lodge, Conan Doyle and other prominent Spiritualists. Conan Doyle's self-righteous rhetoric was much imitated in the Spiritualist press. In October 1925, Madame Estelle, a society *clairvoyante*, was convicted in a court teeming with her supporters, earning the sympathy of the *Morning Post* and, likewise, the *Daily Express*, which printed the pungent reaction of Conan Doyle, who condemned sting operations as 'foreign to the spirit of British law'. Enclosing both clippings, Conan Doyle sallied forth in a letter to the Home Secretary, censuring the police for inciting an offence that the law condemned.

By the 1930s, prosecutions were common and always attracted attention from the press. In 1932, Louisa Meurig Morris, a trance medium, sued the *Daily Mail* for libel and received accolades from, among others, Sir Oliver Lodge, who testified – disingenuously, given his experience in New York a decade earlier – that he had *heard* of fraudulent mediums but had yet to come across one. Harry Price attended all eleven days of the trial (which reached the House of Lords) and was astonished by the cheek of the medium and the credulity of the witnesses. Newspapers worked in tandem with the police. In 1936 the *Sunday Times* exposed psychic photographers the Falconer brothers, after they manufactured a 'spirit-extra' from a painting. But the feeling that reporters were unscrupulous and the police unfair persisted. By the mid-1930s, however, the policy of the Metropolitan Police was explicitly 'not to proceed except (a) where the activities of the fortune teller are such as are likely to become a public scandal – and (b) where the clientele are people of modest means – as distinct from the "idle rich"'. The key factor was money, and even Spiritualists had little time for con artists, or even genuine mediums who abused their gifts out of greed.

In the summer of 1932, Harry Price informed Munich-based Dr Gerda Walther, a corresponding member of the NLPR International Research Council, that what he saw as the pernicious Jewish alliance of Maurice Barbanell and the conjuror Will Goldston was faltering. Not only had a rival conjuror disputed Helen Duncan's genuineness, he said, but Barbanell had warned her in *Psychic News* about the perils of sitting every evening for a fiver. 'One of these days', Price predicted ominously, 'someone will take some action and she will find herself the subject of a prosecution.'

Miss Esson Maule was a stout, no-nonsense forty-something who cut her hair short and dressed imposingly in blazer and tie. A spiritualist with a small 's' at least, she invited mediums to hold seances at her gloomy Victorian townhouse, 24 Stafford Street, a short distance from Edinburgh city centre. Naturally she took an interest in Helen Duncan, by now a celebrity on the psychic circuit, and, following a seance at the Edinburgh College of Psychic Science, obtained some photographs taken by a Dundee press photographer, W. M. Scott. One showed the medium at home, entranced and blindfolded, at her side a papier-mâché coathanger-and-muslin mannequin, looking like Mr Punch from a children's show yet purported to be a materialized spirit.

Meanwhile, Helen had been working closer to home since taking her children out of boarding school owing to Nan's deteriorating health. With the diploma under her belt, she had secured a weekly slot at the Edinburgh College of Psychic Science on Heriot Row – but relations soured after an admiring sitter said she was worth more than his ten-shilling ticket, which alerted her to the fact that the college took as much as £20 at every seance, of which she received only two guineas. Besides, Helen chafed at the lack of freedom. So she decided to go it alone, unprotected but unfettered, and to Maurice Barbanell's alarm began sitting for a few pounds a time. Gena was concerned that her mother always looked so tired, but Henry told her not to worry. In fact, although Helen's earning power had increased, she had less work, meaning an overall reduction in income. By now the London money had all been spent. Together with Nan's disability, the family's reduced circumstances qualified them for a council house on a new but impoverished estate in Craigmillar, south-east of the city, where, according to Gena, Helen became a philanthropist, paying the medical bills of sick neighbours. Helen herself suffered further gynaecological problems and needed a hysterectomy – an operation she survived, it was said, thanks to Albert's advice in the operating theatre.*

---

* A few months earlier, *Light* had reported how the life of the R-101 airship medium, Mrs Eileen Garrett, had been saved by her spirit guide 'Abduhl Latif', who advised surgeons performing a tonsillectomy on how to staunch the bleeding.

Helen relied on her Glasgow seances until private work in Edinburgh picked up. Esson Maule had booked sittings through Henry as early as March 1932 but had been dissatisfied and, after taking expert advice from a contact in London, by the end of the year had decided to set a trap. Early in the evening of 5 January 1933, wearing her favourite tight brown dress, Helen had been performing at the Holland Street Spiritualist Church in Glasgow where she filled the room with the scent of flowers and materialized a woman bearing the red rose her husband had laid on her coffin. Afterwards, the organizer, Mrs Drysdale, informed Helen that while she had been in a trance Albert had warned her to be careful. Packing gifts of homemade scones and jam into her case and pulling on her leather coat, Helen promised she would. She looked at the clock: her next seance was in Edinburgh at eight o'clock, at the home of Miss Maule, and she was already running late. Helen telephoned Hilda Sowden, Miss Maule's secretary, who had made the booking, to apologize. Arriving at Waverley Station shortly after nine, Helen took a taxi to Stafford Street, where she was met by Mrs Sowden, who, Helen noticed, happened to be wearing a red jersey.

As Helen entered the fusty, dimly lit hallway, one of the first things she saw was a wall-mounted cutlass, which it was easy to imagine Esson Maule using in emergencies. She was led up the stairs without a word and into the cluttered morning room, which Miss Maule called her 'den'. After greeting a few sitters, Helen was seated beside a desk, where she lit a cigarette and was handed £4 in ten-shilling notes. Leaving the money on the desk, she stubbed out her cigarette and was led up another two flights of stairs to the seance room on the top floor. There the other sitters (some of whom had seen an advertisement in a local newspaper) were arranged in a semicircle facing a cabinet of chintz curtains suspended across a corner. The only lighting was a forty-watt red electric bulb covered with a turkey-red cotton bag, and a single candle burning on the mantelpiece; the temperature in the room was dropping, the electric fire having just fused. Still wheezing from the stairs, Helen shuffled into the cabinet, the curtains were drawn and, slipping off her shoes, she began breathing deeply as the audience commenced its singing to raise the vibrations.

A long whitish thing appeared and introduced itself as 'Albert' but withdrew when Miss Maule asked to have a better look. Just then another figure appeared who Albert said was a gentleman for the lady in the red jersey. Mrs Sowden recognized the figure at once: it was Mrs Duncan with a length of cloth hanging from her head – and so she was unsurprised that the spiritual gentleman, whose solid form Mrs Sowden patted, was the owner of a large pair of breasts. While this was going on Miss Maule reached into the cabinet, where she could feel that the chair was unoccupied, very much as she had expected it would be.

For an hour a succession of spirits (all of whom smelled of stale tobacco) dropped by to say hello. Finally, Albert took the floor to say how awful he thought Miss Maule's singing was, then handed over to the star turn, Peggy, who popped up behind a vase on the sideboard next to the cabinet and then climbed down to dance. Miss Maule wished Peggy Happy New Year, and then, bored of her chatter, approached the scamp, who everyone could see was Mrs Duncan on her knees manipulating something white and speaking childishly. Then the unthinkable happened: Miss Maule grabbed Peggy. It was immediately obvious that the spirit was made from soft, stretchy material which tore as the challenge turned into an ugly tug of war – a contest won by the defender. As arranged, one of the sitters, a solicitor named Elizabeth MacKay, switched on a powerful hand lamp to reveal Mrs Duncan squatting in the cabinet, frantically bundling the lifeless Peggy under her dress. 'Mrs Duncan, you are taking money for producing fraudulent materialisations purporting to be the deceased friends of sitters,' announced Miss Maule. 'It is disgraceful and I refuse to stand by it any longer.'

Laid bare in the glare of the lamp, the woman who taught her children that to be angry was to lose an argument, felt a blind swell of rage rise inside her and began screaming and cursing. Silenced momentarily by the sitters who were calling out to see the white fabric under her dress, she shouted back that she would not show men her knickers – but Miss Maule, injecting steel into her voice, insisted that she strip. Helen snapped. She raised a heavy wooden chair and swung it at her host, bawling, 'I'll brain you, you bloody bugger!', but missed due to the intervention of one of the male sitters, who then received a blow to the wrist from a flying shoe. With what a sitter described as 'one prolonged, savage yell', Helen swung her arm like a fast bowler and pitched the other shoe at Miss Maule, who ducked just in time.

There was a pause when they all just looked at each other. Helen, panting but calmer, agreed to undress if the men departed, which they did, albeit leaving the door ajar and peeping in from the landing. Under Miss MacKay's spotlight, Helen pulled her dress and petticoat over her head in a single swoop but failed, as she had intended, to make 'Peggy' travel with them. The white stockinette vest fell out and her female examiners simply stared. Hoping to distract them, Helen pulled off her knickers – bright blue bloomers, elasticated at the knee – and showed them the inside to prove there was nothing there. Another pause, then the following exchange:

MISS MAULE (*pointing at the vest*): That is Peggy.
MRS DUNCAN: I'll no say it's no.
MISS MAULE: You cannot deny that is Peggy. Look, there is the tear.
MRS DUNCAN: It might have been . . . you dirty swine.

Hostilities then recommenced. Miss Maule insisted she have the vest; Helen refused, then offering all her clothes said she would go home in the nude. In the end she threw the vest at Miss Maule and again attacked her with the chair, which this time Miss Maule parried. Helen quietened when the men burst back in. Miss Maule explained to them what had happened, and Helen flashed her big blue knickers by way of illustration. Tiring of Helen's 'threatening attitudes and hooligan tactics, swearing and cursing', Miss Maule said she would call the police and left her guest screaming 'The Police!' while Miss MacKay and

Mrs Sowden tried to look unconcerned. When the constables arrived, Helen swooned and asked for glass after glass of water. Accused of fraud, she replied politely: 'If God should stand between us just now I know nothing about it.' One of the men was bleeding from a cut on his head, but no one wanted to press charges, so the constables left.

The tragi-comedy ended in the hallway while they waited for a taxi. It was noticed that Mrs Duncan had managed to reclaim the disputed vest, which after some argument she returned. Then she denied that payment had been arranged, but hesitated to forgo the banknotes Miss Maule was holding. Helen snatched them, whereupon Miss Maule pencilled a receipt on the back of an envelope, which the medium signed with a confident flourish. As her cab pulled up outside, Helen fixed the people in the hall with the dark intensity of her stare and said: 'I don't know how far this, tonight, will go, but I don't want anything in the papers.' And with that she scuttled off into the night.

Eleven days later, Miss Maule and five others appeared before a magistrate to testify that Helen Duncan had been detected in a criminal fraud. They produced their evidence: the grubby undervest, torn and full of pinholes, to which were attached luggage labels, each signed and dated by a witness and sealed with wax. A summary of the facts was compiled, and an indictment framed. Soon afterwards, with clinical precision, Miss Maule hired a photographer to record the entire *mise en scène* at Stafford Street, down to a pile of ten shilling notes to show how things had been prior to the seance. Two months later Miss Maule was called to the office of the Procurator Fiscal, James Adair, to discuss the prosecution. A summons to answer a charge of fraud was sent to the Duncans' home in Craigmillar, causing dismay and despair. A solicitor was hired, who explained the situation to Helen, and she waited.

Proceedings began on the morning of Wednesday 3 May at the Sheriff Summary Court of the Lothians and Peebles. For the first time Helen Duncan, trembling in her Sunday best, felt the architectural and atmospheric power of the law. The court was crowded with reporters, thrill seekers and supporters, the last mostly female Spiritualists. Shortly before 11 a.m., the judge, Sheriff Macdonald KC, called the court to order and the charge was read out. It was alleged that Helen Duncan had pretended to be:

a medium through whom the spirits of deceased persons were openly and regularly materialized in such a manner as to become visible to, and to speak to, and to converse with, those present in a room with you . . . and having each paid to you a sum of ten shillings of money, you did pretend to hold a seance there and to materialize the spirits of certain deceased persons including that of a deceased child named Peggy.

Straining her voice above the hubbub, Helen pleaded not guilty. In keeping with Scottish law, counsel – Mr Adair prosecuting, Mr Ian Dickson defending – made no speeches; a succession of witnesses spoke and were cross-examined. The taxi driver who had brought Mrs Duncan from Waverley Station became embroiled in a debate about where she had said the seance would take place: at Miss Maule's house, or the 'Psychic Research Centre' next door. Dickson also called a doctor, Marguerite Linck Hutchison, who had attended J. B. McIndoe's seances in Glasgow after her uncle – the theatrical producer present at the LSA in March 1931 – thought she might find Mrs Duncan interesting. She rejected the regurgitation theory, not least because she had seen the medium devour a substantial meal of ham and fried eggs before the seance.

On the second day of the trial, when the crowds were even bigger, various expert witnesses were called. J. B. McIndoe recanted his negative opinion of Mrs Duncan's conduct at Stafford Street, a trial of even the most wretched medium being perceived as a trial of Spiritualism itself. Ernest Oaten, too, did what he could. Montague Rust entertained the court with tales of Mrs Duncan dematerializing out of her clothes and lifting him up with a giant snake of ectoplasm. Harry Price was also present. He could hardly believe his ears, though he was impressed by these witnesses' passion, against which the efforts of the Prosecution seemed half-hearted. Sheriff Macdonald reserved judgment for a week – seven days of miserable anxiety for the Duncans.

On 11 May, well-wishers, who had been waiting in the rain, filed into the courtroom, heads bowed in prayer. Ian Dickson, whose maiden case this was, pleaded clemency: Mrs Duncan was only thirty-four (in fact, she was thirty-six in November); she had to support a family of eight (if one included herself and Henry); and, referring to Browning's 'Mr Sludge', said she had just this once 'stooped to manipulation'. Until now, Helen had spoken only to plead and say she remembered nothing of the seance, because she had been in a trance. On hearing Dickson's slur, however, she shouted, 'But I never!', at which the court gasped. Weary of his first client, Dickson closed by saying he hoped the judge would consider the great faith people had in her. Unmoved, Sheriff Macdonald replied: 'Whatever psychic powers the accused may possess, I find that this charge against her has been proved.' Helen Duncan was fined £10 payable within one month, or one month's imprisonment, a sentence which she received stoically until the moment she left the courtroom, when she blurted out, 'God forgi'e ye!'

The local newspapers had a field day. Among many dull stories in Dundee's *Daily Record and Mail* — Highland singers, a stray cuckoo, the Glasgow Local Savings Committee's audit — PRAYERS IN COURT FOR MEDIUM FOUND GUILTY OF FRAUD stood out. The coverage satisfied Harry Price and he returned to London feeling vindicated but still needing to face down critics. Writing in the *Two Worlds*, Ernest Oaten painted him as a sinister presence in court, passing notes to the Bench, a description which once more had Price reaching for his pen. Not only should Spiritualists thank his National Laboratory for purging the movement of frauds, he averred, but he had sent only *two* notes and the verdict was entirely fair: 'I think Mrs Duncan is very fortunate to get off with £10 and I suppose the poor, credulous fools who support her will find the money. And as regards the witnesses for the Defence, I have never heard such a display of the most utter credulity – or sheer lying – as I heard in court last week.'

Harder to deny was the charge, made principally by the Duncans, that Price had set the whole thing up. The machinery of entrapment – advertising for sitters suitable as credible witnesses, making Mrs Duncan accept the money (and sign a receipt), securing the undervest as evidence and making a photographic record – bore his trademark. And the key revelation here is that the 'E. M.' who alerted Price to Kanichka the Human Ostrich was none other than Esson Maule, and the contact in London from whom she had sought expert advice was Harry Price. Between appearing before the magistrate and meeting the Procurator Fiscal, Miss Maule visited the NLPR in Roland Gardens, where, in contempt of court, she delivered a lantern lecture, 'My Experiences with Mrs Duncan'. The police citation calling her to give evidence is filed among Price's papers, although a lack of accompanying correspondence makes it impossible to tell how far Price was implicated in the events of 5 January. Doubtless he followed the investigation and probably suggested that Miss Maule take photographs, a set of which he received together with a print of the 'Mr Punch' spirit. On the back, Miss Maule wrote 'This photograph is for you' and, ignoring Mr Scott's copyright, gave Price permission to reproduce it.

The Duncans were downcast. It remained seven-year-old Gena's habit to retreat into a spiritual bubble, where she hoped to be reassured. After one sleepless night she was rewarded with the comforting vision of a lambent female form, which in the morning inspired her to start singing. 'Shut up,' said her sister Lilian, to which Gena replied: 'I know something you don't know' and ran to tell her mother. Yet the stark reality of the trial seems to have immunized even Helen against Gena's viral optimism: 'She was preparing breakfast, looking so tired, her eyes usually so full of life and joy were now so dull and she appeared absolutely listless. Going up to her and putting my hand in hers, I said: "Please don't worry, it's going to be alright, they promised." Squeezing my hand she nodded and told me to sit down and have my porridge.'

There were reasons to be cheerful. Price was right: £10 was not much for someone with her earning potential and she probably received more from private sources and from the SNU, whose favour she had regained. Maurice Barbanell thought the airing of amazing testimony had done Spiritualism a lot of good: people were listening now when before 'there would have been as little seriousness in such a trial, as in one for witchcraft'. For the SNU a martyred fraud was a martyr first and a fraud second, and for Helen the conviction bolstered a righteous legacy of victimization. That vest became her crown of thorns, and Gena was not the only one to draw parallels between Christ's introspection in Gethsemane and Helen mooching tearfully around the kitchen with a cigarette in one hand and a saucepan in the other. Like God at Calvary, ruminated Gena, Albert had forsaken her mother. Her clients, however, had not. Harry Price's book, *Leaves from a Psychist's Case-Book*, published in October, contained a chapter marvelling at the credulity of the 'cheesecloth worshippers', a mania which had launched Mrs Duncan's 'meteoric flight across the firmament' – although he retracted the image of the medium airborne. But the great pretender was resilient to insults and, resolving in the future to have independent witnesses inspect her clothes (and still never to wear white underwear), she got on with the job.

Many notable engagements were recorded for 1933. Helen was applauded at public meetings, including one where clairvoyantly she saw that a sitter had brought his wife's ashes in a tea caddy. A man named Frank Smith was reunited with his Aunt Lizzie and his nephew who had died in the war; his wife, meanwhile, was thrilled to see her sister Maggie because, even though she was still alive, Mrs Smith did have a dead sister Nellie and thought this was near enough. The Smiths counted eleven manifestations, all recognized except for a lost soul who sank pitifully into the floor. In July a twilight seance was held in a back garden in Liverpool, where, despite the interruptions of a motorcycle and a train, spirit forms manifested between the branches of a rhododendron tree and a flame fluttered in the medium's cleavage. Helen was on top form. Three weeks earlier at the Annual General Meeting of the SNU in Doncaster, a vote of confidence in her mediumship had been carried by fifty-seven votes to two and her diploma renewed. The perceived quality of her seances ensured demand for them in quantity. That summer, to meet all of her far-flung engagements, Helen arranged for the children to be looked after, packing Gena off on holiday with a family friend, Jean Beatson, who lived in a country house in Fife. One day Gena was startled by a fairy dressed in green who doffed his hat and then vanished. Jean told her that fairies were God's gardeners who also helped clairvoyant folk blessed with 'the sight'.

During the Depression, the popular press thrived on the public's addiction to three things: for prosperity, job advertisements; for entertainment, football (which had grown as a spectator sport); and, bridging prosperity and entertainment, the horoscope. Furthermore, as Houdini and Harry Price had discovered, the new tabloid newspapers with their half-size format, copious photographs and accessible style were hungry for tales of mystery and magic and, conversely, provided a vehicle for self-promotion.

So, in September 1933, the Duncans were given a full-page column in the *People's Journal*, a light-hearted Scottish weekly. 'My Second Sight Secrets by Madame Victoria Duncan', which ran for fifteen weeks, was probably ghost-written from Henry's scribblings, and achieved an arid tone stranded between piety, sentimentalism and titillation. 'My role is that of counsellor and friend,' Helen explained on 23 September. 'If I can let in a ray of sunshine where all is sad and dreary how happy I am to guide the brightening beam.' That instalment, which told how clairvoyance was used to reunite a husband and wife, showed Helen clutching a letter and pointing. The photographs had her in various poses: staring madly into a crystal, stroking her chin over an open book; desk-bound, sucking a pencil; and grinning hideously with a new hairdo.

Another week, another problem solved, mostly about relationships, money and travel, with headlines such as MENDING BROKEN HEARTS, LOVE KNOTS WHICH I UNRAVELLED and GIRL WHO WANTED RICH HUSBAND. That last piece was tinged with irony. Having earned the gratitude of the police for helping to trap a burglar, Helen held a seance in a police station, materializing two soldiers who spoke to their uncle about visiting their graves in France. 'I swear that I have given you the whole facts,' she said in another piece, 'and that I have told you nothing but the truth.'

Helen's rehabilitation meant she could return to the Edinburgh College of Psychic Science, where in November 1934 a Mrs Wright from St Albans saw her dead sister step from a foam-like wave billowing out of the medium's body. Local bookings were welcomed, for illness limited Helen's ability to travel and often prevented work altogether. A neighbour, hearing she was laid up, brought her a bottle of whisky, at which she tippled until she passed out. Gena related how the spirit physician Dr Johansen sent her to the kitchen to prepare a reviving snack of tomato on toast, Albert apporting the principal ingredient and thus saving Helen's life by a whisker.

This mantle of protection was extended to the Duncan children when their mother was away. As Helen's youngest son Peter lay crying with earache, cuddled up with Nan in her bed, Albert demonstrated his presence by levitating a full ashtray and setting it down on the floor. The pain subsided and the boy slept. Menial chores were seen to by a new housekeeper, Sadie O'Hara, who had said at Helen's

trial that *she* had torn the stockinette undervest while iron-
ing it. After Sadie moved away, the unhappy, disfigured
Bella cared for her half-siblings until she married, whereupon a new maid arrived, who fled a few weeks later,
taking the family's linen with her. One maid allegedly laced
the leek-and-potato soup with arsenic, hospitalizing Peter,
so naturally she had to go. All of which left the sickly Nan
in charge until Sadie returned, her husband having died
of alcoholism, to see the remaining children through to
adulthood.

Henry also needed attention. For ten months, pleurisy
confined him to the flat to which the family had moved,
where rheumatic fever and his heart condition prevented
him from using the stairs. Helen was also struck down by
pleurisy, diagnosed by Albert at a seance in Glasgow. Their
restricted mobility led them to take out a mortgage on a
small cottage in Kirkhill Drive, which Helen christened
'Albertine' in honour of her guides: Albert Stewart and
Peggy Hazzeldine, who after all had paid for the deposit.
Here, Helen recovered sufficiently to work further afield,
with remarkable results, even though it was obvious she
was in poor health.

A Mrs Broadley attended a seance in Bradford, organized by the Yorkshire Psychic Society, where she was left
speechless by manifestations of her parents. Asked by
what power the spirits returned, Albert replied: 'There's
only one thing that brings them back and that's love.'
Afterwards Mrs Broadley thought the medium looked
very tired, poorly even, although infirmity only underlined the self-sacrificial authenticity of her mediumship.

Mrs Duncan was nothing like that scandalous Mr Wilson in Leeds, thought Mrs Broadley, who just sat there grunting and groaning and then waved a rag doll on a stick – and charged sitters 2s 6d for the privilege.

As well as big northern cities, Helen often visited coastal resorts popular with the elderly – Bournemouth, for instance, where in February 1936 Albert permitted a photographer to record her in a trance, her face swathed in diaphanous ectoplasm. The old folk loved Peggy, who played to the crowd: dancing, drawing and leaving teeth marks in apples. She even, as she grew up in spirit, asserted herself to the medium. When Helen complained that a sitter's sketch of the little girl made her look too old, Peggy demurred: 'Mummie Duncan doesn't ken a bit what I look like now. She thinks I am still like that photograph of me when I was three.' Then she stood up straight, slapped her chest, and declared: 'I am not three. I am ten!'

News of these antics spread through the Spiritualist press, and so Helen Duncan's fame grew. Early in 1937 – a year when the Archbishop of Canterbury conceded that Britain was largely non-Christian – *Psychic News* published an article by Rev. E. B. Fry, who had been dazzled by an 'angel' at a Duncan seance in Monmouthshire:

A form of a young woman appeared in the corner, as if a foot or so off the ground. We were directed to allow the moonlight to shine on it by removing the blind for a moment. The effect was radiant until, in a moment, the form disappeared from our physical sight. The resonant voice of Albert then spoke of a baby which had lived only a few moments. He commanded the medium to stand up and carry the baby out of the cabinet. Then was seen, in the red light, the tall form of Mrs Duncan, in black, and in her arms a snow-white bundle containing the baby.

In February 1937, Helen visited Treherbert, a Welsh mining community. The vicar, Rev. C. G. R. Lewis, was concerned that poor people were saving 3d per week in a club so that they could see her again when she returned in April. After reading Price's *Leaves from a Psychist's Case-Book*, Lewis spoke to the Bishop of Monmouth, who encouraged him to write to Price. This he did, saying that if she was such a fraud, 'is there not some way of preventing her from robbing these people of money they cannot afford to waste?' Price replied with a copy of his NLPR report and offered to lecture in Treherbert – but soon realized the situation was more complicated. Lewis confessed that he was half-persuaded by the local doctor seeing his father and a pit manager kissed by his sister, witnesses described as 'two fairly hard-headed men who would not easily be gulled'.

In the winter of 1937–8, Richard Howe, a young soldier stationed with the Black Watch at Perth, not far from Helen's birthplace, bought a ticket to a seance through the president of the local Spiritualist church, Mrs Macbeth. Although it cost him 10s (a third of his week's wages), to be able to meet the dead and sing 'Sweet Mystery of Life' with Peggy was 'an investment in experience'. Earlier, Howe had seen Helen perform clairvoyance in a public hall and had been captivated by her 'deep, mystical, inscrutable' eyes.

When the conjuror Will Goldston once asked Albert whether he would ever consent to Mrs Duncan performing in theatres he was told: 'I cannot stop her but she will be alone.' But when she did succumb to the roar of the grease-paint and started playing such venues he stuck by her. The performances brought praise and applause, and drew bigger audiences than Harry Price's debunking lectures – even those Price illustrated with lantern slides and recordings of Mrs Duncan putting on voices.

Apart from despising fraudulent mediums, Price believed that explanations for 99 per cent of paranormal phenomena lay in human nature and so, some claim, was motivated mainly by a hunger for publicity. His accounts of a small girl, 'Rosalie', materializing at a South London house in 1937 and, most famously, the haunting of Borley Rectory have been dismissed as sheer inventions – his own brand of fraudulence. Others attribute his commitment to his obsession with the remaining 1 per cent of phenomena; like many sceptical psychical researchers he kept the door of possibility ajar. It's true that Price didn't condemn Spiritualism as such, but rather a growing commercialization of the movement that was saturating it with fakery. What he understood best of all was that society was fascinated by this 1 per cent and that this could be exploited. That, after all, was what orthodox Churches had been doing for centuries.

In 1936 the well-known Oxford philosopher A. J. Ayer advanced the idea of 'logical positivism', arguing that since all meaningful questions were answerable the supernatural was nonsense. But the market was stronger for the opposite view. While Ayer was crystallizing his thoughts in Vienna in 1932, Harry Price was investigating the case of a talking mongoose on the Isle of Man which, it was claimed, sang hymns in six languages, had a smattering of Arabic, Russian and Welsh, and disliked Price as 'the man who puts the kybosh on the spirits'. In the same year, Price took his philosopher friend Professor C. E. M. Joad to the Harz mountains in Germany to cast an ancient spell for transmuting a goat into a fair youth. Such stories offended Spiritualists, alienated psychical researchers and disgusted academics but sold newspapers and books by the van-load. Significantly, the goat experiment was performed at the invitation of the Goethe Centenary Committee, which hoped that witchcraft might do for the local tourist industry something of what the Romantic poets had done for the Trossachs.

According to Price, by the mid-1930s witchcraft was being practised in London 'with a freedom undreamt of in the Middle Ages', and by the terms of the law he was right. Scores of mediums were volunteering for experimentation and so became famous for being infamous – as Helen Duncan's entry in Nandor Fodor's 1934 *Encyclopaedia of Psychic Science* demonstrates. In that year Fodor, the Hungarian journalist handed Mrs Duncan's shoes by Albert, was appointed the assistant editor of *Light* and Research Officer of the newly created International Institute for Psychical Research (IIPR). 'For doing the one hundredth part of what is done by men of science every day,' a promotional article suggested, 'our ancestors would have been burned alive.' Fodor met some bizarre mediums.

Mr Woodward psyched himself up by drinking heavily, fell over trying to levitate a vase, then fell asleep and began snoring. Mrs Hammerton, a squat woman from Chiswick, issued warnings about investments in the basso profundo of her male control, apported trinkets coated in scouring powder and gave off a mouldy smell. Some women narrowed their eyes to claim they had transfigured into Chinese people (photographs of Mrs Everett and 'Woo Fang' being the most extraordinary); others pulled fierce faces to pretend to be Zulus – in the case of Mrs Bullock from Manchester, complete with a bullet wound to the head. The Brighton transfiguration medium Nan Scoggins did a sculptor called Chow and an ancient Persian called Hassef, but best of all, and most tellingly, became her own sister who had died as a child.

Men, too, laid claim to such powers, although male mediumship was tainted with spinelessness or effeminacy. Welshman Jack Webber was an ex-miner who had literally seen the light while lost underground, then became a Spiritualist when he married one. A plain man who preferred comics to books, he had two guides, 'Paddy' and 'Reuben', who helped him levitate and churn out ectoplasm at more than two hundred seances a year, some reported favourably by the press and BBC. Decca even made records of Reuben singing hymns. Webber was also photographed paranormally removing his jacket while lashed to a chair, duplicating his own head, and extending an ectoplasmic tentacle from his mouth with which, once, he played with toys hanging on a Christmas tree. Like Christ, to whom he was compared, he died at the age of thirty-three.

In 1936, Dr Fodor offered another Welsh miner, Trefor Davies of Merthyr Tydfil, £5 to sit at the IIPR and another £20 (plus 50 per cent of the rights) to film him producing ectoplasm with an infrared camera. Yet another miner, Hunter Selkirk from County Durham, held Christmas parties for materialized children. Whether Fodor used infrared on Davies is not recorded, but he did on Dundee engine driver Charles Stewart, 'a slightly built, nervous man, apparently suffering from an inferiority complex'. Intensely shy, he left the talking and the business side of things to his wife. In the early 1930s the Stewarts had met Helen Duncan, who had shared her wisdom, showed them inside her cabinet and encouraged them to form a circle, which they did in their tiny flat in Rose Bank Street. 'Brazen frauds', concluded Fodor, whose photographs show a scrawny man wrapped in a sheet, muslin stretched over his face.

Meanwhile, Harry Price was investigating Kuda Bux, a fire-walking Indian with X-ray eyes, assisted by Mollie Goldney. On behalf of the IIPR, Mrs Goldney exposed a medium named Agnes Abbott, by taking an infrared photograph of a 'floating' luminous trumpet stuck on her thumb and spotting 'ectoplasm' poking out of her dress. Mrs Abbott signed a confession, only to cry that the photographs had been faked. Mrs Goldney also led 'The Probe', a group of SPR members who made war on fraud after Hylda Lewis, a medium who apported flowers, became prominent. In April 1935, Harry Price sent Mollie a card on which he had drawn a poppy labelled 'Apport!', adding: 'Of course you have heard all about the Flower

Medium. Oh dear, oh dear!' Miss Lewis agreed to be examined at Oxford where the Professor of Logic (and future SPR President) concluded that she was a mental case who hid thornless roses inside her body, burned herself with an electric iron and bought toy animals in Woolworth's to pass off as apports; a lead sheep was discovered in her handbag awaiting its moment of psychic glory. The Probe investigators scored a notable success in 1936 when another medium's muslin ectoplasm was grabbed and photographed. Pulse racing, she had promised to mend her ways, while her hysterical daughter distanced herself from her mother.

Probe members insisted that the activities of Hylda Lewis and her like led to 'hundreds of pounds being drawn from the pockets of a gullible or bereaved public'. In 1938, however, complaints about Mollie Goldney's 'wrong temperament' forced her out of the IIPR; Fodor himself was ejected soon afterwards for advancing Freudian sex-based psychoanalytic theories. But the public cost of fraudulent mediumship remained significant. In February 1939 the IIPR's Nora Wydenbruck, an Austrian countess and artist, took a friend to a seance in West Kensington – 'an impertinent and ludicrous exhibition of fraud' – where the medium collected 10s 6d from each sitter, as she did in her two other weekly circles, which had been running for a decade. Assuming an average of twelve sitters and a steady work rate, she would have earned almost £10,000 in this period – equivalent to half a million pounds today. Some said this was just the capitalist world of work. 'It is surely better for a medium to heal broken hearts and prevent suicides, as they often do,' reasoned one Spiritualist, 'rather than scrub floors, wash clothes, peddle matches, or even gamble on the stock exchange.'

A decade which began with the collapse of the New York Stock Exchange ended with a war that most spirits said would never happen. In the mid-1930s the novelist Somerset Maugham had visited a fortune teller who predicted that he would narrowly escape death, that he would be followed by two friends carrying a corpse and that Hitler would die or fall that year. He crashed his car into a tree, his friends picked up a sick man (who died) and, a gossip columnist reported, 'Mr Maugham and his friends are now anxiously awaiting grave news from Berlin.' The news never came and the dictators grew bolder. During Mussolini's war in Abyssinia in 1935, nine-year-old Gena Duncan went to the cinema to watch a Tarzan film and was shocked to see the Pope blessing Italian guns on a Pathé newsreel. Soon afterwards omniscient Albert told her she was too small to take on the world's problems: that was her mother's job. But Albert was one of the few spirits to admit that war was inevitable, and further predicted the coming of a great British leader, the failure of a German invasion, the alliance with Soviet Russia and the survival of the Empire – although memories of this last prophecy were to fade.

In the summer of 1938, as Hitler's designs on Czecho-slovakia grew more strident, Helen Duncan gave regular seances in Glasgow, one of which, held in the basement of a tenement block, was attended by John Winning, a doctor and psychical investigator. Winning reported seeing 'Daisy', a girl in silvery-white robes, reunited with her grieving mother, followed by a woman who had recently died in childbirth holding her spirit baby. Albert also showed sitters Mrs Duncan's two-foot long ectoplasmic trumpet, protruding from her mouth and then gradually reabsorbed. Winning's account of these wonders made the front page of the *Two Worlds*, accompanied by a photograph of a manifested spirit, who closely resembled the medium herself.

The return of dead children at Helen's seances was poignant for Helen herself, given that her eighteen-month-old grandson Thomas, her pride and joy, died that year from meningitis. Thomas's mother, Nan, had been told by doctors that she couldn't have children, so the family feared now she would never have another. Nan's younger sister Gena was haunted by the sound of baby Thomas's voice. These days Gena was often found to be in a 'devham' (a dialect word for 'trance'), and her siblings thought her 'not quite the full shilling', lost in a dream exacerbated by her mother's frequent absences. Helen's seances recalled the last war and anticipated the next. In March 1939, Helen was in Cheltenham, where she astounded sitters with manifestations that not only shimmered and glowed but actually appeared to radiate light. A surgeon was visited by his two sons, both killed in the Great War, and there was an appearance by what looked like Sir Arthur Conan Doyle, like him a serious educated man broken by grief.

By this time, Ena Bügg, the young Spiritualist from

Gosport, had waved her sailor fiancé Ronald off to sea and received ominous messages at a home circle. In August 1939, a *Two Worlds* banner headline read NO WAR, the Spiritualist consensus since the Munich Agreement the previous autumn. But Ena was not reassured, especially when the same month her own spirit guide 'Chiefy' told her a terrible tragedy awaited. It could only be Ronald. The Duncans, too, braced themselves. Helen and Henry's son Peter was nearly old enough to fight, and, when their daughter Lilian married that year, Gena predicted that the marriage wouldn't last long (and was clipped round the ear for it). That summer the Duncan family went away to the coast, and as Helen sat on the beach — her favourite place in the world — feeling a sea breeze blow away the cobwebs of the seance room, she sensed this was the last time they would all be together.

After war was declared, mediums spread confidence in victory, but, as during the First World War, their main role was as private counsellors. Losses were fewer than in the previous conflict, but anxiety was greater, especially from air raids. The Britain of 1939 was also more security conscious and intelligence-obsessed than in 1914 and starved of information. Alternative sources were sought. Mass-Observation, studying social habits and opinions, found that a quarter of the population held paranormal beliefs, reflected in a craze for horoscopes and encouraged by uncertainty and enhanced sensitivity to sound, light and movement caused by the blackout. Air-raid forecasting was a popular service offered by mediums, and Spiritualist churches reported that people of all creeds and classes were attending services, which Catholics disrupted by crying 'spooks!' and other insults from the street. By 1944, Spiritualism was said to have a million believers, worshipping through a thousand churches, the same number of affiliated mediums and over 50,000 home circles.

These beliefs were not just confined to the home front. Lady Rhondda, who visited an army camp for a BBC *Brains Trust* broadcast, found the soldiers innocently open-minded about the occult. In 1942, when the army was at its greatest strength with three million men, even though just 521 soldiers were registered as Spiritualists (and free to worship), many more believers had stated orthodox denominations on joining up or were curious without devotion. In 1941 the Royal Navy recognized Spiritualism as a religion and sailors were allowed to hold services at sea, space permitting. Interest extended up the ranks. Of those 521 Spiritualists registered by the army, 97 per cent were officers. The home circle of Charles Glover Botham, a medium working in London, was said to include generals from the War Office staff, and for three years was visited regularly by Air Chief Marshal Sir Trafford Leigh-Mallory, who conversed with his brother lost on Mount Everest in 1924. After 1939, Leigh-Mallory attended occasionally until 1944 when he, too, was killed in an accident.

War changed life for the Duncans as well. 'Albertine', their home in Kirkhill Drive, was requisitioned as an officers' billet, which was inconvenient, but the income helped them put food on the table. Helen was always short of decent cigarettes, so was thrilled to be given a tin by a grateful sitter whose sailor husband brought them home on leave. Another time, though, she refused a pair of stockings as stolen goods. By the summer of 1940 the war had started to take its toll. Bella's husband was reported missing at Dunkirk, then turned up at Folkestone on a fishing boat; and Nan's husband, a Scots Guardsman, endured the worst of the London Blitz. Lilian's husband Angus was an RAF wireless operator and gunner, leaving her and their baby Dawn in Aberdeen. Harry Duncan, too, joined the RAF in the spring of 1941, soon after he had attended a seance in Kirkcaldy where, lore has it, Albert predicted the war would last half as long again as the last one and would end with two big bangs. By then, the family was in mourning. In February, Lilian, pregnant from Angus's last leave, had heard that he had been shot down and killed over Norway. Helen offered spiritual comfort and drew Lilian's morning sickness into her own body, but her bereaved daughter spent her days in a daze, drifting between picture houses, movies washing over her like waves. When the baby, a girl, was born she took little interest, and was confined to a sanitorium suffering from tuberculosis. Her mother, meanwhile, kept her engagements south of the border while Henry and the girls looked after little Dawn and her new sister, whom they named Joan.

Women like Lilian meant that physical mediums were in demand as never before. None travelled further, or was more eagerly discussed, than Helen Duncan. Jean Baker remembered how in April 1941 Mrs Duncan came to tea at their Gloucester home after a seance at the church where her aunt's baby had materialized, right down to her jacket with ribbons at the cuffs. At a gathering in Paignton in Devon the spirit of Sir Oliver Lodge, who had died in August 1940, reassured a Mrs Barton that their respective sons, in his case Raymond, were friends in the afterlife. In Somerset a widow was reunited with her husband, an RAF pilot recently killed in action. Arthur Oram, living with his parents in Wiltshire while working for the Ministry of Aircraft Production, attended a seance where Albert mocked the audience as a 'pretty hopeless crowd' yet ushered in a gliding procession of spirits, which stopped before each sitter before sinking into the floor. In Suffolk a couple were amazed by a spectral pet rabbit which returned to its tearful owner, who said: 'To think I boiled you in a pot!' At the same seance a manifested German woman spoke to her daughter in their native tongue.

Such stories travelled far and wide. In October 1942 the SPR received a letter from a psychical researcher in Liverpool claiming that Helen Duncan's phenomena were 'at least as remarkable as those which Sir William Crookes is said to have witnessed in the personage of Katie King', to which the SPR replied that their evidence remained 'unfavourable to the genuineness of the mediumship'. But opinion was as divided as ever. In the same year B. Abdy Collins, an SPR Council member, published a laudatory evaluation of Mrs Duncan's powers in *Psychic Science*, of which he was editor, and J. B. McIndoe did the same. By the end of the year, after a stint in Manchester, Helen was back in Scotland. Squadron Leader Ramsden, stationed on Orkney, was astonished by what he saw at the Edinburgh Psychic College in March 1943. He had previously spoken to the medium at one of her Manchester seances, where she insisted she had never seen a spirit form, because she was always in a trance when they manifested, adding: 'I am sure if I did I would die of fright.' Ramsden took to the Edinburgh seance a sceptical fellow officer, who changed his mind when a downed New Zealand pilot explained that he had drowned because he had been unable to open the canopy hatch on his P-51 Mustang.* Ramsden returned to the Psychic College in December, where he met a couple who had brought their eight-year-old son to see his dead older sister. The luminous girl was 'full of life and bubbling over with excitement', reported Ramsden. The siblings stood face to face chatting before the spirit called out to her parents: 'Mum! Dad! Oh, how nice to see you all!'

Helen spent most time where she was needed most. Portsmouth was a secretive, sealed-off naval port, where many families had a husband or son on a ship and the Luftwaffe visited frequently. One-in-five houses had been damaged or destroyed, parts of the city lay in ruins and the effect of the bombing on its population was, according to an observer, 'one of tremendous psychological shock'. The suburb of Copnor had suffered its share of this trauma. Ernest Homer, a pharmacist from Staffordshire, and Elizabeth, a voluble Welsh ex-entertainer who called herself his wife, ran a chemist's shop there at 301 Copnor Road, where they kept an upstairs room for holding se-ances. Known as 'The Master's Temple Church of Spiritual

---

* RAF pilot William Watson of Auckland, New Zealand, died on 18 February 1943.

Healing' (also 'Master's Temple Psychic Centre'), the room was drab and sparsely furnished. A print of Leonardo's *Last Supper* hung on the chimney breast, beside which was a dais with an altar and a wooden crucifix. In the opposite corner, near the bay window looking out on the road, chocolate-brown curtains hung from a curtain pole supported by the picture rails, and within this cabinet stood a solid Jacobean chair with a leather seat and armrests. Many of the mediums were as seedy as the premises, including Llewellyn Rosser and Reginald Scott-Horscroft, both known sex offenders. In November 1943, Dorothy Evans was told by Rosser that her husband, killed on HMS *Illustrious* in 1941, was still alive and would soon be home – news that reached her children, who became irrepressibly excited.

Helen had already visited Portsmouth several times – but by the end of 1943 had become a regular at the Master's Temple, and boarded with a Mrs Bettison in Milton Road. Her reputation had spread locally, a mixture of truth and myth common in wartime and in the Spiritualist tradition. Forever drumming up trade, Mrs Homer fondly told the story of when Helen, holed up in an air-raid shelter, had healed a soldier's baby afflicted with a disease of the legs by laying on hands and saying a prayer. Mrs Homer also put advertisements in the *Evening News* for 'The Great Helen Duncan, the Materialization Medium', with sittings at 3 p.m. and 6 p.m. No admission fee was charged, just a silver collection at the end. But as demand grew, and at each departure sitters clamoured for her return, this was to change. Late in 1943, Helen arranged a fortnight in January at the Master's Temple for which she was promised the sum of £8 per seance (sixteen times the weekly old age pension at that time), and with that booking under her belt left to spend Christmas with her family in Edinburgh.

The seventeen-year-old Gena, in her special way, sensed that this holiday would prove the lull before the storm. On New Year's Day 1944 she dreamed that two sinister men were chasing her mother into a river, where she fell, panicking and thrashing about in the muddy water. The night before Helen left for Portsmouth, Gena lay awake replaying what felt like a prophecy, imagining Christ's final hours and fearing the worst. In the morning, suitcases standing by the front door, Gena pleaded with her mother not to go — but in vain. Watching from the window, she sobbed as the taxi disappeared at the end of their road, fatefully bound for Waverley Station.

6. A Kind of Conjuration: Trial and Denial at the Old Bailey, 1944

On the afternoon of Tuesday 25 November 1941, as Helen Duncan celebrated her forty-fourth birthday, several hundred miles away in the eastern Mediterranean the battleship HMS *Barham* was cruising with HMS *Queen Elizabeth* and HMS *Valiant*, flanked by destroyers. At 4.26 p.m., a barely submerged German submarine, U-331, commanded by Kapitänleutnant Hans-Diedrich von Tiesenhausen, passed through the portside flank and fired four torpedoes. The crew of the *Barham* heard three dull thuds, then the ship began listing as the port battery flooded. Tiesenhausen's engineers put U-331 into a steep dive, narrowly escaping the *Valiant* steaming straight at them, guns blazing. As the angle of the *Barham*'s list increased, sailors were still leaping from the upper deck when a colossal explosion from the 15-inch magazine blasted those remaining into the water. Men sucked down as the ship sank were thrust up through the oil and flotsam on a huge air bubble. HMS *Hotspur* and HMAS *Nizam* picked up over four hundred survivors, who were given blankets and tea laced with rum. They were lucky: 862 of their comrades had been incinerated, blown apart or borne down to the seabed.

The catastrophe contributed to what Churchill called 'a sudden darkening of the landscape' after the fall of Greece and the air raid of 10 May which had wrecked the House of Commons and killed 1,500 Londoners. A fortnight later HMS *Hood* had been sunk and on 12 November, less than a fortnight before the *Barham*, the carrier HMS *Ark Royal* was lost off Gibraltar. Only two British battleships remained active in the region, and by the end of the year even they would be damaged. At first, Kapitänleutnant Tiesenhausen was unaware of what he'd done, guessing he'd hit only a cruiser. Nor did his crew give it much thought as they waited at a perilous depth for the danger to pass, oblivious to the 31,000 tons of the *Barham* falling silently past them. U-331 was hunted until 7 a.m., when Tiesenhausen filed his report and was summoned to Berlin. British Intelligence, who intercepted this on 16 December, already knew from decrypted Enigma messages that the Germans didn't realize they had sunk the *Barham*, confirmed by Italian ignorance of the same. The precious time this bought for reorganizing the Mediterranean battle fleet made it impossible to announce the sinking in Britain; it was not even mentioned in the secret Weekly Intelligence Reports. The news did not break until late January 1942, at which point Tiesenhausen and his crew were celebrated and decorated in Germany. Haunting film recording the death of the *Barham*, taken from the *Valiant*, became a newsreel seen by people all over Britain who, three months after the event, reflected blackly upon the loss.

Spiritualist circles, however, had known about the disaster much earlier. HMS *Barham* was a Portsmouth ship, and it was almost inevitable that a friend or relative of a crewman would attend one of Helen Duncan's seances. The story has several versions with similar features. At a seance soon after the sinking, the spirit of a dead sailor materialized for a female relative – his wife or mother – his cap band emblazoned with the name HMS *Barham*. The next day the woman telephoned the Admiralty to ask for confirmation and was visited by two naval officers demanding to know the source of her news. She told them. Meanwhile, word reached the editor of *Psychic News*, Maurice Barbanell, who arranged to have lunch with his friend Percy Wilson, an official at the Ministry of War Transport, to see if he knew anything. Wilson, who was also a member of Charles Glover Botham's home circle and a future President of the SNU, did not. On returning to work that afternoon, however, he heard that the *Barham* had been sunk but that an announcement was deemed not in the public interest for reasons of military security and the preservation of morale. A delay until after Christmas would allow time to deal with the *Barham*'s loss. For Spiritualists, this episode explains why Helen Duncan was pursued by the authorities; it has even been suggested that they feared she would reveal that Britain had cracked the Enigma code. Any version that placed humble Nell Duncan at the hub of wartime intrigue would be unlikely to be entirely true; but, then again, nor would it necessarily be entirely false.

Declassified records have lifted the lid on wartime intelligence procedures. The investigators from the Admiralty were MI5 officers, either from 'D' Division, responsible for naval security, or more likely from 'B' Division, responsible for counter-espionage. This was not the first time Helen Duncan's name had entered MI5 files. On 24 May

1941, Brigadier Roy Firebrace, the head of Military Intelligence in Scotland, attended one of Helen's seances in Edinburgh, possibly in the home circle of a Mrs Waymark, where Albert announced that a great battleship had just been sunk. Firebrace, a Spiritualist who had seen Helen perform at the LSA in 1931, was a regular member of the Waymark circle, where he received messages from spirits including Sir Arthur Conan Doyle, Lawrence of Arabia and a soldier called Mick he had known at Vimy Ridge in 1917.* Returning to his office, Firebrace telephoned the Admiralty, who said they had heard nothing – but later that evening he received a call informing him that the flagship battlecruiser HMS *Hood* had been split in two by the mighty *Bismarck* after a shell entered her magazine and caused a catastrophic explosion. All but three of the *Hood*'s 1,421 crew perished in the icy waters off Greenland. The news was broadcast by the BBC at 9 p.m. that same Saturday and so shocked the nation that it was perceived to have lowered morale rather than stiffening it. This reaction influenced the more circumspect handling of the sinking of HMS *Barham* six months later.

As a seance-goer, Firebrace admired Mrs Duncan; as an intelligence officer, however, he feared her. A year earlier the *Daily Sketch* had alleged that German agents were attending British seances to glean secrets from the dead,

---

* Later in the war, as well as serving as a military attaché in Riga and Moscow, Firebrace sat on the Executive Council of the International Institute of Psychical Investigation, forever dividing his time between these two sides of his life.

and perhaps something of the rumour stuck. However fantastical it seems that mediums were taken seriously, in wartime secrecy was humdrum and habitual. The security problem was huge, especially 'leakage' of information at ports, matched by a paranoia that extended beyond fear of spies to the belief that a Fifth Column lurked at the heart of the establishment. Churchill, who usually cast an eye over relevant files, had the *Daily Mirror* investigated for criticizing the government's conduct of the war; suspicions were raised that yellow pullovers signalled subversion; and prior to D-Day the *Daily Telegraph* crossword setter was arrested after codenamed beaches appeared as solutions. From 1940, security had been tightened through various committees, notably the Home Defence Executive, which coordinated the efforts of the Home Office, the Admiralty, MI5, MI6 and the police, and pooled information between the Secret Service and the Special Branch of the Metropolitan Police. Mail, telephones and Irish radio broadcasts were monitored, and loose talk by anyone from Jehovah's Witnesses to Finnish officers on American ships – even members of Churchill's Cabinet – was looked into and reports filed.

In fact, the addiction to secrecy – what the Labour MP Richard Crossman later called 'the British disease' – dated back more than a decade to when labour unrest and the fear of socialism had cemented a relationship between the Home Office, the judiciary and the police that in practice worked to suspend civil liberties whenever national security was at risk. Even before the First World War, as Home Secretary Churchill had given the Secret Service powers of arrest without consulting Parliament, and by 1931 MI5 had infiltrated Special Branch to exploit its expertise and use it as a cover. In 1940 the Home Office instructed all chief constables to report security news, however mundane, twice a month to their MI5 Regional Security Liaison Officer and 'matters of special security interest' at once. Soon this became routine administration; likewise communications between the police, the Director of Public Prosecutions and SLB, a legal branch of MI5 that silenced indiscretions in the courts. In 1943, SLB split into two, one section concentrating on prosecutions, the other on leaks; SLB2 had its origins in B19, formed in 1940 to investigate rumours, especially about shipping. By the time Helen Duncan hove in sight, chief constables were accustomed to referring even trivial offences against the defence regulations to the DPP, who then liaised with SLB2.

Aside from security concerns, mediums were seen as a public nuisance, prosecuted for fraud whenever complaints were received. Dorothy Evans, whose children had heard that their dead father was coming home from sea, reported Llewellyn Rosser and so became one of the first people to alert the Portsmouth City Police (which had the very Spiritualist-sounding motto 'Heaven's Light Our Guide') to the activities of the Master's Temple. Helen Duncan, meanwhile, had dissatisfied clients of her own. After a seance at the Devon resort of Torquay in March 1940, a group of friends decided they were the victims of a hoax, and one of them, a Mrs Martin, wrote to the SPR requesting they take some action. The reply was disappointing. The SPR, Mrs Martin was told, existed not to identify frauds but to investigate genuine phenomena, and besides, 'public exposure of any medium, however conclusive to sensible and impartial persons, usually produces a vigorous defence from the medium's less critical supporters'. The following summer Helen was back in Paignton, just down the coast from Torquay. Marion Gray paid 15s to watch 'the doings' (five shillings more than at Torquay), but before things got underway she was asked to help examine the medium, who was waiting in a bedroom. Mrs Gray was in for an unpleasant surprise: 'A coarse and immensely fat woman, partly naked, was sitting on a chair smoking the fag end of a cigarette. The very sight of her revolted me and I'm afraid she noticed my expression. Anyhow she fixed me with a persistent stare, muttering all the time "Oh what shall I do if Albert doesn't come tonight?"'

Albert did come, but he was not the radiant ambassador for the afterlife Marion Gray had hoped for; in fact, all the spirits looked like the medium, the seance was boring and she felt like calling the police. Instead, she wrote to Harry Price, asking: 'Don't you think something should be done to stop these harpies from battening on the misery and agony of others?' Price did, and, agreeing that Mrs Duncan was 'a most repulsive and unpleasant woman as well as a fraud', sent a copy of his NLPR report to Paignton. Mrs Gray also wrote to Maurice Barbanell, who advised her to ignore Price and his 'ludicrous' regurgitation theory. Yet Barbanell did concede that 'Mrs Duncan has been over-sitting and for that reason the phenomena are sometimes weak'.

But the tolerance of the police and courts was running

out. In May 1942 a medium named Stella Hughes, wife of a Hampstead borough councillor, was fined £10 under the Vagrancy Act, a prosecution condemned by Spiritualists given that 'the daily papers are allowed to feature astrological predictions, and fortune tellers openly advertise their trade in the London streets'. A year later the two policewomen who had arrested Mrs Hughes trapped another medium, Gladys Spearman, but were themselves jailed for robbery before her case came to trial. The outrage increased the same month when Brighton magistrates fined a former soldier, Benjamin Misell, who had performed psychometry for another pair of undercover officers. Barely a week later, in June 1943, a request for Stella Hughes to be pardoned was dismissed by the Home Office, which spurred J. B. McIndoe to start a Freedom Fund so that competent (and sympathetic) barristers could be appointed in every instance regardless of merit.

McIndoe felt as he had during Helen Duncan's Edinburgh trial; the cause was more important than the case. And the cases kept coming. One reason that newspaper horoscopes were tolerated, while mediums were not, was the Ministry of Information's view that astrology buoyed up people's spirits, as during the Great Depression, whereas mediums had the opposite effect. Plain-clothes officers from Scotland Yard (the London Metropolitan Police's HQ) warned Maurice Barbanell about this as early as 1940, and by mid-1943 no medium was safe. In August a clairvoyant at Birkenhead was tried for telling one woman that her son, a prisoner of war, would soon be home and another that her missing husband was alive. The charge was fraud;

but for this and at least three other prosecutions in 1943 –
at Cardiff, Birmingham and Great Yarmouth – to the
phrase 'pretending or professing to tell fortunes', which
came from Section 4 of the 1824 Vagrancy Act, was added
a form of words closer to the 1735 Witchcraft Act: 'pretending to communicate with the spirits of dead persons'.

Through the winter of 1943–4, similar cases were heard
in magistrates' courts around the country, where fines
of up to £20 were imposed. This increased volume of
prosecutions was partly due to small groups of private
citizens – like Mollie Goldney's SPR team, The Probe –
who were fed up with bogus mediums, particularly for
exploiting bereavement and damaging morale. Prominent
was the elite conjurors' club the Magic Circle, which had
maintained an Occult Committee as far back as the early
1920s. By late 1943 the work of the committee (chaired by
its founder, Dr Eric Dingwall, who had seen both Rudi
Schneider and Helen Duncan in action) was taken on by
the Magic Circle's Honorary Secretary, Douglas Craggs,
and other magicians, who were organizing members
nationwide into small units to investigate mediums with
the cognizance of the police. Craggs liaised with Scotland
Yard, corresponded with Harry Price and initiated prosecutions. Meanwhile, national security was tightened in the
run-up to the invasion of Europe, and with greater intensity than ever before.

Official interest in Helen Duncan, therefore, lay in campaigns to protect the public from fraud and to protect
military security. Helen was on a collision course with both

because of her unstinting passion for work and growing demand for her services. Thousands of men had been killed or captured, hundreds of planes shot down, dozens of ships sunk, and for every man lost there was a family who either couldn't bear their loss or refused to give up hope. On the anniversary of the sinking of HMS *Barham* in November 1942, the Portsmouth *Evening News* printed 'in memoriam' notices, mainly for sailors still listed as missing because no bodies had been recovered. 'That vague destination seems so nameless and void,' read one. Crowding into this void came Mrs Duncan's ectoplasmic apparitions, to be seen and heard and touched by relatives unable to come to terms with a complete absence. Broken hearts were shattered or mended by materialization seances – but either way the authorities would not abide them.

By December 1943, Helen was being investigated by Detective Inspector Frederick Ford of the Portsmouth police, a ruddy-faced, down-to-earth detective of sixteen years' service, who had received complaints and welcomed help from the Magic Circle. Ignoring a warning from a medium named Charles Burrell, a docker who threatened to expose their 'money racket', Mr and Mrs Homer had continued to behave brazenly, including placing further adverts in the *Evening News* – publicity that assisted the police with their surveillance. It was also well known that the Homers were not just passing round a hat at the end of seances, as claimed, but charging an admission fee of 12s 6d. The file of police reports thickened. One account of a Master's Temple seance described the appearance of 'a white shrouded figure which purports to bring messages from the spirit world in the voices of dead people. Some of the things divulged are shocking.'

One man who found these things shocking was Stanley Worth, a twenty-eight-year-old bespectacled RNVR lieutenant based at a Portsmouth shore establishment. Home on leave at Ashford in Middlesex, he had been intrigued by his mother's experiences at a local Spiritualist group, where she said spirit guides spoke through trumpets, played the piano and performed healing through mediums. On his next leave, however, he became worried by how involved she was, and hearing back in Portsmouth that people went to 'the spooks' above the chemist's shop in Copnor Road, Worth decided to investigate for himself.

That winter he attended several services at the Master's Temple, where a group of mostly middle-aged women sang hymns accompanied by a small organ and clairvoyance was performed. Mr Homer would sit there in a trance, smiling vacantly, and then, controlled by an Egyptian called 'Abdul', would rise to his feet and mumble inanities. Worth might have stopped going had Mrs Homer not told him that in the New Year an amazing materialization medium called Mrs Duncan would be visiting. Worth returned to base, where his interest in Spiritualism was no secret – after all, the Royal Navy now recognized it as a religion. But the commanding officer was concerned that Worth might become hooked, as if drawn into a cult, and spoke with the medical officer, Surgeon Lieutenant Elijah Fowler, who was friends with Worth, requesting that he accompany him to the next seance. Worth consulted

Mrs Homer, explaining that Fowler was not a believer. 'Bring him along to see Helen Duncan', she said. 'I'll give him a seat in the front row and scare him stiff.'

So, at 2.45 p.m. on 14 January 1944, Worth and Fowler arrived at 301 Copnor Road and were met by a northern medium named Taylor Ineson, who led them through the shop, past the glass-fronted cabinets and advertisements for Vaseline and Virol, and into the back room, where others were waiting. At last, with Worth leading the way, the twenty or so sitters, including a soldier and an RAF wing commander, were ushered towards the stairs, where Mrs Homer ticked them off on her list.

In the seance room the first thing Worth saw was the glow of three lamps – red, green and white – daylight kept out by blackout curtains. Each of the seats bore a name slip, an arrangement Mrs Homer was eager to oversee; likewise a ban on blackout torches, which had to be left with Mrs Homer. After the preliminaries of examining the cabinet and the seance clothes, a hush fell as Helen Duncan entered and took up position in the corner. Eyes shut, she slumped backwards – arms loose, head lolling – and began groaning as the curtains closed. Mrs Homer led everyone in the Lord's Prayer, then called upon 'all friends to give their love and sympathy to Mrs Duncan and her guide' before starting up a rendition of Albert's favourite 'South of the Border'. After this had petered out, the white and green light bulbs were unscrewed, leaving just the red one, which was behind the sitters and so made it hard to see anything clearly even after their eyes had adjusted to the gloom.

They were greeted by a voice, apparently that of a man, but higher in pitch, which expressed pleasure to see so many familiar faces, after which Albert appeared, looking like a length of cloth with a face-hole cut into it. Lieutenant Worth was treated to the substantial form of his 'aunt' (dead from bowel trouble, Albert said), even though all his aunts were still alive. Another bulky spirit came through for Taylor Ineson, claiming to be his brother, which shook his hand and in Ineson's own Yorkshire accent said he didn't think much of the medium: *too fat*. A woman whose son was missing received a soldier; a man killed in an explosion in Singapore proffered a stump. To lighten things up Peggy sang a chorus of 'Loch Lomond' before melting into the air with the words, 'I'm gaun doon noo.' Then came Bronco the parrot squawking 'Pretty Polly', followed by a cat and a rabbit, both nondescript white oblongs, the former mewing. For the finale, the medium lurched out flailing her arms and crashed down next to Mrs Homer. At Mr Homer's request, Worth gave her a cigarette and the lights were switched on.

Next morning, Worth visited Portsmouth police station, where he was interviewed by Detective Inspector Ford, who asked him if he would be willing to attend another session the following afternoon. Worth agreed. This turned out to be an ordinary Sunday service where, in broad daylight, a hymn was sung and prayers intoned. Then Helen Duncan, all in white with closed eyes, stood to deliver a sermon in the voice of Albert, exhorting the congregation to aspire to spiritual things. To sustain interest, Helen indicated that the spirit of a girl called Audrey had taken her hand, and pointed to Captain Barnes, a retired army officer known to have lost a daughter – a daughter called Shirley. 'I'm sorry; I made a mistake,' Helen admitted when corrected. 'I should have said Shirley; I got the name wrong.' She sat down, rolling her eyes, and let her new travelling companion, Frances Brown, the wife of a Sunderland collier, do a turn; Mrs Brown, too, saw invisible spirits and waved her arms.

The next day, Monday the 17th, Worth went back to the police station, where he was issued with a torch and whistle, and returned that evening to Copnor Road to book two seats for the next seance, on Wednesday. His companion was to be his friend Rupert Cross, a bookseller and War Reserve Constable he had met through Elijah Fowler. They arrived shortly before 7 p.m. and gave Mr Homer 25s in the kitchen before going upstairs and taking their allotted places in the second row behind seats reserved for the Homers. Then things got started. One of the thirty sitters, Able Seaman Peter Pickett from Sevenoaks, Kent, who had lost his mother as a baby, received a familiar-looking burly woman, shrouded and with outstretched arms. Another spirit form quickly took her place, then another, and it was from this third manifestation that Cross took his cue. Worth reached for the illicit torch in his pocket as his partner raised himself from his chair.

Barging through the front row, Cross tore open the cabinet to reveal Mrs Duncan gathering up several yards of white fabric, which he grabbed. Mr Homer came over and kicked Cross, someone knocked away Worth's torch and the cloth was yanked away. 'It's gone into the audience,' said Cross agitatedly, to which an eerily calm Mrs Duncan replied: 'Of course it's gone; it had to go somewhere.' Worth fixed her in the beam of his torch. Still sitting in the cabinet in her black seance dress, she was bending down, struggling into her shoes. Then in an instant she lost her composure, screaming she was sick – indeed, dying – and needed a doctor. Worth blew his whistle, summoning Ford and three other detectives waiting downstairs.

As they entered the room, Frances Brown told Mr Homer to make sure his daughter Christine, a geriatric nurse, kept her mouth shut. Ford turned on the light and, while a cursory search was underway, asked if anyone had the cloth, but ignored pleas from Christine Homer and others to be frisked; nor did he challenge a woman wearing a sling on her arm. Instead, armed with a magistrate's warrant, he ordered the crestfallen Mrs Duncan to get changed (under the supervision of the policewoman), bundled up her seance clothes as evidence and arrested her on suspicion of contravening the Vagrancy Act by 'pretending to hold communication with the spirits of deceased persons'. All Helen said was: 'I have nothing to worry about' – but she looked very worried indeed. After she had been led away, Ford heard Mrs Homer remind everyone that Jesus had suffered like this and so made a mental note to add blasphemy to fraud.

Accompanied by Nurse Jane Rust (the Defence witness who would soon impress Mollie Goldney so much), Helen was taken by car to Kingston Crescent police station, five minutes away, where she was cautioned. 'What can I say?' she replied limply. She warned them she was a diabetic with coronary problems, whereupon a police surgeon was called who certified that though suffering from 'palpitation due to a fatty heart' she was well enough to be put in the cells. In the morning she was photographed and fingerprinted, given breakfast, tea and a cigarette and then taken before the magistrates, who, at the request of Chief Constable Arthur West, remanded her in custody for five days. Once Ford had collected her insulin kit from Milton Road, Helen, weeping in despair, was driven to Holloway Prison in North London, oblivious to the excited flurry of activity in Portsmouth and beyond.

While Chief Constable West set colleagues in Edinburgh to work on Helen Duncan's case, newspapers, national and provincial, seized on the story. CONSTABLE GRABS 'SPIRIT' AT CITY SEANCE blared Portsmouth's *Evening News*, and the arrest was even announced by the BBC. The Spiritualist press was quick to mount its soapbox, one hyperbolic headline from the *Two Worlds* reading:

FREEDOM VERSUS THE HOME OFFICE

DEAD HAND GRIPS GOVERNMENT

THE GOVERNMENT IS STILL AFRAID OF GHOSTS!

West started receiving angry letters. Squadron Leader Ramsden, veteran of the Edinburgh seances, attested to Mrs Duncan's remarkable powers, insisting that the reality of ectoplasm was 'an established medical fact . . . vouched for by eminent scientific men'. Should the Chief Constable doubt this, Ramsden continued indignantly, he might consider how mediums suffered for their calling.

Perhaps then he would be reduced to a humble silence, 'conscious of the perfect, irrefutable logic which permeates every nook and cranny of our universe'. The next day Ramsden wrote to Maurice Barbanell at the *Psychic News* gallantly reiterating his earlier offer to pay Mrs Duncan's fines should she be convicted.

Upon hearing of Mrs Duncan's plight, Percy Wilson at the Ministry of War Transport, now President of the London SNU's District Council, authorized use of the SNU's Freedom Fund to appoint a barrister, even though representation by a solicitor alone would have been normal at a preliminary hearing. Wilson and his colleagues agreed that there was only one man for the job, Charles Loseby, a seasoned Spiritualist who had defended beleaguered mediums before and had been the chief spokesman for an SNU deputation to the Home Office six months earlier. Loseby accepted the case and after he had been briefed by the SNU's solicitor, Godfrey Elkin, saw the facts plainly. Spiritualism was on trial, and furthermore Helen Duncan was innocent, and he would be the man to prove it.

Charles Loseby would be much criticized by Spiritualists, not for a lack of commitment or effort but because he was young and inexperienced. In fact, he was neither; and it was precisely because counsel at Edinburgh in 1933 had been green and not a Spiritualist that Loseby was chosen. He was sixty-two years old. Called to the Bar in 1913, he had pulled strings to get a commission in the Lancashire Fusiliers, and in thirty months' service in France was gassed, shot through the arm and traumatized. He was haunted by his working-class men, 'like sheep to the slaughter', their expressions indescribable; and he thought of the two square inches a sniper needed to take off a head, the corpses mortared with slime into trench walls and the hum of the rotary fans as German sappers tunnelled beneath them. The war became part of him, as it was part of English culture and belief, and it was more natural than it seems now for the first leg of his honeymoon in 1921 to be spent touring the battlefields of Flanders.

Proud of his service, especially his Military Cross, Loseby retained his commission until 1920, by which time he was a Conservative MP. He campaigned on many social issues, including female emancipation, establishing a Ministry of Health and, most energetically, pensions for disabled and 'nerve-shaken' servicemen, for whom he secured an extra £20 million. In 1921 he joined Lloyd George to fight socialism, but crossed the House of Commons again in 1929 and was returned as the Tory candidate for West Nottingham; in between he worked as a barrister on the Midland Circuit, and in 1922 sent a labourer to the gallows for murdering his sweetheart. Emotionally reserved, he was passionate about the beliefs inspired in him by war, and he liked to play devil's advocate and relished challenges, whether in Parliament or in court. As for so many others, his Spiritualism sprang from agnosticism and a yearning for metaphysical truth to make sense of the past and shape the future. So, by the time that Ernest Oaten pointed him towards 'the irresistible conclusions to be drawn from the accurate observation of phenomena', his conversion was already virtually complete.

At the Home Office, where a file on Helen Duncan had been opened, officials expressed surprise that the SNU should be defending 'such a patent charlatan ... a bare-faced and not particularly skilful fraud'. But Loseby was indifferent to those who rejected incontrovertible truths and took up Mrs Duncan's defence with alacrity. He dug out his dog-eared copy of Ellis Powell's pamphlet *Psychic Science and Barbaric Legislation* (1917), in which, against a passage about gifted mediums at the mercy of ignorant policemen and prejudiced magistrates, he penned a note: 'True a quarter of a century later. Do not rest until an end is put to it.' The Duncan brief could be his finest hour. This ordinary housewife epitomized the persecuted minority, and for that reason the patrician Loseby subordinated himself to her. In an army play on the Western Front he had acted the part of 'Second Slave' to Captain North's 'Plumi Jham', an Egyptian sorceress. There was real irony in this, for farce was about to be repeated as tragedy.

When on 25 January proceedings commenced at Portsmouth Magistrates' Court, the police were surprised to see this gaunt, somewhat elderly barrister, and were surprised still more by his claims. Helen Duncan was a distinguished medium whose life had been endangered, Loseby told the court, and by arresting her, fingerprinting her and denying her bail, the police had turned her into 'a furtive and dangerous criminal', at odds with the Home Secretary's declared wish that the pre-trial procedure of the 1824 Vagrancy Act be dropped. This raised cries of 'hear, hear', silenced by the magistrates. After five days in Holloway, Helen's head was swimming, and she felt as if they were speaking about someone else. Detective Inspector Ford expressed Chief Constable West's request for another two weeks' grace while the Director of Public Prosecutions considered the case, but said the Portsmouth police no longer objected to bail. West, moreover, wanted the Prosecution to be represented by counsel if that was how the SNU wished to proceed. Helen Duncan was released on sureties of £100 (put up by J. B. McIndoe) and another hearing timetabled for 8 February. One can assume that, as chief constable, West had already consulted his local MI5 officer regarding the pronouncements about HMS *Barham*, if not now then fourteen months earlier.

Loseby and the SNU solicitor Godfrey Elkin assured Helen that she wasn't going back to prison. But she feared the worst. Her time on remand in Holloway, she said, had been horrendous. Upon arrival after the seance raid she had waited in a cubicle for an hour until a doctor listened to her heart and a nurse combed her for nits. No one said a word. Standing on a stone floor, she was strip-searched, dressed in overalls (without shoes) and made to bathe. Then she was given a card that read 'Religion: Spirit'; two policewomen laughed at her. Denied insulin, she was put in a cell until morning, when a nurse arrived. Sister Nicholson called her a vile, lazy, filthy woman, and said that wicked mediums like her caused no end of broken homes and suicides. Churches alone, Nicholson chided, were proper places of spiritual comfort. When Helen asked if she could contact her husband, Nicholson said he would do well to divorce her. Mrs Duncan's children, she added, should be ashamed of their mother.

From this time on, Sister Nicholson had made it her business to upset Helen. Prisoners were told to stay away from her because she was infested and, taken sick while tramping round the exercise yard, Helen was made to sit on a water pipe and shouted at. Back in her cell she was forbidden to lie down. Two days later the nurse poured a bucket of hot water over her in the bath, leaving her scalded, wheezing and terrified. It was a relief, then, to be given back her clothes and driven to Portsmouth. The van driver and female warders were, she was surprised to find, 'very kind and most concerned over my condition'.

Meanwhile, much fuss had been made about Loseby's remark in court about the use of the Vagrancy Act. The Home Office was unsure of what he meant, but advised that if he repeated his assertion that the Secretary of State, Herbert Morrison, disapproved of police actions against mediums it should be refuted. Morrison, who the previous year had satisfied himself that the police were acting fairly, declined to contradict Loseby in the House of Commons, which would have been inappropriate given that the case against Mrs Duncan was *sub judice*. Furthermore, the Home Office was not a US-style justice department, but instead relied on a small dusty office known as 'C' Division (Criminal Matters), headed by an assistant under-secretary, Francis Graham-Harrison. His job, in this instance, was to maintain contact with Detective Inspector Ford and the Director of Public Prosecutions, who had agreed to represent the Portsmouth police in court.

On 2 February, Ford submitted a report to the DPP, Sir Edward Tindal Atkinson, summarizing the Duncan case so far, and adding: 'This may or may not be true, but I have reason to believe that she is a person who is addicted to drink.' Every type of personal information was gathered, to which police in Edinburgh were happy to contribute. Records showed that Henry owned the cottage at Kirkhill Drive, but paid no income tax, which was unsurprising given that his wife's occupation was illegal. The police also paid Henry a visit and learned that he settled the household bills, because his wife had no bank account. The Edinburgh Criminal Investigation Department informed Ford that Mrs Duncan, well known as a medium in the city, had been fined for fraud in 1933 and supplied details in an extract of her conviction (for which they charged their Portsmouth colleagues an administrative fee of 2s).

Having read his report, the Assistant DPP, Arthur Sefton-Cohen, told Ford that, considering the flimsy evidence, a charge of conspiracy to defraud would be preferable to vagrancy. That way there would be a jury trial and, in the event of conviction, a custodial sentence. Sefton-Cohen appointed a representative, E. G. Robey – son of Britain's most famous comedian, George Robey, 'The Prime Minister of Mirth' – instructing him to arrange summonses for the Homers and Frances Brown, and to challenge the claim that Mrs Duncan 'was capable of holding communication with deceased persons and causing the spirits thereof to materialise'. The Home Office was notified.

At 10.50 a.m. the next day, 8 February, Helen was charged in the presence of her solicitor, Mr Elkin, who

advised her to remain silent, then driven to the magistrates' court. A queue wound up the steps, people in hats
and coats posing for photographers, all smiling faces and
V-for-Victory signs. Proceedings were brisk. Prudently,
Loseby did not again refer to Home Office policy. When
Helen heard the charge, she fainted and was helped up by
the policemen at her side. Fresh summonses were issued
for Mr and Mrs Homer and Mrs Brown, and the court
adjourned until 29 February. The police called on Frances
Brown at her home in Houghton-le-Spring, County
Durham, where she had fled after the seance raid. The
Homer residence was visited that same afternoon,
although Mrs Homer had disappeared. A journalist from
the *Daily Herald*, W. A. E. Jones, tracked her down to a
bedsit in South Norwood, where she described Helen as
'a comparative stranger' but a natural medium whom she
had paid £8 per seance, amounting to £112 over six days –
the equivalent of three months' wages for a lorry driver.
Ford, meanwhile, made his report to the Home Office,
interviewed the sailor's widow Dorothy Evans and pressed
Edinburgh for more details of the 1933 trial.

Protests continued to pour in. At the *Psychic News*,
Maurice Barbanell's mailbag was full. A woman who had
witnessed Helen Duncan's seances in Yorkshire believed
she had 'done more for convincing sceptics and giving
consolation to mourners than all the bishops in Christen-
dom'. A sceptical Rochdale man had been converted
when Mrs Duncan materialized the twin babies he and his
wife had lost; now they would get to see them grow up in
the spirit world. Mrs Knowles from St Annes-on-the-Sea

in Lancashire told lovingly of a 'disembodied fairy' she'd spoken with at a Duncan seance and had faith that 'English hearts' would resist gross injustice.

Writing to Barbanell from Bourton in Dorset, one Spiritualist was appalled that the authorities could behave thus during a so-called 'war for freedom' and condemned informers as 'imitation Hitlers'. The crusading MP Eleanor Rathbone received a letter from a constituent in a similar vein, enclosing the front page of *Psychic News* and complaining that Mrs Duncan's arrest was inimical to the struggle for liberty in Europe. Miss Rathbone contacted the Parliamentary Under-Secretary of State at the Home Office, Sir Osbert Peake, who, having met the SNU deputation in 1943, was able to inform her that the police used the law only 'to protect the public against those who trade on the ignorant and credulous, and especially those who in wartime exploit the anxiety of people about the fate of relatives and friends serving with the Forces'. Herbert Morrison received a petition from Morecambe in Lancashire signed by, among others, several soldiers and a Glasgow policeman – but used Ford's report to stand his ground.

On the evening of Monday 28 February, E. G. Robey met Chief Constable West at the Queen's Hotel in Southsea to give the charge a final polish, then, like his father before a big show, got a good night's sleep. At the hearing the next morning there were distracting noises off outside the courtroom; someone was playing dance tunes on a piano, overlaid with the dull drone of RAF bombers heading to Germany. Charles Loseby squared up to the youthful Robey, who was full of disparaging theatrical phrases. After the four defendants had pleaded not guilty, Robey gave Mrs Duncan's act the thumbs down as inferior to the great Victorian conjuring shows; but his real point, one persistently stressed by the Prosecution, was that the truth of Spiritualism was not in question, only whether the defendants had conspired to commit fraud. Rupert Cross denied that Mrs Duncan had looked sick or distressed, nor had she fallen over. Ford admitted that her face might have looked a little blue, but, glancing at the dock, added: 'no bluer than she is in court today'.

Other witnesses on the stand that day included Mr Burrell, the dockyard medium, who said he had read about Mrs Duncan and William Crookes's materialization experiments but was disappointed and had his admission fee refunded. William Lock, a licensed pedlar, related that, at the seance on 19 January, the hand of his sister's spirit was cold and flabby; his wife then said that Peggy had made them sing 'You Are My Sunshine', a hit from early in the war, before exiting through the floor. Over twelve shillings 'for the pleasure of this entertainment', remarked Robey drily.

But this would be the end of E. G. Robey's involvement in the trial. The involvement of counsel, the conspiracy charge and the DPP's support all made the relocation of the trial to the Old Bailey, London's Central Criminal Court, inevitable, however excessive that seemed. The DPP's office set to work and the Clerk of the Court framed an indictment that could not be picked apart by a clever barrister. The Clerk's discoveries were significant. Mr Homer could not be indicted as a pharmacist, because according to the Pharmacy and Poisons Act he was merely a drugstore proprietor. Nor could Mrs Homer be indicted by that name, because she was already Mrs Elizabeth Jones, a revelation which solved one problem for the Prosecution, namely that husband and wife could not legally conspire together.

In the first week of March, Robey was replaced as prosecuting counsel. Usually the Central Criminal Bar Mess, a permanent Bar attached to the court, dealt with cases on a rota system, leaving only the most serious trials for Treasury Counsel and the Law Officers of the Crown. Sir Edward Tindal Atkinson, however, considered this to be 'a case of some difficulty', so on the advice of the Attorney General nominated John Maude, whom he thought 'likely to handle this rather unusual case with ability'. Maude, like Robey the son of a well-known actor, and the product of Eton, Oxford and the Middle Temple, had been made Treasury Counsel in 1942 and King's Counsel the following year. Had funds permitted, the SNU would have been well advised to have appointed Treasury Counsel against a KC. Now the odds were stacked against them. Maude's junior would be the gawky and inexperienced Henry Elam, for whom the case was just another brief – until he saw its full implications.

On 15 March, a private meeting took place between Maude, Elam and the DPP that would prove a turning point in the history of Spiritualism. To the DPP and Chief Constable West even a charge of conspiracy to defraud seemed shaky, because they would need to prove that people had paid to see materialized spirits, whereas seance organizers carefully avoided promising anything. Something else was needed to nail the case down. By the end of the meeting, which lasted ninety minutes, a solution had been found in a single clause of a largely obsolete statute: Section 4 of the 1735 Witchcraft Act. When James I's 1604 legislation was repealed, its terms had been imported into a new Act to make explicit their nullification and a section interpolated for 'the more effectual preventing and punishing any pretenses to such arts or powers ... whereby ignorant persons are frequently deluded and defrauded'. Thus, Helen Duncan's emotional protest that she was being tried as a witch was about to acquire some substance, and her mother's prophecy that she would be burned as such borne out to a greater extent than she ever could have foreseen as a second-sighted child in Callander.

Like Mollie Goldney, Harry Price declined to appear as an expert witness – he had been ill with angina – although he was at the Old Bailey for at least one day and contributed indirectly. He sent a copy of *Regurgitation and the Duncan Mediumship* to Chief Constable West, who, in turn, passed it to the DPP with remarks about the disaffected maid Mary McGinlay. Maude thought she might be 'called in rebuttal' should the Defence plead Helen Duncan's good character and especially if the defendant gave evidence herself. Price's stereograms were also invaluable for cross-examination and would corroborate Cross's assertion that the ectoplasm was cheesecloth. The 1933 conviction was also held in reserve; likewise the discovery that Frances Brown had been imprisoned for theft in 1929 – a list of stolen items ran to ten typed foolscap sheets. In mid-March the DPP requested more photographs from Price, who arranged for the Librarian of the University of London to send them to the police.

By the 22nd, the Prosecution's case was complete. Maude and Elam were confident that Loseby's barrage of testimony would fail because witnesses would mostly be describing events from before January 1944, which were irrelevant to the case. The Prosecution would then persuade the jury that Helen Duncan was fraudulent using its own witnesses to the Copnor Road seance, 'which any person with an ounce of common sense would liken to a Punch and Judy show'. The Prosecution had almost no tangible evidence – against the Homers, just a few spirit photographs seized by Detective Inspector Ford – but Maude and Elam knew the Witchcraft Act made this unimportant. They didn't have to prove that Helen Duncan was an impostor, only that she had *pretended* – meaning 'falsely claimed' – to conjure spirits. And the Defence, with its declared intent to prove the resurrection of the dead, would do that for them. Spiritualists advised Loseby to focus on the Prosecution's failure to produce the sheet under which Mrs Duncan supposedly masqueraded as a ghost and to find a witness who could undermine Stanley Worth's credibility. But even if this had mattered that much, Loseby, the quixotic crusader, was too headstrong to listen.

The trial began on the morning of Thursday 23 March 1944 in Court No. 4 of the Blitz-damaged Old Bailey. The public gallery remained out of bounds and spectators squeezed past each other in the precincts and corridors, hopeful of a seat downstairs or at least a spot outside the door. Helen Duncan had arrived early, pulling her coat across her face as a *Daily Mirror* photographer lunged for a snap. Henry, in raincoat and fedora, had calmly steered his wife past the gathering crowd, one hand on her arm, the other cupping a cigarette. Now, as the jury entered the courtroom, Charles Loseby took his place on the Defence side of the Bar table and tried to look confident. He had breakfasted without appetite at his Kensington home, then paced up and down the hallway, suggesting to his wife and daughter that a great burden was weighing him down.

Summoned by the Clerk, Mrs Duncan made her way unsteadily up from the cells, where she and her co-defendants, Mrs Brown and the Homers, had been waiting since they arrived at the Old Bailey. She felt sick, like a condemned felon mounting the scaffold. As the dark stairwell opened up into daylight, an array of faces, loving and accusing and morbidly curious, was spread out before her in that grand, echoing space.

After the judge, the Recorder of London, Sir Gerald Dodson, had made his address, the Prosecution set out its case. Loseby was dismayed by the effect John Maude had upon the court, his strong voice contrasting with Loseby's husky drawl. Loseby was assisted by Mr Simpson Pedler, who, even as the junior, didn't look up to Loseby in the same way Henry Elam did to Maude. Loseby admitted that Maude's arguments were put 'with such adroitness, skill and economy of words that any ill-informed person might well imagine that there could be no effective answer to the case as he set it out'. Most remarkable was the fact that Maude was simultaneously defending a labourer on trial for murder in Court No. 1, a case he would win, and would hurtle between trials, gown streaming, as needed. He habitually fiddled with his wig while speaking but was entirely self-assured. 'Nothing ruffled him,' wrote a reporter for the *Daily Mail*. 'Once, he reached in his inside pocket for a document and accidentally pulled out his identity card and papers, which floated down to the Old Bailey floor. Without a pause in his speech, he bent and picked them up – and as he did so every word was audible.' Bit by bit, Maude's gentle mockery, poised ironies, learned perspectives and appeals to common sense lowered the Defence into a slippery-sided pit from which it would struggle to escape.

The Recorder, a committed Christian long on moral rectitude yet short on patience, even-handedly showed both sides his professional irritability and contempt, while observing the Old Bailey's custom of humanely treating prisoners in the dock. As proceedings wore on, however, even Dodson could not conceal a desire to be elsewhere, perhaps back at the opening night of *The Rebel Maid*, the humorous musical he had co-authored, which may have caused him some wry amusement when he heard about the Duncans' own rebel maid Mary McGinlay.

The spectators were excited, the researchers serious, the Spiritualists tearful. Most witnesses seemed nervous, the exception being Stanley Worth, whose testimony was the jewel in the Prosecution's crown as the charge shifted from vagrancy to conspiracy to witchcraft. At the Portsmouth hearing, War Reserve Constable Rupert Cross had looked ill at ease, whereas Worth, dapper in his naval uniform,

Loseby observed, 'gave his evidence with skill and a good eye to effect, being assisted in the latter by a flickering smile'. Worth could also do all the funny voices, including Albert's. As Loseby cross-examined him, protocols of debate – begged pardons and craved indulgences – gave way to raised voices, causing the Recorder to remind the adversaries that the court could already hear them perfectly well. They squabbled over whether Worth had been a spy, but to Loseby's sarcastic parody of Mrs Duncan 'playing bogey-bogey with a sheet over her head' Worth had nothing to add: that was exactly what she had done. Worth was unshaken and Loseby knew it. More than that, he was utterly persuasive, dismissing inconsistencies over which psychical investigators present had been obsessing pedantically. The Recorder wound up the day's proceedings by requesting a sketch plan of the seance room and releasing Mrs Duncan and her co-defendants on bail.

It didn't help Loseby that his client made such a bad impression, or that the press coverage was so sensational. The journalist W. A. E. Jones of the *Daily Herald*, in court for the entire trial, never warmed to Helen the martyr and her hand-wringing disciples, many of whom had travelled to the capital from Portsmouth. 'As she waddled her way to face the judge and jury,' Jones wrote, 'women threw their arms around her, kissed her, sobbed over her and blessed her in whispering voices.' A reporter from Portsmouth's *Evening News* had followed the legal circus to the Old Bailey and filed thrilling copy every day. London's own *Evening News* and the *Evening Standard* published daily bulletins, as did national newspapers from *The Times* and

Daily Telegraph to the more populist *Daily Mirror* and *The Star*. On Sundays the *News of the World* made the most of 'the witch-trial'. Some papers printed portraits of Helen Duncan, others Harry Price's photos of her emitting ectoplasm. The headlines were things like GHOST INVITED TO GIVE EVIDENCE and SPIRIT CALLED PEGGY LIKED LIPSTICK. The *Daily Sketch* described a seance where Peggy, 'the blithe child spirit', did a jig, a parrot whistled and a ghost said it 'had been downstairs for a torch'. The London *Evening News* and the *Daily Mail* opted for 'the woman's angle', commenting on Helen's outfits although they disagreed about whether or not she was well dressed.

Cartoonists also had fun. The *Daily Express* showed two air-raid wardens, with overhead a witch on a broomstick. 'She'll have to be a bit more careful in future,' one says to the other. 'The courts take a poor view of that sort of thing these days.' The *Daily Mail* used the Duncan case to comment on industrial action by Welsh miners. Whitehall officials were shown binding a 'Coal Industry' medium to a chair, while a malevolent 'Strike Spirit' emerged from the cabinet.

Proceedings on day two opened with Worth, examined by Elam, defending his eyesight – he had a lazy eye – but the Recorder prevented his sharing his optician's opinion. Next up was Elijah Fowler, who, in his diffident Scots voice, confirmed Worth's account of the first seance; then a police photographer explained how easy it was to doctor a negative; Mr and Mrs Lock said their piece, including a story about the return of 'Pinky', an RAF pilot shot through the head; and Charles Burrell likened Peggy to a fairy in a Christmas pantomime. Kitty Jennings, an Air Raid Precautions supervisor, recounted how at an afternoon seance on 19 January 'this wretched Scotch child' (Maude's words), jiggling up and down, had confessed to borrowing Christine Homer's perfume and lipstick. When the witness hesitated in describing Peggy, Maude raised a laugh by asking whether she looked more like Helen of Troy or, say, a pillowcase.

Then it was Loseby's turn. A seasoned actress before the war, Mrs Jennings agreed with Loseby that the spirits' regional accents would be hard to mimic – unless, of course, one were used to doing such a thing. Finally, after Rupert Cross had corroborated the second part of Worth's testimony, Detective Inspector Ford was chastised by Loseby for failing to search the sitters; Ford replied that this would have been unthinkable without a doctor. Again and again, Loseby commented on the strangely absent cloth until the Recorder stopped him, seemingly from boredom, at which point Maude cut in: 'It is obvious there are certain places where things can be concealed?' 'Yes, sir,' replied Ford briskly. And with that, Maude rested the case for the Crown.

It had been an exciting couple of days for Geoffrey Wilson, the teenage son of Percy Wilson, President of the London SNU. Geoffrey had been appointed as Loseby's messenger, meaning he could jump queues, stride through the corridors of legal power and feel important. He also pasted newspaper cuttings into an old scribbling diary from Boots the Chemists. His father instructed him that at the end of the second day he should meet Mrs Duncan and bring her to Merton Park, a garden suburb south-east of the city, where the Wilsons lived. As Geoffrey and Helen arrived at 3 Sheridan Road, Mr and Mrs Wilson and their other son Laurence were waiting to greet them, and the family and their distinguished guest had tea with what was later described as 'some really good red jam'. Then they repaired to the seance room, which the Wilsons had hastily furnished with a movable cabinet made from copper gas piping, black cloth, curtain rings and a modified standard lamp fitted with a red bulb and a rheostat.

The window curtains were drawn, the lamp switched on and dimmed, and Mrs Duncan settled herself in the scratch-built cabinet. No sooner had she entered a trance than she was on her feet, and Percy Wilson, a yard away with the lamp over his head, marvelled at how 'ectoplasm poured in streams, in ribbons, from her nose and mouth, on to her massive bosom, curled up in a ribbon on her bosom, and dropped to the ground'. Laurence was almost knocked over by a tube of rubbery ectoplasm on which a mischievous Albert had invited him to tread. Mrs Wilson received some apported flowers. Then, as the medium stood with outstretched arms, the family saw the shining ectoplasm leap into her hands and instantly disappear. All this Percy Wilson relayed to Charles Loseby, whose idea this test had been to see if he might safely offer a seance to the court when the trial resumed on the 27th.

That weekend at home Loseby paced some more, rehearsing his opening speech and thinking how best to persuade the Recorder to allow his client to demonstrate her gift. On

Monday morning Loseby steeled himself and, before another packed court, tried to discredit the Prosecution's witnesses, while asserting that Helen Duncan was a genuine materialization medium. For now, Sir Gerald Dodson kept his feelings to himself, but they were essentially those of a former Lord Chief Justice: the validity of Spiritualism, far from being a matter for the courts, was 'better discussed in the bracing air at a conference in Blackpool'. Loseby pressed on. He spoke of Mrs Duncan having 'gone down like a shot rabbit' when Worth shone his torch at her and of the burn on her cheek where ectoplasm had shot back. All eyes turned to the dock, but no mark was visible.

Loseby's dilemma – one faced by all Defence barristers – was whether to let his clients, Helen Duncan and the other defendants, testify and risk their incriminating themselves under cross-examination or to deny them the privilege and risk making it seem they had something to hide. For all but Mr Homer, Loseby chose the latter, which Henry Elam thought looked very bad. Sir Gerald Dodson noted this decision and cautioned that if Mrs Duncan were not called now she should not be called later. The whey-faced, unassuming Mr Homer did not incriminate himself – describing a materialization of Mrs Homer's grandmother singing a Welsh hymn – but neither did he exonerate Mrs Duncan, still less support Loseby's argument that the bodies of mediums were portals through which the spiritual dead revisited earth.

Then came the moment for which Loseby had been bracing himself. Mrs Duncan would be willing, he told the Recorder, to perform a private seance for the jury. Sir

Gerald Dodson declined on the grounds that, as he explained later in the trial, such a demonstration 'might operate unfairly against this woman because, supposing the spirit, if such a thing there be, was not mindful to come to her assistance on this occasion, then the verdict would have to be against her'. But, for the moment, Dodson said merely that it was bad enough that London jurors had to try a case that should really have remained in Portsmouth 'without their time being occupied by witnessing exhibitions which may or may not assist them'.

Loseby called his first witness. The twinkle in the eye of George Mackie, the RAF wing commander present at the Portsmouth seance, only confirmed an impression that, like Loseby's other 'skilled investigators', he took himself too seriously. He was certain he had been reunited with his mother, who had died in Australia in 1927. 'A man knows his mother,' he stated, adding, 'I have the advantage also of knowing my father.' To this, the Recorder, eyebrows raised above his spectacles, responded politely: 'Well, that's something', causing some spectators to rub their smiling faces. Harold Gill from Southsea followed Mackie in the witness box. Maude illustrated Gill's recollection of the ectoplasm he had seen by dangling before him a piece of butter muslin which Maude had stuffed in his pocket, to unanimous Spiritualist consternation. Gill's wife Dorothy also testified, saying that she knew ectoplasm could rush back into the medium's body, having heard about it in November 1943 at a lecture by a Mr Lilley of the Portsmouth City Police fingerprinting section – a curious detail not mentioned again.

By the fourth day of the trial, Tuesday 28 March, it

was plain that the repetitiveness of the stories told by witnesses for the Defence, however stupendous and poignant, had nearly exhausted the Recorder's patience. Proceedings resumed with the submission of documentary evidence: some receipts and letters of thanks for seance profits donated to the Wireless for the Blind Fund, the Two Worlds Publishing Company and the SNU Freedom Fund. The Homers claimed all 'surplus money' went to charities, receipts for £450 of which the police had traced, although less than £30 of that revenue had been generated by the Duncan seances.

The first witness that morning was a Mrs Cole, who, describing the manifestation of a friend at the Master's Temple, complained that people in court were laughing at her trying to recall how long Albert's beard was. From then the Recorder's mood darkened considerably, a change that Loseby pretended not to notice. Towards the end of the afternoon, having heard a Royal Marine rhapsodize about the return of his grandparents and unable to bear another second, Dodson interrupted Henry Elam cross-examining a witness about the kind of fairy light seen in Mrs Duncan's hand:

THE RECORDER: We will go into that tomorrow. Mr Loseby, can you give us any help at all with regard to the witnesses?
MR LOSEBY: My Lord, I shall call no more Portsmouth witnesses.
THE RECORDER: Any other sort of witnesses?
MR LOSEBY: Yes, my Lord.

THE RECORDER: How many more? I want to know, roughly.

MR LOSEBY: It is hard for me to estimate. I had in mind forty to fifty.

In reply, the Recorder, craving teatime, said nothing but merely scraped back his chair and disappeared through the door behind the Bench.

Day five, Wednesday the 29th, brought Sir Gerald Dodson no relief. Adding to his malaise, he grew squeamish when Loseby, piqued by the appearance in court of Harry Price, dwelled too long on the appearance of regurgitated cheesecloth. Basil Kirkby, a retired businessman, said he had spent twenty years researching 'the stuff known as ectoplasm', invested, he said, with a power almost as amazing as radium to Marie Curie, and which he had observed in the company of Sir Oliver Lodge and Sir Arthur Conan Doyle. Mention of a talking spirit budgerigar prompted the Recorder to take over the questioning, whereupon he was informed that everyone has a guide on the other side. 'Have we?' Dodson asked incredulously. 'Yes, every one of us,' replied Kirkby, whose guide was 'Chang', a Chinese man with a drooping moustache and swinging pigtail. 'Well, I don't seem to have one with regard to this evidence,' joked the Recorder, mirthlessly.

Next came Captain Barnes, who, overlooking Mrs Duncan getting his daughter's name wrong, praised her for manifesting his son, killed in France in May 1940. There followed: an RAF officer, who at a seance in Preston saw a lady he knew who had died in an air raid; Lilian Bailey, a

medium employed by the IIPR; and Hannen Swaffer, the
journalist who had glorified Mina Crandon – 'Margery' –
when she visited Britain in 1929, and now the first Defence
witness to give Elam a run for his money. After a Glaswegian woman described meeting her dead father in
1931 – complete, if that's the right word, with his missing
eye – it was the turn of the SPR Spiritualist B. Abdy Collins, whom the Recorder treated with respect because he
had been a magistrate and sessions judge in India. Mrs
Duncan's manifestations radiated an unearthly phospho-
rescence, Collins said, offering undeniable proof of spiritual
survival and quite unlike a deception he himself had
exposed at Reading.

The day's testimony ended with a Battersea medium
describing the spirit of her husband Alf, and a man who
had been convinced by his wrinkly granny's Suffolk accent.
The court adjourned. Next morning, day six, Sir Gerald
Dodson's spirits were lifted a little by Loseby's announcement that this was the last day on which he would call
witnesses. First up was Alfred Dodd, the Liverpudlian
Shakespeare hobbyist, who had followed Mrs Duncan's
career since 1931 and was reunited with his first sweetheart Helen. As the Recorder's patience was still fresh,
Dodd was permitted to speak at length, claiming that
Mary, Queen of Scots, a Spiritualist favourite, had tried in
vain to materialize at a seance in 1940 but did manage to
say that she was a lady attired in 'an old-world dress',
spoke Scots tinged with French and had lost her head on
the block – the sort of historical sketch one can imagine
Mr Cumming coming up with at Callander Parish School.

Thus far Helen Duncan's Edinburgh conviction had been kept quiet because, by the law of evidence, it was no indication of guilt, and but for Loseby's strategy it would have gone unmentioned. But during Alfred Dodd's cross-examination, the jury were sent out so that Elam could ask the judge if he could disclose this fact in rebuttal of the Defence's persistent claim that Helen Duncan was a genuine medium. Dodson consented. Loseby protested, insisting that Maude had promised not to use the 1933 conviction. Summoned back from his murder trial in Court No. 1, Maude played this down, and Dodson ruled that since Loseby had chosen to draw upon events from before January 1944 the Prosecution could do the same. Loseby's hopes were fading. The jury returned and were unmoved even when Dodd, describing the Edinburgh trial and affirming the defendant's virtues, reduced a murmuring Mrs Duncan to tears. 'She is a genuine materialization medium,' declared Dodd, 'and anything I can do to help that lady in her distress, I come here to do it, because I owe her a debt.'

Loseby made the most of his last day by calling another fourteen witnesses. Sir Gerald Dodson was impassive. Dr John Winning, Assistant Medical Officer for Glasgow, had seen over four hundred of Helen Duncan's manifestations, who spoke not just in different accents but in Gaelic, German and Hebrew. Spirit relatives he'd met were unlike the medium: his mother was slim, his brother spritely, his uncle bearded, his grandmother eighty-four. Winning was followed by a psychic healer who had seen a spirit child with withered arms; a Frenchwoman whose

one-legged daughter had sung the folk song 'Au Clair de la
Lune'; and a retired sanitary inspector from Kendal who
received a Morse code message from his drowned daughter. Vincent Woodcock, an electrical draughtsman from
Blackpool, identified his wife from a spirit's palpitating
heart, then his stepmother from a fatal wound sustained
in the Manchester Blitz. The only witness with anything
new was Sir James Herries, an Edinburgh journalist and
magistrate, whose friend Conan Doyle had returned to
him at a Duncan seance, albeit only to answer 'yes' to a
question before fading. Herries disagreed with the 1933
verdict and, prompted by Loseby, declared Price's cheesecloth theory 'perfectly absurd'. The afternoon ended in an
evidential blur – more glowing dogs and birds, another
one-legged relative, boasts about spiritual healing, a doctor
talking to his mother (in Swedish), the return of a French
youth killed on the Maginot Line in 1940, and a South
African called Gilbert who perished in a plane crash. At
last, Loseby thought he had called enough witnesses,
whereupon the Recorder requested that the case be
concluded the next day. 'One would like to reciprocate
the patience the jury have shown', he remarked with a
pinched smile, 'by not inflicting more upon them than
we can help.'

That evening, a dinner was held in Helen's honour at
the Bonnington Hotel in Southampton Row. After they
had finished eating, Loseby suggested she try to procure a
spiritual message on a notepad placed under the tablecloth. They continued chatting and smoking, then checked.
On the pad were several words which made the dinner

seem even more of a valedictory last supper: 'Two will be convicted and two will go free.'

In the morning, whereas the jurors and spectators seemed jaded, the defendants, fearing the worst, were alert. For simplicity's sake the charges, including 'effecting a public mischief' by exploiting the bereaved, were all dropped except one: conspiracy to contravene the Witchcraft Act. Loseby's closing speech, the two hours and 11,000 words of which convinced the Recorder that his optimism had been premature, asked the jury whether they felt the Prosecution had proved beyond reasonable doubt that Helen Duncan had exercised or pretended to exercise a kind of conjuration, and whether the 1735 Act was a fit statute by which to try her and her co-defendants. Someone passed Elam a note that read: 'The only evil spirit is now known as Hooch; in 1735 all spirits were evil.' Loseby poured derision upon the Sheriff's Court that convicted her in 1933 and, indeed on Scotland as a whole – a country, he said, which had objected to the introduction of the potato as an act of impiety.

John Maude's cool-headed reply to such floundering was every bit as withering as Loseby had feared, a rhetorical *coup de grâce*. The realm beyond the veil, he suggested to the jury, was a dull and ridiculous place, not awesome, merely awful:

Let me ask you to imagine an afternoon in the Other World. They are sitting round Mary, Queen of Scots. Her head is on. St Sebastian, the pin-cushion saint, is there, perfectly normal. There are various persons who have been mutilated, looking perfectly all right. No arm or leg cut off, no eyes out. Then suddenly someone says something that is sad. Off comes the Queen's head – under her arm, I suppose – St Sebastian begins to bleed, and unmutilated persons become mutilated.

The entire scenario was too fantastical. 'If this is the sort of thing we are coming to,' cautioned Maude, 'it is time we began to pull ourselves together and exercise a little common sense.' And why, apart from Mary, Queen of Scots, did famous people so rarely return in spirit? Never did they see Napoleon, Socrates, Shakespeare, Keats or Shelley, whom Maude quoted in a mocking address to Bronco the Parrot: 'Hail to thee, blithe Spirit! Bird thou never wert', adding: 'For it was not a bird, but a fraud.' Like defending counsel in 1933, he also referred to Browning's 'Mr Sludge, "The Medium"', observing that the occult had attracted charlatans for centuries.

After lunch, the Recorder delivered his summing-up, at two and a quarter hours a masterpiece of compression, shaming Loseby, whose case, he indicated, may have defeated itself 'by being so prolix and multiplied'. Only once did Dodson depart from the notes he had been sedulously scribbling all week, and that was to silence muttered denials from Mrs Homer: 'It is not very much good her emitting noises of a dissentient nature if she does not go into the witness-box when she has the opportunity, and deal with it upon oath.' At 4.32 p.m. the jury retired, returning twenty-four minutes later with four guilty verdicts. Chief Constable West was then invited to give an

account of their records, calmly demolishing the ruins of
Mrs Brown's and Mrs Duncan's credit, referring to the
former helping herself in Selfridges (which had her shout-
ing in denial), and adding the following censure of the
latter, who by now was muttering denials of her own.
Paying little notice, West continued with his vilification of
Helen Duncan:

> This is a case where not only has she attempted and suc-
> ceeded in deluding confirmed believers in Spiritualism,
> but she has tricked, defrauded and preyed upon the minds
> of a certain credulous section of the public who have
> gone to these meetings in search of comfort of mind in
> their sorrow and grief, many of whom left with the firm
> conviction that the memory of the dead had been
> besmirched. She thought fit to come to Portsmouth, the
> first naval port of the world, where she would find many
> bereaved families, and there she practised her trickery.

Halted by the Recorder, West expressed a wish to finish
his point, which was granted. And there came the rub.
West made an unexplained, fleeting reference to the
darker danger Mrs Duncan had presented to the public
and nation since at least 1941, when a report was filed
about her 'having transgressed the security laws, again
in a naval connection, when she foretold the loss of one
of His Majesty's ships long before the fact was made
public'. Now the dead of HMS *Barham* had returned to
haunt *her*.

Sir Gerald Dodson postponed sentencing until 10.30

a.m. on 3 April, Loseby having requested a non-custodial sentence in view of Helen's poor health. He was not optimistic, but at least this way he had time to prepare an appeal application. While Loseby paced and scribbled, Helen and her dishevelled gang spent the weekend in the cells, Albert having at last deserted her. On Monday they were back before the Recorder, who jailed Helen for nine months, to which she yelled back: 'I didn't do anything!' The journalist W. A. E. Jones described how 'she sobbed. She moaned. She groaned. And then she collapsed on the floor, hat off her head, her fur coat flapping round her as prison matrons and the three other defendants helped to raise her to her feet.' Another reporter affected surprise at her keening cry as to whether there was a God: 'For one professedly in touch with the world beyond this one, it was a strange query', and akin to the astrological journal, he said, which had closed down in 1939 owing to the uncertainty of the future. Frances Brown received four months for aggravating Helen's offence, whereas the Homers were saved by their guilelessness, clean records and charity receipts, and were bound over to keep the peace. With the last of his strength, Loseby arranged notice of appeal on behalf of all four defendants, and vainly attempted to have the case declared *sub judice* to restrain the press, who were champing at the bit to get back to Fleet Street to bash out their final witch-trial stories. But the Recorder was in no mood to indulge Losey and concluded by sardonically remarking that it was rich for him to be resisting the press now when all the previous week he had presented 'rather a temptation to them'. 'My Lord, I respectfully agree,' said Loseby with a modest bow.

Later that same day, Victoria Helen Duncan, aged forty-six and suffering from angina, began her sentence in Holloway Prison. Decommissioned, deactivated, she lay idle and inert like a defused bomb, without having had her say or a chance to show what she could do. Her hopes now were pinned on the appeal; her fears were for her family. They, too, were sick with worry, sure she would die a martyr. One night after her arrest, Henry had sat up with Gena and Lilian speculating gloomily, when Gena heard a noise like a window blind wrapping itself around the roller, followed by a discarnate voice which said: 'nine months'. 'No, no, no!' cried Henry when she told him, tears rolling. Lilian, now an invalid, told Gena to shut up; but Henry reprimanded her, believing his youngest daughter – so like her mother! – would be proved right. In the last week of March, Nan, frailer than ever, had accompanied Henry to London for the trial and broke down when the verdict was read out. Outside the Old Bailey, she told a *News of the World* reporter that the Duncans were ordinary working-class folk, adding: 'If Mother were a fraud as a medium, she wasted her time in Spiritualism. She could have made a fortune on the stage.' Over the weekend of 1–2 April, Nan's condition had deteriorated to the point that Henry had to take her back to Edinburgh, leaving Helen to await her fate. Only rats leave sinking ships, sneered one Spiritualist supporter.

Reunited with his other daughters (the spirits had already

told Gena about Nan's state; Lilian had silenced her), Henry carried Nan to bed and called the doctor, who diagnosed jaundice and rheumatic fever. Gena, who had had to stay to look after the sickly Lilian and her children, took the trial hardest, having always trusted in God and Albert. Escaping for a couple of hours, she went to the theatre, but even there a comedian made a joke about 'the witch' and she stormed out. Newspapers were hard to stomach, too, with the dailies taking the kind of sensationalist tone reserved for murder trials.

Reporters bothered the Duncans incessantly. In the end, Henry, under pressure from Helen's estranged sister Florence, gave an interview to a Sunday broadsheet to set the record straight. The resulting exclusive was headed: SEVENTH DAUGHTER OF SEVENTH DAUGHTER CHARGED WITH WITCHCRAFT, which would have horrified the family even if Helen hadn't been the fourth child of an only child.* Bereft that truth had not prevailed, Gena remembered what her mother had taught her: you can bind the hands of a thief but not the tongue of a liar. Bitterly disillusioned, Gena vowed never to become a medium. When word reached Helen's sons – Harry serving with the RAF in Egypt and Peter, a signalman on HMS *Formidable* in the Pacific – both wrote to their father asking him to do something. Peter, believing that his mother was at death's door, was granted compassionate

---

* In her newspaper column, Helen (or Henry) had falsely claimed that her mother was the seventh daughter of the seventh daughter of a seventh daughter: *People's Journal* (9 Sept. 1933).

leave. Broken-hearted, Henry received a request from the Edinburgh City Police that he collect a parcel sent from London containing his wife's clothes, including her confiscated seance outfit.

And so this sad, strange episode drew to a close. The records were made straight: old files closed and archived, new ones opened with a letter here, a cutting there, and the indictments, depositions and exhibits delivered to the Registrar at the Criminal Appeal Office. The receipt for Helen's things, signed by Henry, was posted back to London; her fingerprints were dispatched to 'C' Department (Crime) at Scotland Yard; and Detective Inspector Ford typed up a final report, of which copies were sent to the DPP and the Chief Constables of Sheffield, Sunderland and Edinburgh, all of whom had assisted the Portsmouth investigation. Officers at Scotland Yard, who also received a copy, were especially thanked for their advice and support.

Finally, Ford sent a note to Harry Price enclosing correspondence Price had lent to him, plus confirmation that his photographs were back at the University of London Library. But that was not all. Arriving home in West Sussex for the weekend of 8–9 April, Price found a parcel containing his loaned copy of *Regurgitation and the Duncan Mediumship*, three of his pictures of Helen Duncan in mid-flow and a letter from the Chief Constable of Portsmouth, Arthur West, expressing 'very real thanks and warm appreciation for all the kindly help and assistance you so readily rendered me in connection with this presentation'. And with it West offered an apology: 'The book has been in many hands and it is a matter of some regret to me to find the covers have been somewhat soiled but having regard to all the good it did perhaps you would forgive me for this.' Price didn't mind. Albeit remotely, he had had his day in court after all and could sleep the sleep of the just. The practice he had once branded as 'cheese-cloth worship' had a decade later been formalized by the law as 'a kind of conjuration', and as a result the vilification of hellish Nell Duncan was complete.

PART THREE
Helen Vindicated

7. Squaring the Circle: Fraud and Phenomena at the Seances

In November 1925, fountain pen in hand, Harry Houdini turned to page 666 of the *Atlantic Monthly* for the latest Harvard University report on the mediumship of Mina Crandon. A year earlier, sitting on the *Scientific American* committee with Professor William McDougall and others, he had been sceptical about 'Margery', references to which he underlined, likewise a passage about the luminous levitating doughnuts (actually cardboard rings). 'What I saw holding the doughnut,' wrote Dr Hudson Hoagland, a distinguished neuroscientist, 'appeared to be a human right foot, the toes clamped over the periphery of the disc, creasing it in a way verified by examining the doughnut after the sitting.' 'Aha!' annotated Houdini.

This was more than just a casual interest. Houdini waged war on Spiritualism, demonstrating in Broadway theatres how to fake phenomena – an ironic reversal for an entertainer who started out in dime museums performing feats of escapology copied from Spiritualist stage shows (he even used a curtained cabinet). A passion for debunking was driven by failure to contact his mother, to whose memory he was devoted. His disappointment peaked in Atlantic City in June 1922 when the entranced wife of his friend Sir Arthur Conan Doyle wrote a spirit letter in the correct idiom but the wrong language: English rather than Houdini's mother's inimitable mishmash of Hungarian, German and Yiddish. Four years later, in 1926, the spirits were to warn Conan Doyle: 'Houdini is doomed, doomed, doomed!' Sure enough, on Halloween that same year, he died from a ruptured appendix. In some ways Helen Duncan got off lightly with Harry Price, who by comparison was respectful and restrained in his dealings with mediums, the people the great magician called 'human vultures'.

Fraud mainly concerns falsehood, but through the vagaries of perception also relates to truth – the kind of truth that sees the phenomenal in the mundane and inspires the beholder. In 1944, prosecution witnesses may have shown that poor Nellie was guilty of fraud, but defence testimonies vividly describing engagement with the spirits of the dear departed are remarkable – an alternative reality shaped by emotion. Spoken evidence was storytelling: the manufacture of truth according to desire.

Spiritualist beliefs – perceptions of 'truth' – were unusually foggy. Superficially, Houdini was an arch-scoffer but beneath there lay a yearning agnostic, angry that his spiritual quest was frustrated by impostors. There were many like him: broadly credulous but specifically sceptical. It was all very complicated. Eric Dingwall wavered about Margery yet criticized Houdini as an anti-scientific presti-digitator over his dim view of Eva Carrière, while actually being sceptical of physical mediumship to the extent that he found his Magic Circle colleague Harry Price too credulous. For that, and for not being a gentleman, Price was judged unsuitable as an SPR investigator. One thing on which Price, Dingwall and Houdini did agree was that conjurors were good at detecting fraud because of their skill in what Price called 'the art of mystification' – or, as Houdini put it: 'It takes a flim-flammer to catch a flim-flammer.' Dickens's anti-Spiritualist satires – for example, his 1862 article 'Worse Witches than Macbeth's' – expressed the contempt that, as an accomplished conjuror, he felt for the likes of D. D. Home. Another Victorian conjuror, J. N. Maskelyne, unconvinced by Eusapia Palladino's Cambridge seances yet a believer in apparitions and table-turning, maintained that scientists were easiest to dupe, because they were too lofty to detect simple legerdemain.

Among many books about seance trickery, one of the earliest, *Modern Spiritualism* (1876), was by Maskelyne. Not all were by magicians. *Confessions of a Medium* (1882) speaks for itself, and similar works came from America. Thanks to publicity generated by Spiritualists trying to buy the entire print run, *Revelations of a Spirit Medium* (1891), both an indictment of Spiritualism and a textbook of tricks, had a dramatic impact, not least on the adolescent Ehrich Weiss, who was struggling to escape from Wisconsin to become Harry Houdini. The following year brought Julia E. Garrett's *Mediums Unmasked*, which told of a dupe who thought a medium's foot draped in a handkerchief smelled like a deceased relative. In 1902 the *London Magazine* published an article by Philip Astor, 'A Séance with the Lights Up', and the following year saw his 'Conjuring at Home', also in the *London Magazine*, and the classic work *Modern Spiritualism* by SPR veteran Frank Podmore.

Demand was boosted by the First World War. By 1916 David Phelps Abbott's *Behind the Scenes with the Mediums* had reached its fifth edition, and several new titles appeared each year. During the 1920s, Maskelyne's descendants kept up not only his conjuring but his anti-Spiritualism with exposé articles such as 'Spiritualism Exploited', 'Bogus Séance Secrets Exposed', 'Rogues of the Séance Room' and 'Exposing Ghost Frauds'. Many periodicals carried articles and serializations that spread public awareness. In 1921, the popular magazine *John Bull*, which had demonized Germans during the war, turned on mediums in a piece entitled: 'India-Rubber Spooks: Kings and Clowns on Tap for the Credulous'. A year later Price and Dingwall published a facsimile edition of *Revelations of a Spirit Medium*, the Victorian original of which had by this time become the impostor's bible.

Most fraudulent mediums restricted themselves to clairvoyance and psychometry, where the only hazard was being wrong and for which excuses were legion: spiritual interference, difficulty in raising vibrations, weakness in the communicating spirit or sceptical feelings harboured by the sitter. Good results, by contrast, came from 'pony books': card indexes containing personal details of local Spiritualists which could be lent to visiting mediums. Travelling companions and booking agents could also make surreptitious enquiries. Harry Price advised giving nothing away when visiting a medium to the extent of not speaking and removing rings several days before a sitting to let the marks fade. Once useful information had circulated, a good memory could produce impressive readings. In 1938, Mollie Goldney went back to a medium who mentioned 'Bessie and Alec White', names Mollie had invented at a seance two years earlier.

According to psychic investigator Arthur Wilkinson, forgetting 'when things got sticky' was also important, as were quick wits and an innocent face. A medium's best asset, however, was the client's high expectations, raised further by high fees. Vague insinuations were confirmed by sitters who wanted to help clairvoyants make contact, not to test them. Seances were social engagements where civility took precedence over belief and disbelief alike. Accordingly, shrugged Wilkinson, 'If you have the flair for stunts and some showmanship, well, the field is wide open for you.' Materialization mediums, he added, require only 'muslin, masks, trumpets and a colossal cheek'. Even where ectoplasm was involved, etiquette dictated that physical mediums were forgiven the clumsiest of manipulations. 'With the paid performer you pounce upon him and expose him the minute you have seen through his trick,' observed Sir Arthur Conan Doyle. 'But what are you to do with the friend of your host's wife?'

Darkness also helped: the dim light required to protect ectoplasm provided optimal conditions for conjuring. Even red light was often dimmed as seances progressed. Props were daubed with luminous paint – from Margery's doughnuts to the ubiquitous trumpets and crucifixes – and what helped with visibility also assisted in deception. A luminous business card allowed a medium to read in the dark and luminous plates framed many a ghostly face. Harry Price once saw a medium use a flask of phosphorized oil to project a pale spectral light, and silver of ferrocerium – lighter flints – came in handy. Books and articles on chemical conjuring had been around for years:

John Scoffern's 'Explosive Spiders and How to Make Them' and 'Firework Pie for a Picnic' dated from the 1880s. Light shows, from lantern lectures to the movies, inspired ambitious frauds, a point illustrated tangentially by a German accusation in 1930 that the Angels of Mons had been propagandist motion pictures of projected aeroplanes onto clouds above the trenches to imply that heaven favoured England.

In the end, restrictions imposed by mediums said more about them than about the spirits they invoked. As one sceptic observed, the movement of objects using ectoplasmic rods never exceeded a medium's muscular capabilities. The contrary claim was that spirits rejected extravagant demonstrations as vulgar – a sensibility that would explain why no medium ever caused the laws of physics to be rewritten.

Physical mediumship relied on the same misdirection used by stage magicians. But the context was different, mainly an emotional relationship, often a spontaneous one, between medium and sitter. Consider the words of Albert, Helen Duncan's spirit guide: 'There is a lady here beside me who entered the spirit world quite recently. On the earth plane she suffered from a serious and painful ailment situated in the lower part of the abdomen; eventually her heart was affected and she passed away.' This was a description given hundreds of times: non-specific, open-ended, trite. But the quotation comes not from a disgusted sceptic but from a seance-goer in Blackpool in 1942, who was thrilled by Albert's message and positively

identified the spirit as his deceased wife. Mrs Duncan and
mediums like her – although there was no one *quite* like
her – were only one half of the equation. Helen sometimes
bullied sitters into accepting her messages, becoming red
in the face if they refused; but usually this was unnecessary. The audience were willing if unwitting participants
in the creation of an illusion. The supernatural has no
monopoly over the miraculous: the secular, the banal, the
everyday, all our thoughts and feelings and passions –
these things are full of wonder, too.

Predictions about sinking warships are a case in point.
There were many theories about how news of HMS
Barham leaked out: it came from survivors returning from
Alexandria; a German propaganda broadcast had been
picked up; Mrs Duncan was an enemy spy. A simpler solution is that the prediction was never made, at least not as
reported, and the same applies to HMS *Hood.** In 1941
any medium might have thought of battleships, of which
there were just a handful and all in peril. Italy's entry
into the war in 1940 left the Royal Navy isolated in the
Mediterranean, and it was well known that the *Barham* had
been torpedoed in December 1939 and bombed during
the withdrawal from Crete in May 1941. In that battle,
nine ships had been sunk, including the cruiser HMS
Gloucester, with the loss of over seven hundred men. The
Hood, sunk the same month, had been famously the world's

---

* Since *Hellish Nell* was first published information about the secret
pre-announcement notification of the families of the bereaved has
come to light. See the Postscript.

largest warship in 1939 – an obvious choice for imagining a naval catastrophe. At the seance attended by Brigadier Roy Firebrace, the message was only that 'a great British battleship has just been sunk', which was unremarkable given this was during the Battle of the Atlantic, which had been costly from early in the war when HMS *Courageous* and the battleship *Royal Oak* were sunk. The sinking of HMS *Ark Royal* just days before the *Barham* focused attention, and Portsmouth, where the families of many of the *Barham*'s 1,200 sailors lived, was as much a target for a predatory medium as a battleship was for a U-boat. Percy Wilson considered the sailor's materialization to be 'rather straight evidence of the survival of the boy who came back to speak to his mother'; but one can also see how a cheesecloth shape could have turned into a youth with 'HMS *Barham*' on his hat, either through faulty perception or retelling of the tale. In fact, the classic story was wrong: the sailor was a petty officer and so would have worn a peaked cap, not a round hat with a cap tally. Even if he had been recently promoted, and therefore still 'square-rigged', in wartime all tallies read just 'HMS' for security reasons. Moreover, witnesses reported that, although the *Barham* was mentioned at the seance, the ship's name was extracted from the sitter by Mrs Duncan speaking as 'Albert'.

These explanations are mundane; the wonder lies in the fact that it was really possible for a woman to recognize her son or husband. Of course, the seance conditions at the Master's Temple were ideal for illusion. It was impossible to adjust completely to the darkness, as Stanley Worth testified, and the forty-watt red bulb that Mr and

Mrs Homer described to the police was more like a five-watt. The cabinet concealed all, the music muffled all, the gloom shrouded all, and the show was kept moving by Mrs Brown's and Mrs Homer's commentary, which identified shapes and asked sitters to claim the spirits. The seating plan also helped the Homers control visiting strangers – an old medium's trick to stack the odds in her favour. But the impression was magical. After seeing Helen Duncan perform in 1931, William McDougall said 'that when the general procedure and circumstances demanded by the medium are such as suggest fraud and favour fraud, the observer is justified in regarding the phenomena as fraudulent, even if he is not able to suggest any plausible explanation'. And yet manifestations need not have been genuine to be phenomenal.

Not only was the believer's experience remarkable but the theatrical skill of materialization mediums was remarkable, too. Ectoplasm may well have been butter muslin, blotting paper, wood pulp or egg white – but the artistry of its manipulation was something else. Mediums had long used props. In the 1870s, Madame Blavatsky had been forced to leave Cairo after a ghostly arm was found to be a long glove stuffed with cotton wool suspended by threads, and Maskelyne detected Eusapia Palladino's dummy hands at Cambridge in 1895. But pre-seance searches made prop use difficult – the Homers even obliged a man who asked for the cabinet chair's upholstery to be ripped open – and touring mediums had to use whatever they could hide on or in themselves. Usually this meant fabric, but discreetly inflated balloons and rubber gloves were also used. The clammy matter Dingwall felt on Margery's thigh may have been an animal lung, inflated with a pump hidden between her legs. Others likened her ectoplasm to raw liver, half a brain and an armadillo's back. As a rule, it was best to keep things simple. 'The experimental results are so impossible by fraud', William Crawford said of the Golighers, 'that it would have been quite unnecessary to take any means to prevent fraud.' Yet when Kathleen Goligher came out of retirement in 1936, a camera revealed a thread running down one leg attached to ectoplasm slithering across the floor. C. V. C. Herbert, the SPR's Research Officer, experimented by dragging a handkerchief attached to a length of cotton, slowly winding it towards him round the stub of a pencil. In weak light, observers found the trick almost impossible to detect.

But how were full-figure materializations achieved? Lighting from beneath silk treated with phosphorus, olive oil and alum water produces a luminous vapour, which is perhaps how the illusionist David Devant made a 'ghost in silken gauze' glide across a hall and then evaporate before twenty astonished guests. Helen Duncan essentially played 'bogey-bogey with a sheet over her head', as Charles Loseby put it, and transmuted into six-foot-tall 'Albert' by holding up an arm (tall spirit forms commonly only had use of one arm). The Edinburgh ghostbuster Esson Maule was photographed mocking up Helen's tricks. One shows her with a handkerchief over her face and a vest on her head, face poking through an armhole; in another she draws the cabinet curtains around herself to control how much of her white-swathed body could be seen. Add to this mix thick black stockings, quiet on wooden floors and invisible in semi-darkness, and the effect was that of a slim floating figure. An odd noise heard prior to Peggy's airy entrance was traced to a squeaking floorboard: Helen had lowered herself to her knees to manipulate the vest. Disappearing through the floor was an old trick: working downwards, one gathers up white material behind something dark; the reabsorption of ectoplasm can be faked the same way. At the LSA sessions in 1931, Eve Brackenbury supposed that Helen's face had been shrunk using a dark surround, and that 'the appearance of shortening might easily be produced if the lower end was gradually covered by the black buckram gloves'. By 1944 these were well-established deceits. Elijah Fowler, the naval surgeon, told how plump spirits appeared when the curtains were open, slimmer ones when closed. Stanley Worth remembered heavy thumping as the spirit retreated and also heard cloth rustling – a disturbance Mrs Homer attributed to 'psychic winds'.

After the war, Donald West obtained Harry Price's photo of the 'Mr Punch' mannequin – dubbed 'the old witch concoction' – to illustrate an article he was writing. Unlike Price's stereograms, supposed West, the gargoyle face would persuade anyone that this was just daft puppetry; likewise a visible nail attaching the rag person to the door. Many mediums were compromised by photography. Frú Lára Ágústsdóttir was Iceland's Helen Duncan. Well built, with dark wavy hair, obstreperous and hysterical, she was dogged by poor health yet produced remarkable materializations, such as a Spanish woman who spoke the language like a native. Arriving in England in the summer of 1937,

Ágústsdóttir received national press attention, but the reports were damning. A photograph showed a girl dressed as a nun attached to the comatose medium by a cloth umbilicus. Furthermore, in the IIPR archives there are envelopes containing flakes of pink paint found in Ágústsdóttir's cabinet, allegedly from a papier-mâché mask. Cloth, too, was manipulated in light and shadow then drawn back up under her skirt. Ironically, Margaret Vivian, the Bournemouth doctor, believed Ágústsdóttir to be genuine because 'nobody could fake that dreadful smell which clung to me till the next day . . . We used to get the same smell with Mrs Duncan when her results were genuine.'

Rose Cole, a witness at Helen Duncan's trial, described the odour emanating from the materialized form of her friend Mrs Allen: 'It was just like death and made me feel terrible. I had to stand back because I could not stand the smell. I was told it was ectoplasm smell.' She was followed in the witness box by Bertha Alabaster, who, when asked whether the ectoplasm smelled of vomit, said it was more like what Mrs Cole had said: the smell of death. Perceptions varied. In 1931, Harry Price had described the odour as 'reminiscent of a bit of ripe gorgonzola'. Meanwhile, at the LSA, Henry Duncan had likened it to old cloth, whereas a sitter called it 'strong and objectionable'. Some thought Helen's ectoplasm had an earthy smell, others that it smelled like urine, and one, more courageously, that it had a whiff of semen.

For those who disputed that ectoplasm was what Spiritualists said it was – a plastic sublimate of exteriorized spiritual energy – there was only one explanation: lightweight cloth, tightly packed, was concealed in the body. And so, in 1944 the regurgitation controversy reignited. Price's friend C. E. M. Joad caused outrage by speculating in the *Sunday Dispatch* that physical mediums had second stomachs like cows. Maurice Barbanell reminded Joad that 'we have not yet discovered *everything* about nature', while others referred to the X-rays taken in 1930 and the report certifying that Helen's stomach and oesophagus were normal. The campaigning journalist Hannen Swaffer, a defence witness in 1944, had copies of both the photos and the report with him at the Old Bailey, but was forbidden by the judge to produce them. He vented his frustration in a ditty, which he passed with his regards to Maurice Barbanell:

> I'd swallow until I were drunken,
> But not the bunk on Helen Duncan.
> (If I were swallowing, more and more,
> Things spiritous or beery,
> I'd swallow anything before
> The Price regurgitation theory.)

Spiritualists claimed that doctors in Dundee had laughed at the idea that Mrs Duncan was a regurgitator, especially because it took them half an hour to fit the tube of a pump into her stomach after she swallowed something poisonous (possibly Eusol, as she did in hospital in London). Helen was also sick of being asked if she was a regurgitator – on one occasion in Belfast literally, when she stuck her fingers down her throat at the request of a sceptical sitter and vomited spectacularly.

Price had long been interested in stage swallowing, and all types of tricks and legerdemain. The nucleus of his library was his childhood copy of Angelo Lewis's *Modern Magic* (1876), from which he progressed to own such desirable volumes as his first edition of Scot's *Discoverie of Witchcraft*, the first English book with an illustrated chapter on conjuring. Also in his collection was Peedle and Cozbie's *The Fallacie of the Great Water-Drinker Discovered* (1650), which told of a Frenchman brought to England to work out how he regurgitated two different colours of water. Across pre-modern Europe showmen ate and vomited stones; a sideshow in the Strand in 1788 charged spectators 2s 6d and invited them to bring their own stones. Others swallowed frogs and snakes, glass and nails – feats still being performed in the twentieth century.

In Prague, Price saw a fob watch being swallowed. Houdini saw the glow of an electric light through a man's chest. In May 1944, the swallower Arthur Haylock blocked London traffic with a crowd that had gathered to see him eat razor blades. The SPR thought it should investigate such acts, in Mollie Goldney's words, 'for occasions of the Duncan variety', and so hired Haylock to watch him eat a light bulb, a gramophone record and a bunch of flowers. But, as Price had suggested, stage swallowers like Haylock did not regurgitate, nor could they. In 1935, David Fraser-Harris, the Scottish physiologist who had reported on Helen Duncan at the NLPR, performed an experiment where a stage swallower named Victor Dane regurgitated seven feet of muslin, which came up 'very wet, thick and cord-like'. Fraser-Harris argued that an oesophageal diverticulum – a secondary stomach or pouch – might allow separation of fabric and food and would be hard to detect. Not that physical abnormality was necessary for regurgitation if a medium was well-practised, patient and able to control the gag reflex. An observer likened Margery's ectoplasm to 'lace made of heavy white cord', cool, sticky and malodorous. Once she could also be heard struggling to swallow this vile matter, causing her cruel spirit-guide 'Walter' to joke: 'Put some salt on it, it will go down better.'

Helen Duncan and Mina Crandon were both prone to nosebleeds during seances. Thin material hidden in the nasal cavities was the preferred theory of William Brown, the Harley Street doctor who dismissed Helen Duncan's phenomena as 'clever prestidigitation'. William McDougall first favoured the oesophageal diverticulum idea, then concurred with Dr Brown. Behind this physical explanation lay a psychiatric one. In 1895, Freud had approved nasal surgery on a female patient after cocaine failed to cure her neurosis. When a length of gauze was accidentally left up the woman's nose she haemorrhaged, which Freud put down to hysterical attention-seeking, akin to the conduct of diabolically inspired witches of old, and which in turn made him sympathize with 'the harsh therapy' of witch-hunting judges.

Dr Crandon forbade examination of his wife's digestive tract not only because it 'would be a painful inconvenience' but because the Harvard investigators had decided that her ectoplasmic articles 'must have been stored away internally'. Houdini underlined this judgement five times in the *Atlantic Monthly* report, adding: 'Yes sir'. Yet, as Houdini knew, swallowing was not the only means of concealment (he had hidden tools on his body to escape from dozens of prison cells). Eric Dingwall's suspicions were confirmed by the gynaecologist Florence Willey, wife of SPR founder Sir William Barrett, who told Dingwall in 1925 that 'it would be quite possible to pack a considerable portion of such substance into the vagina . . . By muscular contraction (which however I should think would be obvious) the substance might be wholly or partially expelled.' At a test seance in 1929, Dr Willey found Mina Crandon's vagina and cervix to be abnormally soft for a woman who had not recently given birth; she was also bleeding. The medium said she was menstruating – but Dr Willey had her doubts, owing to the diamond-shaped stain in the medium's underwear that suggested 'something laterally distending the vagina'.

When Detective Inspector Ford hinted that Helen Duncan's sheet may have been secreted thus, he was using information already known to the Portsmouth police. Early in March 1944, Chief Constable Arthur West received a letter from Varina Taylor of Southport, a town in Lancashire. She had helped the medium undress before a seance and thought that 'under the tremendous folds of flesh, or in the vagina, Mrs Duncan could easily conceal the amount of diaphanous drapery used for her various ghostly visitors'. However, Mrs Taylor continued, 'out of decency' no one looked too closely – but 'if a lady doctor were to examine her in these parts (lower abdomen) I am sure they would find room for concealments of this nature'. Back in 1932 a doctor told Esson Maule that when she treated Mrs Duncan for cystitis she found her 'urethra was so stretched with the introduction of abnormal and unnatural foreign bodies, that its natural elasticity was gone, causing frequency of micturition, which her age does not justify'.

Helen Duncan often ate a large meal before a seance, which pressed on her bladder, exacerbating her incontinence – hence the splashing heard from inside the cabinet. This also proved that she and Albert were one and the same. Urine taken from a puddle left where he had been standing during a seance was found to contain uterine blood: 'catamenial discharge in its primary degree'. Miss Maule informed Price that Helen possessed 'enormous depth of pelvis', adding that 'pelvic concealment of articles is one of the commonest acts of insane females, especially if there is any taint of immorality in them. One, two and three large bath towels, secreted in the pelvis, is of common occurrence in any Female Lunatic Asylum.' Consider, too, apported objects: Helen's cucumber; Hylda Lewis's thorn-less roses; Eusapia Palladino's dead rat; Elizabeth Hope's rubber plant; Jack Webber's brass flamingo . . .

Little of Helen Duncan's ectoplasm survives. A small amount, mounted and framed by Harry Price, hangs in the University of London Library, and a square of gauze in an envelope labelled 'Ectoplasm' was stored at the College of Psychic Studies until it was stolen in 1999. The slides made by Montagu Scott in 1931 might be there in a cupboard full of notebooks, portraits of luminaries and luminous trum-pets long silent. But what about a piece big enough to be wrapped around the body? The absence of such a sheet was of course controversial in 1944. Yet if sitters at the Master's Temple had been searched and the cloth still not found it would have embarrassed the police, and in any case the Witchcraft Act made tangible evidence superfluous.

Ford, Worth and Cross all suspected the woman with the sling. But there was another theory. In 1946, Denys Parsons (ejected from the Old Bailey for giving his seat to Mollie Goldney) was put in touch with James Robinson, in 1944 a naval instructor at Portsmouth. Two of his fellow instructors, interested in the paranormal, had sat next to each other at the fateful seance on 19 January: one was called Jacobs, the other Peter Pickett, the Spiritualist sailor from Sevenoaks whose mother had supposedly manifested. This is what Robinson was told:

> Jacobs and his friend were sitting at the front of the audience, and were becoming more and more convinced that the show was a lot of tripe, when, suddenly, there was a disturbance, and Jacobs made a grab at the 'ghost', and contacted with a fistful of cheesecloth, which he immediately stuffed into his great-coat . . . They both made a hasty exit after this and returned to barracks.

Apparently, the piece of cheesecloth, eight feet square, was subsequently put to use as a hammock! Parsons passed the story on to Donald West, the SPR's Research Officer, who traced Jacobs via Henry Elam. At an interview in March 1948, Jacobs laughed at Robinson's account, suggesting that Pickett may have concocted it because he 'was always being teased about his interest in spooks'. And where was Peter Pickett? 'Discharged dead' in 1945 and lying in Naples War Cemetery.* The SPR closed the case.

Before the war, however, another sheet had been seized. On 2 April 1939 a seance was held by Helen Duncan at Cefn Coed in the Welsh valleys, where she was first strip-searched, but without an internal examination. Sitters noticed the medium was out of her chair when she was meant to be in a trance, and a Mr A. J. Miles was unconvinced by a manifestation of his brother as it lacked a distinctive deformity. Deciding enough was enough, Miles and another sitter grappled with the combative Helen, who punched Miles in the eye to keep hold of the cloth – but in vain. Five witnesses signed a statement. A few days later Miles wrote to Harry Price and by May both cloth and statement were in his possession. Price asked Miles about the faint bloodstains, which he hoped to have analysed. Three days after the outbreak of war, Miles obliged with a full account:

> The material was draped over her. That was the reason for my pulling it from her. I could see quite plainly that it was cloth when I was examining the supposed spirit form . . . the cloth was damp but I am not sure whether the stains were fresh. I did not examine it owing to the terrible odour that was issuing from it and the smell

* The inscription on Pickett's headstone reads: 'God links the broken chain as one by one we meet again' – a post-mortem message from his sister and mother.

of it quickly suggested where it had been concealed. I suggest that it was concealed within the lower portion of her body. Although it seems increditable [*sic*] the fact remains that it is possible and the odour says that it is definitely so.

Price was satisfied, as would be the Portsmouth police, for it was Miles's correspondence that Price lent to Detective Inspector Ford in 1944. It is unknown whether anyone considered submitting the cloth as supporting evidence. A photograph from the early 1950s shows Donald West examining the SPR's cabinet of curiosities, including plaster casts of the Polish medium Franek Kluski's spirit hands and a photographic enlargement of one of Margery's spirit thumbprints.* Among other strange items is a length of fabric described as: 'A piece of white drapery, supposed to be ectoplasm, captured from a fraudulent materialising medium.' The old archive handlist confirms its provenance as 'Duncan Mrs Helen Cloth (alleged Ectoplasm)'.

It can be found today in the Manuscripts Room of Cambridge University Library. Inside a cardboard box is a length of cheap white satin, or perhaps cotton silk, measuring over three-and-a-half metres, faintly stained at intervals. These marks, a note by Mrs Goldney suggests, were caused by the cloth being folded and secreted in the vagina where blood seeped in. Single stitches of fine twine can be seen

---

* In 1932, Margery was caught out after a thumbprint left in a piece of dental wax after a seance was found to belong not to her spirit guide 'Walter' but to her dentist – who else?

about a quarter of the way in from each side, suggesting how the cloth might have been invisibly retrieved and perhaps that it was suspended to create a ghost effect. Released at head height, it traps the air, billowing out as it floats to the ground with a tantalizing shimmer.

So the best mediums owed their success to skill and experience but also to the fact that they worked with audiences of true believers, not merely people willing to suspend their disbelief, as in the theatre. Against such strength of conviction, the debunkers' campaigns were futile: Spiritualists had little to fear from demystification. Harry Price was dumbfounded when Mrs Duncan received her SNU diploma after the Edinburgh conviction in 1933, as was Houdini when he demonstrated how to fake Kluski's hand casts only to have an audience member recognize the finger of a girl lost on the *Titanic*. Sir Arthur Conan Doyle was adamant that Houdini was guided by spiritual forces that let him turn his bones to ectoplasm, and, in a perfect illustration of how finely balanced such beliefs could be, confidently proclaimed his friend not only the greatest medium-baiter but also the greatest physical medium.

Many of Helen Duncan's sitters acknowledged that she may have been fraudulent *sometimes*, while insisting this was not what *they* experienced, which could only have been genuine. Their position was reinforced by investigators who had no time for teacup-rattling in the dark but still felt that well-documented exposures didn't necessarily invalidate every paranormal event. Sweeping judgements of that sort would have betrayed the guiding spirit of the SPR. Whether or not one agrees, the fact remains that it's difficult to explain fully the defence testimonies from 1944 and why Mrs Duncan's crude conjuring tricks apparently convinced so many.

Let's suppose some of the materializations were real spirits. By the 1950s, some 20,000 people had seen her perform, some of them interviewed for this book. They seemed perfectly rational describing Spiritualism as a real world shored up by proof not faith and Helen Duncan's seances as absolutely genuine. Spiritualist enthusiasm is impressive without necessarily being infectious. The eighteenth-century empiricist David Hume once said that if a man tells you he has seen a corpse restored to life, both the fact and the man's belief should be treated as phenomena before we decide which is most likely to be true. Perhaps in the end, however, feelings and beliefs cannot be true or untrue: they simply are – and they define us. When the last physiological, chemical and genetic puzzle in the body is solved, the emotions will continue to mystify and most of the world will still find meaning and solace in religion – what Hume termed 'the usual propensity of mankind towards the marvellous'.

This propensity exists because our senses distort data. That the same event could appear different between observers had been noted with respect to materialization before Helen Duncan was born. For his research into the Duncan mediumship, Donald West's mentor Mollie Goldney directed him to a statement made in 1887 by Professor Horace Furness, who drew on a fund of $60,000 that had been bequeathed to the University of Pennsylvania to prove the truth of Spiritualism. Furness was staggered by what he found, but not as the donor had intended:

A woman, a visitor, led from the Cabinet to me a Materialized Spirit, whom she introduced to me as 'her daughter, her dear darling daughter', while nothing could be clearer to me than the features of the medium in every line and lineament. Again and again, men have led round the circle the Materialized Spirits of their wives, and introduced them to each visitor in turn; fathers have taken round their daughters, and I have seen widows sob in the arms of their dead husbands.

The battle for the truth was not just a contest between the men of reason and the rest: they argued with each other and with themselves. Bewitched by the spirit 'Katie King', Sir William Crookes described 'an antagonism in my mind between *reason*, which pronounces it to be scientifically impossible, and the consciousness that my senses ... are not lying witnesses when they testify against my preconceptions'. Charles Richet had harsh words for his fellow Nobel Prize-winner: 'How could I suppose that the savant who has discovered thallium and the radiometer, and foreshadowed the Roentgen rays, could commit himself to be duped for years by tricks which a child could have exposed?' But, of course, Richet himself was duped in the end.

Experiments proved that testimony was made from an unstable compound of belief, environment, vision and memory. Witnesses frequently saw things that never happened and missed things which did. In 1937 a Yorkshire headmaster, concerned that friends had 'come under the influence of Mrs Helen Duncan', was amazed by an observation experiment conducted on his pupils to test a theory that she owed her success to false perception. And in the dark, how much greater the error. In 1931, SPR member Theodore Besterman, inspired by tests from the 1880s, simulated seances using red light where sitters swore they saw stationary objects move, misjudged the passage of time and failed to describe accurately a scene exposed by a camera flash. Commenting on a draft of Donald West's article in 1946, the Cambridge psychologist Robert Thouless explained how people adapt differently to low light intensity, adding, with reference to materialization, 'the relative insensibility of the fovea in semi-darkness makes testimony as to recognition peculiarly uncertain'.

Fatigue played a part. Professor Joad told of seances where the same record was played repeatedly – 'the taste of the spirits is deplorable' – and echoed the investigator who, in 1941, said: 'At the end of a long sitting in semi-darkness, when you are tired, if something appears suddenly, nothing is harder than to say exactly what happened.' Donald West also took advice from Denys Parsons, who in June 1944 had published in the arts magazine *Horizon* an article entitled 'Testimony and Truth' which argued that seeing really was believing, even if belief and proof were different. C. E. Bechhofer Roberts, a barrister and editor of *The Trial of Mrs Duncan*, also counselled the young researcher. Himself the author of a sceptical work on Spiritualism, Bechhofer

Roberts thought that Charles Loseby's defence witnesses 'were trying to tell the truth but were incapable of doing so'. In a *Sunday Times* review of Bechhofer Roberts's book the critic Desmond MacCarthy recalled a seance where a spirit 'was so obviously a fake that I was amazed that others present did not notice it, but, on the contrary, declared afterwards that the seance had been most unusually impressive'. MacCarthy concluded that the hopes and sorrows of such people blinded them to fraud. Brains, it seemed, did not always reliably perceive events but instead predicted them according to need and belief, conjuring up what Ibsen called the 'life-lie' – a fictional confection of meanings that enables human beings to make sense of the world.

Theodore Besterman had not been shy of the word 'hallucination', but his work predated an understanding of how this could be caused by bereavement. Manifestations of deceased partners are common. In 1998 a study of widows and widowers in Sweden and Japan found that hallucinations were experienced by 82 per cent and 90 per cent respectively, and acknowledged that the experience is under-reported in cultures where percipients fear stigmatization; among Hopi Native Americans it is a normal part of death. Grief is an engine of desires that, Joad explained, 'make us extremely receptive to so-called evidence which, if our attitude was purely dispassionate, we should not consider for a moment'. Sitters at materialization seances chose to reserve judgement rather than go home disillusioned. Perceived truth depended on expectation that the dead would come. The vital signs of living mediums, furthermore, confirmed more than they refuted. When the spirit guide 'Bien Boa' turned Richet's barium oxide solution cloudy in 1905 (proving that he exhaled carbon dioxide), everyone applauded. Mrs Hannah Ross, a Bostonian medium of the 1880s, had only to paint a face on a breast and poke it through the cabinet for bereaved mothers to rave about the soft warm skin of materialized babies. Mrs Ross narrowly escaped being lynched after a newspaper exposed her, but the experience of seance reunions was sufficiently intense that neither debunking nor rational explanation ever had much impact.

The history of this predates even the table-rapping Fox sisters in the 1840s. In Cambridge University Library there is a pocket-sized calf-bound volume containing Dr John Ferriar's *Essay Towards a Theory of Apparitions* from 1813. In it, Ferriar criticizes John Beaumont's *Historical, Physiological and Theological Treatise of Spirits, Apparitions, Witchcrafts and Other Magical Practices* from a century earlier, a work in the conservative tradition of Joseph Glanvill, who feared that abolishing spirits would undermine the kingdom of heaven. Yet Beaumont wavered more than Ferriar made out: 'If you ask me, whether I think these Apparitions to be Spirits or only an effect of Melancholy,' he wrote, 'I can only say . . . God knows, I know not, but they appear'd to me Real.' And Ferriar upheld the doctrine of providence, even the idea that ghosts be heavenly messengers. But it is an annotation at the end of the volume that is most revealing about the thread of popular thinking running through the last four hundred years. A reader, probably in the interwar period, wrote in pencil: 'This is all very well, but when one has seen and conversed with a spirit it doesn't exactly satisfy one that it was all bosh! All [that is] proved here is that one may see spectral illusions, which was never doubted.'

Clearly this reader had a story; perhaps it was about Helen Duncan. But stories can be piled up and up and still the question of genuine-versus-fraud remains unresolved. Mrs Duncan's trickery was plain as day – yet belief in her endured. Not all Spiritualists judged her to be on the level and most who did accepted that she cheated from time to time – the idea of 'mixed phenomena'. After seeing Mrs Duncan perform in London in 1942, a Spiritualist wrote to the DPP, saying: 'To my mind the features of every "spirit" that appeared were precisely the same, viz. the thick lips and rather coarse features of Mrs Duncan enshrouded in a muslin veil', yet added: 'I do not contend that Mrs Duncan has not got the power which she professes to possess, but I *do* say that occasionally she appears to lose that power (possibly through overwork) and then stoops to fraud rather than return the entrance money which has been charged.'

It was also suggested that puckish *spirits* produced bogus evidence. Defence witness Dr John Winning was unfazed by the idea that Mrs Duncan used props, believing that 'the controls might be obliged to make use of "earthly" materials'. And B. Abdy Collins wondered 'whether Albert does not apport rubber gloves and cheesecloth and masks on some occasions as a leg-pull for the audience'. Finally, as Margaret Vivian argued, 'If the sitters are strongly persuaded in favour of the fraud theory they will get manifestations that have every appearance of trickery.' Montague Rust agreed and explained the LSA fiasco in 1931 thus: 'One sitter with a hostile critical mind is quite enough to put everything wrong, and this is the element which the London people forget.'

Even if mediumship is ultimately in the eye of the beholder, we might also consider the mind of the medium. What was going on in Helen Duncan's head? Was she a cool, calculating impostor? Or was her mental state incompatible with monstrous deceit? In 1938, Dr Nandor Fodor, ejected from the IIPR for his avant-garde theories, was simultaneously fighting Spiritualists for their miracle-mongering and psychical researchers for their narrow-mindedness. In the autumn of that year, however, he received reassurance from Sigmund Freud, a corresponding SPR member, who had read the manuscript of his book: 'Your turning away from interest in whether the observed phenomena were genuine or fraudulent, your turning toward the psychological study of the medium and the uncovering of her previous history, seem to be the important steps which will lead to the elucidation of the phenomena under investigation.' Perhaps, then, there is more to Helen Duncan than meets the historical eye. Having explained everything in 1931, Harry Price was still perplexed that she had come to London to carry out such a bare-faced fraud, and asked: 'Why did the medium dare to pirouette among us, in a bright light, with a teleplasmic tail trailing round our feet?' Just who the hell did the Duncans think they were?

Henry Duncan's role is yet another grey area. Many mediums had accomplices: Marthe Béraud (later Eva Carrière) and the Arab servant; the confederate whom Price alleged that Rudi Schneider used; even D. D. Home's secret monkey. Some scams were elaborate: in 1930 a trapdoor and remotely operated lights and bells were discovered in premises recently vacated by the British College of Psychic Science. But for a travelling medium like Helen, a companion was essential, and for much of her career this was Henry, who was variously described as booking agent, minder, business manager – even pimp. Almost certainly, he pressured his wife to perform and when things got rough he dematerialized faster than Albert in a police raid. Bechhofer Roberts took Henry's acceptance of the regurgitation theory in 1931 to be his way of admitting that the game was up without implicating himself – but there was more to it than that. A decade of experience had taught Henry that many mediums had childlike dispositions, simple and shy yet frantic to satisfy the expectations of others. Eva Carrière, he said, was a case in point. To that end, he told the NLPR Council, fraud might be motivated subconsciously: he believed Helen to be genuine but also that she possessed an 'automatism of the will' that enabled her to swallow cheesecloth. The NLPR demurred, and yet the theory may have held a grain of truth. The following day, Henry informed the LSA that his wife:

was in the habit of losing her will (entering an altered state of consciousness) for a time about three hours before the sitting and . . . that in a state of unconsciousness resembling hypnosis, Mrs Duncan secreted things in or about her person and that she could retain these things in her stomach and eat and digest food.

Henry may have had a hand in this, for he was adept at hypnotism – a skill he later used to relax his daughter Gena when she was in labour. Victorian SPR pioneer Frederic Myers had noticed how hypnotism could cause automatism in suggestible subjects, an idea popularized in George du Maurier's novel *Trilby* (1894) where a girl is made to sing by the hypnotist Svengali to the extent that, du Maurier suggested, she was not just asleep but ceased to exist. The story was adapted as a well-received feature film in 1931, during the London seances, and 'Svengali' entered the English language.

Anyone who has witnessed stage hypnosis will understand how the effect could be seen as spiritual control. Reading about Margery in the *Atlantic Monthly* in 1925, Houdini was interested in Hudson Hoagland's views about mediumship and hypnotic trance: 'A narrowing of consciousness is obtained by darkness or by concentrating on some simple sensory stimulus ... the subject is urged to render his mind passive. He is then lulled to sleep by the operator ... with the parting suggestion to do what he is told. In a trance, the subject is apparently bereft of a will of his own.'

Acting as guide, the accomplice – Dr Crandon, say, or Henry Duncan – was able not only to manipulate the medium, but could call on sitters to focus their energies to help produce evidence of the truths they had paid to see. But it was possible that even he was seduced by the alternative reality of his own drama. The theoretical psychologist Nicholas Humphrey once suggested that Jesus may have been a conjuror who came to believe in his own powers because of how others responded to his tricks, a virtuous circle where faith and action were self-confirming. Today, psychoanalysts identify similar behaviour in relationships, pointing to 'congruent fantasies' and 'complementary fantasies' where couples act out their desires. The LSA's acceptance of this possibility is indicated in a 1931 letter from the Secretary, Mercy Phillimore, to the SPR Research Officer, which referred to their proof 'that conscious deception had been practised by the Duncans'. Before she sent it, Miss Phillimore decided to be more circumspect, changing 'conscious' to 'conscious or subconscious'.

Mediumship wove spells of mutual fascination between husbands and wives who otherwise may have had little in common. Some mediums could no more renounce their gift (or confess to being frauds) than they could admit their marriages were a sham. The wife of the poet W. B. Yeats scribbled automatic messages to distract her spiritualistic husband from his revolutionary muse, Maud Gonne, and so became, in his words, 'a perfect wife, kind, wise and unselfish'; her revelations helped to inspire Yeats's *A Vision*, published in 1925. In the 1930s, Spiritualism formed a bond of sexual intimacy between Kathleen Goligher and her husband, and Mollie Goldney's exposure of Agnes Abbott revealed that she resorted to fraud because her husband had forced her to perform mediumship even after her powers had waned. How could she disappoint him and risk losing his attentions? What had Mina Stinson, a poor divorcee from Toronto, to offer doughty Harvard physician Dr Crandon except her transformation into the

world-famous 'Margery'? In William McDougall's opinion: nothing, and once Crandon appeared to tire of her,
she invented the mediumship 'with the hope of regaining
his confidence and affection'. Privately, Hudson Hoagland
opined that:

> Dr Crandon is a man who has never learned to play. He
> takes everything very seriously. Mrs Crandon took up
> Spiritualism as a violent hobby and Mrs Crandon played
> it for all it was worth. I think that there may have been
> elements of hysteria that made her believe her own
> phenomena at those early stages but this is relatively
> unimportant. It was all good fun for her anyway and she
> found that her husband was quite fascinated. They both
> found themselves at the center of attention.

Harvard colleagues agreed that Crandon could be both
an accomplice in deception *and* a sincere ambassador for
his wife's mediumship, and that phenomena were 'the
product of an autonomism built up by direct and auto
suggestion in a way of which Dr and Mrs Crandon were
unconscious'. The explanation indicted the mediumship
while partially excusing the estimable Boston socialites
themselves.

Many of the compliments paid to Helen Duncan were
back-handed. To her more cultivated supporters in 1944
she was 'a simple, quaintly gifted, but honest unlettered
woman'; 'not a woman of any great intellectual attain-
ments, but she is a medium'. Charles Loseby remembered
her as 'a humble and ignorant woman with certain physical

attributes in respect of which she suggested no special virtue in herself'. Her childhood may hold the key, insofar as she resembled what the SPR's Frank Podmore termed 'a child of larger growth', displaying the same dissociative, regressive tendencies he had seen in entranced mediums. She was Madame Victoria Duncan, the aggressive hysteric, swearing and blaspheming, swinging chairs and punches at her adversaries; then she was Nellie MacFarlane, the passive child whose dumb compliance during intimate examinations surprised the doctors hired by Harry Price. They noticed an infantile dreaminess about her, a tendency to slip easily into trances from which they roused her by speaking loudly and directly into her face.

Many direct-voice mediums received messages from children or were controlled by them. Mrs Osborne Leonard's juvenile control 'Feda', it was argued, was a classic Jungian complementary character, a dramatic projection of the medium's subconscious self in trance. Freud's parental archetypes and childhood sexual conflicts are plausible seeds of a career in trance mediumship: the austere Eleanor Sidgwick, with her fondness for pure mathematics and the colour grey, always found favour with the childish secondary personalities of mediums who saw in her a strict mother who could be gentle and kind, even though she never had children of her own. Nicholas Humphrey offers an even more tantalizing proposition: young children witness daily the miraculous satisfaction of their needs and must grow out of thinking they are magicians; even sulky adolescents are prone to the fantasy that they are specially gifted and misunderstood by the world. These fixations, at once introverted *and* extroverted, selfish *and* generous, do come close to defining Helen Duncan's personality. By the time she was old enough to make prophecies and perform small miracles, her self-awareness had been shaped by the reactions of her peers, and even when these were adverse the sense of being special was intoxicating, an effect visible in the actions of her mystical daughter Gena and especially every time her sister Lilian told her to shut up. To inspire awe or fear (perhaps both) is to excite the emotions of others, and that can be addictive.

Afraid of dark enclosed spaces, Helen became hysterical if the cabinet curtains closed before she was ready or if the lights went down too soon. She left a room if there was someone present she instinctively disliked. Before seances she muttered fears that Albert would let her down; afterwards, in despair, that the sitters had looked suspicious or disappointed when she had given them everything she could. Her histrionic displays at the Old Bailey persuaded a *News of the World* reporter that 'she is unbalanced, and seems always to be under the compulsion of extreme reactions'. Sometimes, Helen – the ingénue banished from her family home with an unborn child – would assume the character of a lost orphan whose sentimental refrain, 'I don't know where my mammy is', betrayed the darker, deeper and sadder origins of her mediumship.

Contemporary attitudes to women mattered too. Interwar Britain remained a stratified society where the ruling class's indifference to the lower orders met the condescension of liberal elitists. But at least most men, however poor, got to be kings in their own households, backed by the law. Women may have been allowed to vote, smoke and show their knees in public, but they had not slipped the leash: it had just been lengthened. Most women were not suffragettes; they accepted petty inequalities and indignities because they knew no other way, their frustrations internalized and exteriorized in mental illness and religious fanaticism. As a link between the seventeenth and twentieth centuries, the legal label of 'witch' attached to Helen Duncan is superficial compared to how witchcraft and mediumship were sustained by engrained male fantasies of female power. At seances, men paid women to hear what they – or the spirits – had to say. The sort of woman cursed in polite company was, in a trance, congratulated: the chief spirit control of the prim Mrs Piper was a foul-mouthed French doctor. Profanity, blasphemy, exhibitionism – symbolic rebellions against every social restriction – had once been features of the diabolic possession of female adolescents. In England even minor seventeenth-century cases had doctors and clerics from Oxford and London rushing to study the afflicted victims. These girls were exposed as frauds, but only after they had been taken seriously by many people, especially the socially important middle-aged men who managed the subordination of young women.

The hysteria of possession was not necessarily a conscious bid for attention, but rather, predominantly, a symptom of a complex predicament. 'When a child has grown up to be a woman,' Freud suggested, 'she may find all the demands she used to make in her childhood countered owing to her marriage with an inconsiderate husband.' Illness, real or imagined, allowed her to with-draw her obedience and make demands of her own. And many mediums were sickly. Helen Duncan's frequent cuts, sores and burns (almost invariably caused by cigarettes) may have been caused by low self-esteem, even self-loathing, likewise her predilection for swallowing rubbish: matchsticks, cigarette ends and carpet tacks were found in her abdomen during an operation. But these effects still elicited sympathy, and the fact that she really was a sick woman allowed her supporters to magnify the scale of her sacrifice. At this time childbirth was regarded as a form of illness and gave a stage to a certain kind of woman in that it was one vital thing men could not do. In the 1720s, Mary Toft of Godalming simulated delivery of a litter of rabbits by storing them in her uterus – but not before doctors had lent credence to the phenomenon. Even before that, physi-cians had associated the symptoms of possession with gynaecological disorders, hence the term 'hysteria' (wan-dering womb). The parallels to physical mediumship three centuries later are obvious. Montague Rust reported seeing ectoplasm streaming from Helen Duncan's every orifice, a story that J. B. McIndoe embellished into a *tableau vivant* of luxuriant fecundity:

She stood there, in trance, white material of some sort streaming apparently from her eyes, her ears, her nose and her mouth. It seemed a white jelly-like substance right up to the orifices from which it seemed to be flowing. But even more weird and fascinating was the spectacle of a liquid spurting from the nipples of her breasts, apparently transparent as it left them, then becoming white as it fell, condensing into threads which somehow seemed to merge into some sort of fabric which draped the lower part of her body and hung like a kilt down to her knees.

Not content with being a prolific mother, in Helen's body grew the stuff of life for the dead to be reborn. And many people, she found, thanked her for it.

Whenever ectoplasm shaped itself into the dead, 'multiple personality disorder' may have been to blame. In modern psychiatry the condition is better termed 'dissociative identity disorder', but after the First World War it was used to describe abnormal behaviour from the suspended consciousness of shell-shocked soldiers to phobias and obsessions, including the spiritual dramatis personae of the seance room. The famous study of a submissive American student who under hypnosis became demonstrative paved the way. In July 1931, Robert Fielding-Ould, Chairman of the London Psychical Laboratory Committee, said of Helen Duncan that 'her total personality was accustomed to be disintegrated under her husband's hypnotic influence and the fraudulent practices that have been witnessed are due in some measure to her secondary and less responsible personality'. In his presidential address to the SPR in 1939, Professor H. H. Price noted widespread acceptance of the idea, which had 'thrown great light on some of the most obscure phenomena of the human mind'. By 1944 it was a concept even mass-circulation newspapers used to explain Mrs Duncan's mediumship, although for his article Donald West was less forgiving: 'A more likely explanation would seem to be that her personality is subject to some degree of dissociation at all times, but that at her seances it is so extreme that her whole character may change from that of an ordinary, dull, rather clumsy woman, to a very deft and resourceful cheat.'

'Albert', the cultured, confident gentleman speaking in the BBC's accent of authority, made for an ideal alter ego to range against a manipulative and overbearing Henry. Helen's respectable sitters were mocked and mimicked by Albert, and in 1931 he never missed a chance to rebuke Henry, addressing him as 'Duncan', meeting him as an equal in debate and slipping into the vernacular when he told him to go and lose himself. But, like Walter, Albert was also strict with the medium, making asides to her in the darkness when she was supposed to be in a trance. One thing he couldn't stand (apart from Henry) was coughing, from Helen or anyone. At a Glasgow seance in the 1940s, hearing a cough from within the cabinet, Albert said sharply: 'Stop that!', then a few moments later, so quietly hardly anybody heard, whispered: *'Stop smoking.'*

In the mid-1980s, Manfred Cassirer, an SPR Council member interested in Helen Duncan's mediumship, concluded that the balance of fraud and genuineness was 'a problem of such complexity that as yet no conclusive solution can even be imagined'. The quest for definitive answers and squared circles presupposes the existence of a consensual definition of reality inappropriate to the realms of fantasy, belief and spirit communication. Fictions can be as revealing as verifiably true stories. When in

1946 Donald West declared that 'the truth is that Mrs Duncan is an unsolved riddle', he meant the kind of scientific truth that excluded imagined alternative interpretations of the universe. Widening that definition would leave no riddle to be solved. But there were many men and women who did allow for imagined alternative interpretations and, as such, were able in some measure to take the medium Helen Duncan at face value. And these believers were not all simple-minded fools, Freudian basket cases, eccentric scientists or aristocratic dabblers, but rather some of the most publicly influential and politically powerful people in early twentieth-century Britain.

8. Many Mansions:
Public Life and Prominent Men

Through books like Estelle Roberts's *Red Cloud Speaks*, the Gosport girl Ena Bügg had converted her friend Bob Brake to Spiritualism, so that when he was posted to an RAF radar station in Preston, Lancashire, it was natural for him to join his local SNU church. One evening in 1941 he was invited to the President's house, where he met a corpulent woman, who sat by the fireside chatting to other guests, drinking tea and smoking. Suddenly she slumped in her chair and spoke in a deep male voice, which people present said was that of 'Albert', her spirit guide. The light was switched off and the company leaned in for the first message. To Bob's surprise it was for him, from a gentleman who had passed with kidney trouble. Although he found the medium coarse, Bob was impressed, especially when the lights went up and she thought she had just nodded off. Bob was to meet Mrs Duncan again, this time at a trumpet seance, which she attended as a sitter and so herself received messages. The medium's guide, 'Joe', a soldier from the trenches, put Helen in touch with the veteran journalist W. T. Stead, who sang an aria from Gounod's *Faust*, and a wireless operator, who tapped out a message in Morse code. Joe translated this as a distress call from the *Titanic*, aboard which Stead had perished with 1,516 others on the night of 14–15 April 1912.

With his straggly beard and mustard suits, Stead had cut a distinctive figure on Fleet Street, where, as editor of the *Pall Mall Gazette*, he perfected the blend of piety and prurience essential to the modern tabloid press. By the 1890s a crusade against vice had been surpassed by a passion for Spiritualism. Though sceptical about materialization – he once sent his daughter Emma on a tour of drapers' shops to find a match for an ectoplasm sample – he abhorred the SPR and believed in spirit photography. He was not long silent after death. Etta Wriedt, a medium Stead would have met with in New York had the *Titanic* not been sunk, was urged by his spirit to go to England. There she held hundreds of seances, which encouraged Emma Stead to develop her own powers. Other mediums received messages from Emma's dead father. One which began, 'I am one of the passengers on the steamer Titanic. A more awful disaster than the wreck may not be conceived', triggered a dispute about Stead's will.

There were similar cases. W. B. Yeats was contacted by a friend's nephew, Sir Hugh Lane, drowned on the ocean liner RMS *Lusitania* in 1915. The spiritual Lane, however, was less concerned with a codicil to his will than with rumours that he had killed himself. Yeats tended to accept such communications as real (hence his wife's automatic writing) and, like Oscar Wilde and George Bernard Shaw, was influenced by theosophy. On a trip to Paris, Yeats saw something like 'a fragment of the Milky Way' in Eva Carrière's lap, and in 1917 attended a seance with Sir William Barrett, which persuaded him that Lane and other spirits were angst-ridden entities who 'should be treated as a doctor would treat a nervous patient'. This, he argued, would be appropriate even if they turned out to be just the secondary personalities of the mediums.

Spiritualism had been a feature of middle-class life in Britain since at least the 1870s when its American founder, Kate Fox, married a well-connected London barrister named Henry Jencken (the wedding table was said to have reared up on two legs). Respectable Spiritualist demand was met at seances in different ways, but by 1914 academic interest in materialization had abated. Henry and Eleanor Sidgwick's attention now focused on 'cross-correspondences': dovetailed messages received by the likes of Margaret Verrall (a classics lecturer at Cambridge), Leonora Piper in Boston and Rudyard Kipling's sister Alice Fleming in India. This research was driven not just by religion but by a desire for knowledge. Renaissance princes had employed magicians to gain superior intelligence and protect themselves against sorcery: in 1607, James I's Witchcraft Act was amended to make it a more effective shield against treason. It was inevitable, then, that the next time spirits were taken seriously in British society, men prominent in public life would show an interest. Transcending any religious or scientific quest, the story is one of power and those who exercised it.

In 1831, Abraham Lincoln is supposed to have visited an elderly African-American woman in New Orleans, who foretold that he would be President and abolish slavery. During the Civil War, when Spiritualism was flourishing in America, Lincoln was devastated when his young son died of a fever and entertained a medium, Nettie Colburn, in the

White House. In 1891, Colburn wrote the book, *Was Abraham Lincoln a Spiritualist?*, to which the answer remains: no – but for a while he did take mediumship seriously. On the other side of the Atlantic, mediums enjoyed the patronage of the crowned heads of Europe. D. D. Home attended foreign courts as far east as St Petersburg, and, in England, Queen Victoria's mourning for Prince Albert was such that, even if she hadn't flirted with Spiritualism, rumours that she did were inevitable. A watch supposedly presented to the medium 'Georgiana Eagle' by Victoria, and later given to Etta Wriedt by W. T. Stead, was a fake – there was a misspelling in the engraving – but it's more plausible that the Queen's conversations with her Highland ghillie John Brown had a Spiritualist tone. (The story that he was her medium, accounts of which were burned, are unproven.) Evidence for the dabbling of Victoria's longest-serving Prime Minister, William Gladstone, is more compelling. Besides his well-documented approval of the SPR, in 1877 he informed a newspaper that no rule forbade Christians exploring Spiritualism, adding the following year: 'I do not share or approve the temper of simple contempt with which so many view the phenomena.' It seems Gladstone did visit at least one medium, the materializer and Fleet Street editor William Eglinton, who, like Home, toured widely in Britain and Europe and was granted an audience with the Tsar.

Not every great man was impressed. In 1874, Darwin walked out of the only seance he ever attended and was bemused that his contemporary Alfred Russel Wallace thought Spiritualism a 'science of vast extent', an eternal basis for religion and philosophy. Darwin's ally T. H. Huxley declared: 'The only good that I can see in a demonstration of the truth of "Spiritualism" is to furnish an additional argument against suicide. Better live a crossing-sweeper than die and be made to talk twaddle by a "medium" hired at a guinea a séance.' Like many conjurors, Dickens was rumoured to be a medium – but this is unlikely given the cold water he too poured on mediumship.

The fact that such men went to seances at all tells us something. By the Edwardian era it became fashionable to hire genteel mediums on the London circuit. In the 1920s an Irish writer named Geraldine Cummins, grieving for her brother killed at Gallipoli, began a fifty-year career as a medium, dividing her time between the West End and her family's farm in Cork. Her most famous works were *The Scripts of Cleophas*, a supplement to the New Testament, and later *Swan on a Black Sea*, communications received from Winifred Coombe Tennant, the first British female delegate to the League of Nations. Miss Cummins had many well-heeled clients. In 1939 she visited the Surrey mansion of Lord Gerald Balfour, where she was received in the drawing room, entered a trance and produced a sheaf of messages. Then everyone sat down to lunch, during which psychical matters were not mentioned.

Prominence in life increased the chances of returning after death. In 1947 the Irish Spiritualist writer Shaw Desmond addressed a meeting in Newcastle upon Tyne, where he claimed that President Roosevelt, who had died two years earlier, had sought political guidance from mediums. Geraldine Cummins maintained that FDR had, through her, predicted US economic imperialism, labour unrest in Britain and the rise of a strong French leader. In nineteenth-century America the most common communicators were Edgar Allan Poe, Thomas Jefferson and Benjamin Franklin, although these spirits bore out SPR investigator Alan Gauld's dictum that 'if the great minds of this world degenerate so much in the next the prospect for lesser fry is bleak indeed'. The mathematical beauty of Christopher Wren's buildings is absent from Arnewood Tower in Hampshire; rendering improbable its Victorian architect's claim that he was possessed by Wren's spirit. In the 1920s Margery knocked off the odd Wren sketch and also uttered Wildean witticisms; the *Occult Review* reported passable examples of the latter, although lines transmitted to her by Shelley 'would have shamed that genius on earth and certainly outraged his memory in the world beyond'. Verses spoken by a midwife who said she was controlled by the epic poet Homer, according to Harry Price 'might have originated in a box of Christmas crackers'.

Silliness was abundant. A spiritual Sir Walter Scott told Mrs Piper that there were monkeys in the sun, and Gladstone, in life unerringly patrician, confirmed his identity with the words: 'Yis, I'm 'im.' After the war, Alan Crossley, a medium who considered Helen Duncan to be absolutely genuine, met a woman who claimed to be von Ribbentrop looking for his army; when Crossley informed her that von Ribbentrop had been Hitler's Foreign Minister, and had no army, she became abusive. He also told of a sitter controlled by the spirit of her pet dog who, to cries of 'God bless you friend!', frolicked around the floor barking. Transfiguration circles witnessed more than just bellicose Zulus and inscrutable Mandarins. In 1935 a medium straining to produce Lincoln got as far as his mouth, whereas Edith Balmer could do the whole face, as well as Byron, Tennyson, Joseph Chamberlain and Cardinal Newman. A materialization of Lord Northcliffe was seen in Mrs Balmer's ear, and, in 1948, Denys Parsons, though sceptical of Mrs Duncan, was impressed by an SPR test at which elastic Edith assumed the appearance of Queen Victoria, Gladstone and Sir Philip Sidney. Houdini often visited in spirit, but after three years his widow Bess began to doubt she would ever hear their private codeword. In 1936, after a disappointing seance to mark the tenth anniversary of his death, she decided to extinguish the light at his shrine.

The personalities destined to work hardest after death were those who had done most for Spiritualism in life. Many eminent scientists felt that Sir Oliver Lodge, intellect and esteem notwithstanding, went too far with his Spiritualism, which he had taken up two decades before his son Raymond died. The confidant of radical thinkers from Joseph Chamberlain to George Bernard Shaw, Lodge was lambasted by Sir James Dewar, inventor of the vacuum flask, and Charles Mercier, a pioneer of forensic psychiatry. Lodge's empirical rigour, they said, was compromised by emotion.

And yet criticism was more in degree than kind: it was impossible to dismiss the chance that new truths about the universe might be found. Freud, essentially a sceptic, accepted that telepathy might be 'a kind of psychic parallel' to the radio waves and wireless telegraphy in which Lodge's expertise lay; nor was it impossible, he supposed, that mind reading was a form of atavistic communication. For a physicist whose life spanned the Battle of Balaclava and the Battle of Britain, a period of huge technological progress, it was understandable that Lodge's interest in telegraphy would be accompanied by an interest in animal magnetism, mesmerism, hypnosis and telepathy, all invisible media through which physical effects were remotely achieved. The dominant metaphor for brain function, which during the Renaissance had been hydraulic and in our own time is digital, was in Lodge's lifetime telegraphic. In 1886, Marie Corelli's novel *A Romance of Two Worlds* made electricity the connecting matter between God and creation; French peasants recoiled from 'evil' telephone lines; and by the 1920s mediums were being likened to radio transmitters pulling messages from the ether.

Like every great scientist, Lodge had a mind open to new possibilities. In 1931, J. Arthur Findlay's *On the Edge of the Etheric* taught that the universe consisted of orders of vibrations of which the highest – the mind – returned to the ether upon death, an idea that appealed to Lodge, who believed that conventional physics could accommodate mediumship. In the 1920s he took this message on a lecture tour of the USA, where he joined the debate over the 'Margery' mediumship. Initially determined to resist Houdini's prejudices, Lodge's hopes that Mina Crandon would produce Raymond's fingerprints faded, and by July 1925 he had rejected even the idea of her 'mixed mediumship'.

The need to protect genuine mediums, though, remained close to his heart. In 1928 he protested to Prime Minister Stanley Baldwin, who politely suggested his request for legal immunity for mediums might be interpreted 'as a request to the Government to connive at the fraudulent exploitation of the public'. In the same year, the Home Office filed news cuttings reporting two suicides of youths who had dabbled in Spiritualism.

Lodge was above all reluctant to allow the probability of fraud among physical mediums to obscure their significance should they be genuine. Despite his disappointment about Margery, then, he was pleased to be invited by the LSA to one of Helen Duncan's first major performances. On the afternoon of 30 October 1930, Harry Price – conspicuously absent from the guest list – heard noise from 'the people down below' and came out of his top-floor laboratory to investigate: 'Looking over the banisters as they trooped up the stairs, I could not help wondering what the afternoon would bring forth. I was soon to be informed, however, as very shortly the floor of my office reverberated to the "Hurrahs!" and "Bravos!" of those beneath, and I knew that Mrs Duncan had received the *cachet* of the Spiritualists.'

After watching intently while Helen Duncan, sitting still like a sinister doll, was dressed and examined, Lodge escorted her to the seance room where the sitters were waiting. Seven minutes after the medium was tied into her sack and the lights switched off, a foot-long strip of white ectoplasm appeared at the cabinet curtains and Lodge, complimented by Albert on his nice name, was invited to step up and feel it. It wriggled horribly over his hand. Lodge returned to his seat, swapping with another sitter so that he could hear better. As they waited, Albert said, for someone 'to get her out of here and take the atoms to pieces', Lodge peeked inside the cabinet. There, dimly lit, was Mrs Duncan, sweaty and snoring, the ectoplasm dangling from her body. 'It was heavy, cold and clammy,' Lodge noted; 'its texture was like a number of parallel threads forming a bundle two inches thick. It might have been separated into strands. It was not like woven material but was stringy. A curiously unpleasant slight odour remained either on my hand or in my nostrils as an occasional whiff for twelve hours afterwards.' The ectoplasm coalesced into a blob. 'It looks like a baby's head!' enthused Henry, at which Albert snapped: 'It isn't a baby's head, do you think I have no brain!' Lodge, who had a very good brain, was neither impressed nor inclined to criticize. Instead, he continued to act as an ambassador for Spiritualism in all its forms.

Lodge was best known as the author of *Raymond*, the bestselling account of his communications with his son in spirit – communications that had little to do with ectoplasm or any kind of physical mediumship. Lodge had warmed to Eusapia Palladino on the Île Roubaud in 1894, but Mrs Piper and Mrs Osborne Leonard were more his cup of tea. Etta Wriedt, another society medium, Lodge liked so much he gave her a cello, indifferent to rumours that sounds from her seance trumpet were achieved using a pharmaceutical powder. Mrs Wriedt's spirit guide, an eighteenth-century Glaswegian émigré to Indiana, connected her to spirits who spoke in most major European languages, plus Norwegian, Croatian and Arabic. For Lodge, these communications built a bridge of love to his son. He received many letters on the subject. In 1933 a Miss Wainwright, a retired schoolteacher from Sussex, was moved to write after reading his books and receiving messages on a ouija board from an ex-pupil, who, like Raymond, had been killed at Ypres. 'Dear Sir Oliver,' she said, 'what you are to us who grope so blindly cannot be told in words.'

Miss Wainwright's feeling was shared by the Rt Hon. W. L. Mackenzie King, Canada's former Liberal prime minister, who sought guidance from spirits while in the political wilderness. He attended the first of many seances in 1932, and the following year wrote to Sir Oliver Lodge thanking him for the signed copy of his autobiography he had received, adding that he knew Etta Wriedt, who spoke fondly of Lodge and her cello. Mackenzie King also expressed his sadness at the passing of Lord and Lady Grey together with his certainty that they had survived death.

It was at the Greys' home that Mackenzie King and Lodge had met in 1926, at which time he was still premier and in Britain for the Imperial Conference, where equal status for the dominions was established. Lady Pamela Grey was a devout Spiritualist who would send her driver to fetch Mrs Osborne Leonard from her cottage in East Barnet and sometimes went there herself. She also provided a rousing foreword for Rev. Charles Drayton Thomas's *Life Beyond Death with Evidence* in 1928: 'There have been some in all ages who have held they spoke with the dead, and who have given us their message. It may be the message is being recorded, fruitfully, at last.' Back in office in 1936, Mackenzie King resolved to abandon public life and devote himself to Lodge's writings. In that year, on pacifist grounds, he opposed sanctions against Italy for Mussolini's invasion of Ethiopia and made a Remembrance Day broadcast in which he exhorted the world to 'preserve the blessings of peace' and trusted that children's prayers would be heard by 'legions of angels each with its power to save'. When prayers failed in 1939, and after consulting the spirits, Mackenzie King wrote to the dictators urging peace yet fearing the worst. Nor was this the last war he would see coming. In 1947–8, while still in office, he sat several times with Geraldine Cummins and during a seance at the Dorchester Hotel in London was warned to pay attention to serious developments in Asia. He died in 1950, just before the outbreak of the Korean War.

Memories of one war fed into premonitions of the next, as the spirits helped people with what Freud called 'the accumulation of death'. According to Spiritualist lore, Raymond Lodge guided many diffident servicemen (in both world wars) on their faltering journeys to the other side, an idea which acquired an eerie reality at the Cenotaph, London's principal war memorial. In January 1924, Sir Oliver Lodge opened a letter from Sir Arthur Conan Doyle containing a curious photograph. It was taken by a Mrs Ada Deane in Whitehall during the two-minute silence the previous Armistice Day and showed a white cloud studded with faces. 'It is worth examining with a lens,' Conan Doyle advised. 'My son is certainly there and, I think, my nephew.'

Later that year Mrs Deane commenced sittings with W. T. Stead's clairvoyant daughter Emma (now known as Estelle Stead), leading in 1925 to the publication of a booklet, *Faces of the Living Dead*, which shrugged off accusations made by the Magic Circle's Occult Committee that such photographs were fakes. If the Cenotaph symbolized Britain's public acceptance of death, Conan Doyle's nearby Psychic Book Shop, Library and Museum (telegraph: 'Ectoplasm, Sowest, London'), founded in 1925, stood for private denial. As a campaigner, Conan Doyle may have lacked Lodge's academic gravitas but made up for it with wealth and energy, and from 1918 threw himself into touring Europe, the USA, Australia, New Zealand and South Africa. He is said to have spent £250,000 educating the public and badgering politicians, equivalent to more than £10 million today.

His lobbying on behalf of mediums was second to none. In October 1925, writing on Psychic Book Shop notepaper, he protested to the Home Secretary, Sir William Joynson-Hicks, about prosecutions in Brighton, and again the following month when 'Madame Estelle', a society medium, was fined. Conan Doyle argued that the penalties were more severe than for assault or animal cruelty, and that for policewomen to pose as mourners was 'repugnant to one's sense of justice, and foreign to the spirit of British law, which has never encouraged the agent provocateur'. The response of both the police and Home Office was that a person could not be incited to commit a crime they were already committing and saw no reason to change the law despite the support Conan Doyle had from prominent people, among them Sir Oliver Lodge, Lord and Lady Molesworth, Colonel Moore MP and the Duchess of Hamilton. Even so, the argument of Sir Henry Curtis-Bennett KC, Madame Estelle's barrister, that the 1824 Vagrancy Act was 'intended to deal with cases of gypsies upon Epsom Downs' and not mediums, did resonate in legal and administrative quarters.

In the spring of 1929, Stanley Baldwin's Conservative government was facing an evenly three-way general election where competition for votes (including for the first time those of all women) was intense. Conan Doyle had a questionnaire sent to candidates, promising 50,000 SNU votes to any party promising legal reform. The Liberals and Labour both offered written pledges, and the Home Secretary invited the Spiritualists to draft a Bill that would receive sympathetic consideration if the Conservatives were re-elected. In the end support went to the Liberals, although Labour won the election and Ramsay MacDonald became Prime Minister.

The more that the SNU became established in British political life the more its patience with the SPR ran out. In 1930, Conan Doyle led a wave of resignations, realizing that the future lay in practical action, not psychical research. On 1 July he led an SNU deputation to the Home Office, including Hannen Swaffer, Charles Drayton Thomas and Mrs Philip Champion de Crespigny, Principal of the British College of Psychic Science and daughter of the Rt Hon. Sir Astley Cooper-Key. The Home Secretary, J. R. Clynes, heard that Spiritualism had 'a great contribution to make towards the moral and spiritual uplift of society' and that British Spiritualists should enjoy the freedoms already granted in the USA and the Dominions. Clynes sympathized – but the bottom line was the law, which, he said, protected the public against fraud and 'mental terrorization'. Six days later Conan Doyle was dead, though not out of touch. On 13 July the Marylebone Spiritualist Association held a seance in the Royal Albert Hall attended by over six thousand mourners. There on the stage the celebrated medium Mrs Estelle Roberts clairvoyantly saw Conan Doyle in an empty chair and whispered a comforting message to his smiling widow. From that point, Conan Doyle stepped up his campaign, sending messages to an all-night seance in Paris, to Harry Price via Eileen Garrett and to Grace Cooke, another medium, who was inspired to found the internationally renowned Spiritualist society the White Eagle Lodge. The Manchester transfiguration medium Mrs Bullock had her face taken over by Conan Doyle's, and a Canadian medium was photographed vomiting ectoplasm containing not only his image but that of Raymond Lodge. As we saw earlier, Brigadier Roy Firebrace received a message from the great man and Helen Duncan managed a fleeting full-form materialization.

The spiritual Conan Doyle must have been disappointed by Clynes, who had stymied the SNU's ambitions. The Spiritualism and Psychical Research (Exemption) Bill, calling for the licensing of mediums by officially approved churches, was read in the House of Commons in November 1930 and mocked in Parliament and by the press. Sir Oliver Lodge was proved right: pushing for recognition under civil law was too ambitious when the battle against the criminal law had yet to be won. The Home Office, which kept an eye on public opinion, privately branded the Bill 'ridiculous' and after its second reading wrote to party whips to see it was blocked. And so the Tory MP who amused the House with his remark that it would be a shame to spoil the popular association of mediums with witches had his way.

Further behind the political scenes lay a stranger story. In October 1930, Ramsay MacDonald sat down to dinner at Chequers, his prime ministerial country house, feeling uneasy about the maiden flight of the R-101 airship, on which his friend Lord Thomson was a passenger. The terrible news – predicted that same day in a newspaper horoscope – did not surprise him. MacDonald's life had been steeped in grief since the death of his wife Margaret, whose presence he felt often. Shortly before the formation of the National Government in August 1931 his friend Effie Johnson informed him that during an automatic-writing session Margaret had said: 'Tell R. M. I *need* him now; I *need* him now.' In the weeks that followed, Grace Cooke (by now in regular contact with Conan Doyle) received similar messages from Margaret MacDonald, who said her husband was building the brotherhood of man on which the future of the Labour Party depended and advised that Britain should move closer to the USA to guard against global turbulence. Mrs Cooke's claim that she enjoyed a long correspondence with the Prime Minister rings true with MacDonald's biographer.

If it is true, MacDonald was not the first twentieth-century British premier to be this involved with Spiritualism.

Arthur Balfour (Prime Minister 1902–5) had been SPR president in 1893, a position held in 1906 by his brother Gerald (former Chief Secretary for Ireland and President of the Board of Trade), and together their involvement with mediums was common knowledge. Less well known is that in 1924, between his resignation as Prime Minister and election as Liberal leader, David Lloyd George wrote to Sir Oliver Lodge to enquire about a sitting with Mrs Osborne Leonard, to which Lodge replied that he thought it best for him to send a car to collect her as Lady Grey did.

Like Gladstone, MacDonald confessed that he should pay more attention to Spiritualism but unfortunately high office left him so little spare time. But he did attend at least one seance. In April 1925, at the Kingston Vale home of H. Dennis Bradley, a Spiritualist writer, the American medium George Valiantine connected him with the recently deceased Foreign Secretary Lord Curzon, who encouraged the Labour leader to promote spirituality to avert another world war. A decade later, his pacifist dreams crumbling, MacDonald retired to become Lord President of the Council. In October 1936 he made a speech at the opening of a college library in Edinburgh, where, having noticed a 300-volume section headed 'Demonology and Spiritualism', he referred to 'a wave of extraordinary credulity among young and up-to-date people'. No longer young and up-to-date himself, however, a year later he passed away on an ocean liner, and his ashes were united with those of his wife in the same Scottish kirkyard.

*

For Helen Duncan, the price of fame was not just vilification and imprisonment but the damage public life did to
her character, conduct and destiny. The Spiritualist leanings of influential people help us to understand her in
her time, not least because they directly affected the
vicissitudes of her fortunes. Men and to a lesser extent
women prominent in politics, entertainment, science,
the press and the law paid her an extraordinary amount
of attention – not because they loved her but rather
because she was an exploitable resource. This was true
even among her supporters, many of whom reviled the
woman they revered as a medium; vanity and selfish ambition belonged to them as well as to her. Nellie Duncan
came to star in her own pantomime, one where she played
all the parts – the princess and the pauper, heroine and
fool – and found herself alone on stage, blinded by the
footlights, deafened by jeering from the audience.

After the 1944 trial, Spiritualism intruded further into
political debate. Sir Ernest Bennett, who had worked in
Admiralty Intelligence during the First World War, became
a Labour MP in 1929 and joined the British delegation to
the League of Nations in 1934. He listed his recreations in
Who's Who as shooting, fishing and investigating haunted
houses, about which he published a book. In 1930–31,
when Helen was being tested in London, Bennett was
Vice-President of the LSA and attended eleven of her
seances, including her first one (where he saw a small face)
and the one where Sir Oliver Lodge was present. On 5
December he saw the tiny ectoplasmic fingers of a spirit
that removed his watch, and in March the following year a

larger entity shook his hand. By then, Bennett's feelings towards what he called 'that awful female Mrs Duncan' had cooled. On 15 May 1944 he bumped into Harry Price at the Reform Club and spent an hour swapping Duncan stories. Bennett told Price that he had always thought her spirit faces were just her hands draped in cheesecloth. By this time, however, the political agenda had moved on. Now it mattered less what Bennett or any politician thought about Helen Duncan's genuineness or fraudulence, only what her conviction under the Witchcraft Act represented for Spiritualist and, by extension, British liberties. In the spring of that year, it became a matter for the Home Secretary, Herbert Morrison.

Early in 1945, Morrison met his old socialist ally Hannen Swaffer for lunch at The Ivy, where they debated the legal plight of British mediums. As they parted, Morrison grinned and said: 'Well, I'll see you on the Other Side', to which 'Swaff' replied: 'Herbert, you *are* on the other side.' To the tabloid-reading nation, Swaffer was a folk hero and, as the king of gossip and lost causes on Fleet Street, reigned even longer than W. T. Stead. Wearing a cape and floppy bow tie and with a cigarette butt fixed in his drawn face, he looked like a struggling ham actor. A cartoonist in 1935 portrayed him as Don Quixote tilting at windmills with an oversized quill, another saw him as a minister in a fantasy Cabinet, with George Bernard Shaw as Prime Minister and Sir Oliver Lodge as Foreign Secretary ('This World and the Next'). A member of Maurice Barbanell's home circle, he kept in touch with his old boss Lord Northcliffe courtesy of H. Dennis Bradley and was a friend of the occult artist Austin Osman Spare. Like Lodge and Conan Doyle, Swaffer campaigned for Spiritualism and had been part of the 1930 SNU deputation. Corresponding with Morrison about the convicted medium Stella Hughes in 1943, he suggested that to be consistent the Home Secretary should also enforce ancient laws against making mince pies, selling short lobsters and walking along with a lighted cigar: 'I tremble to think what you will do to Winston about this.' Only socialism and Spiritualism, he believed, could save the world from war.

It was a defiant Swaffer who entered the witness box at the Old Bailey on 29 March 1944 and rattled irreverently through the formalities. 'Now take the oath properly,' instructed the Recorder, Sir Gerald Dodson, already nearly at his wits' end. Swaffer had thought to look Dodson up in *Who's Who* and, being a merciless scourge of thespians, was delighted to find he had co-authored a play that Swaffer knew from experience would have been atrocious. Swaffer's testimony was like other witnesses' but delivered with more aplomb, and he was scathing about Albert's allegedly posh accent. Swaffer's first seance with Helen Duncan had been in 1932, the one where she slipped out of the magician Will Goldston's bindings and, he recalled, the flame of a cigarette lighter had made her nose bleed. He had also attended a test seance at Percy Wilson's house – there had been more than one – where ectoplasm poured from her nose like a rope of living snow; only a child, he said, could have mistaken it for muslin. Nor was it possible that Mrs Duncan had been acting, a point that occasioned some drollery:

LOSEBY: Have you been a dramatic critic?

SWAFFER: Unfortunately, yes.

THE RECORDER: For whom?

SWAFFER: What for, my Lord?

THE RECORDER: You said 'unfortunately'. For whom?

SWAFFER: Unfortunately for the poor critic who has to sit through it, my Lord.

Dodson, however, got his own back by denying Swaffer the chance to share with the court his opinion of Helen Duncan's normal oesophagus, nor would he let him try swallowing the cheesecloth brought by the Prosecution. Although he put Henry Elam through his paces (mistaking him for John Maude, indicated by references to 'counsel's actor father'), Swaffer's boast that he ran rings round Treasury Counsel and then stormed out was exaggerated, and the jury had been impassive when he mentioned his spirit guide 'Darak Ahmed'. All this turned the reporter into the reported and gave Swaffer's fellow journalists plenty to chew on. The *Daily Mail*'s headline was: SWALLOWING TEST BARRED BY JUDGE IN 'SÉANCE' TRIAL.

It was to be expected that 'the Pope of Fleet Street' would canonize Helen Duncan as the 'St Joan of Spiritualism'. Her trial, comparable to that of Socrates, was a sign that 'orthodoxy was back to broomsticks' for an establishment indifferent to the ideals of tolerance set down in the Atlantic Charter of 1941. And Swaffer's columns spurred many outraged citizens, from whom the Home Secretary received letters decrying the British Gestapo and their persecution of witches, which, according to Swaffer, had been 'one of the great amusements of the Dark Ages'. In November 1944 a Mrs Vernon-Smith of Folkestone accused Herbert Morrison of betraying his roots and forgetting that socialists used to be 'on the people's side, the side of the under-dog, the side abused by the world, taken advantage of by party politics and repressed by legal jugglery'. Like many others, this badly typed letter was repetitious and festooned with exclamation marks and ink corrections, but it expressed sincere emotional truths, all diligently underlined in blue pencil by a civil servant at the Home Office, where these days sound administration increasingly meant listening to people rather than just telling them what to do.

More eloquent in his protests was Air Chief Marshal Sir Hugh Dowding, a household name since the Battle of Britain when he had used radar to deploy fighters tactically in opposition to the more aggressive strategy of his fellow Spiritualist Sir Trafford Leigh-Mallory. Soon afterwards 'Stuffy' Dowding was ousted and retired to concentrate on teaching the public about the Great Beyond. In 1943 he stirred controversy by reproducing in the *Sunday Pictorial* letters from dead servicemen received in automatic writing – many, his own pilots from 1940 – and the same year published *Many Mansions*, a Spiritualist manifesto rushed into print 'while all these lads are having their souls violently torn from their bodies, and leaving inconsolable dear ones behind'. Inspired by *Raymond*, Dowding also drew on another collection of messages from the spirit of a soldier, published in 1917 by an anonymous serving officer. The eponymous Private Dowding (no relation) described trying to help comrades carry his own body to the dressing station until he realized he was a spirit. Sir Hugh Dowding's messages were similar: a drowned sailor waking up in a strange place; a Norwegian shopkeeper told by God to forgive the Nazis who executed him; a fugitive Polish pilot wondering why he was not tired and hungry; a burned tank officer whose colonel, oblivious to flying bullets, took him by the shoulder and said: 'Don't you see, Kit? We are dead.'

Dowding's contribution was valued by the Spiritualist movement. In July 1943 he led the SNU deputation of which Charles Loseby was spokesman, received at the Home Office by Under-Secretary Osbert Peake, Morrison having refused to see them. Dowding called the recent prosecutions of mediums 'most lamentable' and was praised by a Spiritualist MP present, Thomas Brooks, for raising public awareness of survival. Most of the talking, however, was left to Loseby, who likened the heroic, revolutionary stance of the medium to that of Martin Luther. Morrison found the claims excessive and so the legal demands foundered, although with less finality than in 1930. Whereas Home Secretary Clynes had stonewalled, his successor merely stalled, eschewing 'controversial' legislation in wartime and reiterating that only monetary fraud would be punished. The times were changing. Subsequent correspondence between Morrison and the SNU, some of it acrimonious, was publicized and made the government look intransigent. As a result Morrison made discreet enquiries among chief constables, and in November 1943 issued a circular recommending that the police to stick to preventing the 'exploitation by impostors of credulous members of the public for private gain'. The response of the Metropolitan Police was that this had long been their operational policy – 'the rock bottom point every time'. Nevertheless, the SNU now suspected that a widespread anti-Spiritualist campaign was afoot and warned mediums at greatest risk to exercise extra caution. Helen Duncan was among them.

Dowding sat with various mediums, including Estelle Roberts, and by the end of the war was attending materialization seances. Whether he sat with Helen Duncan is unknown, although Mrs Homer said he had expressed an interest. Having previously thought of ectoplasm only as an 'extremely mysterious but apparently well-authenticated phenomenon', and spirit forms as 'toys of the kindergarten', Dowding was now astounded by what he saw. Like Conan Doyle and Lodge, he went on the road to preach about the ranks of fallen servicemen clamouring to reach loved ones, describing the universe as a set of concentric spheres of personal spiritual development. On 3 November 1943, Dowding addressed a large crowd in Portsmouth, where he expounded the principles of Spiritualism. Present was Harold Gill, an Approved Society official, who until then had thought it all 'a lot of hooey' but was inspired to attend meetings at the Master's Temple, where he and his wife were in the front row on the night Helen Duncan was arrested. Gill went on to give evidence for the Defence at her trial.

The former air chief marshal was invited often to speak at Spiritualist events. On 22 April 1944 he spoke up for Helen Duncan, who had been in prison for two weeks, at London's Kingsway Hall, a concert venue (and canteen for war workers) in Holborn. Programmes were sold for a penny, the proceedings going towards the SNU's Freedom Fund and the fight against the British state's 'bitter and ruthless intolerance' of mediums. That same evening a resolution was passed to protest against the religious injustice of the Witchcraft and Vagrancy Acts. Mrs Duncan's stalwart defender J. B. McIndoe urged the audience to dig deep, predicting that legal action to overturn Helen Duncan's conviction might reach the House of Lords and could cost as much as £2,500.

Dowding also wrote to the Lord Chancellor, Viscount Simon, citing the Home Secretary's previous recommendations, only to be reminded early in 1945 that the Witchcraft Act, like the Vagrancy Act, had nothing to do with religion, only imposture. Another Home Office memo was sent to chief constables nationwide reminding them of this, accompanied by an extract of Viscount Simon's reply to Dowding. Amid laughter in the House of Commons, on 3 May, Thomas Brooks challenged the Home Secretary, who, clearly discomfited, put the issue down to the caprice of legal interpretation. This, however, only exposed the government further, leading Labour's Aneurin Bevan to ask: 'Is not ambiguous law the worst kind of law; and if there is any dubiety about this matter ought it not to be put right by fresh legislation, so that citizens may know what their rights are under the law?' Five days later the war ended and the democratic spirit of Bevan's question soon pervaded every area of British life.

*

Helen Duncan's supporters muttered about conspiracy. The state, they said, had dusted off an archaic statute to stop an innocent woman revealing the secret of the Normandy landings, the greatest seaborne invasion ever. Early in 1944, before the trial, Maurice Barbanell had been writing a propaganda pamphlet that claimed that it was only the Vagrancy Act of 1824 that Spiritualists feared, given that 'the minions of the law realize that to accuse anybody of witchcraft in the 20th century might sound just a little ridiculous'. By the time Barbanell went to press, however, this claim was out of date and a correction slip had to be added, stating: 'No one could have foreseen that in the year 1944 the might and majesty of the law would be invoked to initiate a prosecution under the Witchcraft Act of 1735, as was done in the Helen Duncan case.' No clairvoyant powers were needed though. Not only had that statute been occasionally used for over a century, but more importantly the language of witchcraft had recently been creeping into criminal charges made under the Vagrancy Act.

In June 1805 at Kirkcudbright in Scotland, where a century earlier Elspeth McEwen had been executed for bewitching livestock, Jean Maxwell was sentenced to a year in prison under the Witchcraft Act for telling fortunes from tea leaves, rubbing a potion on a girl's head and frightening people with scratches she said had been inflicted by Satan. The trial of the 'Galloway Sorceress' caused excitement in legal circles and among local people, for whom a bestselling pamphlet was printed. This sensational response suggests that the use of the 1735 Act was something of a novelty, and such cases explain why the Vagrancy Act was passed in 1824 so that fortune tellers could be summarily tried. It was the appeal judgment in the case of the convicted slate-writer Francis Monck in 1877 which brought to public attention the fact that offenders could be tried under the more serious Witchcraft Act and reminded the courts that there was no need for them to manipulate the 1824 Act.

Mediums who objected to being branded as vagrants were now made to feel grateful that they had not been tried as witches. A Cornish cunning man was indicted under the Witchcraft Act in 1894, although the judge was uneasy about this 'almost obsolete statute', a feeling shared by a London magistrate ten years later when the fortune tellers Charles and Martha Stephenson were committed for trial. In this instance the Act was physically out of print and for that reason the Stephensons were acquitted. Distaste for the term 'witchcraft' notwithstanding, Section 4 of the Witchcraft Act did cover the offences committed by mediums and fortune tellers, so the police continued to use it. In the 1920s at least two gypsies were tried according to its terms: one in Northamptonshire received a month's hard labour for selling charms; the other in Cornwall was sentenced to six months' imprisonment for taking £500 from a sick man to counteract the effects of the evil eye.

In 1935, Bournemouth magistrates issued warrants against several mediums, including a Welsh clairvoyant, Nesta Lewis; she had already been fined £7 the previous year, a judgment questioned in the House of Commons by Manchester MP Edmund Radford, later a member of the SNU deputation. This time round Mrs Lewis – alias 'Nesta of the Forest' (her husband was a Druid) – was fined £25 under the Witchcraft Act after an undercover policeman visited her business premises in Gloucester. The Home Office received a letter of protest from Lady Margaret Knollys and opened a file. In 1936, Nesta Lewis sued the magazine *John Bull* for libel at the Court of King's Bench – an indirect attempt to have the Witchcraft Act repealed – where she was represented by Quintin Hogg, the future Lord Hailsham. Lewis lost, but Lord Chief Justice Hewart could not resist asking her about the fate of Spain, then on the brink of civil war, to which she replied: 'The King and Queen will return there.'

Nesta Lewis was able to fight her own battles and admitted that the publicity generated by her lawsuit brought her many new clients. For lesser mortals the Spiritualist movement was there to help. In 1937 *Psychic News* took up the cause of J. Clive-Holmes, a materialization medium imprisoned for, in effect, the crime of conjuration; a seance sitter had grabbed a spirit form made of crêpe bandage (a piece of which survives in the IIPR archives). Maurice Barbanell badgered Sir Samuel Hoare at the Home Office, spoke of how Clive-Holmes, who had been buried alive in the trenches, was terrified of his cell and set up a fund to support his family.

The prosecution of Helen Duncan, therefore, cannot have surprised Barbanell as much as he made out, nor was he unprepared. Earlier in the war, battle had already been joined around the country. In 1942, following a sting operation by two policemen dressed as convalescent soldiers,

mediums Austin Hatcher and Emily Little were imprisoned at Cardiff for 'pretending to hold communication
with departed spirits to deceive persons'; when Hatcher
was denied Spiritualist ministration the SNU swiftly used
his case as a lever against injustice. All this suggests that
Helen Duncan was prosecuted not so much as a threat to
national security as simply a nuisance who lowered public
morale – and in Portsmouth, a key point of departure for
D-Day, at the most crucial moment of the war. To cap it
all, the Witchcraft Act had even been used before by
Portsmouth magistrates. In 1939 a gypsy called Bessy
Birch was cautioned for dishonestly receiving money after
she advised a woman that her ring was bewitched and she
should bury a pound of steak with a human hair, then
burn a glove stuck with a needle and a pin. This case
would prove an important legal precedent in 1944.

After all, the authorities wouldn't really have been afraid
of Helen Duncan's powers . . . would they? The Nazis, of
course, took the occult seriously. Obsessed with astrology, mesmerism and spiritism, SS chief Heinrich Himmler
set up an 'Occult Bureau' and an academic team to study
the witch craze. Hitler believed his fate was determined by
providence, an idea he elaborated with Hans Goldzier's
'earth electricity' creation theory and von Reichenbach's
'Odic force', which some detected in luminous emana-
tions from crystals. Dowsing maps with a pendulum to
find warships was another of Hitler's eccentricities. Little
about British attitudes can be inferred from this, and yet
modern intelligence agencies like to think the unthinkable
just in case their enemy does. Dr Walter Stein, a Viennese

occultist, escaped being pressed into the Nazi Occult Bureau, and fled to Britain, where he became an adviser about Hitler's beliefs, which he said included an obsession with the power of a relic alleged to be the lance used to pierce Christ's side. The War Office employed an astrologer in Grosvenor House, Louis de Wohl, who cast Hitler's horoscope to predict his moves, and after the war a shadowy figure by the name of Ernesto Montgomery claimed to have been part of an MI5 psychic unit from where he ventured behind enemy lines in astral form – presumably like Henry Duncan visiting his sister in Arbroath but more dangerous.

One might expect the history of the occult in wartime to be awash with fantasies, but we shouldn't dismiss everything. Between 1940 and 1944, Geraldine Cummins performed psychic work 'of an investigative nature undertaken for patriotic motives', one record of which is said to remain in the custody of a government department; another, made in 1949, is under lock and key in the SPR archives. The witchcraft expert Cecil Williamson claimed that in 1938 he was asked by Lieutenant Colonel Edward Maltby, an MI6 officer (and brother-in-law of the occultist Dion Fortune), to make a list of high-ranking Germans who dabbled in the occult, work which led Williamson to establish the 'Witchcraft Research Centre'. At the outbreak of war Williamson served in the Royal Corps of Signals and, as well as monitoring the work of Nazi astrologers, broadcast propaganda and 'degenerate' jazz to U-boat crews. Maltby thought the occult was nonsense, but that wasn't the point. The intelligence services collected information; sources were secondary to that purpose. Williamson, a believer, also claimed to have witnessed 'Operation Mistletoe', a ritual performed by Aleister Crowley in a Sussex forest at the behest of MI5, where a dummy in Nazi uniform was burned, surrounded by white-robed soldiers. After the Fall of France 'Operation Cone of Power' was launched by witches in the New Forest to prevent a German invasion, and groups such as the Society of the Inner Light performed similar ceremonies, known collectively as 'The Magical Battle of Britain'. Lord Dowding was a supporter of the 'Cross of Light' campaign, where Grace Cooke's White Eagle Lodge put up posters across London hoping to concentrate positive thought and invoke spiritual power against forces of darkness.

Perhaps the security services didn't have to believe that Helen Duncan was a genuine medium to be concerned. Information flowed from her at a time when victory depended on secrecy, and MI5 were unlikely to have ignored that. There was something unusual about her treatment. The Home Office's excuse that the responsibility for sending a case to the Old Bailey lay with the committing magistrates was dubious, and similarly the claims that it was convenient to hold the trial in London because many of the witnesses lived there (few did) and that the case would otherwise have had to wait until the next assizes. It could have been dealt with summarily by Portsmouth magistrates under the Vagrancy Act or it could have gone to the local quarter sessions. Neither of those things happened; nor is it entirely true to say that the decision rested with the magistrates: the Clerk at the Old Bailey sent them a notification that the case would be removed to London 'for the special reason that there are special circumstances which make the case an unusually grave and difficult one and that delay and inconvenience would be occasioned by committal to quarter sessions'. Why was it so important not to delay a simple case of vexatious imposture?

Although the Metropolitan Police have no records relating to Helen Duncan, Brigadier Firebrace alleged that, after the sinking of HMS *Hood*, Scotland Yard solicited his advice about how best to silence her and believed that she was targeted because 'from the point of view of the authorities Mrs Duncan was a dangerous person'. Targeted by whom though? Accusations against Stanley Worth that he was a mole, a spy and a stooge are unsubstantiated. And yet, although little was said in court about his links to the police, his father, a senior sergeant in the Metropolitan Police, had been transferred to Portsmouth, and Worth's uncle, Percy Worth, was the Chief Constable at Scotland Yard. Furthermore, before the war Stanley Worth himself had been a Special Constable in the Metropolitan Police in Middlesex and became friends with Chief Constable Arthur West and his family after they attended a function at his naval base. It's fair to suppose that, as Percy Wilson's son Richard believed, 'the whole affair was a conspiracy by the Portsmouth police, which proved more difficult than they expected'.

And from the Wilsons came an astonishing claim. At Christmas 1943, John Lock, a storeman at the Cowley motor works, visited his parents in Portsmouth: William and Bessie, the licensed pedlar and his wife present at the Master's Temple on 19 January 1944. William Lock told his son that a naval officer called Worth had joined their Spiritualist church a few weeks earlier and that he, Lock, an ex-policeman himself, suspected that Worth was working undercover to expose Mrs Duncan. At the trial the Locks denied this, although they were friends with Charles Burrell, the disgruntled Spiritualist to whom Mrs Homer had given a refund. Nor did Worth admit to knowing the Locks before proceedings began. The Wilsons alleged, furthermore, that on 3 January, a fortnight before the raid, John Lock had been discussing materialization with William Spencer, a foreman welder who was convinced by Helen Duncan's seances. Lock bet him five shillings she would be arrested within weeks – and so it proved. Percy Wilson arranged for Spencer to appear as a witness at the Old Bailey but he was never called. The story influenced both the Prosecution and Defence but is impossible to verify. In 1958, Percy Wilson recounted his version of events at the College of Psychic Science conference in Brighton, adding not only that it was actually *Spencer* who was privy to the secret information but that he was Worth's nephew!

Stanley Worth denied being a police stooge or that he was involved with anyone except Detective Inspector Ford regarding Helen Duncan; his uncle was never involved, nor did he have any nephews. Clearly, however, he held back a little. When the SPR researcher Donald West spoke with him, West found him 'much more frank and revealing than when put on the defensive by badgering in the witness box'. Although he may not have dealt directly with Worth, Chief Constable Arthur West did oversee the investigation personally, and in a BBC interview in 1975 admitted that the Admiralty had wanted Helen out of the picture, without too much concern for how she had obtained knowledge about the sinking of warships. By the start of 1944 he felt that something had to be done and after he sent his report to the DPP a prosecution under the Vagrancy Act was discussed. 'But none of this seemed to cover what we were getting at in these circumstances,' West recalled, 'and therefore the Director said, look here, we'll use the old Witchcraft Act. Old it is, he said, but it'll cover what we want. And that's the one we took.' The Admiralty's approval soon arrived.

West did not mention the complicity of Douglas Craggs and the Magic Circle. In a letter to Harry Price dated 29 January 1944, Mollie Goldney shared her suspicions that Craggs had been involved in Mrs Duncan's downfall – but then Price already knew this. The next day Craggs wrote to him saying that the Magic Circle's investigation at Portsmouth was now a police matter and that, 'We are asked to help and wish to if in any way possible'. Craggs added: 'We have recently been in *constant* touch with Scotland Yard and I am hopeful that we may eventually get results.' Price's response is unknown, but he certainly lent his expertise, books, photographs and correspondence to Chief Constable West, and the trial went much as he had predicted. On 9 February 1944, West sent Price's *Regurgitation and the Duncan Mediumship* to the DPP's representative, E. G. Robey, saying that he had reviewed the case in relation to the charge and was 'satisfied that these four people will have some difficulty in proving their innocence'. Another clue: among Harry Price's papers is a compliment slip from the small Portsmouth bookshop run by War Reserve Constable Rupert Cross, which has to be more than coincidence.

However satisfied the police, DPP and Admiralty were before the trial, afterwards the Home Office became concerned. Assistant Under-Secretary Francis Graham-Harrison contacted his superior, Sir Frank Newsam (both present when the Home Office received the SNU in 1943), after hearing from Robey that the Prosecution had added the witchcraft charge without consulting the DPP. Newsam asked Under-Secretary Theo Mathew to check this, and on 6 April 1944 Mathew wrote to the DPP Sir Edward Tindal Atkinson to ask why the Witchcraft Act had been used, indicating that the Duncan episode was becoming a headache for the Home Secretary. Instead of trying this medium for fraud, Mathew said, the authorities had played into the hands of the Spiritualists, who 'will exploit to the utmost the fact that Helen Duncan was convicted under an Act which they can with some reason represent to be an anachronism and quite out of harmony with contemporary feeling'. Tindal Atkinson replied that although he would have preferred the principal charge to have been common law conspiracy to defraud he usually allowed counsel to frame their own indictments. On this occasion, he explained, the Attorney General had nominated John Maude KC, who thought the case would best be proved with the Witchcraft Act.

One final point has gone unnoticed: the presence of a

Secret Service officer at Helen Duncan's trial. If MI5 were to prosecute persons who contravened security laws, it made sense for them to see their cases through to the end, as happened at the trial of the traitor William Joyce, alias Lord Haw-Haw. Some officers were reluctant to appear as witnesses, for fear of revealing their identities, but this doesn't mean they weren't there, either in the background or in plain sight out of uniform. A Major Nicholson present at a meeting of chief constables on 17 May 1945 to discuss fraudulent mediums was, given his military rank, almost certainly an MI5 officer, and argued that greater coordination was needed due to the 'difficulties he had experienced in the recent prosecution in this area', presumably the Duncan case. Preparations for D-Day made from 1943 by the Inter-Services Security Board – a body that united the Admiralty, Air Ministry, War Office and MI5 – included at every meeting discussions of the latest public rumours. To gather stories, 'B' Division of MI5 (Counter-Espionage), led by a former Scotland Yard subversion expert, relied on a network of Regional Security Liaison Officers, to whom chief constables reported 'matters of special security interest'. Since 1939 MI5 had been recruiting 'men of discretion': Britain's natural rulers hailing from the great public schools, who followed class instincts rather than the dictates of what was seen as a corrupt 'European' bureaucracy. Many were drawn from the legal profession and were given the honorary rank of major in the Intelligence Corps.

One of these men of discretion was John Maude. In 1939 he had joined MI5, and, as usual, was given the job description of 'Temporary Civil Assistant to the General Staff at the War Office'. At the outbreak of war, he received his Intelligence Corps commission, and in December 1939 was put in charge of a section dealing with leakage of information. In spring the following year, this work was done by B19, of which Maude was also head until the section was reconstituted as B1K, by May 1943 it had been absorbed by SLB2, the subdivision of MI5's legal unit responsible for leaks. Maude himself travelled undercover to investigate the source of rumours (on at least one occasion to Scotland) and devised a scheme to plant agents in foreign embassies posing as domestic servants. From 1942 he worked specifically for the Offices of the War Cabinet. Surely, then, when the Attorney General chose Maude for the difficult case of Helen Duncan he had this experience in mind. Mollie Goldney, who had her ear close to the ground, suspected that the Magic Circle had a hand in things, and that they were working with the Admiralty, which would explain why a naval officer had been called as the Prosecution's star witness. B. Abdy Collins told her that he believed not only that the Duncan trial stemmed from the *Barham* incident, but that prosecuting counsel had offered to scale down the charges if the Defence agreed to Mrs Duncan being locked up for six months 'over the coming offensive'. Charles Loseby refused. Could it be that the 'witch-finding activities' Churchill once criticized in MI5 had come literally true?

Spiritualists have long cherished the idea that Churchill was outraged about Helen Duncan's conviction because he was one of their number. Escaping from a prison camp during the Boer War, it is said, he plotted his orientation with a planchette, a pencil mounted on a wheeled cradle used for automatic writing. As a politician he attracted considerable attention from Spiritualists. In 1922 a Canadian woman sent him poems from the spiritual Shelley, including all 7,350 words of 'A Song of Italy', which told of Christ approaching the darkened earth through the etheric spheres of light. Conan Doyle also wrote. 'I wish you would yourself look into this psychic question,' he implored in 1923. 'It is far the most important thing upon the earth and we want leaders of energy.' That Churchill would become Prime Minister had been predicted by the spirits in a message sent to him in 1915 when he was one of Asquith's ministers. After the Dardanelles disaster, Churchill served in the trenches with the Royal Scots Fusiliers, and, although there is no proof for the Spiritualist claim that he and Charles Loseby were comrades, they may have met as battalion commanders at Ploegsteert in 1916. They were well acquainted after the war. In 1919, as Secretary for War, Churchill received a deputation from Loseby about the promotion of other ranks to commissions and dealt with him in connection with war bonuses. Covering the period 1918–22, Loseby's curriculum vitae reads: 'Worked closely with Winston Churchill for whom I did several missions – never lost touch', which was borne out in correspondence from the 1920s and confirmed by Loseby's daughter, who remembered Churchill's visits. All this may explain cryptic references to Loseby having been one of Churchill's spies, without proving that Churchill shared Loseby's Spiritualist sympathies.

From the letters he received in 1944, Churchill must have been aware of public opinion about Helen Duncan. After her arrest, a housewife from Bath drew the Prime Minister's attention to police harassment of mediums, who had 'brought knowledge and spiritual comfort in these dark days', and that her son, missing since the Battle of Crete, was 'just one [of] many who fought, and still fights, for the preservation of an idealistic way of life for these islands'. News of Mrs Duncan's conviction moved her good friend Mr Latimer in Alloa, twenty miles from Glasgow, to inform Churchill about the wonderful things he had seen – spirits in shimmering robes, light divided prismatically – but said he was sure Churchill knew all about spiritual power already, 'for no mere man could have carried your burden without help'. Like many others, Latimer's letter ended with a plea: 'You are a great man but be a just man and see that this woman gets justice or your Charter is in vain and the Gestapo of religion still lives.'

Typically, such correspondence was forwarded to the Home Office, and may not have reached the Prime Minister's desk, but Churchill nonetheless heard about Helen Duncan's case and was impelled to comment. On Monday 3 April 1944, he sent a personal minute to Herbert Morrison which read:

Let me have a report on why the Witchcraft Act, 1735, was used in a modern Court of Justice. What was the cost of this trial to the State, observing that witnesses were brought from Portsmouth and maintained here in

this crowded London, for a fortnight, and the Recorder
kept busy with all this obsolete tomfoolery, to the detri-
ment of necessary work in the Courts?

Morrison immediately forwarded the note to Theo
Mathew, who composed a reply stating: first, that it was
not the Home Secretary's job to interfere in a criminal
prosecution; secondly, that the police had been right to
act against fraud, especially 'in wartime when relatives of
men killed or missing are easy victims'; and thirdly, once
again, that magistrates, not the police, were responsible
for allocating cases to courts. The question of the Witchcraft Act was left open, proposing further consideration
after a full report had been made. 'I put in this sentence',
Mathew told Morrison, 'in case we have to do something
to placate the prevalent opinion that a law is unsatisfactory because it is old. My own view is that the Act of 1735
is a very sensible and natural measure which compares
favourably with the superstition and irrationality rampant
in 1944.' Finally, Mathew insisted that expense and inconvenience were 'part of the price to be paid for maintaining
the right to be tried by a jury'. The Home Secretary excised
a passage conceding that 90 per cent of trials were han-
dled summarily, which would only have emphasized that
Helen Duncan's case *was* peculiar. And with that the
answer was retyped, signed and sent on 6 April, and
doubtless Churchill was satisfied.

Churchill's minute was not quite 'the call for an inquiry
and a reprimand' Spiritualists have made it out to be, nor
did he stand up in the House of Commons to 'let the world

know where he stood about the trial of Helen Duncan'. If anything, he was irritated that resources were being wasted at a time when national efficiency was key, and in any case was emotionally preoccupied at that time by the death of Orde Wingate, the leader of the Chindits in Burma in whom Churchill saw himself as a young man. Besides, the personal minute received by Morrison was just one of several Churchill sent on 3 April. Other business of concern to the Prime Minister that day included the dangerous political situation in Italy and the Russo-Japanese agreement about North Sakhalin. Churchill and Morrison met that same day in the War Cabinet, where they focused on bombing policy in occupied territories, fears of industrial unrest and reports of a successful attack on the German battleship the *Tirpitz*; nor was the Duncan case mentioned during the rest of the week's business, whereas inland transport, national water policy and civil aviation all were.

At times in the past when Churchill had been required to deal with Spiritualism, he had shown the constructive pragmatism one would expect from a leader who counted bricklaying among his recreations. As Home Secretary in 1910–11, he did nothing to restrain the Metropolitan Police in their raids on fortune tellers and mediums and may even have sanctioned them. Challenged on the issue in the House of Commons in 1911, he blithely referred his opponent to the terms of the 1824 Vagrancy Act. As Chancellor of the Exchequer in 1928, Churchill was called upon to suppress a lecture by the widow of Captain Walter Hinchliffe, whose aeroplane had been lost over the Atlantic that year. Mrs Hinchliffe told of her husband's return

through mediums such as Estelle Stead and Eileen Garrett, whom she had been encouraged to meet by Sir Arthur
Conan Doyle, and how the spirit of W. T. Stead had
helped her husband to get in touch. Churchill was all for
remonstration, but the Public Trustee advised against
antagonizing 'the Stead-Conan Doyle gang' and instead
the lecture was just mildly censored.

Stories of Churchill the seance-goer who visited Helen
Duncan in Holloway and had a private sitting in her cell
have accumulated since the war. The Prime Minister is
supposed not only to have apologized and promised to
make amends, but to have sought psychic counsel for how
to prosecute the last phase of the war, for which the family
received 'personal notes of appreciation' (unfortunately
lost in the fire that ravaged Henry Duncan's archive). It's
strange that no Cabinet colleague, civil servant, prison
official, warder or prisoner remembered this visit, and the
idea that an imprisoned medium might be allowed to hold
seances at all seems fanciful. According to one account,
Holloway's wartime governor was a sympathetic Spiritualist woman who had allowed Helen Duncan to continue
working, and that during air raids Helen was given the
keys of the cells so that inmates could be together. But
this cannot be true. The governor was a man – HMP
Holloway did not have a female governor until 1945 – and
not a Spiritualist, and cells were routinely left unlocked
during air raids anyway.

The idea that her other clients included Mackenzie King,
General de Gaulle and the Queen Mother should be treated
with similar caution. From autumn 1945, Mackenzie King's

friend Mercy Phillimore did arrange seances for him at the LSA, and in 1947 promised him 'some of the best mediums', although whether these included Helen Duncan (as Spiritualists assert) is not recorded. He definitely sat with Lilian Bailey, whose own development as a medium was inspired by Helen's materialization of an officer from the First World War, but that was probably as close as Helen ever got to a head of state. The suggestion that, as Sagittarians, Helen and Winston understood one another might be true but says nothing about the great man's beliefs. He didn't use a planchette pencil to escape the Boers, yet that was the metaphor he chose to describe the instinctiveness of his trek. Remembering his South African adventure, Churchill spoke of 'the assistance of that High Power which interferes in the eternal sequences of causes and effects more often than we are always prone to admit'.

As well as being a ruthless pragmatist, Churchill was a romantic freethinker – spiritual without being Spiritualist. Nor was he, as some claim, a Druid.* Like Hitler, he saw himself as a man of destiny. He was also capricious in his attitudes and can no more be summed up by an antireligious phase he went through after reading W. E. H. Lecky's *History of the Rise and Influence of the Spirit of Rationalism* than he can by the metaphysical turn of mind which inspired him, in the late 1940s, to write a story where he dreamed that the spirit of his father returned to quiz him about the twentieth century. For, like the questing virtuosi of the

---

* In 1908, Churchill joined the Ancient Order of Druids, a non-religious masonic fraternity with no apparent neo-pagan connotations.

seventeenth century, Churchill was interested in everything. He owned at least one book about spirits, possibly
Joseph Glanvill's *The Vanity of Dogmatizing* (1661), which
in 1904 he lent to Pamela Tennant, a writer who later
became the second wife of Sir Edward Grey. Her letter of
thanks when returning the volume said that the Grey
family, with whom she was already acquainted, owned 'a
copy of Glanvils book on Witchcraft' – *Saducismus Trium-
phatus* (1681) – and she expressed horror at the injustice
of the burning times. 'These poor innocent witches', she
lamented, 'were no doubt people with psychical gifts.
How much more advanced we might have been in that
direction if so rigorous a treatment of this subject had
never been.' The Spiritualism Pamela Tennant flaunted
after she became Lady Grey in 1922 was therefore already
in evidence long before she met Etta Wriedt or Mackenzie
King.

Like many of his contemporaries, Churchill neither
ruled spirits in nor ruled them out. On 25 November
1947, three days after a sitting with Geraldine Cummins,
Mackenzie King met Churchill and informed him that
Roosevelt had sent him a message from the other side.
Churchill asked to borrow a transcript. Who knows what
he thought of it, but Mackenzie King believed he took the
transcript seriously, recording in his diary that it had been
returned to him accompanied by 'a most significant little
note'.

The openness of Churchill's mind is demonstrated by
his correspondence with an astrologer in Norwich called
R. G. Hickling, whose rambling predictions Churchill

shared with Cabinet colleagues, including the Prime Minister H. H. Asquith and Foreign Secretary Sir Edward
Grey. Hickling's first letter, warning of the worst planet-
ary conjunctions for forty years, was received in August
1911, just days before the Admiralty and War Office began
strategic planning for war with Germany. Messages over
the next three years concerned such matters as industrial
disputes and instability in the Balkans, and after Hickling
correctly foresaw an abrupt end to the miners' conference
in 1912, Grey wrote to Churchill to ask: 'Have you any
indication of the nature of events of a far graver character that are to supervene?' In 1914, Hickling told of the
danger of conflagration but thought the planets would
ensure British victory as they had during the Boer War. As
First Lord of the Admiralty the following year, Churchill
continued to study Hickling's forecasts concerning the
optimal moments to initiate sea battles, although it's doubtless significant that the last letter, dated 28 April 1915,
predicted that the Dardanelles campaign would be Churchill's greatest personal victory.

In 1964, Wellesley Tudor Pole, the anonymous editor of
the communications of 'Private Dowding' in 1917, wrote
to the novelist Rosamond Lehmann, with whom he maintained a long correspondence. Like John Maude, he had
been an MI5 officer at the War Office, where he warned
the Prime Minister about bugs in the House of Commons
and believed that 'Churchill has always feared the supernatural not because he thought of it as bunk but because
he believed in it.' As Churchill lay dying a few months
later, what did he think would become of his soul? There

is no proof that he believed in an afterlife, and he was joking when he said brandy and cigars kept ghosts at bay. And yet the evidence that he allowed for the possibility of a superior existence is compelling. In 1942 he told the House of Commons that the recently deceased Duke of Kent had 'gone to join a happy family', leading the Spiritualist MP Thomas Brooks to ask Churchill privately whether he really believed that. 'I do,' came the reply. 'Is it true then?' pressed Brooks, to which Churchill answered: 'No doubt about it in my mind.'

Churchill's memo to Morrison about the 1944 trial can then be interpreted in a different light. Although Hannen Swaffer's disclosure to a journalist that three members of the War Cabinet had attended seances (thereby contravening the Witchcraft Act) seems improbable, it is just about plausible. Perhaps, after all, Churchill watched Helen Duncan's appeal against conviction with more sympathy than his declared concern with economic efficiency and public accountability would have us believe. That he visited her in Holloway is beyond credibility – but he may have spared a thought for her plight as she marked off the days of her sentence.

9. Nellie, Keep Your Chin Up!: The Path to Liberty

Holloway Prison in North London was a century-old Gothic fortress complete with loopholes and battlements, where hunger-striking suffragettes had once been force-fed and Oscar Wilde reflected on the iniquities of English justice. For forty years it had been a women's prison, the largest in Britain, and, although the walls had been repainted a softer cream now, a pall of timeless, nameless wrong hung over the cell blocks which radiated from an open atrium like the spokes of a wheel. Individual cells were reached from galleries lining the perimeter, a network of mesh-covered walkways and spiral staircases connecting them to one other and the main concourse. It was, in short, a panopticon where surveillance and servility were meant to bring the fallen closer to God and the ideals of the state.

The senses of new arrivals were assailed by the reek of boiled cabbage and disinfectant and the echoing sound of raised voices, slammed doors and jangling keys. Helen Duncan and Frances Brown repeated the routine they had been through before: separated into gloomy reception cells, and from there to cubicles where a nurse weighed them, examined their hair and scalps and asked about varicose veins, fits and periods. Finally, a female doctor came round with a stethoscope and an indifferent manner, and decided that in Helen's case, once she had been bathed and dressed, she should receive treatment for her diabetes and angina. Like most of her fellow prisoners – pickpockets, cheats, prostitutes, derelicts and backstreet abortionists – her wits were at once flattened by despondency and heightened by fear. She felt faint and expected to die.

In wartime Holloway everything was in short supply, including hot water, soap and clothing. The contents of the bundle each new prisoner received were invariably soiled, including the calico chemise, voluminous drawers and knitted black stockings, which, without garters, drooped ceaselessly. The shapeless blue frock was no longer patterned with what Mrs Pankhurst had called 'the broad arrow of disgrace', but was nonetheless degrading attire. Shoes were mismatched, handkerchiefs scarce and against the cold (fuel economies were obsessive) each prisoner was given a grimy serge cloak to wear to chapel and during the daily hour of outdoor exercise.

Cells measured thirteen feet by seven with a barred window and armoured door. Cold and sour, they contained only basic necessities: an iron bed, table, chair, jug, bowl, mug and covered pail. Baths and the issue of clean underwear were supposed to occur weekly, but a wait of a month was not unusual. Toilet paper was highly prized and women often used pages from the bibles provided for their moral reformation. The food was monotonous – coarse bread, oily meat stew, dirty greens – and might cause either diarrhoea or constipation depending on how a prisoner's digestive system reacted to the shock. The only 'treat' was the cloying ship's cocoa, from which the women would skim the grease to use on hands chapped from long toil.

Arranging to see the Medical Officer ('booking for the MO' as it was known) meant being locked up while one waited, missing not only work but meals, recreation and exercise, so was not a soft option for malingerers. Even then, women reporting sick were treated with suspicion, although Helen Duncan's abnormal pulse and bluish pallor were convincing enough. The prison hospital in which she found herself was no light antiseptic haven but just another cell, where she was confined to bed, isolated and incarcerated around the clock. As in all cells, there was an emergency bell – but it often went unheeded as the ringing annoyed the wardresses. Helen was measured, probed and medicated, treatment which she received in the same passive manner as when she'd been examined before a seance or studied by psychic investigators. Her diabetes was regulated with precise doses of insulin and a strict diet, which she would have minded more had her voracious appetite not deserted her. She craved cigarettes, but smoking was forbidden in the infirmary and there were no cigarettes to be had anyway. Nor was there much in the way of privacy, and little sympathy or comfort from the unsmiling staff monitoring her. Once Helen's condition was stable, she was back on the wing.

Whether Helen had much to do with Frances Brown, or even saw her, is unknown, nor is there any indication she made new friends. Once a prisoner was used to the spartan regime, her greatest enemy was monotony. As

Helen's strength had returned, the doctor had permitted her to spend time in the workroom engaged in handicrafts. Now properly up and about, she may have attended classes in making soft toys and home economics, and prisoners could earn pocket money doing menial tasks, which was spent on cosmetics, so they no longer had to make rouge from exercise-book covers. Anything that stopped their being locked in a cell every day from 4.30 p.m. to 7 a.m. – the prison's greatest source of mental distress – was appealing. Apart from work there were few distractions. Old insipid novels were available in the library and Maurice Barbanell sent Helen books – but she was not a big reader, having always preferred Henry to read to her: poems and stories and, cocooned next to him in bed, nuggets of psychical research. Alone at night, her bed surrounded by well-wishers' cards and notes, her thoughts turned to her family, and she did her best to put her trust in God and Albert. Holloway's cells were dark but never dark enough, and sobs and screams reverberated through the still prison. Sleep came to Helen in irregular waves and waking offered small relief from the nameless menace of her dreams.

Prisoners were deprived of news, although Helen may have guessed what was being said about her in the world outside. In wartime a dearth of notable criminal cases meant that those that did come along generated feverish interest in the bored populace. As she walked free from court, Mrs Homer told journalists that she would carry on at the Master's Temple 'in the ordinary way', but in fact she kept a very low profile. The London *Evening News*, keen to know what had happened to the takings from Helen's seances prior to her arrest, sent a reporter to Portsmouth who found 301 Copnor Road closed, a notice about cancelled services chalked on a board and the sole occupant apparently a chow dog. Over-excited about tracing the carpenter who made the seance room's crucifix, the *Daily Mirror* managed to refer to Helen as *Hilda* Duncan. Charles Loseby blamed these travesties on the Prosecution, who he said had spun a story at the Old Bailey which was 'clear, simple, blatant and vulgar and lent itself to headlines which were freely given'. To Mollie Goldney, however, Spiritualist propagandists and the tabloid newspapers were as bad as each other, dubbing them all the 'FFFs' because they were fifty-fifty in frightfulness. The *Times*, by contrast, used the same sober headline day after day: ALLEGED SÉANCE DECEPTIONS.

Alone among the tabloids, the *News of the World* was sympathetic, having sensed a feeling beyond the Spiritualist movement that the prosecution of witches and the war to liberate Europe were incompatible causes. The historical image of the witch craze symbolized a class-ridden, patriarchal past at a time when British people were demanding a new world in reward for their sacrifice. Helen Duncan was thus portrayed as an infirm philanthropist whose annual income had never exceeded £200 – less than half the national average for a man. The liberal and serious *New Statesman* realized that a conviction for exercising 'a kind of conjuration' had potentially serious implications for ordinary Spiritualists and suggested that Mrs Duncan's conviction was unjust if that were not the case. An article in *Truth* regretted that the 'mediaeval savour' of the 1735 Act allowed Spiritualists to claim that they were being persecuted even when they were not and to elevate Mrs Duncan to sainthood. Likewise, the *Glasgow Herald* called for a new legal style, suggesting that 'in the coming epoch of reconstruction Parliament may take the view that a rewording would be worthwhile'. The Marquis of Donegall, who had been present at the Old Bailey, wrote in the *Sunday Dispatch* that he saw no difference 'between a person who obtains money under false pretences by pretending to be a witch and one who does the same thing by selling shares in a non-existent goldmine. Why should the former be accused under a special archaic Act? To my mind, the so-called witchcraft part of it is purely incidental.'

At the Home Office, news clippings were pasted onto sheets of paper – as an economy, cut-up propaganda posters – and filed with letters of protest. Both E. G. Robey at the DPP's office and Chief Constable West in Portsmouth were asked for reports to help the Home Office reply and, in his letter of 6 April to DPP Sir Edward Tindal Atkinson, Theo Mathew referred to the Marquis of Donegall. Under-Secretary Francis Graham-Harrison, who had also seen the *Sunday Dispatch* article, noted that: 'On the face of it, it is a pity that Duncan was convicted under the Witchcraft Act and not simply of conspiring to obtain money by false pretences. It is already clear that the Spiritualists will make the most of the fact that she was convicted under an Act 200 years old, which they can represent with some show of reason to be archaic and out of harmony with modern feeling.' Mathew used almost identical words.

But the DPP was unmoved: proving conjuration had obviated the need for proof of intent to defraud and the Witchcraft Act had therefore been appropriate. The Home Office objected to the imputation that a citizen, innocent until proven guilty, *had* to be convicted and that a statute's existence justified its use.

Parliamentary representation and popular literacy had made people less passive in the face of injustice – some called it tyranny – than in the previous century. Added to rants about the British Gestapo were more measured criticisms from melioristic non-Spiritualists defending liberty for the postwar world. A York man said there were more harmful things on which to spend money than seances, and another (admittedly writing from a mental hospital in Kent) felt the country had returned to the mentality of the reign of James I and that, like the witch-hunters of old, the Chief Constable of Portsmouth had lost his head.

As anticipated, Chief Constable Arthur West himself received letters from Land's End to John o'Groats, which, he said, were broadly fifty-fifty for and against the action he took against Helen Duncan. He was quiet about a critical article in the *Police Review*, which, taking a similar line to the *New Statesman* piece, argued that the conviction of a medium whose fraud was unproved seemed to undermine the Home Secretary's assurance of November 1943 that imposture alone would be pursued by the police. It was hard to disagree, and an embarrassed Home Office was forced to take refuge in its inability to comment while an appeal was pending.

Among psychical researchers, Donald West felt that if Helen Duncan had disclosed war secrets, she should have been tried for that – but most of his colleagues were interested in not justice, nor even the truth about her alleged manifestations, but rather the testimonies that Charles Loseby had submitted as evidence. Waiting for a train to Putney after the trial, Mollie Goldney, who believed that the verdict and sentence had been just, spotted the champion witness for the Defence, the Glaswegian Dr John Winning, and asked him if he now thought Helen Duncan was a fraud. Smiling, he replied quietly that he did not, and said he had photographs of the spirits of his relatives – but refused to show them to Mrs Goldney, on the grounds that he didn't know her. She politely remonstrated until his train arrived. Back at the SPR, the President, W. H. Salter, was unhappy. 'I wish the police had left Mrs D. to stew in her own ectoplasm!' he railed. 'She isn't worth all this fuss.' Even so, he thought someone should write a proper report on her mediumship, but forbade Mrs Goldney or any other member to visit Helen in prison or contact her in any way without the express consent of the SPR Council.

Not that Helen was short of visitors. It was difficult for Henry to travel, because of his poor health and domestic responsibilities, but the girls came when they could. Helen's friend Jean Beatson, who had taught Gena about the fairies, travelled from Fife every week bearing cigarettes concealed in bunches of violets. B. Abdy Collins visited, too, and felt she was being well treated, which he attributed to the guilty conscience of the authorities. Helen was also one of the first prisoners to receive Spiritualist ministration. A decade earlier, the Prison Commission had refused to recognize Spiritualism as a religion, but the SNU campaign on behalf of Austin Hatcher, the incarcerated Cardiff medium, forced a reconsideration in October 1943. Despite reservations that allowing ministration would instigate the crime for which prisoners were serving time, it was conceded that Spiritualism deviated from orthodoxy hardly more than Christian Science or Buddhism and the rules were amended. It's reasonable to guess, too, that Helen, now famous, gave psychic readings in return for cigarettes, pennies or favours. According to Spiritualist mythology, she held full seances to which a blind eye was turned by sympathetic wardresses, who in any case refused to lock her cell door. In another version 'Albert' came to her as she slept and, like the Angel of the Lord dissolving St Peter's chains when he was jailed by Herod, dematerialized the lock.

Reports in the Spiritualist press fuelled the campaign against Helen Duncan's conviction and Britain's ignorance of the miraculous. As the editor of *Psychic Science*, Abdy Collins published an article by defence witness Alfred Dodd, who shared his wondrous experiences with tub-thumping righteousness. 'With the advancement of knowledge,' railed Dodd, 'we shall cease persecuting the prophets and the smelling out of witches.' Activists received hundreds of letters from high and low. Lady Eleanor Smith, the novelist daughter of Lord Birkenhead, informed Hannen Swaffer:

Although I'm no Spiritualist, I regard Mrs Duncan's conviction as a disgrace to English justice, and another detestable attempt to interfere with our personal liberty. I don't want to go to one of her séances – that's all right – but why the devil shouldn't other people go, if they want to? Anyway, if she was tried under a Witchcraft Act of 1735, I'm only astounded that she wasn't sentenced to be burned at the stake. Wishing you every success in your campaign.

Maurice Barbanell had a diverse mailbag. Superintendent L. R. Russell of the Indian Police thought it scandalous that England, whose democracy was a model to the world, persecuted witches when India did not. According to Gunner T. A. Mead, a Spiritualist serving in Italy, the case mocked the cause for which he was fighting. The arguments were ingenious. Donkey rides on Sundays were technically illegal but went unpunished, and it was hypocritical, some believed, to pay the Archbishop of Canterbury £15,000 a year for interceding between God and man when a poor medium could be banged up for a few shillings. On 8 April 1944, writing in *Psychic News*, Barbanell pointed out the absurdity of a situation where resurrection was central to Christianity but was forbidden at seances, speculating that 'if every medium and Spiritualist who is wiping away the tears of mourners is to be imprisoned, then the building of jails will have to become a new war-time priority'. Finally, he assured his readers (who included Theo Mathew at the Home Office) that the fight would continue. A fortnight later the *Daily Mail* reported the SNU's intention to raise £5,000 to meet the costs of an appeal and reiterated its determination to take the case to the House of Lords if necessary.

As well as thinking about Henry and Albert, Helen must have thought about the man most likely to get her out of prison, Charles Loseby, unaware that five miles away in Kensington he was thinking of her as well. Holed up in his study preparing his case, once more he sought inspiration in Ellis Powell's pamphlet, which described the 1542 Witchcraft Act as 'the first anti-psychic statute', and argued that 'the demon of Law, not the goddess of Justice' was the pre-eminent arbiter of truth. That much Loseby knew now. At the end of the trial, the judge had refused to grant a certificate of appeal, but within two hours Loseby and the SNU's solicitor, Godfrey Elkin, gave notice they would be appealing anyway. The grounds were threefold: use of the Witchcraft Act had been inappropriate; the verdict had been 'unreasonable and perverse' given the Prosecution's lack of evidence and its abundance with the Defence; and Sir Gerald Dodson's refusal to accept that the defendant might be a genuine medium was unjust.

However futile the appeal seemed – Harry Price dismissed it as 'mere propaganda' – interest stirred among lawyers. The editor of *Archbold's Criminal Pleading, Evidence and Practice* obtained a copy of the indictment. The *Law Quarterly Review* devoted a paragraph to the appeal, noting that 'an otherwise sordid case was given a dramatic quality' by the Witchcraft Act. Contrary to W. H. Salter's opinion that Stanley Worth was a 'rotten bad observer and a rotten

bad witness', C. E. Bechhofer Roberts, editor of the Old
Bailey Trial Series, thought he was 'clearly a witness of trust
in all essential matters', whereas his opponents – Loseby
above all – had been barking up the wrong tree trying to
prove post-mortem survival. Initially, the subtlety of the
point had been lost even on junior prosecuting counsel
Henry Elam, who in court seemed to Mollie Goldney 'very
much at sea, afraid of bungling it in consequence'. Notes
by someone on the Prosecution side (possibly Elam himself) included this nervous observation: 'Issue is: Have
Crown proved that Mrs D = Fraud?', when really this
wasn't the issue at all. Another note to the effect that the
jury's refusal to attend a test seance was significant also
missed the point. The jury were right to refuse, not because
the test was unlikely to yield results, nor even because it
would have amounted to an ordeal, as the judge argued, but
rather because it was irrelevant to the question of whether
or not, in January 1944, at 301 Copnor Road, Helen Duncan
had conspired to pretend to exercise a kind of conjuration.
The wily Maurice Barbanell was undeceived, recognizing
that 'under the Witchcraft Act there was no possible
defence because it all turned on the word *pretending* to conjure up spirits, and legally it was maintained that *pretending*
meant if you said you could produce materializations . . . it
was witchcraft'.

By the time Helen Duncan's appeal case was heard, on 8
June 1944, D-Day had happened and there was now a
secure beachhead at Arromanches. The big secret no
longer had to be defended, the feint that the landings

would be at the Pas-de-Calais was over. The official reason why the appeal had taken ten weeks to come round was that a full transcript of the eight days of proceedings had to be prepared. As news spread of the Allies fighting their way into France, British spirits soared – and for a while so did those of Mrs Duncan and Mrs Brown as the police van carried them from Holloway to the Law Courts in the Strand where they met the Homers again. Far from being the wan and wasted figure Helen's supporters had expected, they noticed she had lost a bit of weight and looked quite well, certainly better than in April.

Three judges presided at the Court of Criminal Appeal that day: Viscount Caldecote, the Lord Chief Justice and pillar of the Church of England; Mr Justice Birkett, Methodist son of a Cumbrian draper and an adviser on defence regulations; and Mr Justice Oliver, who had won the Military Cross in the First World War and in 1932 represented the Bishop of Norwich to prosecute the debauched Rector of Stiffkey, Harold Davidson.* Together, then, these judges brought experience of religion, war and national security; perhaps Helen never stood a chance. The mood on the day was inauspicious. The courtroom was packed with tearful Spiritualists, idle servicemen (including an American flying officer), curious lawyers and over-eager journalists. Everyone noticed the books

---

* Davidson found fame as a fairground attraction where he stood in a barrel 'starving to death', for which he was arrested for attempted suicide. Davidson's fate lay not in the courts, however, but in a cage in Skegness where in 1937 a lion, also starving, ate him.

piled on the counsel benches – calf-bound, time-worn tomes of irregular sizes from the libraries of the Law Courts and Inns of Court – both sides in the case having sought the wisdom of the past to make sense of the present.

The rousing speech Loseby had painstakingly prepared was deflated by persistent judicial interruptions and, however admirable the skill and grace of his replies, hope was stirred in Spiritualist hearts alone. On the question of the Recorder's bias at the Old Bailey trial, Loseby was required to retract an allegation of impropriety, but, when asked by Birkett whether he would have objected had the bias been in favour of the Defence, he laughed sardonically and replied that he should not be in court today had that been the case. A debate about the disallowed test seance followed, with Birkett asking whether the jury might have been allowed to touch the materializations, after which John Maude rose to speak. Debate about the precise meaning of 'conjuration' ensued, Loseby protesting that the word did not appear in the Bible, which was countered with the argument that invoking spirits (and not merely evil ones) was as close to a legal definition of conjuration as could be conceived. A protracted discussion about the meaning of 'pretend' stemmed from this, the judges upholding Maude's definition of 'to claim untruly', the inference being that Helen Duncan was an impostor as well as a necromancer.

Over on the press bench there was much scribbling, but Maurice Barbanell just sat there wondering what the spirits would be thinking. Sitting far back from the lawyers,

Helen listened to all the mealy-mouthed pedantry, looking flushed and anxious, and was silent except for the occasional sob that she muffled with a handkerchief. Her confederates were less emotional, although Mrs Brown shed a few tears.

For two long days the discussion wore on, touching on such recondite matters as the translation of the Old and New Testament, the true story of the Witch of Endor, variety in the Witchcraft Acts from the reigns of Henry VIII, Elizabeth I, James I and George II, and the sententious opinions of Dr Samuel Johnson. Witchcraft, sorcery, conjuration, invocation, magic and enchantment were all dissected and parsed in meaning as had not happened in an English court for over two centuries. Intellectual issues that triumphant rationalists assumed had died at the dawning of the Enlightenment seemed merely dormant. Loseby read from a 1727 edition of the seventeenth-century magistrate's vade mecum, Dalton's *Countrey Justice*, to argue that the spirits once linked to witches were diabolical familiars, a belief consigned to the dustbin of redundant superstitions. Nathaniel Bailey's dictionary of 1735, of which there was also copy in court, served the Prosecution best in that the definition of the verb 'to conjure' encompassed not only 'to raise or lay spirits' but 'to conspire' as well.

Volume after marked-up volume was passed to the Bench, ushers were sent to fetch more and the court officials began to yawn and doze. 'Look,' whispered Barbanell, nudging his neighbour, 'here is another going into trance.' Snoring could be heard above the nitpicking etymological exchanges, the bored riffling of pages, coughing and the shuffling of fidgeting backsides. At the end of the second day the judges leaned towards each other, muttering in consultation, then announced that judgment would be given at the next sitting in ten days' time.

The following Tuesday, just as Churchill was stepping off a landing craft at the Normandy bridgehead, Hitler took his war back to the heart of Britain. The first V-1 flying bomb, known as a 'doodlebug', landed in East London, killing six people. Swelling optimism in the capital was now punctured by uncertainty; even the government didn't know what to expect and set up defensive belts of barrage balloons, anti-aircraft guns and fighter patrols, fearing that ten thousand people might be killed every day.

Prisoners in Holloway, unable to join the million Londoners who had fled the capital by the end of July, were especially anxious. Helen Duncan became frantic at the droning of the V-1 engines, which was followed by a few seconds of silence as the bomb exhausted its fuel and began its deadly descent. Her reaction was not unusual: many prisoners were depressed or hysterical, symptoms that the Holloway medical authorities did little to acknowledge or alleviate. Ironically, there was one V-1 that may have given Helen some quiet satisfaction: the one that landed on the Law Courts, wrecking the chamber where she had attended the learned symposium on witchcraft just a few days earlier. Had this really been a witchcraft trial, such a timely misfortune would doubtless have confirmed and compounded her guilt.

On 19 June, with the business-as-usual sangfroid at

which wartime London excelled, an air-raid shelter was swept and furnished with plain wooden tables and benches, and there the spectators queued just as they had at the start of the hearing. Fewer than fifty people managed to cram themselves inside. And there they waited, huddled together in their seats, Spiritualists cheek by jowl with reporters and lawyers, even alongside Helen and her fellow applicants.

At least the proceedings were brief, not that the Spiritualists gave much heed to mercy once the doughty Viscount Caldecote began to read the judgment, the speed of which sent the journalists into a flat spin. 'You'll never get this down,' whispered Maude to the pressman squashed next to him. In the end it took the Lord Chief Justice just twenty minutes to get through four thousand words – three a second. Even the expert shorthand writers knitted their brows. But the gist was clear. The grounds of appeal, eleven in all, were dismissed and Sir Gerald Dodson's judgment upheld. Regarding the legal interpretation of historical terms, it was plain that even after the repeal of the 1604 Witchcraft Act the statute that replaced it and on which Helen Duncan had been convicted 'did not go the length of allowing anyone to make the pretence of engaging in converse with spirits, not being evil spirits. Such a distinction would raise an issue of fact incapable of determination and based on no intelligible principle of law or religion.' Summoning any spiritual entity, evil or benign, was covered, which made the Act applicable to the conspiracy alleged. In conclusion, Caldecote explained that the Prosecution had set out to prove not the impossibility of materializing spirits, but only that Helen Duncan had falsely claimed to do so on the occasion in question. A demonstration of her powers in court, he continued, would never have acquitted her on this count and might even have been misleading.* Frances Brown, it was decided, had served her sentence, less remission for good behaviour, and should be freed at once.

The second round lost, Loseby applied to the Attorney General for the case to be heard in the House of Lords: the highest court in the land. But that would not keep Helen from returning to prison that same gloomy day. She looked utterly forlorn, her face red and blotchy from crying. Before she was led out of the frowzy shelter, Maurice Barbanell snatched a few minutes with her. Smiling stoically, he told her to keep her chin up and reassured her that the fight would continue and that she would be vindicated. Saying nothing, she simply groaned as she was taken away.

More Spiritualist ink was spilled in correspondence and in the press. The Lord Chief Justice was criticized for misreading the Bible and attention drawn to the irony that he had rejected Spiritualism but elsewhere declared the Resurrection 'a fact beyond dispute'. But hot air quickly dissipated and did nothing to make the four walls of Helen Duncan's cell less real. At the Home Office a civil servant stuck the last clipping about the appeal (from the *Yorkshire Post*) to a scrap of old Auxiliary Territorial Service recruiting poster

---

* Today, the ruling *Rex v. Duncan* is best known among lawyers in relation to the power of a judge to exclude evidence likely to cloud the issue before a jury.

and the file was closed. Loseby probably did not expect the Attorney General to send the case to the House of Lords and was already planning to draw a line by writing a book, *The Vindication of Helen Duncan*, where 'the evidence will be made to speak for itself'. The eight days of the trial, and three days of the appeal, had done little to alter Loseby's understanding of the legal realities. Yet when he noted incredulously that the implication of the DPP's case was that Mrs Duncan was *defenceless*, he was closer to the truth than he knew: that was the ancient magic of the Witchcraft Act. This time, Abdy Collins packed his criticism of Loseby into a Psychic Press pamphlet, never published because of libel, and Percy Wilson pointed the finger, too. J. B. McIndoe was also writing a book, for which Loseby provided an introduction suggesting that the only person Loseby was really interested in vindicating was himself. He soon lost interest in Helen the felon and only held a torch for her as a figurehead for the Spiritualist cause. The fact that he had begun carelessly to misspell her name 'Hellen' may not have been significant, but his allusion to her ectoplasmic manifestations as 'parlour games' certainly was.

Only at home was support for Helen unconditional and pure. Her children had held out for the appeal, praying to God for a miracle and Albert for strength and guidance. Henry, too, never lost faith. By now he was being cared for by his daughter Lilian while Gena, who had qualified as a nurse, was out at work. Without Helen's income, the household was beset by money worries, especially since Henry had stopped accepting a dole of £3 per week from the Edinburgh College of Psychic Science in protest against their quizzing Gena about whether he had found a job yet. 'Do you not think your mother has kept him for long enough?' they asked.

Increasingly desperate, Henry decided to petition the Home Secretary, the Prime Minister and the King. On 24 June 1944 he wrote three letters, each a variation on the same theme: his wife was a good woman who had helped thousands but now languished in prison broken in body and spirit. Buckingham Palace forwarded their letter to the Scottish Office, who passed it to the Home Office; Churchill's Private Secretary did likewise; and Morrison's landed on Francis Graham-Harrison's desk, where it was reunited with its siblings and logged in a ledger. The Home Office had the perfect excuse to do nothing, having heard from the Governor of Holloway that Helen Duncan had made an application to the Attorney General, which meant the case remained *sub judice*. The first step towards the House of Lords was for the Attorney General, Sir Donald Somervell, to grant a fiat – a certificate – stating that the appeal ruling involved a matter of exceptional public significance; until Somervell made a decision, Graham-Harrison explained to Henry Duncan, his hands were tied. Henry had their family doctor summarize Helen's medical history in a letter which he sent to the Home Office, begging compassion on the grounds that the earliest Lords hearing would not be until October. The Home Office reiterated that they were unable to help while the case was under review – but were careful not to promise future action either.

This was prudent, for, in August, Somervell refused the

application, thus ending the fight to overturn Helen Duncan's conviction. Meanwhile, the Home Office, wary of making martyrs, had sought the opinion of the Medical Officer at Holloway. Given everything they had heard, officials were surprised by the MO's report, which began by saying that Mrs Duncan's diabetes was under control: 'Her present condition is entirely satisfactory as there is no evidence of any sugar in the urine with this treatment. As regards her heart there is some myocardial regeneration due to fatty infiltration of the heart muscle but this has been benefited to some extent by a loss in weight.' She had weighed 236 lbs upon arrival, which had fallen to 212 lbs. The report went on to note no problems with her gall bladder or digestive system. The only deterioration in her condition was mental. The flying bombs had caused 'mild depression' and in general she was 'very emotionally hysterical', although the MO thought twice about this and put 'emotionally *unstable*' instead. News that the appeal had failed left Helen more downcast than ever. She arranged an interview with the Deputy Governor so that the prison authorities would know that her present course of legal action was at an end, and they, in turn, informed the Home Office. The next day, an official at the Home Office wrote to Henry Duncan to reassure him that his wife was in good health.

Spiritualist confusion about what had been achieved by the Helen Duncan campaign was made depressingly clear by the continued activity of the police and courts. Within weeks of the Old Bailey trial a magistrate at Hull offered to dismiss the case against a fortune teller, charged under the Vagrancy Act, if she could predict how much he had decided to fine her. When she declined – the answer was £3 – he called her a fake.

Even more ominously, on 10 July 1944, Jane Yorke, a seventy-two-year-old medium, was arrested at her home in Forest Gate, East London. 'Why, after twenty-three years?' she asked the police. Mrs Yorke held seances in her basement, where the spirits spoke through a Zulu guide who impressed sitters with his war cry 'Umba, Umba, Umba!' Queen Victoria was a frequent communicator (Mrs Yorke scrunched up her face) and Sir Arthur Conan Doyle had been known to drop by. Her messages were not just vague but wrong, which she blamed on the bombing. Acting undercover, a police inspector was told that he had lost his father in the First World War; a policewoman that her dead baby was beside her holding a bunch of roses; and a sergeant that his brother had been burned alive on an RAF bombing mission. When Mrs Yorke hit upon the truth, however, the effect could be devastating. Already deeply upset by the medium impersonating her son, an airman who *had* been killed, a woman was warned that 'a loved one is going to meet with a serious accident but I fear it will be fatal'. She was told to watch out for her husband.

Jane Yorke's case was referred to the DPP, who paused while the Court of Criminal Appeal reached its judgment in the Duncan case then, confident he had escaped criticism, pressed ahead. He appointed as prosecuting counsel Henry Elam, who, surer of himself now, framed an indictment under the Witchcraft Act using a near-identical formula to that used against Helen Duncan, the only change, albeit a significant one, being a greater emphasis on the fraudulent receipt of money. On 12 September, Jane Yorke was convicted at the Old Bailey, but presumably due to her age and disability the Recorder, Sir Gerald Dodson, mercifully consented to bind her over for three years.

Jane Yorke's example was not directly comparable to that of Helen Duncan: she had divulged no state secrets, unless one counts Queen Victoria guaranteeing the success of D-Day ('Get your red-white-and-blues ready!') or Conan Doyle predicting that the war would be over by October 1944. The reason that the authorities used the Witchcraft Act against Jane Yorke is simple: after Helen Duncan they knew that they could.

This legal confidence is further reflected in events at Altrincham, near Manchester, where two weeks after Jane Yorke's conviction the police banned a public Spiritualist meeting – an address by a spirit guide, 'Dr Letari' – on the grounds that it would constitute an act of conjuration. The London and North-Eastern Railway had already stripped advertisements from their stations, the Altrincham Corporation withdrew permission to use the municipal hall and printers refused to print propaganda that the SNU had planned to send to MPs. Hannen Swaffer rushed gallantly to Altrincham but was forbidden to speak there so decamped to nearby Sale.

Such was the fear of the Witchcraft Act, cried the Spiritualists. In the House of Commons, Herbert Morrison laughed the whole thing off, but his officials were less sanguine. The DPP was twitchy after an MP asked a parliamentary question alluding to antiquated legislation and only relaxed when the Law Officers' Department informed him that the MP had been referring to a prosecution for failing to display notice boards outside a house the Salvation Army used as a Services' Club. In December 1944 a draconian ban on mediumship imposed by the police at Redhill in Surrey was met with mixed feelings by the authorities. The President of Redhill Spiritualist Church had been warned that clairvoyance and psychometry constituted conjuration indictable under the Witchcraft Act and was asked for a written undertaking that these practices would cease. Public protests followed, and the Home Office started looking at ways to weed 'crazy old nuisance laws' from the statute books.

By the time the news about Jane Yorke reached Helen Duncan she had less than a fortnight of her sentence left to serve. To her last day in prison, she remained tormented by the bombing and, unlike many London mediums, found little solace in her spirit guide. By then many of the V-1 launch sites had been overrun by the Allies, and 80 per cent of the doodlebugs that did make it over the Channel were intercepted. However, the announcement that the Battle of London was over proved premature once the first supersonic V-2 rocket smashed into the capital on 8 September. In Holloway, the circle of anxiety and depression became yet more vicious. Helen later remembered a wardress who came nervously to her cell, seeking comfort after a rocket exploded nearby, but it's more likely that it was the wardress who comforted Helen, the 'child of larger growth', shaking and weeping, alone and afraid.

On the morning of Friday 22 September, fear of the war became fear of the world as Helen was bathed, examined (usually the mere touch of a stethoscope) and her clothes and possessions returned. Less the usual remission, she had served 172 days of her sentence and, free to go, she was met at the prison gates by members of her family, with whom she caught a train home from King's Cross.

The girls were overjoyed to see her, and back in Edinburgh were moved by the sight of their father crying as he watched his cherished Nell snoring in a chair, napping away an afternoon. Extremely tired all the time, she seemed somehow diminished and was plainly unwell with her heart. A doctor referred her to Edinburgh Royal Infirmary, and she caught up on correspondence while waiting to be admitted. A letter from her dear friend Maurice Barbanell arrived, saying she 'must be overjoyed at the fact that the ordeal is over, but the fight goes on'. Barbanell urged her to take a holiday and allow herself to be guided by 'Albert'. She replied at once – he called her 'Nellie', she called him 'Barbie' – to say that she was indeed relieved to be out of 'that awful place', which had made her ill, although she had 'picked up wonderful' in the past week. Clearly Barbanell wanted Helen not just to recover but to reflect, but she didn't waste much time getting back into the swing of things.

The first thing that happened involved the SNU. The Freedom Fund committee issued a press release which stated: 'We are satisfied that Helen Duncan . . . was completely innocent of the charge of pretending brought against her, that her trial violated elementary principles of justice, and that she was wrongly convicted.' Yet they were unable to hide their self-interest, concluding that the affair had been a 'grave blow to investigation, advance and progress'. Helen, her hackles already up from the SNU's failure to help, formally withdrew her services as a medium. They had paid Charles Loseby's legal fees, but what good had that done? When word reached Harry Price that Mrs Duncan had retired from mediumship – her announcement was published in *Psychic News* – he was deeply sceptical. At the time when she was just beginning her sentence, he had ended a letter to Mollie Goldney with a wry prediction: 'One last certainty: when Mrs D comes out, she will be at the old game again!'

Price was correct. Recovering in Edinburgh Royal Infirmary a few days later, Helen wrote to the *Two Worlds* saying: 'My Spiritualism is my life, and for all the laws of the country I could not and will not give it up.' But there was more. Although she was sick, a condition made worse by prison, and couldn't bear the conditions imposed on her previously, she intended 'to keep my mediumship active'. And so, not long after she was discharged from hospital, she started to give private sittings near to home. Henry, who at least pretended to blame himself for having developed his wife's mediumship, was uncomfortable but was reassured by her promise that there would be no more nationwide materialization seances. For one thing, Helen regretted that by touring constantly and then going to prison she had missed so much of her children's young lives. She started spending more time with Lilian, Gena and Nan, and her grandchildren, telling them jolly stories from her childhood and reflecting grimly on the second shock wave of war she had experienced in her lifetime.

In December 1944, the SNU began compiling a national register of accredited mediums and to that end sent out a declaration to be signed by holders of its diploma. Helen Duncan received a letter, together with a notification that her five-shilling subscription for 1945 was due. The SNU knew from the *Psychic News* announcement that Helen had withdrawn her services, but persisted anyway. In February 1945, having received no reply, the SNU's Dorothy Wilson, the wife of Percy Wilson, at whose home Helen had performed during the trial, sent her a personal reminder. Helen signed and returned the declaration but said she couldn't afford the fee: she had no income and besides, after all she'd been through, she expected free membership. Mrs Wilson reassured Helen that she and Percy would pay her subscription, adding: 'I think you are wise to take a long rest from séance work. I hope you will soon get back to health and strength.' If only Dorothy Wilson had known!

A spirit once told Gladys Osborne Leonard that unreleased ectoplasm builds up in the muscles and can cause cancer, but the reason that Helen returned to materialization was more prosaic: it was simply what she did best, or at least it had been. Within a month she had broken her promises to Henry and everyone else and made short trips to Lancashire and North Wales, up to her old tricks. In these places she found the golden beaches she loved so much, which had been de-mined and cleared of barbed wire so that holidaymakers could return. Plenty of Spirit-ualists retired to such places, too. At Blackpool, the kiss-me-quick jewel of the north-west coast, it was said that sandwich-board men advertised her seances on the seafront, though this may have been just a malicious rumour put about by Spiritualists who felt her standards had fallen.

It was true that the psychic results were uniformly poor. Helen was booked to hold a seance in Ashton-in-Makerfield, a town outside Wigan. The sitters – three men and fourteen women – met for lunch at a hotel and were in good humour as they arrived at the venue, a remote cottage. But there they sat in a small room, twelve feet by fifteen, for two hours waiting for Mrs Duncan to show up. She arrived alone in a taxi, wearing a navy blue dress and seemed drunk. As soon as she had taken off her coat and settled herself in the cabinet the seance began. A voice called for the lighting – a storm lamp covered in red cloth – to be dimmed further, then a figure appeared, which one of the sitters, John Lane, thought was 'plainly that of the medium, draped in something white'. The spirit forms spoke incoherently, waving about and then retreating behind the curtains. Albert sounded tired, almost bored, speaking in a voice that 'dropped to a weary whisper at the end of each sentence'. He used the same stock phrases again and again – 'very tragic circum-stances', 'died from consumption', 'sing a hymn' – then wrapped things up by saying 'he hoped he had made eve-ryone very happy'.

The sitters were not happy: the flappy fabric spirits all

smelled of whisky, a seance suit had not been worn, the seance had lasted less than half an hour, and a cupboard or drawer was visible inside the cabinet. But they were all too polite to make a fuss, handed over 12s 6d each and returned to the hotel for tea. They were unanimous in their opinion that Mrs Duncan was a ventriloquist and not a very good one. John Lane, who until now had felt sympathetically towards her, changed his mind about the raid in Portsmouth and the trial, although he suspected she might still be unaware of what she did during a seance, which would explain why she was sincerely mystified about being accused of fraud. He just wished she would take a break.

Maurice Barbanell received complaints from Mr Lane and others – Helen performed a second chaotic seance in Wigan on the same day – and put a notice in *Psychic News* warning readers that whatever Mrs Duncan was producing they were not genuine materializations. 'That does not surprise me,' Barbanell added sympathetically, 'in view of the ordeal through which she has passed.' But he was powerless. 'She is a free agent, and there is nothing I can do to stop her,' he told Lane. He wrote to Helen, urging her to wait until her powers were restored or risk further imprisonment and damage to the reputation of the SNU, whose diploma endorsed the quality of her mediumship. On 13 April 1945, the SNU's General Secretary sent her a stiff letter about the seances in Lancashire and North Wales, which by all accounts had been 'entirely, and even dangerously, unsatisfactory and indicative of a very serious deterioration in your mediumship'. On those grounds, they said, the SNU had decided to withdraw her diploma. Helen replied to say that she wished the cowardly sitters had said something at the time; this was obviously a case of 'kick a dog when it is down'. The imputation that she was drunk was 'a damn cheek', she added, not least because she hadn't touched a drop since she was arrested in Portsmouth. Helen said she wanted nothing more to do with the SNU, signing off: 'Please don't trouble to reply.'

The war ended in May 1945. Helen and Henry's sons came home, Harry suffering from amoebic dysentery (he was in hospital, then married his nurse), Peter traumatized by a kamikaze plane that had struck HMS *Formidable* and killed his best friend. The Japanese surrender in August brought peace and new dangers. The bombing of Hiroshima and Nagasaki (which Albert had predicted), combined with the penetration of Britain's island security by the V-weapons, suggested that the next war would mean obliteration, perhaps on a global scale. Back in 1942 a spirit speaking through Mrs Osborne Leonard had warned that storms, earthquakes and tidal waves would follow the war, a message repeated at seances nationwide from 1945. Utopian Spiritualist aspirations for a new order of peace, light and the brotherhood of man seemed even more relevant in this new nuclear age than they had in 1918.

More immediately, Helen was pleased to help a fresh cohort of war bereaved, though she attracted all sorts, including a persistent woman seeking tips for the greyhound track. Her friend Lily Greig established a development circle at the Duncans' home, but this was disbanded when Albert said that no one there would ever develop as a physical medium, including Helen's daughter Gena. Helen arranged sittings in Edinburgh, where her manifestations, received less critically than in Wigan, included an African boy who conversed with a colonial farmer in Swahili. She also returned to her old haunt, the Spiritualist church in Glasgow. Then bad luck struck again.

The story goes that on one of her trips to Glasgow she agreed to take her granddaughter Dawn. Henry accompanied them to Waverley Station, but as they approached the platform Helen was struck by a premonition. Telling Henry to take the child home, she continued regardless. Stopping to buy cigarettes at a kiosk, and finding she had no change, she refused the vendor's offer of tick, because she was not sure she would be coming back. Just before the train arrived in Glasgow it crashed. Seconds earlier Helen had heard Albert's warning and hurled herself into a lavatory cubicle, which afforded some protection from the impact. She remembered being upside down among the splintered woodwork and arms reaching in towards her, and then woke up in hospital, where she was observed for a few days and then discharged.*

Even while she was recuperating at home, clients were knocking at the front door, invading her privacy, hemming her in. She breathed deeply and looked to Albert and the occasional stiff drink for sustenance. One evening

---

* This story is hard to verify. There were serious crashes on the Edinburgh–Glasgow line in 1915 and 1984, but none is recorded in the immediate postwar period.

Gena brought home a soldier she had met at a football match. His name was George Brealey. The house was quiet and dark, except for the fire in the dining room, so the pair left the light off before settling themselves on the sofa. Suddenly, Albert's voice boomed out a greeting and Gena realized that her mother was sitting in the room. Perhaps the strangest part of the story was George's reaction. It turned out that he was an aspiring medium himself, so when his future mother-in-law left her trance and introduced herself, he was quite unperturbed. But then Helen already knew all this. It was who she was and what she did. Wishing the young couple good night, she trudged up to bed, tired – so tired – and yet fed up with being at home: its dull routines, the constant interruptions, the lack of glamour. Helen was restless, ready, itching to get back on the road.

10. The Kiss of Death: Spiritualism's Triumph and Decline

In the late 1940s, June Moore attended a seance in a semi-detached house in Warrington, Cheshire. She had been raised a Spiritualist – her headmaster father had a home circle – and, now in her twenties, June was eager to witness a materialization. Aware that Helen Duncan had been in prison just a few years earlier, the organizers were secretive and protective. Collecting the medium at the station, they took the back streets and 'wrapped her up in cotton wool a bit', even refusing to let the handful of sitters meet her in person. Mrs Duncan sat at one end of the dimly lit downstairs room looking 'fishwifey', thought June, and around her a fog began to form, which drifted towards the audience. Inside this cloud, June saw a spectral old lady, whom she recognized as a woman from her village who had been knocked down by a bus. There she was, just as she had been in life. In a quailing voice, the spirit said: 'I don't know whether I should have come.' Her niece, who was present, reassured her, kissing her on the cheek and saying: 'It's lovely to see you Auntie.' And after that the spirit, who had felt as solid as a living person, began to fade and the fog rolled back towards Mrs Duncan.

By this time Helen was firmly back on the old circuit. Reports of her seances, ranging between the rapturous and the highly critical, had reached the ears of Maurice

Barbanell and the SNU, infuriating them. But there was nothing they could do: Mrs Duncan was now a law unto herself. In July 1945, Lena Hazzeldine, the mother of Peggy, the child Helen Duncan claimed was her spirit guide, had written to Barbanell. She had heard that Helen Duncan had resumed her seances and that 'Peggy' had been appearing, but said this couldn't be a genuine manifestation. These days Mrs Hazzeldine visited a reputable medium, where her daughter told her that she no longer saw 'Mummy Duncan', who now only pretended to be her. Seance-goers, warned Mrs Hazzeldine, should guard against imposture. Early in 1946, Mollie Goldney wrote to her SPR friend Lady Ruth Balfour, a distinguished doctor, to say that the Spiritualists were furious with Helen Duncan and had disowned her. 'She is giving sittings right and left', said Mrs Goldney, 'and drinking hard.' Some believed it was her fondness for whisky that most turned the SPR against her. Donald West was convinced of it.

It was Mollie Goldney who suggested that Donald, her protégé, should write an article about Helen Duncan, Harry Price having declined to conduct a joint study with her. To this end, she had asked Ruth Balfour about meeting Dr John Winning in 1944, at which time Lady Ruth was on war service in Winning's native Glasgow. Ever since Mollie had encountered him on the station platform, the SPR had wanted to see his photographs, but he was reluctant. Ruth Balfour, however, had seen all eight of them, the most striking of which showed 'Abdul', a black-bearded Arabian 'physician' who was ignorant about medicine but did know the names of all the nurses at the city hospital. When she asked Winning about Price's regurgitation theory, he had struggled to contain his anger, forcing her to make a hasty exit.

Mollie Goldney had liaised with others on Donald's behalf, including Price (who resented this Liverpudlian upstart) and Eric Dingwall, who offered to read West's draft, saying: 'I want this to be *the* paper on fat Helen.' Donald also benefited from long conversations with Mrs Goldney herself, who thought he needed educating in metropolitan ways and steering through the minefield of SPR protocols. She teased him for his 'leftish mind', played him Bach and was gratified to hear his Mersey accent fade. When the time came to publish his study in the SPR's *Proceedings*, President W. H. Salter feared libelling the subject, especially about her drinking. Donald protested that he had 'piles of witnesses' for this, including B. Abdy Collins, who, despite having backed Helen Duncan and visited her in prison, now said, 'Mrs D. is a dreadful woman and has always drunk something like a bottle of whisky a day.' In the end, Donald toned things down and in April 1946 submitted his article, in which he made it clear that his involvement with Helen Duncan was over. In October he received a belated reply from Elizabeth Homer in Portsmouth, 'Certified Masseuse, Diploma Holder, Healer, Speaker and Demonstrator'. Mrs Duncan, she assured him, was an honest medium but regretfully she had heard nothing from her since the trial.

Unlike Helen Duncan, Mollie Goldney was neither a drinker nor a smoker: she preferred to waste money on gramophone records, she confided smugly to Donald

West. However, apart from the odd attention-seeking burn, Albert's languorous slurring and a whiff of the saloon coming off the spirits, Helen's vices never did her much harm – she was too ill for that – but they were another stick to beat her with in a society governed by strict expectations of how a woman should behave. She couldn't allow herself to care that much: odium was the price of fame. And for every lacklustre performance there was one like that which June Moore witnessed in Warrington and would remember for the rest of her life – a tour de force recalling former glories, back when the ectoplasm billowed like a quicksilver cloud and Peggy sang 'You Are My Sunshine' like a mischievous angel. When Susie Hughes, a well-respected medium, entertained Mrs Duncan at her Liverpool home, her cousin, killed in the war, materialized, followed by her father. A big man in life, he embraced his widow, Mrs Hughes's mother, then lifted her over his head in a performance that was half tearful reunion, half strongman act. Susie Hughes also attended one of Helen's meetings at the local Spiritualist church, where she saw a Dublin colleen with long dark curls take shape from tendrils of mist rising before the girl's father, who was sitting agog in the front row.

By the later 1940s, Helen Duncan had settled into a pattern of work that kept her close to the devoted and, for the most part, away from critics. The venues were invariably small, discreet and manageable – poky Spiritualist churches in the margins of northern towns, sour rooms above pawnshops and chemists and Cooperative Societies – but demand for her seances was brisk, nor did losing the SNU diploma diminish her in the eyes of those devoted to her as a medium rather than just an emblem of mediumship. Helen's martyrdom was safe with such people, and at post-seance teas she told stories of degrading searches at the hands of Harry Price and Mollie Goldney, like an ancient Quaker speaking of past sufferings. Some new admirers heard for the first time that she had been tried for 'witchcraft' and were appalled.

And so, in her own way, Helen Duncan thrived. In 1948 Charles Findlay, the director of the Institute of Metaphysical Research, attended a seance in Glasgow, where, from a mass of ectoplasm, emerged Estelle Roberts's famous spirit guide 'Red Cloud', a Native American in a feathered bonnet. 'It was abundantly clear that this was an immaterial figure,' recorded Findlay. 'Any suggestion of its being fraudulent is quite inadmissible.' Findlay was also dumbstruck to be reunited with his sister, who had died before the First World War at the age of seven, and his grandfather, who was 'still the same bullying, overbearing person, loud voiced with a hair-trigger temper'. So impressive were the phenomena that when eighteen months later Findlay attended another of Helen Duncan's seances and saw her standing on a chair, 'deliberately and consciously duping her sitters', he put it down to personal hardship and mental strain.

Helen frequently crossed the Firth of Forth to Dunfermline, where she performed in the Cooperative Hall, the basement of a Presbyterian church and the cramped attic of a Mr and Mrs Lingwood. Eileen Lingwood, a friend of Helen's daughter Lilian, saw the usual glowing

parade, plus the cavorting Peggy and a glowing fairy twirl-
ing on Mrs Duncan's palm. Eileen's brother Harvey, who
had to tidy away toys to make room for the sitters, was in
the same Cub Scout troop as Lilian's son and was invited
to tea at the Duncans' house. Helen, bespectacled these
days, her hair pinned back in a severe bun, forced cake upon
him and told him he had healing powers. At a seance
twenty miles west of there, in the town of Tullibody, there
appeared a strapping Sikh in a jewelled turban and an even
more racially stereotyped 'Chinaman' with what a witness
described as 'large teeth and obvious Chinese features'.
The same sitter was overwhelmed to see his father, who
had died in the First World War. Albert's scornful remark
'I do wish Mrs Duncan would stop smoking!' only made
the display even more believable.

Despite the family's avowal to shun the Edinburgh
College of Psychic Science, Helen continued to work
there, too. Test conditions were applied, with vaginal and
rectal searches by a 'committee of lady sitters', although
since the war verbatim records of seances had been
discontinued – the excuse Donald West heard when he
enquired about sources for his article. In 1949 a young
woman named Denise Hankey flew from London to
Edinburgh to visit her mother Muriel, the college's
Deputy Principal, and attended a seance. Milky ectoplasm
spilled from Mrs Duncan's nostrils like solidifying egg
white, she recalled; sinking to the floor, it ebbed and
flowed in a swirling carpet smelling of body fluids. Albert
told Denise that a girl who had 'passed with a condition
of the lower part of the body' was present, upon which

the ectoplasm around Denise's ankles rose to form the well-defined face of a schoolfellow who had died from uterine cancer. The spirit asked Denise to pass on a message to their former headmistress, which she promised she would. Mrs Duncan struck Denise as a heap of flesh who drank like a fish – in other words, the perfect vehicle for materialization. She also had bad manners. The following year Laura Culme-Seymour attended a seance at the Edinburgh Psychic College, where she was reproached by the spirit of her dead daughter: 'You must hold yourself up and not stoop, it makes you look older.' It struck Lady Culme-Seymour as out of character for Marjorie to be so rude.

Sitters often found some parts of a performance suspicious, others utterly convincing. Mr S. M. Gardiner, a non-Spiritualist SPR member, attended eleven of Helen Duncan's seances in Dunfermline and, although he dropped her at the station on his way back to Glasgow, he was no fan of her as a person, nor, it would seem, as a medium. He was sorry that all a materialization of his father had done was point at his moustache, and he thought that 'Albert' was probably just Mrs Duncan's secondary personality. Gardiner hoped to borrow an infrared telescope from the Admiralty, where he worked, to find out what was going on. Yet the materialization of his young daughter gave him pause. Peering at him, her face eighteen inches from his, she said: 'I'm going to touch my daddy' and patted him on the head. His wife had a conversation with the child's luminous form and was convinced. Aware of Mrs Duncan's past, the Gardiners knew what they had seen and believed that not all her phenomena were fraudulent.

A similar conclusion, where truth was suspended between positive and negative poles, was reached by a seance-goer named Leah Longman. One evening in 1949 she arrived at a private flat in Edinburgh and heard the 'powerful masculine voice' of Mrs Duncan, who was chatting with her sitters, each of whom had paid 10s 6d to see her perform. A tiny alcove had been made into a cabinet, from which a spirit form appeared. 'It bore no resemblance whatever to any communicator,' Mrs Longman felt, 'but a marked resemblance to Mrs Duncan.' The spirits which followed, however, were more convincing – differentiated, voluble and emotionally alive – reducing several women to tears. 'My view at the moment', she informed the SPR, 'is that it is as difficult to explain the phenomena of Mrs Duncan on normal lines as it would be to accept the forms at the face value.' One of Helen's friends, Ivy Northage, formed the opinion that, although she possessed remarkable powers, Helen was nonetheless 'a very foolish woman' who was 'battened on' at home to make money, implying that she needed to resort to fraud to eke out her rapidly depleting energies.

Reports that arrived from time to time at the SPR's London headquarters always attracted interest. Donald West still hankered after a proper test seance like the one Helen Duncan had done for Harry Price yet denied the SPR. By now the SPR had increased its prize for proof of physical mediumship from £250 to £1,000, and some years earlier Donald had asked the Glasgow-based Mr Gardiner to approach Mrs Duncan on his behalf. She was indignant, asking whether by 'the SPR' he meant Price and Goldney before launching into the full story: the choking seance bag, the sanitary towel, the double stomach and the now-unemployable maid Mary McGinlay. She said she wouldn't do it for a million pounds. Refusal, sniffed Donald, served only to harm her reputation – but perhaps he just found it hard to accept that her popularity had survived and would flourish for as long as the law remained unchanged.

It was also hard for Donald to accept that the Duncans had again reversed their fortunes. They had moved a mile away to 36 Rankeillor Street, a four-storey sandstone town house on the edge of Holyrood Park, where Helen and Henry spared themselves the stairs by sleeping on the ground floor and letting the upstairs to lodgers. The Duncan household was a favourite with tramps, who called by for food, marking the doorstep with chalk as a sign to others. Helen saw her young self in a pregnant Welsh girl she took in. And likewise in Maggie, a despairing eighteen-year-old with alopecia, whom she met while out shopping. Helen invited her to tea and bought her a couple of wigs, and she stayed for four years. But even with guests in residence there was always plenty of space. Henry kept his books in a room he called 'the library', and another was kept empty except for a pianola. The busy, homely kitchen had a scrubbed pine table, a washing machine and a walk-in pantry stacked up with pickle jars.

Gena came every day to help, accompanied by her children, the infant Sandra (born on Helen's birthday) and a baby, Sheila – both destined to be psychics. When they were a little older they grew afraid of the rumbling of the water tank, which Helen told them was the sound of a bogeyman called 'Alligator Bill'. The environment in which

Gena's children grew up was as invested with spiritual power as that in which she herself had been raised, especially for Sandra, who chose to live with Grandma Nellie and was fiercely protective of her. Helen had known that Gena was pregnant with Ann even before Gena did and had asked her spiritual physician Dr Johansen, who saved her from a whisky-induced coma in the 1930s, to give her a health check. Perched on Helen's lap, the girls would write questions on pieces of paper which she burned, rubbing the soot on her arm, thrillingly, to reveal the answer.

In the world beyond Rankeillor Street, the religion of Spiritualism was losing vitality. Many had renounced their faith, especially after the spirits predicted peace in 1938, and new converts were few. The flowering of Spiritualism after 1918 was not repeated in 1945: the loss of life was smaller, its public impact lessened by experience. Of course, the grief of individual households – a third of a million of them – was no less devastating than it had been in the previous war, and for these mourners mediums were on hand. Minnie Harrison (the sister of the exposed Agnes Abbott) helped hundreds of widows and orphans between 1946 and the mid-1950s with her ectoplasmic extrusions, materializations and trumpet levitations. At a special Armistice Day seance in 1947, a poppy and a Royal Artillery tunic button were apported.

First World War soldiers in the afterlife, whose leader remained Raymond Lodge, complained that there were too few mediums to go round. The end of an era was approaching. In 1952, *Psychic News* reported a decline in psychic phenomena, which mediums themselves had noticed. Belief in the supernatural was not the problem. A Mass-Observation study of postwar London indicated that two-thirds of men and four-fifths of women believed in God, a majority of whom believed in an afterlife; one vicar said his flock still envisaged the world of carefree leisure inhabited by 'Raymond'; and over a third believed in contactable spirits, half in clairvoyance. It was just that enthusiasm for acting upon such beliefs had subsided. In 1944, Maurice Barbanell reckoned there were a million Spiritualists in Britain, but by the 1950s the SNU laid claim to a fraction of that figure. Originally a weekly, the LSA's newspaper *Light* had become a monthly in 1944, then in 1955 a quarterly no longer devoted solely to Spiritualism; in the same year, the LSA was renamed the College of Psychic Science to reflect changing interests and attract members drifting away from the SPR.

Spiritualism and psychical research, long at odds in outlook and purpose, suffered similar fates to each other. In 1932, C. E. Bechhofer Roberts had predicted that Spiritualism would be 'doomed to perish by the hand of its own child, psychical research'. He was right, albeit for the wrong reason. There was simply less active interest in the paranormal than there had been before the war. In 1948, W. H. Salter wrote a self-congratulatory history of the SPR suggesting that the ambitions of its founders remained as relevant as ever. The reality was otherwise. Postwar Britain had moved a long way from the intellectual *noblesse oblige* of Sidgwick, Myers and Gurney and their search for salvation from godless Victorian modernity.

Nandor Fodor, who had escaped to the more intellectu-
ally relaxed haven of New York, argued that 'psychical
research has tried to be too scientific for years and has
gone bankrupt as a result'.

This shift was reflected in the media revolution. Radio
waves, which had been linked to psychic communication,
were established as a means of communication in their
own right. Any territory occupied by Spiritualism in the
name of national unity had been ceded to the BBC, and
even interest in radar and extraterrestrial radio waves was
of little significance compared to the transformation of
popular entertainment. The new realms of experience
existed in this world alone. In 1939, 40 per cent of the population went to the cinema once a week, but with victory
even this was threatened by television. Ownership of TV
sets grew exponentially once transmissions, suspended
during the war, resumed in 1946, especially once coverage
reached beyond the south-east. Whereas only a few thousand saw the 1946 Victory Parade, two and a half million
households tuned in to watch the Coronation in 1953. In
television lay a paradox which would prove a bitter blow to
Spiritualism: people went out less, but they knew more and
they questioned more. Interwar Britain had largely accepted
what it was told, whether by BBC newsreaders or a commanding spirit guide. Spiritualism had also been a public
religion for gregarious activists; television was domestic,
personal and passive. Generations raised on instant gratifi-
cation would never spend the hours novice mediums had
formerly put into their development circles and used their
senses differently. Furthermore, light was let in on magic in

a more practical way with the increased availability of infra-red cameras and optical equipment. In 1936, Harry Price was on the verge of being able to film a seance and antici-pated the day it would happen. 'When we reach it,' he predicted, 'the day of the fraudulent medium will be over.'

Helen Duncan had enjoyed Spiritualism's best years, but now she, like the movement in which she had so inspired and vexed, was in decline. Spiritualist churches still exist, but materialization seances are rare and not open to the public. It's easy to see why. A photograph of Minnie Har-rison supporting a trumpet on an ectoplasmic pseudopod clearly shows a piece of cloth stretched from her teeth to a bandaged rod held between her legs on to which the trumpet has been fitted. There are no photographs of Mrs Duncan at work in the early 1950s, but this was the sort of thing she did, too. She admitted that prison had made her deceitful and stage fright affected her worse than ever, requiring a few slugs of Dutch courage. Seances went badly and ended disastrously. At the Alloa home of Mr Latimer (he who had appealed to Churchill), the sound of breaking glass – the Latimers' young son, unable to turn the handle of the lavatory door, had escaped using a hammer – had her suddenly pack up her things. She said that a torch had caused the ectoplasm to rush back into her body and returned to Edinburgh with a burned stom-ach. Evidently the memory of the Portsmouth raid remained fresh in her mind. Six months later Helen col-lapsed into a diabetic coma, her kidneys were found to be damaged and she was rapidly becoming infirm.

She refused to stop working, but needed a companion. Henry was confined to their home in Edinburgh, and Helen could hardly ask Frances Brown. In the end she found that companion in Gert Hamilton, who kept a seance room above her grocer's shop in Stoke-on-Trent. There Helen materialized an airman, a printer who had lost his fingers on a cutting machine and a woman who illuminated her face to show everyone her harelip; this time white light did the medium no harm. On the strength of this performance, Gert became Helen's personal assistant, making sure she took her insulin and keeping suspicious sitters off the front row. Albert continued to do his bit too, waking Helen in the night to warn her about a man with red hair who would come to the next seance. Gert kept an eye out for him and directed him straight to the back row, her suspicions deepened by the fact that he seemed to be wearing a wig.

Helen was in and out of hospital. Eileen Lingwood, then training to be a nurse, saw her for the last time leaning out of the toilet window in Edinburgh Royal Infirmary having a crafty cigarette, but Eileen didn't stop to chat, because it was raining and her starched cap was getting wet. Helen's medical complaints multiplied. Her eyesight had deteriorated (her letters had to be read to her); a trip to Paris was cut short when her blood-sugar level soared and Gert rushed her home; she suffered a minor heart attack; a huge abscess in her groin was drained, at which point she was diagnosed with shingles; and she was admitted to a Welsh hospital one Christmas with her diabetes. Most devastating of all was the news that came as she and Gert

were travelling back from Wales. Henry had sent a telegram to Gert so that she could break it to Helen that their
daughter Nan, sickly and long suffering, had died.

The phenomena went from bad to worse. Muriel
Hankey and her daughter Denise attended a seance in a
large hall in London, where Mrs Duncan managed to get
some ectoplasm on her face, but that was about all. Tony
Cornell, an SPR investigator, attended a Spiritualist gathering off the Seven Sisters Road, where the floundering
medium, somewhat the worse for drink, jiggled cheesecloth from a metal coathanger. Albert's sentences trailed
off distractedly and formalities were dispensed with. One
hand would poke out of the cabinet, click its fingers and
point; the other, concealed behind the curtains, invariably
held a cigarette, the smell of which was unmistakable.

Gert Hamilton did her best to keep things together,
and to the end Helen had the power to awe credulous
audiences. Tony Cornell admitted that the women around
him were in raptures – and this was far from being an
isolated occurrence. Chris Newberry had just finished his
National Service when he spent a pound on a ticket to see
a Duncan seance in a Nonconformist hall in Plymouth.
Various spirit forms manifested, one of whom Chris
recognized as his grandfather, a lay preacher, who seemed
astonished that he had not had to wait for the Last Trump
in order to return. Gert, who sat at a table next to the
cabinet, opened the curtains to reveal the medium still in
a trance, and the audience were tickled to see the hunched
spirit of an old lady who asked whether Helen was all right
and whether she should take her a glass of water. As a finale,

Gert helped to her feet an apparently oblivious Helen, who opened her hand to reveal, once more, the glowing fairy, who did a little turn on her palm. Everyone gasped.

Helen pressed on into 1954. Alan Crossley, a medium shaken by the war (his spirit guide was a soldier killed at Dunkirk), met Helen in Liverpool and was smitten, despite sitters muttering that she was not as good as she used to be. Alan went on to see dozens of materializations, including his friend's father (who encouraged his widow to get on with her life), twin babies in Helen's arms bawling their heads off, and the Mayor of Tewkesbury, resplendent in his chains of office. Alan also saw Helen do a double act at Southend-on-Sea with Maud Gunning, another well-built materialization medium; they turned water into wine and apported fruit and flowers, which they donated to a local hospital. On another occasion, he saw Helen dematerialize the contents of a cup of tea that a sitter had spilled down her dress. In London an investigator who had quit the SPR for the LSA found the medium dull and monosyllabic yet didn't doubt that his mother had returned wreathed in a white mist.

In the same year, though, Mollie Goldney received a complaint from 'a sensible sort of girl' about a seance she had attended with her flatmate. A faceless 'Albert' had Mrs Duncan's arm for a backbone, and an Arab who appeared was still sticking on his beard. A manifestation that one lady swore was her daughter 'looked exactly like Mrs. D. and more 70 than 17'. A Lancashire Spiritualist wondered if Helen should be told what was happening, fearing her possession by 'Powers of Darkness'. Mrs Quinlan from Manchester was grateful that Helen materialized her brother, who, she was informed, had died in New Zealand, but three months later was angry (as well as overjoyed) when she discovered he was alive and well.

Such recklessness suggests that Helen Duncan had given up pretending and was not even trying to be convincing, merely attempting to put on a half-decent show. At an after-hours seance in a hairdresser's shop in Glasgow, the spirits of a woman and her baby, victims of a fire, reduced sitters to tears – a sad mood lifted by the spirit of a merry fellow who sang 'The Lily of Laguna' and did a soft-shoe shuffle, then an elderly Highland gentleman, complete with crooked staff and pet Shetland pony, which, a sitter recalled, 'stood and nodded its head, as ponies do'. Around the same time, in 1955, in Gloucester, a woman named Jean Frost struggled to see a friend in the ectoplasmic form of a young woman and had reached no firm conclusion when it melted away; nor did the sad spirit utter a word. In West Kensington, Richard Sheargold, an SPR member, saw Albert – 'a long white streak with barely discernible features' – appear between Helen and Gert Hamilton. Albert showed the sitters his 'voice box', described by Sheargold as 'a peculiar object rather like a large white potato', and by others, in previous years, as a large pair of pendulous lips, a square box on a rod of ectoplasm and Mrs Duncan's draped fist held vertically. A dozen spirits or so came through, one of which looked like Helen Duncan in a grey hooded dressing gown. 'Another purported to be Latvian,' recorded Sheargold, 'but in response to floods of eloquence in that tongue from a lady sitter it made an unrecognizable sound which might have been anything and disappeared.' The following year saw Helen attending to the poignant desires of more refugees, this time from the Hungarian Uprising, many of whom had found jobs in the coal mines around Dunfermline. Harvey Lingwood witnessed the spirit of a woman speak to her son at the Cooperative Hall and, although no one knew if these words really were Hungarian, the man's tears seemed to speak for themselves.

Whatever scathing words Helen Duncan had to weather, she was at least safer than she had ever been before. All mediums were. Although the SNU deputation to the Home Office had failed to repeal the Witchcraft and Vagrancy Acts, the war years had seen a number of small victories: ministration for prisoners; recognition for Spiritualists in the services; promising challenges to the BBC's embargo on Spiritualist broadcasts; protection of Spiritualist churches and their endowments; and the right to hold Spiritualist burial services. And the bigger prize remained in sight. When the Labour leader, Clement Attlee, became Prime Minister in 1945, he appointed a Home Secretary who was Nonconformist in religion and libertarian in politics: James Chuter Ede. Attlee's choice was propitious for the SNU, which redoubled its lobbying efforts, sending a deputation to the Home Office soon after the general election and, overall, channelling the righteous indignation of 'An Amazed Citizen of Gateshead' and others who had written to Herbert Morrison. The Labour government were modernizers to whom the Witchcraft Act smacked of the Middle Ages, making witch-hunters of the police and turning the courts into an inquisition. Changing the law was a small price to pay to prevent state policy on Spiritualism becoming a symbol of British backwardness. The Attorney General had denied that Helen Duncan's case was a matter of public importance; Maurice Barbanell for one was determined to make him eat his words. And the fact that some legal experts were sympathetic meant he had a chance. 'The present situation, in which both Spiritualists and quacks are prosecuted under two obsolete Acts', *The Solicitor* had argued in 1944, 'is highly unsatisfactory, and calls for investigation.'

So far as the police were concerned, it had been agreed in 1945 that discretion over whether to prosecute mediums lay with chief constables, who, due to the publicity generated by the Duncan trial, were expected to refer all cases to the DPP. The Home Office too advised caution and took seriously an argument in Desmond MacCarthy's review of Bechhofer Roberts's book that 'the effect on a medium of public exposure is not what one might suppose: it brings a larger following and an increase in faith'. By degrees, the SNU was getting its way, and in 1948 Chuter Ede's Criminal Justice Act stopped the police arresting suspected mediums unless there was good reason to suppose they would abscond. Prosecutions grew rarer, although every time a fortune teller was tried under the Vagrancy Act – thirty-nine of them in 1949 – it was a reminder that a judicial sword of Damocles still hung over Spiritualists.

This sense became more vivid in June 1950 with the Old Bailey trial of Sir Trafford Leigh-Mallory's medium,

Charles Glover Botham. Glover Botham had promised the widow of a former Tory MP that £1,500 left behind a cushion would be dematerialized by her husband's spirit and given to charity. It was Mollie Goldney who exposed the con trick and Glover Botham was tried for obtaining money by deception. However, the charge was supported by an indictment under the 1735 Witchcraft Act in case it turned out that the hoodwinked woman had believed her husband would actually appear, which was an offence now well established at law as pretence to conjuration. The words of the judge, once again Sir Gerald Dodson, marked a significant departure from 1944 and were therefore straws in the wind. At his conviction, Dodson reprimanded Glover Botham for his 'great disservice to Spiritualism, which is held in great reverence by many devout people'. As it happened the fraud was so blatant that the judge spared the jury from returning a verdict on the subsidiary charges, but the SNU could still capitalize on the fact that the Witchcraft Act had been mentioned at all.

In the same year, Charles Loseby, who, despairing of England, had emigrated to Hong Kong, received a letter from Percy Wilson with all the latest gossip. The editor of the *Two Worlds* was a communist; Ernest Oaten was ageing fast; the secular Spiritualists were at war with the Christians; Hannen Swaffer had been having blackouts; Maurice Barbanell had 'fallen on evil days', embezzling the proceeds of propaganda meetings to pay for a lost libel action; and 'Mrs Duncan is misbehaving again!' The biggest news was that, as a Unitarian, the Home Secretary supported their fight for liberty and, although their draft legislation had been rejected, an alternative had been drawn up by the Home Office and Parliamentary Counsel.

On Monday 16 July 1951, the Spiritualists' Parliamentary Committee hosted a convivial dinner at the House of Commons in honour of the Spiritualist MP Thomas Brooks and Sir Hugh – now Lord – Dowding to celebrate their Bill receiving Royal Assent three weeks earlier. It had been read for the first time in November 1950 by Walter Monslow MP, not a Spiritualist but rather a Methodist passionate about freedom of worship for all nonconforming believers. Chuter Ede and his fellow Unitarians in the Commons, joined by Congregationalists, Catholics and Jews, across the political parties, endorsed the principle. Indeed, before the general election in February no fewer than two hundred MPs had pledged support for the SNU's aims. Brooks seconded the motion, calling the 1735 and 1824 Acts 'terrible measures to apply to decent folk' and alluding to the injustice of the Glover Botham trial.

After concern about exploiting the war bereaved had been expressed, Chuter Ede rose to speak. The day before, he had visited the Home Office library, where he found a 1616 edition of James I's *Daemonologie* and pondered what witchcraft had meant to previous governments. His speech was the epitome of reason. Next, an under-secretary from the Home Office apologized for joking about the obsolescence of broomsticks during the 1945 election campaign, which had been his reply to a question about the Witchcraft Act while speaking in public about the mass production of vacuum cleaners. Everyone in the House laughed. One backbencher remarked on the peculiarity of the English:

that only last night they had been discussing a looming war in Korea, and today not only were the front pages smothered in the Australian Test Match but here they were, chewing the fat about witches. Yet the cause was important. And Chuter Ede was sure that fraud would now be tried as fraud and witchcraft consigned to history.

A standing committee recommended minor amendments after the Bill's second reading and in May 1951 it passed to the House of Lords, where it was read by Lord Dowding. The former Lord Chancellor Viscount Simon agreed that using antique legislation against Spiritualists was shameful. The following month the Fraudulent Mediums Act of 1951 repealed the Witchcraft Act and substituted certain provisions of the 1824 Vagrancy Act, the central point being that intent to deceive or defraud would need to be proved. A clause provided a special defence for 'anything done solely for the purposes of entertainment' and all prosecutions would need approval from the DPP. Spiritualists were at last free to worship without the stigma of a magical, maleficent past that the Witchcraft Act inflicted upon them. Whatever her merits or demerits, Helen Duncan had accelerated this change – her case had been cited in the first reading of the Bill – and all Spiritualists knew it. The trial had refreshed old arguments and generated publicity that extended the debate. Chief constables were notified by the Home Office, and Theo Mathew, now DPP, asked to see only the most serious cases, 'not those merely relating to a gipsy fortune teller on Epsom Downs' – a phrase he borrowed from an old file. On the ground, the police were unsure how to adapt to the new definitions, causing one senior officer to make the following recommendation: 'I think the time has come to scrap all the existing instructions and make a fresh start.'

And what of Spiritualism in its hour of triumph, blessed with its new lease of life? There lay the greatest irony. A movement that for so long had thrived on being maligned and misunderstood, and had built its aims on persecution, found itself accepted and protected. It was no longer possible to rail against bigotry in the name of justice – that good old cause so ingrained in Spiritualist culture it largely defined it. Now was a good time for a medium like Helen Duncan to bow out, not just because materializing spirits had had its day but because there was nothing left to decry, and people stayed at home listening to the wireless, watching television and speaking on the telephone. In 1961, Bill Neech, the editor of *Psychic News*, neatly summarized the decline: 'Doyle died, the Second World War came and went. Swaffer stepped more and more out of public life, Spiritualism was recognized in an Act of Parliament. It was the kiss of death.'

In the darkest hour of the night, Henry Duncan woke up to see Helen fully dressed standing at the foot of the bed. She had been away to give seances in Nottingham and he hadn't expected her back so soon. Switching on the lamp, he saw her face was deathly pale and tears were rolling down her cheeks. He asked what was wrong and she replied only that she had been going to leave him – after forty years of marriage – but couldn't bring herself to do it. Perplexed, Henry reached for her hand, upon which her wraithlike form dissolved back into the shadows and was gone.

Unable to go back to sleep, Henry got up, dressed and made a pot of tea as the sun rose over the hill of Arthur's Seat. The postman would not call for another two hours and Gena not till nine. Restlessly, he put on his coat and set off into the chill of the autumn morning to buy a newspaper. Returning home, he let his eyes swim over the latest on the Suez Crisis: it looked like Britain would soon be at war again; what more was there to say? When at last Gena's face appeared round the door, he told her of his fear for her mother and she tried to reassure him, but she, too, was afraid. There was a knock at the door – a telegram, which they could hardly bear to read. It was from Gert Hamilton and stated only the barest details: the police had raided a seance, Helen was seriously ill and Gert would be bringing her home at once.

It was Tuesday 30 October 1956. Rushing outside to meet the taxi, Gena helped her wincing mother into the house, where she found even the gentlest kiss or embrace pained her. While Gert explained to Henry what had happened, Gena took Helen into the bedroom, began to undress her and, removing her corsets, found the cause of her discomfort. Even as a nurse she was appalled and let out a scream that brought Henry and Gert rushing in. On Helen's right breast was a burn the size of a tea plate, and on her stomach another as big as a saucer – injuries, Gert said, caused by the reabsorption of ectoplasm. Henry took over, easing his trembling wife into her nightdress. The doctor arrived and gave his opinion that the burns were electrical, whereupon Henry asked if they might have been self-inflicted. The doctor doubted it, adding that she would have to go to hospital anyway for her diabetes to be treated. Henry swore that this time he would sue the police and, after Helen had been made comfortable in the Western General, he sat Gert down and made her go over again what had happened in Nottingham two nights earlier.

They had been invited to stay for a weekend with Joe Timmins, a chiropodist and 'divine healer', who lived in a quiet avenue of semi-detached villas in West Bridgford, a suburb south-east of the city. Helen and Gert had been there many times, and people were forever ringing up to see when they would be returning. Helen, feeling better than she had in a while, held a seance on the Sunday afternoon and then rested before the evening session. At 7.25 p.m. Mr Timmins and his wife Amy ushered their visitors – fourteen regular sitters and six guests – upstairs to the back bedroom used for seances. One man, introduced by a sitter as her husband, Timmins had met only once before and two of their friends never. Everyone paid ten shillings and the door was locked. Gert gave a short introduction and then went to fetch the medium. As Helen took her place in the cabinet, a pair of female helpers attested that they had witnessed her change into her black satin outfit. Then the white light was switched to red. During a rendition of the Twenty-Third Psalm, Albert greeted everyone before introducing the first apparition.

Twenty minutes later, by which time two of the spirits had been claimed, the seance was brought to an abrupt

halt by banging on the front door and a continuous ringing of the doorbell. The four suspicious sitters, actually
plain-clothes police officers, leapt through the front row –
an uncanny re-enactment of Copnor Road twelve years
earlier – and tore down the cabinet curtain. Seconds later
a swarm of officers were in the room, torches shining,
cameras flashing, pinioning Helen to the floor where she
had tumbled. The main light was switched on to reveal
the room in utter disarray. Helen, her face a ghastly grey,
in the voice of Albert reassured Gert that she wasn't dead.
The policewomen searched down the front of her dress
and in her underwear. A distressed Gert asked: 'Whatever
are you doing?' to which one of the officers replied: 'We
are looking for the shroud and masks.'

Seated back on the cabinet chair, Helen was cautioned.
Still speaking as Albert, she asked for a doctor. The police
ignored this request, so Gert went to telephone herself.
Someone brought Helen a glass of water. A detective
inspector, whose name was Smalley, asked Mr Timmins
where the disguises were, to which he retorted: 'Don't be
silly, she's a genuine medium.' The sitters were kept there
for an hour or so while the police searched the house.
They even rummaged through Gert and Helen's suitcases,
while ignoring Mr Timmins's indignant demand that he
and everyone else should be searched. Instead, they were
all sent downstairs.

The doctor arrived and Helen was laid down in her
bedroom. Detective Inspector Smalley asked him to
search the suspect's anus and vagina, but he refused and
simply examined her (finding no burns) and gave her an

insulin injection. The doctor came back into the seance room and said she was dangerously ill. 'My God, to do this to an innocent woman!' cried Mr Timmins. The doctor left and Timmins went downstairs, where his wife was serving tea, sandwiches and biscuits to the concerned sitters. Helen, still prostrate on the bed, was questioned at length. The guests left at 10.15 p.m., the police three-quarters of an hour later. They took away the cabinet curtains, a red bulb and other seance-room paraphernalia, and some letters and personal possessions, though Gert persuaded them to leave Mrs Duncan her cigarettes. Standing at the door, Smalley assured Mr Timmins that they were only doing their duty, to which he replied with barely suppressed fury that an honest woman had been attacked 'in Gestapo fashion' and he never thought such a thing could happen in England. Timmins also accused the police of being 'godless' – like communists.

At 11.45 p.m. Detective Inspector Smalley phoned Mr Timmins to say that he had been thinking about what he had said about mediums being hurt by white light and had decided to offer Mrs Duncan a test seance with a police photographer and an infrared camera. If she were genuine, Smalley said, the police would drop the charges. Timmins told him it was for the police to prove her guilt, not for Mrs Duncan to prove her innocence and, besides, she might now never perform again. Then Joe and Amy, Helen and Gert, all went to bed, shocked, upset and exhausted.

The next morning, Monday 29th, the doctor returned and expressed grave concern for Helen's health. The police didn't come back until late afternoon the next day. Helen, who had not left her bed, was told by Detective Inspector Smalley that if she 'came clean', he could make it easy for her. She was distraught, sobbing. Prison was unthinkable; yet how *could* she come clean? Smalley took statements from Gert Hamilton and the Timminses and was handed two books on mediumship, one illustrated with alleged spirit photographs, which Joe said would make him a wiser man. Spiritualism, he assured the nonchalant inspector, was 'God's gift to mankind'. Smalley simply answered that Mrs Duncan might be charged with 'pretending to be a medium' and he and Mrs Timmins with aiding and abetting fraud. Just before he left, Smalley made Mr Timmins retract his accusation that the police were communists.

Helen and Gert were free to leave Nottingham, but they stayed another night until Albert felt confident that Helen was well enough to travel. Not wanting to worry Henry when he was powerless to help, it was only then that Gert had sent her telegram. On 3 November, Henry wrote to Joe and Amy thanking them and lamenting the 'duplicity and ignorance' of their enemies. Mr Timmins had already contacted the SNU's lawyers and Henry had written to Maurice Barbanell and other figures in the Spiritualist press seeking support. His wife was not the woman she had been before, he informed them, and it seemed as if her life's work was over and that she had come home to die. The *Two Worlds* reported the outrage, and in an open letter to the Chief Constable of Nottingham *Psychic News* accused his officers of behaving like the Gestapo, citing the Fraudulent Mediums Act of 1951, namely that mediumship was an offence only if intent to deceive were proven. By now, Gert Hamilton had asked a solicitor to look at the 1951 Act, and he advised that they had a case against the Nottingham police – although Gert was concerned that money had changed hands.

On 12 November, the *Daily Telegraph* and *Daily Mail* told the nation what had happened, after which Joe and Amy Timmins received letters of support, even from non-Spiritualists. They were convinced the police should not have entered the house without a warrant unless they suspected a felony was being committed. The next day Percy Wilson, on behalf of the Spiritualist Council for Common Action, wrote discouragingly to Timmins. Contrary to SNU advice, he said, strangers had been admitted to the seance, which disqualified Mrs Duncan from financial assistance in any legal battle. Henry, who was in regular contact with Timmins, began to lose hope both that they could sue the police and that his wife would ever recover.

Either the Director of Public Prosecutions or the Chief Constable of Nottingham must have contacted the Home Office, because, on 15 November, Helen Duncan's files from 1944 were called up from the archive. One imagines the police would have been advised to drop the case even if her health had not been poor. Given the inevitable publicity and possible martyrdom, she was best left unmolested. Besides, the charge – that a materialization had pretended to be the spirit of a man who was alive – was insubstantial, the photographs taken were inconclusive and there was no other evidence.

Without the Witchcraft Act, they would need more than that.*

Helen passed her fifty-ninth birthday joylessly in hospital. She had been there three weeks now, being stabilized and monitored, and was troubled in mind. Henry, still awaiting clear legal advice, visited regularly, passing on messages from well-wishers, but Gert Hamilton couldn't leave her shop, because times were hard, she said. 'She is like someone lost and forsaken', Gert told Joe and Amy Timmins in a letter. 'She cannot do with her own company at all.' A few days later, Helen was home in Rankeillor Street, but as November turned into December the family could do nothing to lift her spirits. Confined to an armchair, the pain in her back worsened, she ate little and couldn't sleep without tablets. Gena made her daily pilgrimage down the Dalkeith Road and found her father morose, her mother anguished. That morning Helen had received a letter from the Chief Constable of Nottingham informing her that her case had been passed to the DPP. Describing it as 'a calculated piece of cruelty', Henry forwarded the letter to the editor of the *Two Worlds*. Gena stayed with her mother, who was in such pain she wished she had the courage to end her life. Breathless from angina, Helen took to her bed and waited for the doctor. He could do little except inject her with morphine.

That evening when he returned to repeat the dose, Helen's condition had deteriorated, and Henry was told to

* On 28 November, the Chief Constable of Nottingham told Joe Timmins the case had gone to the DPP's office, but there is no record of this, presumably because the DPP dismissed it.

prepare for the worst. The next day the doctor administered more morphine and Helen faded further from the world of sorrows. On the Wednesday she gave out the few Christmas presents she had bought already and spoke tearfully of her mother, with whom she would soon be reunited in love and forgiveness. Nan, Etta and Alex, her children in spirit, were waiting for her, too. Her son Harry came and, choking back his tears, sniffed the strange floral perfume in the room where by now his mother was ebbing in and out of consciousness. It seemed her prophecy that she would never live to see another trial was to be fulfilled.

Later an exhausted Gena kissed her mother's head and went home to see her own family and sleep. At about 11 p.m. the doctor came to give Helen morphine and left Henry reading to her at the bedside. Before long he fell into a doze and did not wake up for several hours. Between three and four in the morning, with Albert and the legions of the beloved dead beckoning in her dreams, Helen pushed softly through the veil, not so much raging against the dying of the light as drawn to the light that had guided her life. Gena, who knew from a solemn knocking at the front door that her mother had passed, was ready when summoned at dawn. It was 6 December. The family made no formal statement, nor did they show any interest in Spiritualist pledges to petition the Home Secretary and have questions asked in Parliament. 'We want to be alone with our grief' was all they said. Maurice Barbanell travelled to Edinburgh to offer financial support and found the family calmly determined to seek legal redress. The story was covered in the local and national press: MEDIUM'S DEATH BLAMED ON RAID was the headline in the *Daily Express* for 8 December. From overseas, Charles Loseby issued a rare public statement: 'Helen Duncan was murdered!' Her death certificate, however, recorded diabetes and cardiac failure caused by angina.

Helen's body was brought home from the Cooperative Society funeral parlour and laid out in Henry's library, surrounded by books and papers and piles of letters and cards of condolence. Gert Hamilton – Auntie Gert to the grandchildren – took ten-year-old Sheila in to see her. Peering into the coffin, Sheila saw a woman serene yet bloated 'like a beached whale', even though she had lost a considerable amount of weight. 'That's not my grandmother', the child told Gert with tearful defiance. Henry, too, knew that what lay in the coffin was merely a lifeless cadaver and that his wife lived on in spirit and that she was nearby.

On the morning of Monday 10 December, Harvey Metcalfe, an SNU minister (and family friend who had photographed Helen's spirits in Dundee in 1928), arrived at 36 Rankeillor Street. After a short private ceremony for Henry and close relatives, Metcalfe accompanied them by car to Warriston Crematorium, three miles away, where wider family, friends, clients, ex-lodgers and the presidents of Spiritualist churches nationwide had gathered beneath a louring sky. A representative came from the Edinburgh Psychic College, where a minute's silence had been observed at their last meeting. Maurice Barbanell returned to pay his last respects. Rev. Thomas Jeffrey, a Spiritualist Church of Scotland minister who had attended many of Helen's seances, conducted the service, describing her as Scotland's Joan of Arc.

Beforehand, Gena had gone alone to the chapel of rest and, standing over the open coffin, had whispered that she loved Helen and laid a red rose on her chest – a rose, she was assured by a medium, that one day would be returned to her. Gena gave the ashes to her sister Lilian, who would treasure them in her bedroom beneath the framed photograph of the bust of Albert. Later, Helen's remains were brought home to Callander and scattered among the graves of the MacFarlanes in the ancient cemetery at Kilmahog.

After the funeral, Henry, exhausted by reporters, went to stay with his daughter Lilian in Dunfermline, returning on Saturday 15 December. He retired at 11 p.m., read for an hour or so, then switched off the lamp. As he lay there, turning things over in his mind, the room became very cold. A dark cloud, barely visible in the moonlight through the curtains, drifted towards the bed. Henry pulled up the sheets, but they billowed around him, and a hand emerged from the mist and grasped his, softly but firmly. Sensing his wife's presence, Henry cried out: 'Ma, oh! Ma, my dear!' The spirit gripped his hand more tightly, as if reassuring him everything was going to be all right. And then it was gone. The next evening was Helen's memorial service at Gayfield National Spiritualist Church in Morrison Street. In his eulogy, Henry told the story of his wife's spiritual return, which had given him the calmness and courage to face the future. 'The reality of the truth of Spiritualism', he concluded, 'is indeed the truth.'

Epilogue: Beyond the Veil

The campaign to remember Helen Duncan and clear her name began soon after she died. The *Two Worlds* appealed for contributions to a memorial fund and the Home Secretary, Gwilym Lloyd George, was pestered until he responded that complaints should be addressed to the Chief Constable of Nottingham. Mr J. Routledge of Gorleston-on-Sea in Norfolk wrote on New Year's Eve 1956 and receiving no answer – a new Home Secretary, Rab Butler, took over on 14 January – Routledge wrote to *Psychic News* enclosing a ten-shilling postal order for Mrs Duncan's fighting fund and encouraging Spiritualists to write to the Home Office. Routledge himself wrote again to remind Butler that 'Spiritualists are decent citizens of our country and are entitled to a citizen's privileges without fear of interruption by the police.' These were the 1950s, he protested, not the 1850s! Finally, a civil servant replied that this was a matter for the Nottingham police but assured Routledge that his 'comments about the danger of awakening mediums suddenly from trance have been noted'.

Fred Archer, who had succeeded Maurice Barbanell as editor of *Psychic News*, received many other letters and donations – a few pounds here, a few shillings there – from as far away as South Africa and New Zealand. Helen Duncan – 'immortal Helen', one admirer called her – had been 'deplorably degraded', her suffering comparable to that of Christ; clearly Britain had not left behind the days of inquisitions, torture and witch-hunting. Witnesses to her mediumship said they would swear under oath that she was genuine. A widow from Manchester gave five shillings and related how Mrs Duncan had brought back her son, who held her hand – 'no muslin about that', she said. From Sussex came an account from a man who saw a manifestation of a friend who had recently hanged himself, playing a tin whistle just as he had in life.

In the end the fighting fund was not spent as had been intended. Henry Duncan, upset and crumbling inside, being cared for by Gena, was in no fit state to organize his own affairs, let alone a lawsuit. He did manage to consult a solicitor in Dunfermline and applied for legal aid. Meanwhile Fred Archer instructed the London lawyers Hale, Ringrose & Morrow, who decided the whole case was embarrassing and passed it to another firm, who found they were duplicating the work of Henry's solicitor in Scotland. Besides, they said, he would never qualify for legal aid – nor were burn marks on his wife's body mentioned in the medical reports. A red patch on Helen's stomach 'may or may not have been connected with violence', and the Duncans' GP, Dr Lugton, refused to give the cause of death as 'emotional upset'. Even so, a barrister was briefed, who in November 1957 advised that the case against the police was not worth pursuing. Within a week it was all over. Joe Timmins also dropped his action, announcing that turning the other cheek was more befitting of a Spiritualist. Now it was time to decide who would pay the legal bills, with Fred Archer arguing that the fund should be for all mediums and that *Psychic News* could only make a small contribution.

Why Helen Duncan had been raided again remains a mystery. There were no rumours of conspiracy as in 1944 and it seems most likely that local police simply received a complaint and intervened to protect the public. Prosecutions under the 1951 Fraudulent Mediums Act were very rare, though, which does raise the question of what charges the police intended to bring. There is one final intriguing piece of evidence: the Anglo-French landings to reclaim the Suez Canal, which involved the British Secret Service, were the largest British seaborne military operation since D-Day. The coincidence – and probably it's no more than that – is stranger because the raid occurred less than thirty-six hours before the assault began.

The legend of Helen's life grew but commanded less public interest than would have been so before the war. Maurice Barbanell printed some salient memories, including an impromptu performance for Estelle Roberts where Helen, wearing nothing but a red tablecloth, materialized the racing driver Sir Henry Segrave killed on Lake Windermere in 1930 attempting the world motorboat speed record. Segrave appeared to his widow as he had in life and left his autograph on a notepad. Barbanell also recalled how Helen could make spirit messages appear on a slate – the trick she had been performing since her days at Callander Parish School. Other tributes were published in the *Two Worlds* and *Psychic News* – and yet what before 1951 would have become a crusade to emancipate Spiritualists amounted to little more than a trickle of nostalgia.

Fred Archer heard complaints that Helen Duncan's story was not getting the coverage it deserved. The last thing Spiritualists needed, they said, was trivial articles about ESP and reincarnation and flying saucers – but the times were changing, and a younger readership had less interest in the old ideas and causes. And the movement as a whole seemed more preoccupied with spiritual warnings about the Hydrogen Bomb.

Helen found her most fitting and enduring memorial not in the press but in the private recollections of people she had helped. 'It was as though the gates of heaven had opened and let me in for a short time,' said a housewife from Stockport of a seance she had attended. 'I cannot put into words the joy I felt.' An ex-miner from Yorkshire, who met his deceased mother and saw Peggy guzzling chocolates, ended a letter to Helen's friend Alan Crossley with these words: 'At the age of eighty-eight, one is getting to the end of life's road, but it does not worry me as I shall only pass through a veil to a better life where I shall meet all my loved ones again.'

Another life transformed by Helen Duncan was that of Ena Bügg, the shy girl from Gosport whose fiancé Ronald went to sea and whose friend Bob Brake was stationed with the RAF in Preston. Ena and Ronald were married in January 1940, but a month later he died when his ship was sunk by a U-boat. Although the spirits had prepared her, she was devastated and had no grave on which to focus her grief. All she had were his pyjamas. Ena sought solace in Bob and by the end of the year had agreed to marry him if Ronald gave his blessing from the spirit world. In the spring of 1941 Ena took Bob to one of Helen Duncan's seances, where 'oceans of white' poured from her mouth. Ena's grandmother appeared, then Albert announced a young man whose body lay at the bottom of the sea. With Bob's arm around her shoulders, Ena pleaded: 'Come on, Ron darling, come and speak to me', whereupon the cabinet curtains opened and out stepped Ronald wearing a uniform of glowing ectoplasm. 'Hello, darling,' he said, 'I've come to give you my blessing. I want you to know that your happiness is my happiness always. Take care of her, Bob, until she can join me.' Helen had done this before. Vincent Woodcock, a witness at the Old Bailey, received a similar blessing from his dead wife when he wanted to remarry; there was also the widowed mother of Alan Crossley's friend, told to get on with her life. But what makes Ena and Bob special is that they lived long lives, happily married with children and grandchildren, during which they continued to speak of their small miracle – and of Helen Duncan – with the same reverence and gratitude they had felt sixty years earlier.

Back in the late 1990s, when I met Ena and Bob, one could still find people who attended Helen Duncan's seances, although most of the key actors from the 1944 episode were already long dead. Charles Loseby lived out his days as a tax exile in Guernsey; Maude and Elam became respectable judges. Hannen Swaffer died in 1962 and swiftly sent a message to Maurice Barbanell: 'Dear Barbie, it is quite untrue that I am dead, Swaff.' Harry Price, the man whom Swaffer so reviled, died of heart failure in 1948, smoking his pipe after lunch; he was rounded on at once by colleagues in the Magic Circle, and Spiritualists and psychical researchers have been bashing his memory ever since. His sidekick – some said lover – Mollie Goldney was awarded the MBE (for work with the Blood Bank) and remained a stalwart of the SPR, crossing swords with credulous members until dementia claimed her. Donald West became a psychiatrist, Professor of Clinical Criminology at Cambridge, President of the SPR and a committed campaigner for gay rights. To the end he believed that, although Helen Duncan was a fraud, the case against her was unproven. Percy Wilson retired from the Civil Service in 1949 suffering from 'nervous overstrain', and as President of the SNU watched its prestige and finances go into steep decline – much as the spirits had predicted a decade earlier. His son Geoffrey, messenger for the Defence at Helen's trial, emigrated to America, where he recalled mostly how boring the whole thing had been. Stanley Worth stayed in the Royal Navy until 1953, when he emigrated to New Zealand, where he worked in real estate until retirement; he always denied that he had spied for anyone except himself. In 1949, he married the sister-in-law of War Reserve Constable Rupert Cross, who himself later left England for New Zealand. The shop in Copnor Road, Portsmouth, to which they brought such chaos in January 1944, was renovated and became the premises of a firm of estate agents. Demolition work on the old Holloway Prison began in January 1971. The Labour Party never did embrace 'the fundamental law of Spiritual Brotherhood' which the spirit of Ramsay MacDonald's wife predicted was the only hope for them and the world. The threat of nuclear war receded. The ghosts of the two world wars have thinned out now that there are fewer survivors to haunt.

And what of the Duncans? Henry died in Edinburgh in 1967, his second wife having failed to penetrate the cocoon of sentimentality he had spun around himself. Helen's granddaughters Sheila and Ann, who both became nurses in Staffordshire, shared their mother Gena's conviction that the legacy of persecution caused family members to neglect their psychic gifts and that the burden of blessed memory caused the break-up of their parents' marriage. Cousins, nieces, nephews and grandchildren were spread across Scotland, England, Australia and America, some more curious than others about their famous ancestor. There are still MacFarlanes living in Callander, where in the shops and pubs Helen is remembered with both forthrightness and furtiveness as 'Hellish Nell', although the origin of the nickname – her tomboyish appearance and behaviour – has long been surpassed by the memory of her conviction at the Old Bailey. In 1997–8, controversy flared up when a Spiritualist group, the White Rose Fellowship, presented a specially commissioned bust of Helen Duncan to Callander Community Council, who, after much deliberation, consigned the bulky bronze to a museum in Stirling.

Few other relics of Helen Duncan's life survive. The portrait of 'Albert' remained in the family, but the gold watch given to her by the 'Double Chance' gambler suddenly vanished after it was inherited by Gena, who inferred that no one else was supposed to own it. The fine furniture and books at Rankeillor Street were sold off, and her clothes destroyed or given away, as Henry retreated into his shrunken world. Photographs are scattered in archives, libraries and among her family. It is said that her trumpet was still in use in a home circle in Wiltshire in the 1980s; others she used are in the cupboard at the College of Psychic Studies. Helen's ebony mirror upon which spiritual fingerprints were left is there – at least it was in the 1990s – broken and dulled. The ectoplasmic sheet seized in 1939 is safe in the Cambridge University Library.

The wax cylinders on which Harry Price captured Albert's voice have not survived, although other recordings exist. Around 1955, Alan Crossley made one with his Grundig reel-to-reel tape recorder. The accents of the female sitters suggest the seance was in Lancashire or Cheshire, but the quality is poor and it is hard to hear what was said. 'Albert' we can hear: he slurs and sounds breathless, wavering between a parody of clipped middle-class English and coarse Australian, much of which is muffled gibberish and may have been so at the time: 'I wahnt someone – jus' like thees, but furthair beck, towards the cor-nah thay-are – to ask a yang laydee aaht that passed . . . Now, I hev a feeling that she's hed an operation of sam koynd.' And so on.

Helen's earthly legacy was augmented by her influence from the spirit side of life. On the day she died, a Nottingham shopkeeper and his wife, both Spiritualists, experienced a bad smell, which they tried to cover up by spraying perfume everywhere until they realized that the cause was Mrs Duncan's passing. In Glasgow, also on 6 December, a medium found she could smell ectoplasm and within a few hours had received a message from Helen. Sending love to Henry, she said she had been greeted by Albert and reunited with Nan and that the spirit world was even more wonderful than she had ever imagined. The news was passed to Henry, who was soon to have his own encounter with Helen's spirit: her firm hand from a dark cloud.

Much later, Helen Duncan's presence was detected at Gena's home circle, and once a trumpet levitated but without her voice. Elsewhere, Helen communicated many times and acted as a spirit guide to several mediums; and yet, except for her admonishing arm in 1958, she had never actually materialized. Physical mediums capable of such feats were a dying breed and, in any case, it was suggested, Helen had been so disillusioned with life on earth she never wanted to return. But in the early 1980s it emerged that a medium in Leicester, Rita Goold, was holding seances where Helen Duncan was the chief communicator (Raymond Lodge was another), appearing in full materialized form in the darkness. In 1983, Alan Crossley not only witnessed this, but spoke to Helen for three-quarters of an hour, felt the see-saw effect as she joined him on a sofa and nearly had the life squeezed out of him. Some of this he taped, including Helen's advice that he should take care, 'because you know what happened to me'. Helen protected Rita: once a man had tried to shine a torch yet failed because Helen dematerialized the batteries, dropping them into his hand before he was banished. A year earlier, a reporter from *Psychic News* took Gena Brealey along, where for over an hour a shadowy spirit resembling her mother engaged her in private conversation. Objects were apported, including a red rose on a long stem, sprinkled with dew as spirit flowers usually were.

Helen still sends messages from time to time and, free of her various ailments, is said to be happy in God's palace, basking in the Communion of Spirits and the Ministry of Angels. One of the most famous communications occurred in 1994, the fiftieth anniversary of the trial, at a home circle at Scole in Norfolk. Sitters heard 'a soft plop' on the table, and 'Mrs Bradshaw', a spirit helper, informed them of Mrs Duncan's presence. Unable to speak, she brought a relic 'from an unhappy time in her life': a pristine copy of the *Daily Mail*, dated 1 April 1944, in which the lead story was her conviction. The Scole Circle had grown out of the Noah's Ark Society, founded in 1990 to revive physical mediumship. Disagreement over the genuineness of their spectacular effects (apports from Churchill, extraterrestrial voices, coloured lights and images on unexposed film, including of St Paul's Cathedral during the Blitz) divided the Council of the SPR.

Modern parapsychology pays little attention to spooks and ectoplasm, and more to telepathy and precognition. The public is no longer much interested in it as a discipline. Like today's Spiritualists, who still worship in most towns, parapsychologists tell themselves comforting stories which help them to believe they are winning a war of revelation, and abide by the dictum attributed to Sir James Dewar, inventor of the Thermos flask, that minds are like parachutes: they only work when they are open. Others prefer the advice of philosopher Jacob Needleman, who once cautioned against being 'so open-minded that your brains fall out'.

In modern Britain, widespread belief in the supernatural has so many shades and outlets that most of us hardly notice it. Christianity, Hinduism, Islam, Judaism, Buddhism and so on are all established codes whereby mortals have faith in forces and entities for which no tangible evidence exists. Wicca – New Age paganism – is a growing religion. Others engage with imaginary forces by reading horoscopes, walking round ladders and avoiding travel on Friday the 13th. In 1993, four members of a jury at Hove in Sussex used a ouija board to contact a murder victim's spirit to help them in their deliberations, then convicted the person named. And we should remember that the Western world is the *most secularized* corner of the globe, a place where for over two centuries people have worshipped technology, industry and consumerism, and by and large have stopped going to church.

Elsewhere, belief in witchcraft as a harmful and a healing power is indistinguishable from beliefs endemic in pre-modern Britain. In 1997, Syria executed a man for the crime of witchcraft. And in the last thirty years there have been witch lynchings in India, South-East Asia and Papua New Guinea and throughout sub-Saharan Africa, including Tanzania, where 5,000 suspects died between 1994 and 1998. In the Indian state of Andhra Pradesh arrests for burning alleged witches are a frequent occurrence.

Just three hundred years ago, at Kirkcudbright, Dumfriesshire, this was how governors and governed alike dealt with the luckless Elspeth McEwen.

All of which leaves Helen Duncan as a more mainstream representative of human nature than she might at first appear. Animism – the belief in spirits – is the oldest religious belief, anxiety for survival our oldest emotion, stretching back hundreds of thousands of years to when hominids became conscious they would die yet were unable to contemplate their own extinction. Imagining death remains a sublime paradox. Because of this, perhaps, and because we seek to control destiny, our innate mentality is not secular but magical. Our ancestors, like people in the developing world today, believed in witches because intuitively it made sense to explain the world that way. Many of us resist the idea that our lives are shaped by intangible forces and that an afterlife exists, and yet are surprised to find ourselves praying at times of crisis. We can't prove that God and the devil are scholastic fictions, that the heavens are empty and that Raymond Lodge is not up there sipping a whisky and soda as his father believed. No matter: the sheer *desire* to imagine an enchanted universe is enough.

The comfort of speaking with the dead might make Helen Duncan's trial in 1944 seem unjust after all. Perhaps she did have an unselfish love for humanity, a tap you couldn't turn off. Some, of course, would go further: her sentence was unjust because she genuinely raised the dead. In 1997, the centenary of her birth, a campaign to have her conviction quashed was revived by a group of

Spiritualists advised by a retired Quaker barrister. When
the Criminal Cases Review Commission refused to refer
the case to the Court of Appeal (because the conviction
predated the Fraudulent Mediums Act), campaigners
moved to secure a Free Pardon by exercise of the Royal
Prerogative of Mercy – granted only once before, in 1966,
in the case of Timothy Evans, hanged for murder in 1950.
The press showed an interest, the headline in the
Guardian – PARDON HOPE FOR LAST WITCH BRANDED A
WARTIME TRAITOR – being broadly typical. The *Times*
showed a cartoon of Home Secretary Jack Straw recommending clemency to the Queen after his transformation
into a toad.

Who knows what Helen Duncan wants? Even in death
she has been pulled this way and that. The leading activist
Michael Colmer claimed to have been warned by her
spirit to 'Steer clear of the family, laddie'; but then by
and large her relatives believe she only wants to rest in
peace. 'It seems to matter a great deal more down there
than it does up here,' the spiritual Helen told the SNU
President. Colmer appealed to his MP, Michael Ancram,
to put pressure on the Home Office to act, leading the
Italian parapsychology journal *Luce e Ombra* to revisit the
Helen Duncan story in an article entitled 'Tony Blair and
the Last English Witch'. Yet what was true of the Home
Office in 1944 remains true: the Secretary of State cannot
reverse decisions made by the courts. By the summer of
1999 the case was no longer under active consideration
and Michael Ancram returned the papers sent to him by
Michael Colmer. The campaigners remained optimistic,

however, insisting that their work had entered a 'discreet phase'.

'One day the truth will come out,' Alan Crossley predicted, 'it's all there in the archives, and when it does she'll be hailed as a martyr.' It will never happen, nor will campaigners get their way. There is no truth to uncover, at least no single version of events to banish speculation and controversy for all time. Solving historical mysteries often gets harder the deeper one delves – the muddy water rises, the sides of the hole fall in – especially concerning matters of wartime secrecy. As Churchill said about the preparations for D-Day: 'Truth is so precious that she should always be attended by a bodyguard of lies.' It all comes down to interpretation. The research materials for this book lend themselves more to fiction than would be usual in a historical biography, which is why I have limited how far the narrative steps outside the world those materials purport to describe. That my personal opinions seep through is inevitable, but as far as possible the seance-goers and psychical researchers have been permitted to tell their stories in their own way.

Besides, the purpose of this book is not merely to valorize, vilify or vindicate Helen Duncan, but to do all those things – and with an ulterior motive. At one level her life, viewed in the round, has as much potential to entertain as any adventure. There's no denying the truth of Alan Crossley's remark that her story is 'one of tragedy and absurdity, yet at the same time one of triumph over adversity', and as such that it deserves to be told. But there's something else. Her story opens a window on the twentieth century, not merely as a sequence of events but as a cultural drama where unspoken assumptions and ambivalent attitudes were as influential as concrete statements and actions. In a children's history book her trial is illustrated by a cartoon of a woman in 1940s clothing tied to a stake and about to be burned, at which point a member of the crowd turns to another and says: 'You don't think we might be overreacting just a bit?' The appeal of the joke suggests that the story of Hellish Nell is important not just because it is her due, nor even because it teaches us about a wider historical terrain, but because it provides a commentary on the human condition, on love, truth, power and death – all things children understand as instinctively as they understand the allure of witchcraft.

Postscript: Nell Revisited

Soon after *Hellish Nell* was first published, in 2001, I gave a talk at the Cheltenham Festival of Literature. I was standing on the stage of the town hall and, as my eyes adjusted to the footlights, I could see there was a full house. I did my standard turn on Helen Duncan and invited questions. To my right, in the front row, an elderly woman in hat and coat raised a hand. 'Young man', she began, 'I lost my father in the First World War, and it destroyed our family. Then Mrs Duncan brought him back and made us whole again. So, when you stand there telling stories of fraud and witchcraft, all I can say is you don't know what you're on about.' A heartbeat of silence. 'Thank you', I replied, my mouth dry. 'Please let me explain.' But she was already on her feet, leaning on a stick. 'I'm sorry', she said with show-stopping defiance. 'I have to catch my bus.' Then she made off into the gloom and with a clunk of the fire door was gone. Rows of heads turned from the exit back to me. I felt as exposed to scrutiny as any medium when the curtains parted, and with no 'Peggy' or 'Albert' to help me.

It was embarrassing, but also electrifying. The room had heard the voice of a bereaved child cutting through the decades, unmuffled by time. And the interjection had made my point better than I ever could. Behind the delusions of the seance room lay real emotional power and, controversially, real value in the therapeutic power of mediumship. Belief in an immortal soul is a conviction, not a choice, a devotion of the heart rather than the mind. The colourful eccentricity of Spiritualism obscures its power as a means of self-expression, and the same is true of its scientific cousin psychical research. Finding meaning and solace in an intangible realm is a defining human characteristic, more ancient and prevalent than disbelief in such a realm.

A quarter of a century has passed since I started researching Helen Duncan's story.

When the book first came out, some readers were unhappy. *Psychic News* reviewed *Hellish Nell* twice, first calling it 'a character-assassination disguised as a serious study', and then, in effect, an attack on Spiritualism. Others thought I should have tightened my grip. What had *actually* happened? The novelist Julie Myerson would have liked to be guided through this 'downright weird material' – the seance-room puppetry and mimicry, alternating moods of levity and schmaltz and the misdirection of histrionic swoons and intimidating outbursts. But all these things were part of a unified historical picture, which I'd wanted to describe intact. I was explicit about Mrs Duncan's fraudulent methods and yet stopped short of condemning mediums. Sitting on the fence, however awkwardly, was the only way to capture the emotional force of Helen Duncan's story.

Seance phenomena are easily explained; quirks of perception are endlessly mysterious. Like Jung, who once said it was irrelevant to him whether rapturous Catholics had actually seen the Virgin Mary, since his interest was only in how such visitations were experienced, the parapsychologist Donald West was fascinated by beliefs he didn't hold. He had witnessed Helen Duncan in action, and saw in *Hellish Nell* a sympathetic portrayal of Spiritualism suited to recovering a complex historical reality. He also understood why Mrs Duncan's followers revered her as a true yet flawed medium. 'Provided miracles conform to prevalent religious beliefs, as Helen's manifestations conformed to Spiritualist traditions of her daya,' he wrote, 'they become for the faithful undeniable occurrences, unaffected or even reinforced by evidence of fakery, which can always be interpreted as the imitation of something genuine.' Hilary Mantel noted in her review of the book the 'position of observant neutrality' from which I surveyed not only supernatural belief but the suffering of twentieth-century working-class women, much as her novel *Beyond Black* entered the twilight world of unhappy mediums for whom the pestering dead were just another misery to endure. Mantel also described the trickiness of the paranormal, which exposed writers 'both to accusations of crankiness and to a sort of self-disgust about the sensationalism involved'. 'It is hard to sift out an acceptable truth,' she continued, 'given the human tendency to confabulate, the fallibility of memory, the wide scope for interpretation and the prejudice which invests the whole subject.'

Mantel picked up on my desire to vanish in the presence of my subject. 'He would not like to think', she said, 'that, like some spirit guide made of papier-mâché, he is now Helen's announcer, her mouthpiece, and that his dematerialisation amounts to crouching in the half-light behind a torn curtain on a rickety rail.' I've come to feel very much like Helen Duncan's announcer, however, and could never have imagined how mightily she would continue to dwell in me. Whether you believe in Spiritualism or not – and I still don't – a biographical subject who made a career from the belief in life after death remains stubbornly present, like a guest on the verge of outstaying their welcome yet worryingly comfortable in that armchair. I subsequently returned in my writing to an earlier historical era where everyone is unequivocally dead, unlike the twentieth century, where spirits and the people who saw them linger. I have felt close to my seventeenth-century subjects, but none has ever left me phone messages or had me over for tea and cake.

My disbelief notwithstanding, I admit that while researching the book I had some odd experiences. One night the TV and radio in my bedroom switched on when I was asleep. Visiting a chaotic second-hand bookshop in Cambridge, I was drawn to an unlabelled packet of family photographs, just lying there, all of Main Street, in Callander, the town where Helen Duncan was born and grew up. At a flea market in Guernsey, where I'd gone to examine Charles Loseby's archive and interview his daughter, I noticed a few old copies of *The Times*, which turned out to be exclusively from March and April 1944 and covered the whole of the Duncan trial. Weirdest of all, perhaps, as I was writing this book the date on my computer changed to 6 December 1956 – the day Mrs Duncan died.

I can't explain any of this, but I'd swear I imagined it all before I'd suppose that a discarnate spirit was playing tricks on me. If I were a Spiritualist, I probably would have shared these occurrences with my fellow worshippers, but disbelievers who experience the uncanny have no one to tell, unless they want to be thought dishonest or deluded, even psychotic. Spiritualists may suppose that I'm in denial about life after death, as Conan Doyle insisted Houdini was. Who knows? Spiritualism is subjective, free of orthodoxy. In its Victorian heyday this had been the appeal: an end to blind faith and obedience for the age of science, technology and mass movements.

No surprise, then, that Helen Duncan's legacy continues to divide opinion. Even her supporters disagree, some believing she was an absolutely genuine physical medium, others that she had real powers and yet sometimes resorted to fraud. Her diehard champions emphasize different things: she was a wonderful person and an eternal inspiration to psychics; she was the victim of a miscarriage of justice, a martyr; she remains a neglected source of proof for postmortem survival.

In preparing this postscript, I literally dusted off a box file labelled 'Hellish Nell: Recent Research' and tipped the contents onto my desk. There were articles, clippings, Xeroxes, notes, letters, photographs and pamphlets – all related to things that had come to light since 2001. I was immediately re-enchanted by that phantasmagoria of hauntedness, voyeurism and indignation. The first thing off the pile was an article by Victor Zammit, a retired Australian lawyer, claiming that belief in Spiritualism is irrelevant in the face of proof. His website linked to a sound recording of a conversation, apparently with the spirit of Houdini, and had a film clip of Zammit promoting a book written with his wife Wendy. According to the Zammits, Helen Duncan was 'one of the most important women in psychic history', a pilloried martyr denied natural justice. The state-led conspiracy against her was 'outrageous, immoral, unconscionable and violated every human and legal right of a human being'.

For thirty years there has been a campaign to clear Helen Duncan's name. The British Society of Paranormal Studies, and its founders Michael Colmer and James MacQuarrie, led the way in association with the Noah's Ark Society for Physical Mediumship. In 1997 the Criminal Cases Review Commission turned down an application for Helen Duncan's conviction to be quashed, deciding that her conviction had been 'fair' back in 1944. But in January 2001, just before *Hellish Nell* came out, the *Sunday Telegraph* reported that there was fresh hope. An appeal court ruling in another case by the Lord Chief Justice, Harry Woolf, had shifted the justification for verdicts from contemporary standards of fairness to today's; this, said Lord Woolf, was the only way to ensure the safety of historic convictions. Encouraged by this line of reasoning, the legal director of the Helen Duncan pardon campaign, Derek Wilmott, felt that justice was now 'inevitable'. Petitions were, however, rejected by both the Scottish Parliament and the Home Office, and then, in June 2002, Wilmott died. Colmer, his sights now set on the European Court of Human Rights, sought 'earthly advice' and £50,000 to fund a case likely to last three years. An advert in *Witch-Craft Times* appealed for free legal counsel and 'a company or a wealthy individual to help fund the project to get justice beyond the grave for Helen'.

The story hit the press again at the end of 2006. The Helen Duncan campaign was reinvigorated by two developments, neither concerned with Spiritualism. The first was an announcement in August that the 306 British and Commonwealth servicemen shot for cowardice or desertion in the First World War were to be pardoned; the second, in November, was Prime Minister Tony Blair's expression of 'deep sorrow' – stopping short of an apology – for Britain's role in the slave trade. The sympathy of the present for the past seemed promising. In October the *Edinburgh Evening News* printed the memories of Mary Martin of Craigmillar about the persecution of her grandmother, Helen Duncan. 'It's upsetting thinking about it. The whole family were devastated.' When Helen was released from prison, recalled Mrs Martin, she had lost the will to live and never really recovered. Mrs Martin was in no doubt about Grandma Duncan's honesty and goodness. 'I am so proud of her – she did nothing wrong. I loved that lady and I still miss her after all these years.' An English newspaper picked up on Mary Martin's story in January 2007. 'Our troops were preparing for D-Day,' she was quoted as saying. 'Why did they spend ten days trying an old lady for witchcraft?' Mrs Martin remembered being mocked at school for having a grandmother tried as a witch. 'It was all in the papers, and of course the evil eye, witch-spawn – you name it, we were called it.'

Another petition was sent to the Home Secretary, John Reid, requesting a pardon for Helen Duncan. Now the impetus came from Gordon Prestoungrange, the incumbent of a medieval barony at Prestonpans, near Edinburgh, who had exercised his seigneurial right to pardon eighty-one local women and men executed as witches. 'The prosecution and conviction of Helen Duncan', said Dr Prestoungrange, 'was clearly as much of an injustice as those of the sixteenth and seventeenth centuries.' Others lent support. Full Moon Investigations, a group of Scottish clairvoyant paranormal detectives, wrote to the Holyrood Petitions Committee, demanding that it lobby the Home Office in Westminster. A petition was sent to Home Secretary Jacqui Smith in February 2008, but nothing came of it. Around this time, the education director at the Salem Witch Museum in Massachusetts remarked that Helen Duncan was 'very much victimized by her times'. Salem's example gave Helen Duncan campaigners hope. Michael Colmer argued that pardons issued to the twenty women and men executed during the trials of 1692 should have come from the UK government, given that Massachusetts was an English colony at the time. And if Britain were to pardon Americans, speculated Colmer, 'What about the Scots woman they have been trying to ignore for all of this time?'

The Scottish Parliament rejected another petition in 2008, and yet another in 2012. In that year Michael Colmer died, robbing the campaign of its leading light. To mark the fiftieth anniversary of Helen Duncan's death, in 2016 five hundred pages of legal argument were sent to the Criminal Cases Review Commission but were returned unread because the application was deemed 'not in the public interest'. The following year, however, the Policing and Crime Act gave campaigners their best chance for years – or so they claimed. This Act contained the so-called 'Turing Law', an amnesty for men convicted of homosexual acts before 1967, named after the mathematician Alan Turing, granted a royal pardon in 2013. Lord Woolf's revised concept of fairness came into play: convictions for decriminalized activity cannot be upheld. Graham Hewitt, a retired solicitor acting for Helen Duncan's grandchildren, the son of a materialization medium himself, asserted that Turing's pardon 'has set a precedent for Helen's pardon to come. The circumstances are almost identical.' Plans were announced to lobby the Scottish Parliament, but whether they came to anything is unclear.

Victor Zammit has said that Helen Duncan's name will be cleared only by adjudication at the UN Human Rights Commission. Failing that, her followers should send a delegation to her birthplace to stage a 'symbolic exoneration'. To my knowledge no such delegation has gone there – though it might be warmly received. Helen Duncan is remembered in Callander with curiosity and sympathy. In 2019 a proposal to name a street after her was under consideration, and the medium's granddaughter, Margaret Hahn, who lives in Tennessee, was enthusiastic. Mrs Hahn fronts the official Helen Duncan website, which has a petition to clear the name of 'an extraordinary woman and a wonderfully caring mother and grandmother'.

The legal rationale for Helen Duncan's conviction has secured her a place in the history of witch trials. In the sixteenth and seventeenth centuries, witchcraft was the capital crime of using illicit magic to cause harm and of conjuring spirits, as opposed to *pretending* to conjure them, as outlawed by the Witchcraft Act employed in 1944. Historical comparisons remain instructive. In 1951, the Fraudulent Mediums Act replaced the 1735 statute, and then in 2008 the Fraudulent Mediums Act was itself replaced by the Consumer Protection from Unfair Trading Regulations. Whereas the 1735 Act had prohibited pretended conjuration, its 1951 successor had allowed mediums to undertake paid psychic work if classed as entertainment. But if fraud were alleged the Crown needed to prove intent, and so to remedy this the EU Unfair Commercial Practices Directive paved the way for the 2008 Regulations. The onus was thus put back on mediums to prove they didn't swindle people. The Spiritual Workers Association (SWA) protested to the government about the implied commercialization of Spiritualism. 'The Fraudulent Mediums Act protected the medium,' argued the SWA's founder, Carole McEntee-Taylor, 'because it meant the person receiving the information was taking personal responsibility.' As a civil rather than a criminal matter, though, cases are judged according to the balance of probabilities. If a verdict hinged on whether a medium was genuine, most trials would collapse, because this couldn't be proved one way or the other. The defendant's bona fides would be, as in so many other legal suits, a matter of interpretation.

Other papers in my dusty box file concern later myths and legends about Helen Duncan's life. Supporters have long dined out on links to Winston Churchill. Although his memorandum calling the trial 'obsolete tomfoolery' referred only to distraction from the war effort, some Spiritualists continue to see outrage at the persecution of a great medium. So we have Churchill protesting in Parliament (nothing about this in *Hansard*), remonstrating with colleagues (nothing in the Cabinet minutes) and expressing displeasure to family and friends (nothing in his correspondence at the Churchill Archives). In 2007, Michael Colmer renewed his insistence that the great man had visited Mrs Duncan in prison, although 'in keeping with the Spiritualist tradition of confidential seance room ethics' her spirit refused to tell mediums what had passed between them. There is no proof that Winnie could have cared less about Nellie, nor was he obviously bothered with the beliefs and ideals of the movement she represented.

We actually now have more evidence of Churchill's indifference towards Spiritualism. His cousin the sculptor Clare Sheridan became a Spiritualist after her husband was killed in the trenches in 1915, but in death she found him as overbearing as he had been in life, and although she and Churchill were very close he showed no interest in her beliefs. He received several letters from another cousin, Desmond Leslie, a Spitfire pilot (and later an avid believer in flying saucers), who had grown up with Spiritualism. Writing from an RAF base in 1943, Leslie opined that postwar improvements 'will not make us the least bit better until we give a little more thought to the Immortal Soul which will be disinfected and regulated out of existence'. Clementine Churchill invited Leslie to tea at Chequers – the only sign of any reciprocation. In June 1950, Churchill's private secretary asked if he would like to send Leslie a telegram reading, in its entirety, 'Thank you so much for your most amusing letter.' As an afterthought, 'most' was scribbled out, perhaps by Churchill himself.

Currents of wishful thinking also flow beneath the HMS *Barham* story. But some revealing letters have surfaced since *Hellish Nell* was first published. On 6 December 1941, Sir Henry Markham, Permanent Secretary to the Board of the Admiralty, wrote to the parents and wives of deceased crewmen informing them of the tragedy and requesting that they should 'not communicate this sad news to any but your immediate relatives, who should similarly be asked to regard it as highly confidential'. The Admiralty even sent Christmas cards to the dead, afraid that failure to do so might arouse suspicion. Officials must have known nonetheless that the idea of maintaining confidentiality was unrealistic. People find hiding grief harder than keeping secrets, and word must have circulated in the close-knit working-class neighbourhoods and extended families of Portsmouth long before the *Barham*'s loss became public knowledge. In fact, by January 1942, people in Portsmouth were frustrated that the cause of their grief was still being kept from the nation, especially now that rumours were rife. On the 27th, the First Lord of the Admiralty, A. V. Alexander, received a letter from Patrick Donner, MP for Basingstoke, concerned about disquiet regarding the *Barham*. Alexander passed it on to Churchill, and the Prime Minister authorized a press statement explaining that the news had been suppressed because the Germans had not at first realized they had sunk the *Barham*.

The next day *The Times* reported, tellingly, that bereaved families in Portsmouth had been 'inclined to the suspicion that the Admiralty's continued silence ... indicated a departure from the declared policy of frankness regarding British losses'.

The key question, however, remains the exact date of the seance where Helen Duncan supposedly manifested a sailor from the *Barham*. There's no reason to think that it predated receipt of the Admiralty's letter. 'It is a matter of record', asserts Roy Stemman, a former editor of *Psychic News*, 'that leading Spiritualists were aware of the Portsmouth revelation within twenty-four hours of it occurring', which is possible, but still doesn't confirm when the seance took place. The order of events is key here. If the seance was on the same day that the *Barham* was sunk, it is more impressive than if it came after the letters of condolence were sent on 6 December. The researcher Simon Young notes that four hundred men survived, each with a story to tell as they awaited redeployment in Egypt, and that thousands of other sailors and Royal Marines had witnessed the sinking from their ships in the Mediterranean convoy of which the *Barham* was just part.

Something else I hadn't known in 2001 was that the sailor in question was Sydney Fryer, a thirty-one-year-old Acting Stoker Petty Officer, an unmarried man (which means the woman at the seance was definitely his mother rather than his wife). Not only did Fryer come from Portsmouth, according to a Channel 4 documentary broadcast in 2009, he came from Copnor, the same small part of the city where his spirit is said to have returned. The programme features Roy Stemman surveying the room once occupied by the Master's Temple Church of Spiritual Healing and informing the presenter, Tony Robinson, that no one knew about the loss of the *Barham* before Helen Duncan's seance, because it was 'top secret'. This is only half right: it *was* secret and yet, given that the families had been informed, not *top* secret. A writer named Graeme Donald made an interesting calculation:

> Letters of condolence were sent out to families of the 861 dead, asking them to keep the secret until the official announcement. So, allowing for perhaps ten people in each family, there were about 9,000 people who knew of the sinking; if each of them told only one other person, there were 20,000 people in the country aware of the sinking, and so on – hardly a closely guarded secret.

Under the circumstances, Donald concludes, Helen Duncan 'simply picked up the gossip' and worked it into her Portsmouth seance routine. This is more likely than that she raised the dead or, as has been suggested, spied for the Germans. Naturally, modern mediums claiming to be in touch with Mrs Duncan have asked her what happened. The reply, in every case, has been the same: she knew nothing about government secrets and how could she ever have known? This remains an impeccably reasonable position – a note of clarity from beyond the grave.

Helen Duncan's supporters continue to believe that she was the victim of a government conspiracy to silence her before the D-Day landings. And, in a way, they are right: there definitely was a policy of halting loose tongues and it was a sensible course of action. After all, the Allies were trying to plan an invasion of Europe and, incredibly, keep it secret from the enemy just across the Channel. Blabbermouths had to shut up and it was the job of the security services to ensure they did. We now know the *Barham* news leaked out even before the families were notified on 6 December. In 2005 the wartime diaries of Guy Liddell, director of MI5's 'B' Division (counter-espionage), were published. These indicate that the leaker was a man named Postan working in the Ministry of Economic Warfare (MEW). This may have been Michael Postan, a medieval historian recruited as an adviser on Soviet affairs, or Konstantin Postan, whose job, according to Soviet intelligence, was to gather information about military and economic targets in the USSR. Both were White Russian émigrés, hostile to communism, and one of them, wrote Liddell, had 'clearly talked very indiscreetly'. MI5 felt their case against him was weak because he would claim 'that the loss of the *Barham* had a very important bearing on work that he was doing and that the Admiralty representative had mentioned the matter to him in this connection'.

What Postan's work was and why it involved the *Barham* remain obscure. Early in December 1941, soon after the sinking, an MI5 agent named Edward Cussen interrogated Postan and other MEW employees, but it was decided that a prosecution under the Defence of the Realm Act would not reflect well on either the government or the security services. Three weeks later, on the 26th, Liddell wrote in his diary: 'The *Barham* case has come up once more. A medium has produced a drowned sailor called Syd who was recognized by several people present at the séance and said he was one of the crew. Edward Hinchley Cooke and Edward Cussen are once more taking up the trail.' Cussen, who had a legal background, and Hinchley Cooke, a determined half-German bloodhound of spies, probably went to Portsmouth to investigate, but there is no further record of what they found. Evidently no action was taken against Helen Duncan then, but we might suppose that her card was marked by the incident.

The problem shared by Helen Duncan's admirers and detractors is a tendency to paint everything in black and white, whereas the true meaning of her story lies in shades of grey. Incensed by Tony Robinson's TV documentary, Lew Sutton, an advocate of physical mediumship, wrote to *Psychic News*: 'Die-hard sceptics with an almost mocking self-satisfied attitude shouldn't get away with their totally inadequate claims going unchallenged.' But sceptics are challenged all the time, just not with evidence that many would find persuasive. Moreover, non-believers are often just relativists, immunized against the supernatural by awe for nature itself. As Joseph Conrad observed: 'The world of the living contains enough marvels and mysteries as it is; marvels and mysteries acting upon our emotions and intelligence in ways so inexplicable that it would almost justify the conception of life as an enchanted state.'

Some sceptics are more hostile. Responding to the new

consumer protection regulations, the British Humanist Association (now Humanists UK) welcomed an end to a situation 'where psychic practitioners are permitted to make completely unsubstantiated claims and to take payment for their services, without fear of legal action'. The writer and broadcaster Charlie Brooker is militant on the issue. 'I think every psychic and medium in this country belongs in prison,' he wrote in 2006. 'Even the ones demented enough to believe in what they're doing. In fact, especially them.'

This seems harsh, somehow at odds with the humanity in humanism. Mediums should be allowed to exist and, as the law has long recognized, there is usually no reliable means of challenging their sincerity. The obvious exception would be where seance encounters with Helen Duncan have gone beyond mere messages relating to, say, the reason for her arrest and her dealings with Churchill. Alleged physical manifestations of her, famously in the 1980s through the psychic Rita Goold, are not only implausible but cast doubt on the medium's good faith. The ghost hunter Tony Cornell was unimpressed by Goold's seances. The 'Helen Duncan' he saw was much smaller than the living woman, indeed more like Goold herself. After Mrs Duncan's supposed return to the astral plane, Cornell also noticed that one of the medium's trouser legs was rolled up and a shoe was different, as if she had got changed during the seance.

By this time, mediums preferred to materialize objects rather than human forms, such as the 1944 newspaper sent to the Scole Circle. Helen Duncan continued from time to time to show up in person, as happened at a seance in Scarborough, when she 'stood in full tangible form in the middle of the circle' and held the hand of the medium, Mary Armour, to thank her for her good work. The Zammits also claim to have witnessed the Australian medium David Thompson, at one of his Circle of the Silver Cord seances, resurrect Helen Duncan out of shining ectoplasm. This sort of thing infuriates sceptics. Unlike stage performances, though, physical mediumship is a private affair for believers. Even if they pay, participants are told they are taking part in an experiment, not procuring a service where grief is exploited. So, who are they deceiving except themselves?

As ever, the extraordinary testimony that has bubbled up since 2001 lacks extraordinary proof and yet resists easy dismissal as fiction or fraud. Donald Bretherton, an Anglican clergyman interested in parapsychology, sent me recollections of interviewing a medium who had known Helen Duncan: they had 'a fervent conversation in which it was affirmed that she [Mrs Duncan] had produced genuine and remarkable phenomena, but under pressure . . . was tempted to cheat'. Farce rubs along with pathos. An obituary for Ursula Roberts, a Spiritualist from Chichester, told of how Mrs Duncan 'had such an excess of ectoplasm that on one occasion she and a friend were washing up dishes at a kitchen sink, when suddenly streams of ectoplasm began to flow from Helen's solar plexus, pouring onto the water in the kitchen sink!' Apparently, she was ashamed of these spontaneous evacuations but was unable to control them.

Helen Duncan has revisited me in other ways. In the archives of the Edinburgh College of Parapsychology, Gerald O'Hara discovered a crackly eighteen-minute gramophone recording of a Helen Duncan seance from December 1937, which he had cleaned up and digitized. The accompanying booklet contains an arresting photograph from the 1950s showing Mrs Duncan sitting in an open circle, a thread of white ectoplasm attached to her nose. According to Lew Sutton, my review of the CD was 'laced with innuendo, assumptions and misquotes'. He admitted that Helen Duncan resorted to fraud but wanted to know how some of the phenomena could have been faked 'in the days well before holographic images and the like'.

Among the sitters present when the recording was made was Laura Culme-Seymour, who had been a guest at one of Helen Duncan's London seances in 1931 and whose seventeen-year-old daughter Marjorie had subsequently drowned in a canoeing accident. The distraught mother took part in many seances searching for her daughter's spirit, including one given by Rudyard Kipling's psychic sister. In 1936 a spirit photographer made two plates showing a young woman's face in a cloud above her parents' heads. Lady Culme-Seymour was convinced. The following year she began attending Mrs Duncan's materialization seances in Edinburgh. 'I was terribly nervous,' she recalled, 'but knew it was our beloved child and managed to control myself.' She called to Marjorie, and what looked like a girl wearing a long white robe appeared from behind the cabinet curtains. At a private sitting on 25 October 1937, the spirit guide 'Albert' invited Lady Culme-Seymour to stand on 'a large psychoplasmic rod', and then dematerial-ized Marjorie, shrinking her until nothing remained. On the gramophone recording, made just a few weeks later, we can hear a pitifully disjointed conversation: the mother desperate for comforting communication; the daughter, fey and distracted, airily signing off with the words: 'I am going away, dearie, goodbye.'

Archival treasures have turned up in the Cambridge University Library, which has learned to love the Society for Psychical Research's archive housed there. When I went through the collection in the late 1990s, it was disorganized, the catalogue confused. 'May I ask why you are looking at all this *rubbish*?' enquired an archivist so drily it was hard to tell if she was joking. Among dozens of 'medium files' Helen Duncan's was unlisted, and I found it only by chance when I was taken into an off-limits storeroom. There it was on a shelf, silently screaming at me. Since then, the collection has been re-boxed and re-catalogued and new items have emerged, including Geoffrey Wilson's scrapbook about the Helen Duncan trial. Other relics have surfaced in the Harry Price archive at the University of London, including boxes of half-plate negatives and stereoscopic slides, even an X-ray of Helen Duncan's skull, showing several missing teeth. A pair of oak chairs on one or both of which the medium sat for Price's tests in 1931 are not listed as such, but by comparing them to laboratory photographs of her sitting bound and blindfolded, in full ectoplasmic flow, it can be seen that these are the same ones.

In the end, Helen Duncan's story always leads back to ectoplasm. Thanks to Paul Gaunt's online journal *Psypioneer*,

I came across a remarkable photograph from 1938. Mrs Duncan peeps out from the cabinet curtains, her expression one of shy modesty, all downcast eyes and meek smile. One assumes she's in character, perhaps impersonating someone. Most startling, however, is that her head and neck are wrapped in cloth so that only her features are exposed. The picture is grainy, yet obviously the cloth is not only pale but has a silky sheen – exactly like the cloth seized at the seance in Wales a year after the picture was published. There's a very good chance that this shows Helen Duncan using the same length of sheer fabric that I was once ticked off by the disapproving archivist for throwing in the air. For all we know, the person she was pretending to be was Marjorie Culme-Seymour.

Even this most troubling of artefacts has been rehabilitated at the Cambridge University Library, whose *Curious Objects* exhibition in 2016, marking the library's 600th anniversary, saw it displayed in a case devoted to Spiritualism and psychical research. Since I first encountered the ectoplasm, others have had their own private audiences with it. Marina Warner ignored the archivist's warning that it was 'very nasty' but promised to 'be discreet'. She describes it thus:

> a folded heap of dressmakers' lining silk, the cheapest kind of fabric, a man-made fibre, once white but yellowed by age. About four yards had been cut straight from the bolt, left unhemmed, the selvedge plain. It had been washed and ironed, but the creases where it had been crumpled were still marked; the pattern of these

showed it had been tightly wadded. There were traces of old blood that the laundry had not erased.

Yet Warner saw something mysterious and potent there: the belief that the medium's body 'occupied the role of transmitter, in an analogous fashion to the wireless receiver, catching cosmic rays whose vibrations produced intelligible phantoms and presences'. The seance room was a camera obscura where ectoplasm was light making impressions on a blackness sensitized by emotion and belief. Since then, the Helen Duncan ectoplasm has been displayed at the Ashmolean Museum in Oxford, as part of *Spellbound: Magic, Ritual & Witchcraft*, an exhibition I helped to curate. This exhibit, together with my panels and labels, angered some visitors, one of whom found it 'ludicrous, deeply offensive, and factually inaccurate', and begged the museum to remove the display to avoid accusations of religious discrimination.

The success of Helen Duncan's seances depended not just on Spiritualist devotion but also on reluctance to admit that she could have done the distasteful and degrading things she undoubtedly did. In 1957, Laura Culme-Seymour dismissed the idea of Mrs Duncan concealing butter muslin anywhere on her body as 'all too ridiculously impossible'. Dark truths lie there. Samples of ectoplasm are more than just stage props from a more innocent (if that's the right word) age of entertainment: they point to the physical expression of sublimated desire – numinous, sexual and procreative. This typically meant female desire in a world dominated by men. Ectoplasmic tendrils, however mundane their ingredients, reached out to new frontiers of wisdom and fulfilment. Nothing but cardboard and cloth, yet still they symbolized an evolutionary phase in Western Christianity between faith and doubt. Spiritualists made a science out of religion, and ectoplasm was, for a while, both the holy metaphysics and quantum mechanics of a new way of seeing.

Art and literature also help us to interpret experience and consciousness, drawing on signs and rituals essential to religion. 'I was not immune from fellow-feeling,' wrote Hilary Mantel after seeing a stage medium perform in Windsor. 'Which other self-employed persons stand up in public to talk about non-existent people? Novelists, of course. We listen to non-existent voices and write down what they say. Then we talk with passion and conviction about people no one can see.' Like ectoplasm, art shows us our feelings. *The Last Person*, a 1998 video installation by Susan MacWilliam, staged the drama of Helen Duncan's seances in a zone of dreamlike unease: a medium writhes in a chair, ectoplasm from her mouth supporting a floating voice trumpet. We know it can't be real, and yet we see it. As Clare Grafik, the curator of an exhibition, said of the piece: 'It flips between being a re-enactment and being a real event.'

Uncertainty of feeling and perception is essential to making sense of life. In 2007, I received a letter from Keith McFarlane, Helen Duncan's great-nephew, who until recently had known nothing of her story. Keith sent me a poem, 'The Medium', which he had published in a literary journal:

She sat entranced, between two worlds,
Her body lost to her command,
While from her mouth like mist advanced
The red-lit substance of her flesh.
She wove a veil of silver weft
that pooled beneath her, rose as vapour;
condensed as something, some one, other;
what forms the spirits would impress.

These lines capture the pure experience of the seance, pressing against what the poet called 'the ineffable, the limits of what is explained or explicable, the mysteries of consciousness itself'. This, and the juxtaposition of the sublime and the ridiculous, make *Hellish Nell* what it is – all the humour, pathos and tragedy of one person's existence. As Mrs Duncan said herself, admittedly at a seance forty-four years after her death but with a voice both cryptic and clear, no-nonsense and all nonsense, and so winningly authentic: 'if that was my life's work, then I bloody well done it'.

Acknowledgements

I am grateful to so many people, in particular Hilary Mantel, who supported me for so long and will be an inspiration for ever, and Donald West, who kindly read the prologue in which he appears as a character, casting his mind back fifty-six years to save me from errors. Over lunch in Cambridge, Donald had already laid the intellectual foundations of the book by insisting that it was impossible to prove negatives and explaining how things can seem simultaneously true and false. Both are remembered in my dedication.

The encouragement of friends and family has been invaluable, before and since *Hellish Nell* first appeared. My dear friend Rosamond Roughton read a draft of the original text and made valuable suggestions, as did my wife, Sheena Peirse, who has shown me boundless love and patience over the years. Since 2001 we've had three children, who drive me mad and keep me sane, as children are meant to do. Like most of my projects, this book began with one of my father Ed Gaskill's postal dispatches of newspaper cuttings – predating a time when people emailed each other weblinks – and I'm indebted to him, and to my lovely mum Audrey, for this and so much else besides. Dad: thanks for everything, this book is for you.

My literary agent Felicity Bryan, who died too young in 2020, believed in *Hellish Nell* as a book and gave me my first break. I am eternally grateful to her. Felicity put me in the hands of Clive Priddle at fourth Estate, an editor who together with Mitzi Angel helped me realize my vision for the book. Since then, I have been looked after by Natasha Fairweather at Rogers, Coleridge & White, and edited at Penguin Books by Tom Penn and Eva Hodgkin, who have been enthusiastic champions and a pleasure to work with, as have Maddie Watts and Mairéad Zielinski in publicity and marketing respectively. I would also like to thank Ruth Pietroni for seeing the book through its production stages, and my copy editors, Stephen Ryan and Louisa Watson. To my loyal film agent and friend Rebecca Watson at Valerie Hoskins Associates I owe so much.

The staff of many archives and libraries helped me, memorably at the Cambridge University Library, the National Archives at Kew, the former British Newspaper Library at Colindale, the University of London Library, the Island Archives Service in Guernsey, the Churchill Archives Centre and the College of Psychic Studies. I would also like to thank the record management departments of the Crown Prosecution Service and the Home Office, both of whom allowed me to examine restricted files. Jenny Lee showed me round the old London Spiritualist Alliance and let me nose around in their archive cupboard. Arthur Oram, who died in 2005, took me to see his medium: Helen Duncan allegedly communicated – with a warning. Roger Caldwell at the Home Office and the Rt Hon. Michael Ancram kindly brought me up to speed on the pardon campaign. In Scotland, Sheila Livingstone provided sources relating to witch trials, and Andy

Thomson escorted me round the pubs of Callander, photocopied a rare book kept behind the bar at the Crown Hotel and by introducing me to Helen Duncan's childhood nickname unwittingly gave me the title of this book.

I am also indebted to Helen Duncan's granddaughters Sheila Downie and Ann Pooey for their generosity and permission to use their mother Gena Brealey's unpublished work. Others who shared memories include Mary Armour, Bob and Georgina Brake, Tony Cornell, Alan Crossley, Jean Frost, Richard Howe, Denise Iredell, Lucian Landau, Harvey Lingwood, Dorothy Mahoney, June Moore, Chris Newberry, Arthur Oram, Eileen Philp, Diane White, Geoffrey Wilson and Stanley Worth. These people belonged to a generation now rapidly fading away; I was lucky to have spoken with them. I am grateful to Helen Weinstein, with whom I made a radio documentary about Helen Duncan, and to the BBC for permission to quote from another documentary, *The Last Witchcraft Trial*, broadcast in 1979, for which Maurice Barbanell, Gena Brealey, Henry Elam and Arthur West were interviewed. Thanks also to the repositories mentioned above for permission to quote from their archives, and to the Crown with regard to copyright documents held at the National Archives.

After the first publication, other people helped me take the story forward. My dad continued to send newspaper clippings; Allen Packwood, archivist at the Churchill Archives at Churchill College, Cambridge, supplied references; Donald Bretherton, who died in 2016, sent me a useful article; and Leslie Price and Paul Gaunt have provided valuable information. I am especially grateful to

Leslie for alerting me to documents in the Cambridge University Library that otherwise I would have missed, and for sending a transcript of Helen Duncan's remand diary. I would also like to thank Sophie Page for a guide to the reorganized Harry Price archive and for finding a strange, compelling pair of chairs, which I mention in the Postscript. Thanks, too, to my brilliant former research assistant James Brown, and to Nadia Wilson and Phoebe Judge, who in 2017 invited me on to the *Criminal* podcast 'Secrets and Séances' and got me thinking about Helen Duncan again. Their show connected me with the LA-based screenwriter Chris Basler, with whom I've since had many inspiring conversations.

No amount of gratitude to Helen Duncan's supporters and detractors can hide the fact that their accounts disagree. I have tried not to privilege one version over another, but rather to present different angles on the same story. The 'one real world' that the philosopher and historian R. G. Collingwood thought the exclusive objective of both his disciplines doesn't quite apply. Historical truths are kaleidoscopic; singular perspectives deceive. So, for this revised edition my emphasis has remained on open-minded interpretation; in fact, it's a book *about* interpretation. Collingwood's dictum that history should aim to be 'the re-enactment of past experience', however, I wholeheartedly endorse. I don't judge 'hellish' Nellie Duncan; my intention has been only to recover and re-animate her, to give her another kind of resurrection.

Notes

General

The most informative guide to Helen Duncan's life, had it survived, would have been Henry's journal. There are traces of it in their daughter Gena Brealey's indispensable biography, *The Two Worlds of Helen Duncan* (1985). An extensive ghostwritten section describing the Old Bailey trial paraphrases Maurice Barbanell's angry yet readable *The Case of Helen Duncan* (1945), based on his reports in *Psychic News*. Fans of courtroom drama might prefer C. E. Bechhofer Roberts's edited transcript, *The Trial of Mrs Duncan* (1945), which has an insightful introduction.

Alan Crossley, who knew Helen in her later years, wrote touchingly about her in *The Story of Helen Duncan: Materialization Medium* (1975), drawing on information from Gena Brealey and Maurice Barbanell. Manfred Cassirer's *Medium on Trial: The Story of Helen Duncan and the Witchcraft Act* (1996) evaluates the Duncan mediumship for psychical research and is cautiously optimistic. My conversations with Sheila Downie and Ann Pooey were as revealing as the accounts left by their mother, Gena Brealey. Thanks to them I also learned much from Gena's unpublished autobiography and from a letter written by Gena's brother Harry in 1981.

What follows is a guide to these and other sources. It credits authors whose works have been consulted and may guide further reading on Spiritualism and psychical research, although little of the secondary literature published since 2001 has been included for the revised edition. A notable exception is Jenny Hazelgrove's *Spiritualism and British Society between the Wars* (2000), a book published too late for me to exploit fully first time round. Important works that appeared too late for me to make use of in this edition include Kyle Falcon, *Haunted Britain: Spiritualism, Psychical Research and the Great War* (2023), and Michelle Foot, *Modern Spiritualism and Scottish Art: Scots, Spirits and Séances, 1860–1940* (2023).

There have been more books about Helen Duncan: Mary Armour, *Helen Duncan: My Living Has Not Been in Vain* (2000); Nina Shandler, *The Strange Case of Hellish Nell: The Story of Helen Duncan and the Witch Trial of World War II* (2006); and Robert Hartley, *Helen Duncan: The Mystery Show Trial* (2007). None of these add much to the story, although by reproducing the Timmins correspondence, Armour does shed light on the 1956 seance raid. The argument of Simon Featherstone's article 'Spiritualism as popular performance in the 1930s: the dark theatre of Helen Duncan', *New Theatre Quarterly*, 27 (2011) is suggested by its title. Marion Gibson writes sympathetically about Mrs Duncan in *Witchcraft: A History in Thirteen Trials* (2023), ch. 10.

These notes are of necessity highly selective, and many titles and references have been simplified. Page and chapter numbers are given only where failure to do so might be confusing or otherwise unhelpful.

Prologue: Under Fire

Together, Bechhofer Roberts and Barbanell provide a satisfactory account of the trial. Additional detail came from newspapers,

local and national, kept today at the British Library in London
(BL) – formerly Colindale – although the Home Office was
assiduous in keeping clippings; see also Geoffrey Wilson's scrapbook in the Society for Psychical Research (SPR) Helen Duncan
archive in Cambridge University Library (CUL). The legal files
are in the National Archives at Kew (TNA), HO 144/22172. A
restricted file gathered in 1944 by the Director of Public
Prosecutions – TNA, DPP 2/1204 – was made available to me
at the Crown Prosecution Service's offices in Ludgate Hill, but
has now been declassified and is freely accessible at Kew. On the
Defence side, Charles Loseby's private papers are held by the
Islands Archive Service, Guernsey. His notes relating to Helen
Duncan's trial are in the SPR archive in CUL ('SPR, Loseby').

The SPR archive contains several invaluable folders on the
Helen Duncan mediumship: Reports, 1931–56; Correspondence,
Folder 1, 1931–44; Correspondence, Folder 2, 1945–86; and
Press Clippings, 'Duncan Case'. During my original research at
CUL, in July 1999, I found just one scuffed cardboard wallet in
a box labelled 'Duncan, Mrs Helen, 1944–46–49'. It wasn't
even mentioned in the old typed handlist but was simply one
folder among many alphabetically arranged SPR 'Mediums
Files'. The material is now better organized and cared for.

Chapter 1. You'll be Burned as a Witch!:
The Child-Prophet of Perthshire

The secondary literature on witch trials is extensive. One might
begin here: Malcolm Gaskill, *Witchcraft: A Very Short Introduction*
(2010); Brian P. Levack, *The Witch-Hunt in Early Modern Europe*,

4th edn (2015); and Robin Briggs, *Witches and Neighbours* (1995). Christina Larner's *Enemies of God: The Witch-Hunt in Scotland* (1981) is especially relevant. On witchcraft and the law, see the essay by C. R. Unsworth in T. G. Watkin (ed.), *Legal Record and Historical Reality* (1989).

Keith Thomas, *Religion and the Decline of Magic* (1971) remains the best introduction to popular beliefs about the supernatural; for Scotland, Robert Kirk, *The Secret Commonwealth* (c. 1691), available in modern editions, is essential. The execution of Elspeth McEwen is described in Sheila Livingstone, *Confess and Be Damned* (2000) and Brian P. Levack (ed.), *Witchcraft in Scotland* (1992). The Kerrick haunting is described in Alexander Telfair, *A True Relation of an Apparition . . . of a Spirit* (1696). On James I, see Christina Larner's chapter in A. G. R. Smith, *The Reign of James VI and I* (1973) and Brian P. Levack, *Witch-Hunting in Scotland* (2008), ch. 3; and for witch beliefs more generally, Julian Goodare, Lauren Martin and Joyce Miller (eds), *Witchcraft and Belief in Early Modern Scotland* (2008).

Social historical insights come from T. M. Devine, *The Scottish Nation, 1700–2000* (1999) and John Stevenson, *British Society, 1914–45* (1984). Alastair Thompson, *Callander through the Ages* (1985) is excellent on Helen Duncan's home town; Sarah Murray, *The Beauties of Scotland* (1799) and John Thomas, *The Callander and Oban Railway* (1990) were also helpful. Other local colour came from crumbling copies of the *Callander Advertiser* in the BL. For the belief in prophecy, see Norman McCrae (ed.), *Highland Second-Sight* (1908).

Genealogical information was obtained from the General Register Office for Scotland. Other details of Helen's early life are inconsistent and impossible to corroborate; yet an outline emerges. Gena Brealey was the principal source here, but articles from 1933 published in the *People's Journal*, a Scottish Saturday newspaper, under the heading 'My Second-Sight Secrets by Madame Victoria Duncan', were also helpful and are nearer in time to the events described.

The quotation from Mrs Foster Turner's seance comes from p. 298 of Nandor Fodor's *Encyclopaedia of Psychic Science* (1934). For other predictions about the First World War, see F. C. S. Schiller writing in the *Journal of the SPR*, 37 (1916) and Frederick Bligh Bond, *The Hill of Vision* (1919).

Chapter 2. Developing God's Gift:
Labour, Love and the Arrival of Henry

Most of the family details at the start of this chapter were provided by Sheila Downie. The birth certificate of the illegitimate Isabella corrects Gena Brealey's account. Other relevant works here include Gillian Bennett, *Traditions of Belief: Women and the Supernatural* (1987); W. Lance Bennett, *Reconstructing Reality in the Courtroom* (1981); and Ethel S. Person, *The Force of Fantasy* (1996).

For the history of Spiritualism, Lisa Morton, *Calling the Spirits: A History of Seances* (2020) is a good start. Ruth Brandon, *The Spiritualists* (1983) ranges widely, and Simeon Edmunds, *Spiritualism: A Critical Survey* (1966) and G. K. Nelson, *Spiritualism and Society* (1969) are useful. On the Victorian and Edwardian eras, see Logie Barrow, *Independent Spirits: Spiritualism and English Plebeians, 1850–1910* (1986); Janet Oppenheim, *The Other World: Spiritualism and Psychical Research in England, 1850–1914* (1985);

Efram Sera-Shriar, *Psychic Investigators* (2022); and, on the Fox sisters, Barbara Weisberg's compelling *Talking to the Dead* (2004). The ideals of the age are captured brilliantly in Philip Hoare, *England's Lost Eden* (2005), esp. chs 4 and 8.

Brian Inglis, *Natural and Supernatural* (1977), a history of the paranormal to 1914, and Alan Gauld, *The Heyday of Mental Mediumship* (2022) are useful. Among other good works on the shifting relationship between religion, science and philosophy are Peter Washington, *Madame Blavatsky's Baboon: Theosophy and the Emergence of the Western Guru* (1993) and Alison Winter, *Mesmerised: Powers of Mind in Victorian Britain* (1998).

The Great War's boost to Spiritualism is covered in ch. 3 of Jay Winter's *Sites of Mourning, Sites of Memory* (1993), and David Cannadine, 'War and death, grief and mourning in modern Britain', in Joachim Whaley (ed.), *Mirrors of Mortality* (1981). On beliefs among soldiers, see Leo Ruickbie, *Angels in the Trenches: Spiritualism, Superstition and the Supernatural during the First World War* (2018); Owen Davies, *A Supernatural War: Magic, Divination, and Faith during the First World War* (2019); and Hereward Carrington, *Psychical Phenomena and the War* (1918).

Eric and Andro Linklater, *The Black Watch* (1977) enabled me to imagine Henry Duncan's war service; and Gena Brealey's *Two Worlds of Helen Duncan*, the *People's Journal* articles, and genealogical records supplied details for the rest of his young life. Military service records relating to Henry's father can be consulted at TNA, WO 364/1072. To understand Sir Oliver Lodge's reaction to the loss of his son, look no further than his *Raymond Revised* (1922).

Chapter 3. Radiant Effects:
'Albert' and the Spectacle of the Seances

Helen Duncan's granddaughters, Sheila Downie and Ann Pooey, told me the story that opens the chapter. Copies of Ellis T. Powell, *Psychic Science and Barbaric Legislation*, 3rd edn (1917) and *The Medium: A Journal Devoted to Mediumship* (Sept. 1926) can be found in the Loseby collection at the Islands Archive Service (IAS), Guernsey (shelfmark: AQ 197/1) and CUL respectively. J. Arthur Findlay's study of John Sloan was expanded and became a bestseller, *On the Edge of the Etheric* (1931).

The story of Henry's astral journey is taken from the *People's Journal* (14 Oct. 1933), subsequent events from other editions of the same and from Brealey's *Two Worlds of Helen Duncan*. Peggy Hazzeldine's death certificate is reproduced in *Psypioneer Journal*, 11 (Feb. 2015).

Information about William Eglinton comes from his SPR Mediums File in CUL. On Crookes, see Trevor H. Hall, *The Spiritualists: The Story of Florence Cook and William Crookes* (1962). The investigations by Sidgwick, Lodge, Richet, Myers et al. are retold engagingly in Alan Gauld, *The Founders of Psychical Research* (1968).

On Schrenck-Notzing, there is no substitute for his illustrated 1913 book, translated as *Phenomena of Materialization* (1920). For the Golighers, see *The Experiences of Dr E. E. Fournier d'Albe* (1922) and W. J. Crawford, *Psychic Structures of the Goligher Circle* (1921); Crawford's obituary, by W. Whatley Smith, is in *Proceedings of the SPR* (Nov. 1920). Jenny Hazelgrove's *Spiritualism and British Society* surveys physical mediumship after 1918, as does John Beloff's *Parapsychology: A Concise History*

(1993). For more credulous guides, see Linda Williamson, *Mediums and the Afterlife* (1992) and Alan Crossley, *A Journey of Psychic Discovery* (1993).

In *Science and Parascience* (1977), Brian Inglis continues his history of the paranormal up to 1939; his discussion of the work of Kathleen Goligher, Mina Crandon ('Margery'), Eva Carrière' and others I exploited thoroughly. On Mina Crandon, see J. Malcolm Bird, *'Margery' the Medium* (1925); her mediumship is also well documented in the SPR archives. There are SPR Mediums Files on other key figures, too. Essential was Fodor's *Encyclopaedia of Psychic Science*, more particularly the 1966 edition with its valuable introduction by Leslie Shepard.

Gena Brealey's autobiography, and Harry Duncan's letter referred to above, give the child's perspective on Helen Duncan's seances at Dundee in the later 1920s. The reports from 1930 were found in the Harry Price Library (see below). Harvey Metcalfe's photographs are reproduced in Crossley, *Story of Helen Duncan*.

Chapter 4. Darkness and Light: Research and the Search for Respectability

Ena Bügg's story is told in an autobiographical booklet, Georgina Brake, *My Spiritual Quest* (1999); I also interviewed Mrs Brake (née Bügg) and her husband Bob. On the Armistice, see Charles Drayton Thomas, *Life Beyond Death with Evidence* (1928), ch. 34, and Cannadine, 'War, death, grief and mourning'.

The barrister C. E. Bechhofer Roberts's *The Truth about Spiritualism* (1932) is a fine guide to the interwar period, as are W. K.

NOTES

Lowther Clarke, *Spiritualism and Psychical Research* (1941) and G. W. Butterworth, *Spiritualism and Religion* (1944). The controversial Montague Summers, *The History of Witchcraft and Demonology* (1926) puts the Catholic case. F. W. FitzSimons, *Opening the Psychic Door* (1933) is worth a read, if only for the creepy pictures.

On the early history of the SPR, Alan Gauld's *Founders of Psychical Research* is a stylish guide; W. H. Salter, *The Society for Psychical Research: An Outline of its History* (1948) and Renée Haynes, *The Society for Psychical Research, 1882–1982* (1982) are less stylish but nonetheless informative. For paranormal research being done elsewhere at this time, see Muriel Hankey, *J. Hewat McKenzie: Pioneer of Psychical Research* (1963) and Harry Price's *Fifty Years of Psychical Research* (1939), which covers the early years of the SPR as well as later developments; chapter 11 begins: 'The history of Spiritualism is a history of fraud.'

The story of Mrs Duncan's London tests is told in reports published in *Light* – the journal of the London Spiritualist Alliance – in 1931–2, and in Harry Price, *Regurgitation and the Duncan Mediumship*, published by the National Laboratory of Psychical Research in 1931. The 'Materials Relating to Helen Duncan' in the LSA's archives at the College of Psychic Studies in London, and what used to be called 'Helen Duncan Box' in the Harry Price Library (HPL) at the University of London Library – shelfmarks: HPC/3D, HPC/3H, HPC/4A–C, HPF/2B–C, HBF/3A – add colour and depth to events. The HPL records had not yet been properly catalogued in 1999 (former shelfmark: HPL MSS 6/4) but are now well organized and meticulously listed.

Harry Price glossed the story of the 1931 tests in his *Leaves from a Psychist's Case-Book* (1936), ch. 9. Price has taken some knocks. To Paul Tabori's mistakes in *Harry Price: The Biography of a Ghost-Hunter* (1950), Trevor Hall added vitriol in *Search for Harry Price* (1978), although John Randall, 'Harry Price: the case for the defence', *Journal of the SPR*, 64 (2000) tries to set the record straight. To summarize reactions to the 1931 tests, I relied on Helen Duncan's SPR archive. On Price's admiration for Hitler, see his *Search for Truth* (1942), ch. 12.

Testaments to Helen Duncan's mediumship in the early 1930s crop up in *Psychic News* and *Two Worlds*. The Manchester seances are described in George F. Berry, 'Impressions of Mrs Duncan's mediumship', *National Spiritualist* (May 1932) and James Leigh, 'Dramatic interview with materialized spirit form: "Albert" talks about his life and work', *Two Worlds*, 45 (1932).

The story of Mary McGinlay is taken from the *Daily Mail* (7 Mar. 1932) and from her declaration (22 Feb. 1932), a copy of which survives in the HPL. The turning point in Price's thinking sparked by Kanichka the Human Ostrich is also documented in the HPL.

Chapter 5. Changing Fortunes:
A Brush with the Law and the Coming of War

The story of the Tomsons came from the *Sunday Chronicle* (12 Feb. 1928); a letter from Houdini about them is item 766 of Lodge's correspondence in the SPR archives.

For prosecutions under the Vagrancy and Witchcraft Acts, I used Owen Davies, *Witchcraft, Magic and Culture, 1736–1951* (1999) and James Hayward, 'Mediums, psychics and the law',

Criminologist, 19 (1995). Details of the Metropolitan Police's purges – and Spiritualist reactions – came from TNA, MEPO 2/1323 and TNA, HO 144/1806; the latter, which contains the royal petition of 1921, was still closed to the public in 1999 but has now been declassified. A letter – CUL, SPR, Lodge 759 – was revealing. Police policy regarding mediums can be studied at TNA, MEPO 2/9158.

The story of the 1933 seance and trial in Edinburgh was reconstructed from documents and photographs in the HPL and a police report (dated 1 Feb. 1944) in TNA, DPP 2/1204. The *People's Journal* articles can be found in the BL; the HPL also has a selection. The works of Brealey, Crossley and Cassirer supplied details of the 1930s seances, and I also drew on personal correspondence with witnesses. The story of Mrs Broadley's Bradford seance comes from an account (Feb. 1944) in Helen Duncan's SPR archive; that of Peggy growing up in spirit is from Mary Winifride Slater, 'Spirit eats an apple', *Two Worlds* (25 Sept. 1936).

The Treherbert incident is recorded in correspondence in the HPL. Price's other exploits in the mid-1930s are related in his *Confessions of a Ghost-Hunter* (1936), see esp. ch. 20, and the story of the talking mongoose is also covered in Christopher Josiffe, *Gef!* (2017). The files of the International Institute for Psychical Research (IIPR) can be found in the SPR's archives in CUL.

Stories of the male mediums were drawn from Harry Edwards, *The Mediumship of Jack Webber* (1940); Harry Emerson, *Listen My Son* (1984); and the SPR Mediums File on Charles Stewart. There is also a Mediums File that documents extensively the peculiar mediumship of Hylda Lewis. The quotation about mediums and capitalism comes from Harry Boddington, *The University of Spiritualism* (1947), p. 447.

The Glasgow and Cheltenham seances are described, respectively, in the *Two Worlds* for 26 Aug. 1938 and 17 Mar. 1939. Accounts of Helen's seances from the early 1940s come from the sources already cited. Arthur Oram describes his experience in his book *The System in Which We Live* (1998) and expanded on it to me personally. Other accounts come from the SPR Helen Duncan archive in CUL. For Ramsden, see J. H. Webster, *Voices of the 'Passed'* (1948), pp. 106–15.

On the effects of bombing in Portsmouth, see Gibson, *Witchcraft*, p. 193 (quotation). The Master's Temple Church of Spiritual Healing is described in Bechhofer Roberts (ed.), *Trial of Mrs Duncan* and in the TNA files HO 144/22172 and DPP 2/1204. For seance advertisements, see Portsmouth's *Evening News* for 15 May 1943 and 15 Jan. 1944. More about wartime beliefs can be found in Miriam Akhtar and Steve Humphries, *Far Out: The Dawning of New Age Britain* (1999), chs 2–3. Details of Spiritualism in the armed forces were found in TNA files ADM 1/23868 and PCOM 9/1482.

Chapter 6. A Kind of Conjuration: Trial and Denial at the Old Bailey

The sinking of HMS *Barham* was reconstructed from Admiralty records to be found in TNA, ADM/1/11948, 186/801, 223/152; I owe the point about the Enigma decrypts to vol. 2 of F. H. Hinsley (ed.), *British Intelligence in the Second World War*, 5 vols (1979–90) – see the note on p. 329. The story of the sailor's spirit appears in many places. I used Percy Wilson, 'Evidence for survival: the historical significance of physical mediumship', *Light*, 79 (1959); Mollie Goldney's notes on Wilson's 1958 lecture; and the account given by Gena Brealey. On HMS *Hood*, see Bruce Taylor, *The Battlecruiser HMS Hood: An Illustrated Biography, 1916–1941* (2004), ch. 9, and Simon Young, 'Helen Duncan and HMS Hood: a coincidence?', *Beachcombing's Bizarre History Blog* at www.strangehistory.net.

Useful works on wartime secrecy include John Court Curry, *The Security Service, 1908–45* (1999); Nigel West, *MI5* (1983); and Christopher Andrew, *Secret Service* (1985). The Home Defence Executive minutes are in TNA at CAB 93/2–3; see also the committee on Overlord preparations: CAB 98/40.

For the complaints of Mrs Evans, Mrs Martin and Mrs Gray, see TNA, DPP 2/1204; CUL, SPR, Helen Duncan file; and the HPL respectively. B. Abdy Collins's quote comes from *Psychic Science*, 21 (1942), and for Stella Hughes, see *Psychic News*, May–June 1943. *Psychic News* (21 Sept. 1940) was also where Maurice Barbanell reported his warning from Scotland Yard. Information about other police activity comes from Edward Smithies, *Crime in Wartime* (1982). Evidence of the involvement of the Magic Circle is in the HPL's Helen Duncan box. The 'in memoriam notice' about HMS *Barham* comes from Portsmouth *Evening News* (25 Nov. 1942).

The rest of the chapter was assembled from the sources cited for the Prologue, especially TNA files HO144/22172 and DPP 2/1204 and Bechhofer Roberts (ed.), *Trial of Mrs Duncan*. Additional material includes reports in the Portsmouth *Evening News*; W. A. E. Jones writing in the *Daily Herald* (4 Apr. 1944); Barbanell's *Case of Helen Duncan*; and an interview with Charles Loseby's daughter Diane White. Loseby's First World War service record is at TNA, WO 339/14142. The account by Helen Duncan of her five days on remand (20–24 Jan. 1944) can be found in CUL, SPR, Mediums, Helen Duncan: Reports, 1931–56.

The trial records are in TNA: CRIM 1/1581, 4/1709 and 2/256. The sketch of Maude in court comes from the *Daily Mail* (5 Apr. 1944). Geoffrey Wilson's scrapbook is in the SPR's Helen Duncan archive in CUL ('Duncan Case', press clippings); his father Percy Wilson told the story of the Merton Park seance in his 'Evidence for survival'.

The newspaper cartoons mentioned come from the *Daily Express* (1 Apr. 1944) and *Daily Mail* (3 Apr. 1944). For an account of the prediction that Helen Duncan made at the Bonnington Hotel, see *Psychic News* (29 Dec. 1956).

Chapter 7. Squaring the Circle:
Phenomena and Fraud at the Seances

Houdini's annotated copy of the *Atlantic Monthly* is among the SPR's 'Margery' files in CUL. On Houdini, see Inglis, *Science and Parascience*, ch. 5; Milbourne Christopher's *Houdini: The Untold Story* (1969); and Christopher Sandford, *Houdini and Conan Doyle* (2012), esp. chs 4–6. Houdini's association with Mina Crandon is comprehensively covered in David Jaher, *The Witch of Lime Street* (2015).

Among many exposés of trickery, Harry Price and Eric J. Dingwall (eds), *Revelations of a Spirit Medium* (1922) is the best introduction, and Price's *Short-Title Catalogue* (NLPR *Proceedings*, Apr. 1929) lists similar works. Arthur Wilkinson's *Spiritualism on Trial* (1953) is particularly enlightening.

The discussion of the *Barham* episode in Edmunds, *Spiritualism* is useful; for McDougall's report, see Price, *Regurgitation*. Price's photographs can be seen in the HPL. Frú Lára Ágústsdóttir has a Mediums File in the SPR archives in CUL.

The 'secondary stomach' debate can be followed in Joad's article in the *Sunday Dispatch* (2 Apr. 1944) and a reaction to the piece in the *Psychic Times* (May 1944); see also Barbanell, *Case of Helen Duncan*. Hannen Swaffer's poem is in the HPL. On swallowers in history, see Price, *Regurgitation*. The Freud story from 1895 is told in Roy Porter, *The Social History of Madness* (1987).

Varina Taylor's letter is in TNA, DPP 2/1204, and Esson Maule's report in the HPL. The story about the sailors' cheesecloth hammock comes from the SPR's Helen Duncan archives and is summarized in Cassirer, *Medium on Trial*. The Cefn Coed cloth from 1939 is in CUL; letters relating to its seizure in the HPL.

My thinking about seance phenomena here was shaped by Nicholas Humphrey's *Soul Searching: Human Nature and Supernatural Belief* (1995); see also David Hume, 'Of miracles', in his *Enquiry Concerning Human Understanding* (1748), §x – on extraordinary testimony requiring extraordinary proof – and C. G. Jung, *Psychology and the Occult* (1978). Horace Furness's description is quoted in Gauld, *Founders of Psychical Research*.

Two works – Theodore Besterman's 'The psychology of testimony in relation to paraphysical phenomena', *Proceedings of the SPR*, 40 (1930–32) and Denys Parsons's 'Testimony and truth', *Horizon*, 9 (1944) – helped to inspire Donald West's 'The trial of Mrs Helen Duncan', *Proceedings of the SPR*, 47 (1942–5). Also valuable are chs 2–3 of West's *Psychical Research Today* (1954), which discuss the phenomena and psychology of mediumship. David Marks and Richard Kammann offer further insights in this direction in *The Psychology of the Psychic* (1980); and on multiple personalities see Stephen Braude, *First Person Plural* (1991). On the way that brains predict rather than perceive reality, and Ibsen's 'life-lie', see Sam Knight, *The Premonitions Bureau: A True Story* (2022), pp. 74–5, 186–7.

On the hallucinations of the bereaved, see W. Dewi Rees, 'The hallucinations of widowhood', *British Medical Journal*, 4 (1971) and Sylvia Wright, 'Experiences of psychokinesis after bereavement', *Journal of the SPR*, 62 (1998). For the dialogue between Fodor and Freud, see Shepard's foreword to Fodor's *Encyclopaedia*. Henry's confessions are recorded in Price, *Regurgitation*, and *Light* (17 Jul. 1931). For striking parallels with seventeenth-century possession, see James Sharpe, *The Bewitching of Anne Gunter* (1999); and on Mary Toft, see Karen Harvey, *The Imposteress Rabbit Breeder* (2020). J. B. McIndoe describes the medium in full flow in 'The phenomena of Mrs Helen Victoria Duncan', *Psychic Science*, 21 (1942).

Chapter 8. Many Mansions:
Public Life and Prominent Men

Bob Brake kindly read his story to me from his unpublished memoirs. Information about W. T. Stead was taken from Fodor's *Encyclopaedia*; the spirit account of the *Titanic* disaster is in the SPR archives in CUL. For W. B. Yeats, see Brenda Maddox, *George's Ghosts* (1999); a letter by Yeats is among Barrett's SPR papers. On royal and political connections, see David Herbert Donald, *Lincoln* (1995) and Elizabeth Longford, *Victoria R.I.* (1964); and for Gladstone, see *Two Worlds*

(18 Nov. 1887) and Nandor Fodor in the Glasgow *Sunday Mail* (15 Nov. 1936).

Charles Fryer, *Geraldine Cummins: An Appreciation* (1990) speaks for itself. For Shaw Desmond on Roosevelt, see *Psychic News* (29 Mar. 1947); Arnewood Tower can be seen in Ronald Pearsall, *The Table-Rappers* (1972). Details of transfiguration come from SPR Mediums Files.

Lodge's dealings with Stanley Baldwin are recorded at TNA, HO 45/14235; and with Helen Duncan in Price, *Leaves from a Psychist's Case-Book*, and the College of Psychic Studies's 'Materials relating to Helen Duncan'. On Lodge in general, see W. P. Jolly, *Sir Oliver Lodge* (1974). Miss Wainwright's letter is in an SPR 'Research File' ('Seances'). The letters from Mackenzie King are at CUL, SPR, Lodge 994–5; see also C. P. Stacey, *A Very Double Life: The Private World of Mackenzie King* (1976).

The letter from Conan Doyle is at SPR, Lodge 455. On Conan Doyle, see Kelvin I. Jones, *Conan Doyle and the Spirits* (1989); Daniel Stashower, *Teller of Tales: The Life of Arthur Conan Doyle* (2000); and Andrew Lycett, *Conan Doyle* (2007). Details of his campaigning come from: Churchill Archives (Churchill College, Cambridge), CHAR 22/240; the College of Psychic Studies archives; and TNA, HO 45/11968.

The Home Office file on the Spiritualism and Psychical Research (Exemption) Bill is TNA, HO 45/14235. On Lloyd George, see CUL, SPR Lodge 643; on MacDonald, see TNA, PRO, 30/69/834; David Marquand, *Ramsay MacDonald* (1997), p. 407; and H. Dennis Bradley, *The Wisdom of the Gods* (1925), p. 402.

Hannen Swaffer's own *My Greatest Story* (1945) is the key work on the great campaigning journalist; see also Tom Driberg,

'*Swaff*': *The Life and Times of Hannen Swaffer* (1974). Mrs Vernon-Smith's letter is at TNA, HO 144/22172.

For Dowding, see Basil Collier, *Leader of the Few* (1957) and Hugh Dowding's own *Many Mansions* (1943). The Kingsway Hall convention is described in the *Sunday Express* and *News of the World* for 23 April 1944, and in the event programme – 'The Witness of Spiritualism' – a copy of which is in the SPR's Helen Duncan archives. See also *The Report of the Deputation of the SNU to the Home Office* (1943); TNA, MEPO 2/9158; TNA, HO 144/22172; *Hansard* (Commons), 3 May 1945.

For prosecutions under the Witchcraft Act, see Davies, *Witchcraft, Magic and Culture*; Hayward, 'Mediums, psychics and the law'; and Eric Maple, *The Dark World of Witches* (1962). 'Nesta of the Forest' – Nesta Lewis – has an SPR Mediums File; see also *Hansard* (Commons), 5 Jun. 1934, and TNA, HO 144/20121. The Cardiff case is mentioned in TNA, PCOM 9/1482.

For the occult and the war effort, see Akhtar and Humphries, *Far Out* and Dion Fortune, *The Magical Battle of Britain* (1993). Peter Brookesmith (ed.), *Cult and Occult* (1985), pp. 156–67 is good on the Nazis, and Clifford L. Linedecker, *Psychic Spy: The Story of an Astounding Man* (1976) concerns Ernesto Montgomery.

Details of Worth's role in the 1944 raid come from Mollie Goldney's notes on Percy Wilson's lecture, Loseby's notes in the SPR archive, and personal correspondence from Stanley Worth. Other details are from the HPL, the DPP's file and TNA, HO 144/22172. For the chief constables' meeting, see TNA, MEPO 2/9158.

Evidence of MI5 activity can also be found in TNA, WO 283/11; Curry, *Security Service*; and West, *MI5*. The files of the

Metropolitan Police's Special Branch (TNA, MEPO 38) were still closed at the time of writing, but appear now to be open; more facts may be found there. Maude also features in West, *MI5*, and in A. B. Schofield, *Dictionary of Legal Biography* (1998).

For Churchill, see Churchill Archives, CHAR 2/123/12–35, 72–96; 2/126/35; 2/71/81; 1/165/34; 2/67/30. David Stafford, *Churchill and Secret Service* (1997) was helpful. For Mr Latimer's letter, see TNA, HO 144/22172. Loseby's involvement is recorded in the Guernsey archives: IAS, AQ 196/7, 10, 19, 27, and the Hinchliffe incident in the Churchill Archives, CHAR 1/200/59, 60, 61, 63–82.

The query put to Herbert Morrison is in the Prime Minister's Personal Minutes, April 1944 (copy in the Churchill Archives), and the original correspondence in TNA, HO 144/22172. For other Cabinet business, see TNA, CAB 65/42. Robin Foy, *In Pursuit of Physical Mediumship* (1996), pp. 302–6, suggests that Churchill attended a seance in Kingston Vale in April 1925, but this was Ramsay MacDonald – see above p. 270.

On Churchill's supposed visit to Holloway, see Michael Colmer, 'Churchill *did* visit Helen in Holloway', *Psychic World* (*c.* Apr. 2007). See also William Colvin's claim: Andy McSmith, 'Toil and trouble: The last witch?', *Independent* (29 Feb. 2008). Other claims appear in Colmer's *Churchill's Witch* (2009), p. 38, and Mary Armour's *Helen Duncan*, pp. 35–6. See also Daniel Yates, 'Obituary: Lady Taylor', *Independent* (7 Jan. 1998), and Harley Cronin, *The Screw Turns* (1967), p. 154. For sceptical comment, see Leslie Price, 'Bewitched by the Duncan myth', *Psypioneer*, 5 (2009).

On the Boer War escape, Churchill is quoted in *Psychic News* (29 Mar. 1947). The Tennant letter is at Churchill Archives,

CHAR 1/43/13; the Hickling correspondence at CHAR 2/53, 57, 62; 13/47, 49, 51. The memories of 'W. T. P.' come from Elizabeth Gaythorpe (ed.), *My Dear Alexias: Letters from Wellesley Tudor Pole to Rosamond Lehmann* (1979). Brooks's story is in the *Report of the SNU* (1943).

Chapter 9. Nellie, Keep Your Chin Up!:
The Path to Liberty

To reconstruct Helen Duncan's incarceration in 1944, I relied on Kathleen Lonsdale et al., *Some Account of Life in Holloway Prison for Women* (1943) and John Camp, *Holloway Prison* (1974). A key source for the appeal is the DPP's file (TNA, DPP 2/1234); see also Bechhofer Roberts (ed.), *Trial of Mrs Duncan*; Barbanell, *Case of Helen Duncan*; and Brealey, *Two Worlds of Helen Duncan*. Details are recorded formally at TNA, CRIM 2/256 and J 81/48.

Newspaper clippings came from the HPL and TNA, HO 144/22172; other reactions to the trial and appeal can be found in the latter, and from the SPR's Helen Duncan archives. For the case of the Rector of Stiffkey see A. J. P. Taylor, *English History, 1914–1945* (1965), which is rich in the flavour of the period. Also helpful was Stephen Inwood, *A History of London* (1998). Legal outcomes are detailed in the *Law Quarterly Review*, 61 (1945) and *Halsbury's Laws of England* (1990), volume 11 (2).

Loseby's papers in the SPR and Guernsey archives expand the story; the latter contains his introduction to McIndoe's book (IAS, AQ 196/25). For Henry Duncan's letters, see

TNA, HO 144/22172, which also contains the medical report. Jane Yorke's file is at TNA, CRIM 1/1617. On Redhill Spiritualist Church, see Nelson, *Spiritualism and Society*, p. 166. Helen Duncan's undated letter to Maurice Barbanell, received 3 Oct. 1944, is in Folder 2 (1945–86) of the SPR's Helen Duncan Correspondence, and Barbanell's letter, dated 29 Sept. 1944, is in Folder 1 (1931–44).

On Helen Duncan's relations with the SNU, and the Wigan seance, see Paul J. Gaunt, 'Why did the SNU remove Helen Duncan's diploma in 1945?', *SNU Pioneer Journal*, 2 (2015), and various letters in the SPR's Helen Duncan Correspondence, Folder 2, for March 1945 (esp. re John Lane). Price's prediction to Mollie Goldney was made in a letter (4 Apr. 1944): SPR Mediums File 'Schneider, Rudi'. Mrs Osborne Leonard's prediction is in Box One of the Bosanquet material in the SPR archive in CUL.

Chapter 10. The Kiss of Death: Spiritualism's Triumph and Decline

June Moore told me her story in a letter, Denise Iredell (née Hankey) in person; the Lingwoods sent emails. See also Laura Culme-Seymour's sad memoir *Marjorie* (1957), p. 61. Lena Hazzeldine's letter is in the Britten Memorial Museum, reproduced in *Psypioneer Journal*, 11 (Feb. 2015). For the Tullibody seance, see the letter from Bill Robertson, reproduced at https://helenduncan.org/?page_id=66. Mrs Goldney's letter to Lady Balfour is in the SPR's Helen Duncan archive, as are papers relating to Donald West; statements made by S. M.

Gardiner and Leah Longman are there too. Charles Findlay's account is in 'The case of Helen Duncan: an appraisal', *Your Fate and Horoscope*, 8 (Sept. 1962), pp. 53–7.

Family details here come from Gena Brealey's accounts and from her daughters. On Minnie Harrison, see Tom Harrison, *Visits by Our Friends from the Other Side* (1989). The Mass-Observation study is *A Puzzled People* (1947); see also Edmunds, *Spiritualism*; and Cannadine, 'War, death, grief and mourning'. Ivy Northage's recollections are in her book *While I Remember* (1998).

Brealey, *Two Worlds of Helen Duncan* is the principal source for Helen Duncan's later life. Tony Cornell, Chris Newberry, Jean Frost and Alan Crossley told me their stories; other accounts were taken from Crossley's book, the SPR archives, Cassirer's *Medium on Trial* and the 'Sitters' Accounts' at https://helenduncan.org/?page_id=66. For the Glover Botham case see Hayward, 'Mediums, psychics and the law' and his SPR Mediums File. The letter from Percy Wilson is in file AQ 196/27 in the Guernsey archives (IAS).

For the story of the Fraudulent Mediums Act, 1951, see *Hansard* (Commons), 1 Dec. 1950; *Hansard* (Lords), 3 May 1951; and Davies, *Witchcraft, Magic and Culture*, pp. 73–5. For police reactions to the change in the law, see TNA, MEPO 2/9158. Bill Neech's quote is from Edmunds, *Spiritualism*, p. 99.

Chapters 1, 2 and 22 of Gena Brealey's *Two Worlds of Helen Duncan* are the main source for Helen's final months. Drawing on *Psychic News* reports, ch. 4 of Crossley's *Story of Helen Duncan* is also informative. The police raid at Nottingham is covered in Mary Armour's *Helen Duncan*, which reproduces Joe Timmins's extensive correspondence. See also accounts in

Psychic News (15 Dec. 1956) and *Two Worlds* (8 and 15 Dec. 1956). Mollie Goldney's notes from Percy Wilson also contain relevant material.

Details of the funeral came mainly from Sheila Downie's own reminiscences, but also from a report in the *Two Worlds* (15 Dec. 1956) and the SPR's Helen Duncan Correspondence, Folder 2 (Henry Duncan, Dec. 1956).

Epilogue: Beyond the Veil

For the aftermath of Helen Duncan's death, see *Two Worlds* (5–12 Jan. 1957), *Psychic News* (29 Dec. 1956 and 2 Feb. 1957) and various letters in Folder 2 of the SPR's Helen Duncan Correspondence.

Maurice Barbanell's memory of spirit writing can be found in his book *This is Spiritualism* (1959); the words of the Stockport housewife are quoted in Manfred Cassirer, 'Helen Victoria Duncan: a reassessment', *Journal of the SPR*, 53 (1985); and for the Yorkshire miner, see Crossley, *Story of Helen Duncan*, pp. 57–8. For Ena and Bob Brake, see Brake, *My Spiritual Quest*. The supposed spirit of Swaffer is quoted in Edmunds, *Spiritualism*, p. 92. Alistair Hendry told me about the bronze bust.

For Helen Duncan's return in spirit, see *Two Worlds* (15 Dec. 1956 and 5 Jan. 1957). Alan Cleaver and Alan Crossley told me about Rita Goold; see also Andrew Collins, *The Circlemakers* (1992), pp. 224–5. The communications at Scole are respectively valorized, vilified and vindicated in Grant Solomon and Jane Solomon, *The Scole Experiment: Scientific Evidence for Life After Death* (1999); Bryan Appleyard in the *Sunday Times Magazine*

(27 Jun. 1999); and Montague Keen et al., *The Scole Report, Proceedings of the SPR*, 58 (1999).

Jacob Needleman is quoted in Jon Klimo, *Channeling* (1987), p. 9. On modern witchcraft and witch-hunting, see Wolfgang Behringer, *Witches and Witch-Hunts* (2004), chs 6–7. On writing about ordinary people in history, see Jill Lepore, 'Historians who love too much: reflections on microhistory and biography', *Journal of American History*, 88 (2001). The cartoon of Helen Duncan at the stake can be found in Terry Deary, *Horrible Histories: The Twentieth Century* (1996).

Postscript: Nell Revisited

The *Psychic News* reviews, from May and June 2001, were by John Samson and Lyn Guest de Swarte respectively. Julie Myerson was writing in the *Guardian* (31 Mar. 2001). For another allergic reaction, see Anna Burnside in *Sunday Herald* (1 Apr. 2001). See also criticisms made by the sociologist of religion David V. Barrett, *Independent* (2 Apr. 2001). On Jung, see his *Symbols of Transformation*, trans. R. F. C. Hull (1956), pt 1, ch. 4. Donald West reviewed *Hellish Nell* for the *Journal of the Society of Psychical Research* (Apr. 2002). Hilary Mantel's review appeared in the *London Review of Books* (10 May 2001). *Beyond Black* was published in 2005. Writing in the *Guardian* (30 Apr. 2005), Fay Weldon praised Mantel's novel for having 'taken that ethereal halfway house between heaven and hell, between the living and the dead, and nailed it on the page', which fairly sums up my intentions for *Hellish Nell*.

On differences of opinion about Helen Duncan's legacy, see

'Spiritualist disarray over Duncan death', *Psychic Pioneer* (Apr. 2001), which is a review of Armour's *Helen Duncan*. I cite p. 147 of Victor Zammit and Wendy Zammit's *A Lawyer Presents the Evidence for the Afterlife* (2013), and a 1999 version of an online article by Victor Zammit, 'The irrefutable objective evidence'.

On the pardon campaign, see 'The lying, the witch and the war probe', *Fortean Times* (Nov. 1998); Ian McKerron and Jonathan Petre, ' "Last witch" set to win posthumous pardon', *Sunday Telegraph* (14 Jan. 2001); Fiona Macgregor, 'Spirited fight to clear name of Hellish Nell', *Edinburgh Evening News* (22 Jul. 2002); and 'Sponsor and help needed for European Court witchcraft appeal', *WitchCraft Times* (Summer, 2002). Michael Colmer is quoted in Jim Gilchrist, 'A spiritual healing', *Scotsman* (27 Jul. 2002). Mary Martin's story comes from Stephanie Bungay, 'Tribute to Britain's last "witch" ', *Edinburgh Evening News* (28 Oct. 2006), and Severin Carrell, 'Campaign to pardon the last witch, jailed as threat to Britain at war', *Guardian* (13 Jan. 2007). See also the *Glasgow Herald* (2 Feb. 2008), and Jonathan Petre, 'Campaign to pardon last witch jailed in Britain', *Daily Telegraph* (29 Feb. 2008). Michael Colmer is quoted in Lorna MacLaren, 'Witch-hunts go on trial', *Herald* (1 Jun. 2002). For the judgment of the Barons Courts of Prestoungrange and Dolphinstoun, Trinity Session, 2004, see www.prestoungrange.org.

Other legal developments are covered in Sarah Knapton, 'Calls grow for formal pardon for "Britain's last witch" ', *Daily Telegraph* (3 Nov. 2016), and www.helenduncan.org, the website of 'The Official Helen Duncan Organization'. This website, at the time of writing run by Helen Duncan's granddaughter Margaret Hahn, claims to have attracted 60 million users and that Mrs Duncan 'now reaches more people in a single month via the web than she did in her private sittings'. See also Chris Marzella, 'Street may be named after last ever "witch"', *Stirling Observer* (18 Oct. 2019).

Details of changes to the law regarding Spiritualist mediums are available online: www.legislation.gov.uk/ukpga/ Geo6/14-15/33/contents (Fraudulent Mediums Act, 1951); and www.legislation.gov.uk/uksi/2008/1277/contents/made (Consumer Protection from Unfair Trading Regulations, 2008). See also Bruno Waterfield, 'Mystics see trouble ahead over EU law', *Daily Telegraph* (18 Apr. 2006), and the debate between David V. Barrett and Martin Jenkins in the *Fortean Times*, 239 (2008).

On Clare Sheridan, see Midge Gillies, *Army Wives* (2016), ch. 8. And for Desmond Leslie: Churchill Archives, CHAR 1/368/83; 1/374/64–5 (quotation); CHUR 1/48/2–12 (telegram of 6 Jun. 1950 at 1/48/2); David Clarke and Andy Roberts, 'The saucerer's apprentice', *Fortean Times*, 225 (2007).

For recent updates to the HMS *Barham* story: George Knowles, 'A battleship, a U-boat and a witch', www.controverscial.com; Simon Young, 'Helen Duncan and HMS Barham: a sceptic speaks', *Beachcombing's Bizarre History Blog* at www.strange history.net; 'Programme marred by inadequate research', *Psychic News* (17 Jan. 2009) – including the quotation from Roy Stemman; *Tony Robinson and the Blitz Witch*, Channel 4 (UK), broadcast 29 Dec. 2009; and Graeme Donald, *Loose Cannons: 101 Things They Never Told You About Military History* (2009), p. 48.

Examples of the Admiralty's letters of condolence can be found online, see http://www.hmsbarham.com/pressletters/letters.php; the Christmas-card story comes from Iain Ballantyne,

Warspite (2001). On public disquiet about the sinking of the *Barham*, see Churchill Archives, CHAR 20/57A/63–4; *Gloucestershire Echo* (27 Jan. 1942); and *The Times* (28 Jan. 1942). The Commonwealth War Graves Commission's website records Sydney Fryer's details, including that he was unmarried and that his parents' names were Horace and Emma Fryer of Copnor, Portsmouth: https://www.cwgc.org/find-records/find-war-dead/casualty-details/2492684/sydney-arthur-fryer/. For Helen Duncan's denial from the spirit world, see Mary Armour's *Helen Duncan*.

The military intelligence angle is covered by Nigel West (ed.), *The Guy Liddell Diaries: MI5's Director of Counter-Espionage in World War II*, 2 vols (2005), I, pp. 199, 203. On Michael Postan, see Martin H. Folly, *Churchill, Whitehall and the Soviet Union, 1940–45* (2000), pp. 16–17. On Konstantin Postan, see Nigel West and Oleg Tsarev (eds), *Triplex: Secrets from the Cambridge Spies* (2009), p. 320. Edward Hinchley Cooke is mentioned in Christopher Andrew, *The Defence of the Realm: The Authorized History of MI5* (2010), pp. 56, 68–9, 78, 81, 143; for Cussen, see ibid., pp. 219, 275–7, 296, 344. In 1944, Cussen met P. G. Wodehouse, describing him as 'a stupid old man who has made so many blunders that he had brought himself perilously near the clutches of the Treachery Act': West (ed.), *Liddell Diaries*, II, p. 231. The head of Scotland Yard did not mention Helen Duncan in his memoirs, but reinforced the sense of the routine nature of her arrest, saying of Special Branch it 'goes about its job quietly and unostentatiously ... keeps tabs on everything and puts the Government in the picture ... No cloak-and-dagger stuff': *Commander Burt of Scotland Yard by Himself* (1959), p. 113.

Other references here are Lew Sutton, 'Sceptics' "inadequate claims" shouldn't go unchallenged', *Psychic News* (17 Jan. 2009); Bruno Waterfield, 'Mystics see trouble ahead over EU law', *Daily Telegraph* (18 Apr. 2008); Charlie Brooker, *Guardian* (4 Dec. 2006), p. 5. The Joseph Conrad quotation comes from *The Shadow-Line: A Confession*, 2nd edn (1920), author's note.

On Rita Goold and seance phenomena after Helen Duncan's death: Alan Crossley, interview, 22 Dec. 1999, and Crossley's book, *A Journey of Psychic Discovery* (1993), p. 105; Tony Cornell, *Investigating the Paranormal* (2002); Solomon and Solomon, *Scole Experiment*, p. 51; Zammit and Zammit, *A Lawyer Presents the Evidence*, pp. 153–4; Armour, *Helen Duncan*, p. 50.

The personal letter from Donald Bretherton was dated 4 July 2001, and the tribute to Ursula Roberts came from the website of Doug Osborne, medium and healer. The recording came from *Mrs Miller's Gift: The Helen Duncan Séance: December 1937* (2009). See also my review in the *Journal of the Society for Psychical Research*, 73 (2009), and the exchange with Lew Sutton in the next issue. Helen Duncan seances are described in Culme-Seymour, *Marjorie*, pp. 15–16, 35–7, 63–5, 71–2, 74–6. According to *The Peerage*, available online, Marjorie Culme-Seymour was born 17 Feb. 1916 and died 21 Jan. 1934.

The relevant HPL materials are HPG/3/559–582, Box 39, and 583–608, Box 40 (slides and negatives); HPG/1/4/3, no. xix (X-ray); and HPI/1/I–II (chairs). The photo of Helen Duncan wrapped in fabric – mentioned in chapter 5 – first appeared in John Winning, 'Materialisation', *Two Worlds* (16 Aug. 1938). Marina Warner describes her encounter with the cloth in *Phantasmagoria: Spirit Visions, Metaphors and Media into the Twenty-First Century* (2006), pp. 299–300. The letter of complaint was sent to Alexander Sturgis, 18 Aug. 2018. See also Sophie Page and Marina Wallace (eds), *Spellbound: Magic, Ritual & Witchcraft* (2018), pp. 138–9.

Repression and expression of female desire are explored in Alex Owen, *The Darkened Room: Women, Power and Spiritualism in Late Victorian England* (1989), esp. chs 1–2, 8. Hilary Mantel's comments come from 'The message that inspired *Beyond Black*', *Guardian* (28 Jan. 2006). Clare Grafik is quoted in Charlotte Cripps, 'The spirit enquiry', *Independent Extra* (14 Nov. 2007), p. 13. Keith McFarlane's poem can be found in *Acumen*, 57 (Jan. 2007), pp. 52–3. The quotation from Helen Duncan's alleged spirit comes from page 126 of Mary Armour's book.

Index

Abbott, Agnes, 152, 245

Abbott, David Phelps, *Behind the Scenes with the Mediums*, 217–18

Abdy Collins, B., 159, 201, 241, 290, 307–8, 318, 334

Adair, James, 138

Adventism, 31

Ágústsdottír, Frú Lára, 225–6

Ahlefeldt-Laurvig, Countess Ingegerd, 104

Air Ministry, 289

Alabaster, Bertha, 226

Albert, Prince Consort, 257

'Albert Stewart' (HD's spirit guide): bust made of, 78; HD names house 'Albertine' in honour of, 146; as HD's alter ego, 252, 357, 359; HD's performance of, 224, 231; manifestations and photographs of, 78; origins of, 60; performance during seances, 95–9, 109–10; portrait of, 371; prediction of Second World War, 154; role of, 79–80; voice recognized as HD's, 111; voice recordings, 372

Alexander, A. V., 1st Earl Alexander, 392

Alexandra, Queen, 41

Altrincham, Cheshire, 322

American Society for Psychical Research, 73, 118

Ancram, Michael, 377

angels, 13, 32, 33, 147, 265, 308

'Angels of Mons', 42, 220

Anglo-American Bio-Tableau Cinematograph, 22

animal magnetism, 32, 65, 261

animism, 376

Anne of Denmark, 5

apportation, of objects, 60, 86, 111, 120, 145, 151, 152–3, 231, 341, 347, 374

Arbroath, Scotland, 40, 53

Archer, Fred, 365, 366–7, 368

Ark Royal, HMS, 164

Armour, Mary (medium), 398; *Helen Duncan* (2000), 410

Arnewood Tower, Hampshire, 259

Arnold, Matthew, 33

Ashmolean Museum, Oxford, 402

Ashton-in-Makerfield (Wigan), 327, 328

Asquith, H. H., 298

Institut Métapsychique
International, Paris, 102
International Institute for
Psychical Research, 150,
152, 153
Iredell, Denise *see* Hankey,
Denise
Irwin, Flight Lieut. H. C., 101
Isle of Man, 150

James VI and I, King,
Daemonologie (1597), 5, 352
Jefferson, Thomas, 259
Jeffrey, Rev. Thomas, 363–4
Jehovah's Witnesses, 167
Jencken, Henry, 256
Jennings, Kitty, 195
Joad, Prof. C. E. M., 150, 227,
238, 239
Joan of Arc, 55–6; HD
compared to, 274, 364
John Bull (periodical), 218, 281
Johnson, Effie, 269
Johnson, Dr Samuel, 13, 33
Jones, W. A. E., 185, 193, 207
*Journal of the Society for Psychical
Research*, 62
Joyce, Gilbert *see* Monmouth,
Bishop of
Joyce, William ('Lord Haw-
Haw'), 289
Joynson-Hicks, Sir William,
266
Jung, Carl, 118, 247, 382–3
Justice of the Peace (periodical), 129

Kanichka the Human Ostrich,
124–5
Kardec, Allan, 32
Keats, John, 9
Keighley, Yorkshire, Spiritualist
church in, 35
Kelley, Edward, 32
Kent, Duke of (Prince George),
299
Kilmahog, Perthshire, 14, 25, 364
Kipling, Rudyard, 37–8, 256, 399
Kirk, Robert, 13, 412
Kirkby, Basil, 200
Kirkcudbright, Scotland, 3–4,
279, 376
Kluski, Franek (Polish medium),
234, 235
Knollys, Lady Margaret, 281
Koons family, Ohio, 31
Korean War, 265, 353

Labour Party, 267, 269, 349, 370
see also socialism
Lane, Sir Hugh, 255
Lane, John, 327–8
Lang, Cosmo, Archbishop of
Canterbury, 147
Lankester, Edwin Ray, 128
Larkin, Philip, 24
Last Person, The (video
installation, 1998), 403
Lavradio, Countess de, 104
Law Quarterly Review, 310
Lawrence of Arabia, spirit
messages, 166

Price, Harry – *cont'd.*
  photographs, 115, 225, 333,
    344; investigates HD as fraud,
    123–5; reports on Tomson
    trial, 126; attends Louisa
    Morris's trial, 130; warns of
    HD's downfall, 131; at HD's
    Scottish trial, 139–41;
    debunking lectures, 149;
    beliefs about paranormal
    phenomena, 149–50;
    investigates Kuda Bux, 152;
    declines to appear as witness at
    HD's Old Bailey trial, 189;
    attends HD's trial, xx, 200;
    provides evidence and
    photographs for HD's trial,
    210–11, 233–4, 287–8;
    exposure of fraudulent
    mediums, 216–19; on smell of
    ectoplasm, 226; and
    regurgitation theory, 228; on
    HD's audacity, 242; on HD's
    LSA seances, 262; sceptical of
    HD's retirement from
    mediumship, 325; death and
    reputation, 369–70; *Leaves from
    a Psychist's Case-Book*, 142–3,
    148; *Regurgitation and the Duncan
    Mediumship*, 116–18, 189, 287
Prison Commission, 308
Probe, The (SPR investigators),
    152–3, 171
Psychic Book Shop, Library and
    Museum, 266

Psychic News, xxiii, 104, 122, 147,
    165, 185–6, 281, 309, 325, 328,
    342, 359, 365–7, 382
Psychic Science (periodical), 159, 308
psychometry, 53–4, 60, 80, 170,
    218, 323
Psypioneer (online journal), 400–1
Punch (periodical), 92

Queen Charlotte's Midwifery
    Hospital, 107
Queen Elizabeth, HMS, 163
Quinlan, Mrs (of Manchester),
    347–8

R-101 airship disaster, 101, 116,
    132n, 269
Radford, Edmund, 280
radio and television, effect on
    Spiritualism, 343–4, 354
Ramsden, Squadron Leader,
    159–60, 178–9
Rathbone, Eleanor, 186
Rayleigh, Lord (Robert
    Strutt), 91
Redhill, Surrey, ban on
    mediums, 323
regurgitation controversy,
    69–70, 113–14, 116–19, 125,
    139, 227–30, 243, 334
Reichenbach, Karl von, 282
Reid, Dr E. S., 104
Reid, John, 387
Revelations of a Spirit Medium
    (1891), 218